Managerial
Breakthrough

Other Books by J. M. Juran

Bureaucracy: A Challenge to Better Management, 1944

Management of Inspection and Quality Control, 1945

Quality Control Handbook, First Edition 1951; Fourth Edition 1988

Case Studies in Industrial Management (with N.N.Barish), 1955

Lectures in Quality Control (in Japanese), 1956

Lectures in General Management (in Japanese), 1960

The Corporate Director (with J. Keith Louden), 1966

Quality Planning and Analysis (with Frank M. Gryna), First Edition 1970; Third Edition 1993

Juran on Planning for Quality, 1988

Juran on Leadership for Quality: An Executive Handbook, 1989

Juran on Quality By Design, 1992

Managerial Breakthrough

The Classic Book on
Improving Management
Performance

J. M. Juran

Revised Edition

McGraw-Hill, Inc.

New York   San Francisco   Washington, D.C.   Auckland   Bogotá
Caracas   Lisbon   London   Madrid   Mexico City   Milan
Montreal   New Delhi   San Juan   Singapore
Sydney   Tokyo   Toronto

Library of Congress Cataloging-in-Publication Data

Juran, J. M. (Joseph M.), date.
    Managerial breakthrough : the classic book on improving
management performance / J. M. Juran. — 2nd ed.
        p.   cm.
    Includes bibliographical references and index.
    ISBN 0-07-034037-4 (alk. paper)
    1. Management.   2. Personnel management.   I. Title.
HD31.J815   1995
658—dc20   94-34023
                                                         CIP

1 2 3 4 5 6 7 8 9 0   DOC/DOC   9 0 9 8 7 6 5 4

ISBN 0-07-034037-4

The sponsoring editor for this book was Philip Ruppel, the editing supervisor was Paul R. Sobel, and the production supervisor was Donald F. Schmidt. It was set in Palatino by McGraw-Hill's Professional Book Group composition unit.

Printed and bound by R. R. Donnelley & Sons Company.

McGraw-Hill books are available at special quantity discounts to use as premiums and sales promotions, or for use in corporate training programs. For more information, please write to the Director of Special Sales, McGraw-Hill, Inc., 11 West 19th Street, New York, NY 10011. Or contact your local bookstore.

INTERNATIONAL EDITION
Copyright © 1995. Exclusive rights by McGraw-Hill, Inc. for manufacturer and export. This book cannot be re-exported from the country to which it is consigned by McGraw-Hill. The International Edition is not available in North America.

When ordering this title, use ISBN 0-07-113404-2.

 This book is printed on recycled, acid-free paper containing a minimum of 50% recycled de-inked fiber.

Contents

Preface to the Revised Edition

It has now been 30 years since the publication of *Managerial Breakthrough*. More than any other book, *Managerial Breakthrough* captures the essence of Dr. Joseph M. Juran's many contributions to modern management. The "Breakthrough Sequence" he so aptly captured and clearly explained in this book has now been copied, modified, relabeled and rediscovered so many times in the past 30 years that many truly feel it is theirs alone.

Not long ago I was teaching a senior management workshop in London, and a participant from one of the world's leading companies and winner of numerous quality awards sought me out during the first break. He stated that he was so pleased to see that Dr. Juran had so carefully adopted their Quality Improvement Process. I laughed and agreed. Juran had like it so much, I said, that he had adopted it 30 years ago. The executive was puzzled. "But we've only been using it for the past eight years."

Many people throughout the world have given Juran credit for "inventing" this breakthrough sequence or structured quality improvement process. "Discover" is a far better term.

I first stumbled on this book almost 15 years ago when I started teaching graduate courses at Columbia University. I had no trouble finding numerous texts for the statistical quality control part of my "Quality Control and Management" course. But finding good management texts was a far more difficult task. One of my friends at Bell Labs, Ramon

Leon, asked if I had read *Managerial Breakthrough*. Many years have passed and I still haven't found a better text to explain the two key managerial processes of control and improvement.

Not long after these first classes, I gave the book out as a reference for a management workshop at AT&T. One of the managers read it from cover to cover on his return flight and called to ask for 200 more copies. He wanted one for every manager in his entire organization. He had found exactly what he was looking for.

Such is the effect this book has had on people for 30 years. The derivatives of the breakthrough sequence are everywhere. We frequently see "8-step quality improvement sequences" or 12-step or 7-step or even 4-step. Many have different names, but they share the same simple explanation of the scientific method Juran so aptly captured 30 years ago. Many of these processes were probably truly rediscoveries, many others direct descendants. I am sure Juran doesn't care either way. For as he said several years ago when stealing a joke from his longtime friend, W. Edwards Deming, "When you find something this good you should copy it, improve upon it, use it often, and soon you'll believe it is your own."

For many years Juran has said that he wished he had time to rewrite *Managerial Breakthrough*. He feels he could now do a much better job explaining the control process. And he feels a great need to add the missing key managerial process, planning. He would no doubt add many new examples from the past 30 years. He has continued to do research, teach and write. Two of these books, *Juran on Quality Planning* and *Juran on Quality By Design*, have directly addressed the critical planning process.

In creating this anniversary edition, we have resisted the temptation to update the anecdotes, examples and case studies. Too many are classics and should be read or reread by everyone interested in management. We have limited ourselves to freshening the graphics, and adding two chapters. Josette Williams, Anna Occhuizzo, Beth Schauber, and Mike Costantino have worked hard on creating new graphics. Josette has also made a number of small improvements throughout the text. The first addition is a chapter on quality planning, the missing part of the trilogy. Jane Roessner has taken *Juran's Quality By Design* and extracted the essential ideas to make this text somewhat more complete. There has been no attempt to rewrite *Managerial Breakthrough*, just to add a critical missing piece. Ken Katzeff has added many thoughts and clear graphics to this chapter.

The second addition is a brief biography of Joseph M. Juran. For the past several years, Howland Blackiston, President of Juran Institute, has been working on a labor of love—a television documentary of Juran's life. John Butman and Jane Roessner have been preparing the script and have written this short biography from the script. Much has happened in quality management in the past 30 years, and Joseph M. Juran has played a pivotal part in many phases of this "quality revolution."

In reviewing the book, these new chapters and the new graphics, I have once again discovered the many nuggets in *Managerial Breakthrough*. Although I, like so many others, have learned, relearned and used the breakthrough sequence for many years, I continue to find new insights with every reading. We wish you the best, whether it is your first reading or your nth. We are sure you will find that *Managerial Breakthrough* remains a treasure.

A. Blanton Godfrey
Chairman & CEO
Juran Institute, Inc.
Wilton, Connecticut

Preface to the First Edition

Every conscientious manager periodically sits back to ask "What is my role as manager?" "What am I really here for?"

This book offers a new approach to defining and acting out the manager's role, to answering the question "What am I really here for?" This new approach starts with the proposition that all managerial activity is directed either at:

(a) breaking through into new levels of performance, i.e., Breakthrough, alias creation of change, or alternately,
(b) holding the resulting gains, i.e., Control, alias prevention of change.

This book claims that:

(1) There is a universal sequence of events by which the manager achieves Breakthrough.
(2) There is a second universal sequence of events by which the manager achieves Control.
(3) The manager can better carry out responsibilities for Breakthrough and Control through deliberate, organized use of these two universal sequences.

These claims have been tested against the reactions of thousands of industrial managers.

The first extensive tests took place during 1952-1953, when the author, as a Fellow of American Management Association (AMA), launched the Planning and Controlling unit of AMA's Management Course. During those years the author was in close contact with hundreds of industrial executives, each studying, in depth, the problems of planning and controlling.

As the meetings progressed, there began to emerge various management "universals", i.e., rules of practice which seemed to be applicable to any problem in planning and controlling, irrespective of the particular product, process, or function involved. A collection of such "universals," published in an early AMA paper,[1] included the "unvarying sequence of steps which is necessary to regulate anything," i.e., the Control sequence.

Evolution of the theory of a universal sequence of events for Breakthrough was sharply accelerated by the publication of "Cultural Patterns and Technical Change." This book, by an eminent anthropologist,[2] examined the causes of failures of experts who went to foreign countries on missions of introducing technical change. For the present author, the book was a revelation. He had devoted much of his industrial career to creating and introducing technical change, and had experienced his share of failures. Suddenly, the causes of his most baffling failures became obvious, so obvious that he dropped everything else to write a paper[3] on the application of the book to the problems of industry.

This reexamination of the role of "cultural patterns" in "resistance to change" led the present author to a broader examination of the problem of creating change. In addition, his paper (which had become known as the "Cultural Patterns" paper) aroused considerable interest among industrial managers. One consequence was that the author was invited to discuss the paper in many seminars. The feedback from these audiences of managers likewise illuminated the entire activity of creating change. As a result, there emerged a rudimentary statement of the theory of a universal sequence of events for Breakthrough, again in an AMA publication.[4]

---

[1]Juran, J. M., "Universals in Management Planning and Controlling," *The Management Review*, November, 1954.

[2]Mead, Margaret, ed., "Cultural Patterns and Technical Change," United Nations Educational, Scientific and Cultural Organization, Paris, 1954. Reprinted as a Mentor Book by the New American Library, 1955.

[3]Juran, J. M., "Improving the Relationship between Staff and Line," *Personnel*, May, 1956.

[4]Juran, J. M., "Industrial Diagnostics," *The Management Review*, June, 1957.

This rudimentary theory underwent much refinement and emerged as the "Breakthrough" lecture, which the author has presented to many audiences of managers, in AMA, before various professional societies, at various universities, and in the executive development meetings of various companies. This audience, already international in scope, was broadened considerably when AMA invited the author to put the "Breakthrough" lecture on motion picture film. Through this medium, AMA has made the lecture readily available to many company training programs as well as to many AMA functions.

The theories of these two universal sequences, for Breakthrough and Control, have been fleshed out with experiences supplied mainly by the many managers who have served as the proving grounds. The author is grateful to all of them for their forthright challenges to the theories and for their contributions of practical examples of success and failure in Breakthrough and Control.

Finally, the author owes a special debt of gratitude to American Management Association for having served as the principal forum in which the thesis of the book germinated and developed to maturity.

J. M. Juran

Foreword:
An Immigrant's
Gift

One of the Vital Few

Both the life and influence of Joseph M. Juran are characterized by a remarkable span and an extraordinary intensity. Born in 1904, Juran has been active for the bulk of the century, and influential for nearly half that period. From his entry workaday position as a factory troubleshooter, he has created a richly varied career as writer, educator and consultant. Raised in dismal poverty, he has attained a position of respect and prosperity.

Juran's major contribution to our world has been in the field of management, particularly quality management. Astute observer, attentive listener, brilliant synthesizer and prescient prognosticator, Juran has been called the "father" of quality, a quality "guru" and the man who "taught quality to the Japanese" (a claim he refutes). Perhaps most important, he is recognized as the person who added the human dimension to quality—broadening it from its statistical origins to what we now call Total Quality Management. Although Juran's name may have received less exposure

Adapted from the script for "An Immigrant's Gift " a film, produced by Howland Blackiston that explores quality's impact on society and the life and career of Dr. J. M. Juran.

than others, his impact on managers, businesses, nations—and the products and services we buy and use each day—has been profound.

Accurately defining Juran's role in the quality "movement" is as challenging as defining quality itself. Both seem quite basic and yet, on closer inspection, are revealed to be enormously complex. Juran himself speaks of quality as having two aspects. The first relates to product features: higher quality means more and better product features that meet customers' needs. The second aspect relates to "freedom from trouble": higher quality consists of fewer defects. But, as elementary as that may sound, every manager knows that achieving higher quality is no simple task. For Joseph Juran, planting the seed of quality in the consciousness of the world has constituted the task of a lifetime.

Certainly, Juran's body of work abounds with "features" that have anticipated and met the needs of his worldwide "customers". A list of only the brightest career highlights swiftly proves that assertion. In 1937, Juran conceptualized the Pareto principle, which millions of managers rely on to help separate the "vital few" from the "useful many" in their activities. He wrote the standard reference work on quality control, the *Quality Control Handbook*, first published in 1951 and now in its fourth edition. In 1954, he delivered a series of lectures to Japanese managers which helped set them on the path to world quality leadership. This classic book, *Managerial Breakthrough*, first published in 1964, presented a more general theory of quality management, comprising quality control and quality improvement. It was the first book to describe a step-by-step sequence for breakthrough improvement, a process that has become the basis for quality initiatives worldwide. In 1979, Juran founded the Juran Institute to create new tools and techniques for promulgating his ideas. The first was *Juran on Quality Improvement*, a pioneering series of video training programs. *The Quality Trilogy*, published in 1986, identified a third aspect to quality management—quality planning. In addition to these accomplishments, there is Juran's seminal role as a teacher and lecturer, both at New York University and with the American Management Association. He also worked as a consultant to businesses and organizations in 40 countries, and has made many other contributions to the literature—in more than 20 books and hundreds of published papers (translated into a total of 17 languages) as well as dozens of video training programs.

But even the most comprehensive accounting of Juran's achievements (and the many honors and awards they have brought him) cannot express the richness and intensity of Juran's influence. Managers who have learned from Juran—and there are thousands and thousands of them worldwide—speak of his ideas with a respect that transcends appreciation and approaches reverence. Steve Jobs, founder of Apple Computer and NeXT, refers with awe to Juran's "deep, deep contribution." Jungi Noguchi, Executive Director of the Japanese Union of Scientists and Engineers, states categorically that, "Dr. Juran is *the* greatest authority on quality control in the entire world." Peter Drucker, the writer and theorist, asserts that, "Whatever advances American manufacturing has made in the last 30 to 40 years, we owe to Joe Juran and to his untiring, steady, patient, self-effacing work." Lawrence Appley, chairman emeritus of the American Management Association, uses a metaphor to express his admiration for Juran. "Joe is like a river," says Appley. "He just flows on and on. You don't know where it starts, you don't know where it ends. You just know it's rich and there's always water in it and it's always for good use."

These managers, leaders and fellow theorists attach so much worth to Juran's ideas for many reasons. Perhaps most important, his work has been devoted to revealing and promulgating bedrock principles. He is no faddist, he has not sought fame as a trend-spotter or futurist. Particularly today, when we are bombarded with a jumble of information, buzzwords, manifestos and old ideas repackaged as new, Juran's messages come across as the genuine article—down-to-earth, helpful, common-sensical and wise.

Of course, it is impossible to separate the character of the man himself from the impact of his work. Juran does not match the popular profile of the best-selling author and globe-trotting consultant to the powerful leaders of the world. To read Juran's work, to talk with the man, is to come in contact with a keen mind and a generous spirit passionately devoted to quality and improvement in the broadest sense of those words. His strengths lie in his ability to listen, to synthesize ideas and articulate concepts in a way that renders them unusually precise and accessible. His whole life has been characterized by a respect for facts; he refuses to overstate them when it comes to measuring the value of any one individual, including himself. He always has been reluctant to claim credit for ideas not wholly his own, has shunned self-promotion and been content to take less than his share of the limelight. In one journal entry he confided, "It wouldn't bother me if I'm not remembered at all."

Grim Beginnings

Like many managers who look forward and see only a great struggle in achieving higher quality, Juran's early years were anything but free from trouble. Joseph Moses Juran was born December 24, 1904 in the city of Braila, then and now part of Romania. His father, Jakob, was a village shoemaker. Sometime after 1904, the family moved to Gurahumora, a Carpathian mountain village then a part of the Austria-Hungarian Empire. Here, Juran writes, "They had no quality problems. Never had a power failure, never had an automobile fail. Of course, they didn't have power, they didn't have any automobiles." In 1909, Jakob left Gurahumora seeking a better life in America. His father's goodbye to five-year old Joseph remains one of Juran's earliest memories—the boy would not see his father again for three years, when the entire family joined Jakob in Minnesota in 1912.

Life in America did not immediately change the fortunes of the Juran family. They exchanged the dirt-floored house in Gurahumora for a tarpaper shack in the woods of Minneapolis. To make ends meet, the children went to work at whatever jobs they could find. Joe drove a team of horses, he worked as a laborer, a shoe salesman, bootblack, grocery clerk and as a bookkeeper for the local icehouse. During those years, he undoubtedly began to develop a visceral understanding of the practical workings and underlying principles of business.

Joe was a bright, even brilliant, boy. He so excelled in his school classes—math and physics, in particular—that he was repeatedly pushed upward through the grades and wound up three years ahead of his age group. Always a small boy, now he found himself as the youngest in class, as well. To make matters worse, he possessed the quick, acerbic tongue that often accompanies a sharp mind. Small, young smart alecks are the natural prey for school predators and Joe became the favored target for flying snowballs and pummeling fists. The grind of school, poverty, never-ending jobs and chores at home combined to produce a high school graduate who, in his own words, "was pretty soured on the world. I had a grudge against the world for a long, long time."

In 1920, Joe enrolled at the University of Minnesota, the first in his family to attend college. Here he discovered an activity that profoundly changed his outlook on life: chess. His analytical mind reveled in the intricacies and complexities of the ancient game; he became the university champion and performed well in state-wide competitions. For the first time, he felt the warmth of admiration and the pride of respect from others. This success at chess helped Joe revise his opinion of himself. Gradually, he shed the image of the skinny misfit and outsider; now he knew that his difference was in the nature of a gift, rather than a curse.

Discovery Quality

In 1924, Juran graduated with a BS in electrical engineering and took a job with Western Electric Company, the manufacturing arm of the Bell Telephone System. He was assigned to the Inspection Department of the vast Hawthorne Works in Chicago, where 40,000 people worked, more than 5000 of them in inspection alone. Juran was intoxicated with this life characterized by steady work and steady pay, and—despite a complete ignorance of inspection or quality—plunged into his work with vigor. The Hawthorne plant spread out before him like a giant, three-dimen-

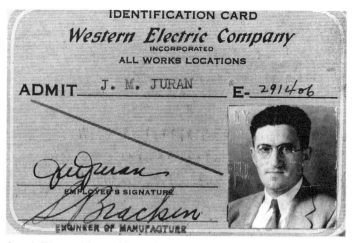

Juran's Western Electric I.D. card. The card is signed by Stan Brackin, chief engineer, who later became president of Western Electric.

At New York University, 1945.

sional chessboard, bristling with opportunities for investigation and learning. With his capacious brain and indefatigable memory, Juran soon developed what he calls "an encyclopedic knowledge of the place." It would have been impossible for Hawthorne's managers to miss Juran's intellectual and analytic gifts, and he quickly moved through a series of line management and staff jobs.

In 1926, a team from Bell Laboratories made a visit to the Hawthorne factory. The team was made up of some of the pioneers of statistical quality control—including Donald Quarles, Walter Shewhart, and Harold Dodge—and their intention was to apply some of the tools and methods they had been developing in the laboratory to operations in the Hawthorne plant. Since the factory lacked people trained in statistical methods, a young professor from the University of Chicago, Walter Bartky, was invited to conduct a training course for about 20 managers and engineers. Juran was selected as one of the 20 trainees, and then as one of two engineers for the nascent Inspection Statistical Department. It was one of the first such departments established in industry in this country. In retrospect, the greatest significance of this department may have been that it set Juran firmly on the path toward his life's work. But, although honored to be chosen for the department, Juran felt uncomfortable in his growing role as middle manager. Once again, he experienced vicissitudes similar to those of the school playground—youthful, green and sharp-tongued managers can be the natural prey of envious colleagues. Juran took this experience as evidence that his talents did not lie in people management. Nevertheless, he persevered.

In 1928, Juran authored his first work on the subject of quality, a training pamphlet called *Statistical Methods Applied to Manufacturing Problems*, which explored the use of sampling in analyzing and controlling manufacturing quality. It became an input to the well-known *AT&T Statistical Quality Control Handbook*, still published today.

During the Depression, Juran witnessed a shrinking of the workforce at Hawthorne that would rival any of the "downsizing" and "rightsizing" adjustments made during the 1980s and early '90s. The factory population shrank from 40,000 to about 7,000. Some 33,000 people who had imagined their jobs secure and lives in order found themselves jobless and without any of the compensations we are accustomed to today: pensions or parachutes, extended benefits or unemployment insurance. As a hedge against his own dismissal, Juran took advantage of his shortened work hours to earn a law degree from Loyola University. Although he did not lose his job, the Depression experience certainly demonstrated to him that, ultimately, no position is secure—a realization that was to encourage him to try his hand as an independent some years later.

In 1937, Juran found himself as the head of Industrial Engineering at Western Electric's corporate headquarters in New York. During this period, he became a kind of in-house consultant, visiting and exchanging

In 1954, the Union of Japanese Scientists and Engineers and Keidanren invited Juran to deliver a series of lectures on managing quality. Juran is seen here with Japanese executives during a tour of a Japanese manufacturing company.

Juran received the National Medal of Technology from President George Bush in 1992 for, "...providing the key principles and methods by which enterprises manage the quality of their products and processes, enhancing their ability to compete in the global marketplace."

ideas about industrial engineering with many U.S. companies. It was on one such visit, to General Motors in Detroit, that he first conceptualized the Pareto principle. This intensive, first-hand exposure to the working realities faced by managers in a variety of industries formed the basis of Juran's extraordinary mental database on quality management issues.

In December of 1941, Juran took a "temporary" leave of absence from Western Electric to serve in Washington as an assistant administrator with the Lend-Lease Administration, which managed the shipment of goods and material to friendly nations deemed crucial to the war effort. Here, Juran became enmeshed in managing governmental processes, including a massive problem in what today might be called "renumerating government," or "business process reengineering." He led a multi-agency team that successfully eliminated the paper logjam that kept critical shipments stalled on the docks. The team redesigned the shipment process, sharply reducing the number of documents required and significantly cutting costs. Juran's temporary assignment stretched to four years.

Launching a Canoe

On September 1, 1945, Juran left Washington and, at the same time, disembarked what he called the "ocean liner" of Western Electric and launched his untested and unproven "canoe" as an independent. He would, he had decided, devote the rest of his life to the subject of management. His plan was to do it all: philosophize, research, write, lecture and consult. After more than 21 years with Western Electric, Juran had concluded that he didn't belong there any more; in his own estimation, he was "too individualistic." In his letter of resignation, Juran wrote, "It is mainly because the road of opportunity has recently seemed for me to be approaching a barricade that I have concluded I should take another road." Later in the same letter, referring to deeper personal motivations, he adds, "The problem which confronted me has its roots in the dim past, long before there was any Bell System. For that problem, there will be, even in my century, no complete solution."

Juran, with a growing family to provide for, was far too practical a man to set off down this new road without prospects. He had already identified a temporary harbor for his newly launched canoe at New York University, where he served as Chairman of the Department of Administrative Engineering. But he had a vision of a much broader life, and he deliberately began piecing it together—building a consulting practice, writing books, developing his lectures in quality management for the American Management Association.

The seaworthiness of Juran's canoe was proven decisively in 1951, with the publication of his *Quality Control Handbook*. The *Handbook* established Juran's reputation as an authority on quality and became the standard reference work for quality managers throughout the world. On the strength of the book, Juran found himself in great demand as a lecturer and consultant, and its reputation extended well beyond the borders of the United States.

In 1954, the Union of Japanese Scientists and Engineers and Keidanren invited the celebrated author to Japan to deliver a series of lectures. These talks about managing for quality were delivered soon after another American, W. Edwards Deming, delivered his lectures on *statistical* quality methods. Taken together, the visits represent the opening chapter of a story that every business manager in every country in the world knows by heart—Japan's remarkable ascent from its prewar position as a producer of poor-quality, manufactured goods for export, to its current reputation as a world paragon of manufacturing quality. Although Juran downplays the significance of his lectures there, the Japanese themselves do not. Nearly thirty years after his first visit, Emperor Hirohito awarded him Japan's highest award that can be given to a non-Japanese, the Order of the Sacred Treasure. It was bestowed in recognition of his contribution to "the development of quality control in Japan and the facilitation of U.S. and Japanese friendship."

This is not the only recognition Juran has received from a head of state. In early 1992 President George Bush awarded him the National Medal of Technology "for his lifetime work of providing the key principles and methods by which enterprises manage the quality of their products and processes, enhancing their ability to compete in the global marketplace."

With the publication of *Managerial Breakthrough* in 1964, Juran's sphere of influence broadened further still and he became a trusted authority to general managers—in addition to quality managers—who came to rely on him as a source of knowledge and guidance. Gradually, Juran became recognized as a insightful analyst of developments and trends throughout the field of management theory and practice. As early as 1966, Juran warned Western business that "The Japanese are heading for world quality leadership, and will attain it in the next two decades." In 1969, he noted the growing dependence of the technological society on effective quality control. He has often referred to the "quality dikes" which serve as our best protection against such catastrophic breaches of quality as the Chernobyl and Bhopal disasters. In 1973, he argued that the "scientific management" model first espoused by Frederick Taylor in 1911 was antiquated and needed replacement. In the same year, he began to advocate that quality concepts are equally as applicable to service activities as they are to manufacturing.

In 1979, after 28 years of what Juran calls a "blissful life as an international author, lecturer and consultant," he changed course once again.

Overcoming his reluctance to create an institution—which he feared would become his master rather than his servant—he founded The Juran Institute. The immediate purpose of The Institute was to provide a continuity of Juran's ideas through an emerging form—video programs. The video series, *Juran on Quality Improvement*, met with great success and the proceeds served to fund a host of other activities. Juran found himself back aboard an ocean liner, albeit a small one, and in a position he had intentionally abandoned some thirty-four years earlier: manager.

Even with the responsibilities of this new role—which never ceased to be a burden to Juran, despite the Institute's success—he continued to write, lecture and consult. In 1986, Juran expanded his analysis of the role managers must play in the quality process with publication of *The Quality Trilogy*. Also in that year, he helped with the creation of the Malcolm Baldrige National Quality Award, testifying before Congress and serving on the Board of Overseers. In 1987, Dr. Juran, with a sigh of relief, relinquished his leadership of The Juran Institute. After a triumphant series of lectures in 1993-94, "The Last Word" tour, he ceased all public appearances in order to devote his time to writing projects and family obligations.

A Final Contribution to Society

As a result of the power and clarity of Joseph Juran's thinking and the scope of his influence, business leaders, legions of managers and his fellow theorists worldwide recognize Dr. Juran as one of "the vital few"— a seminal figure in the development of management theory. Juran has contributed more to the field—and over a longer period of time—than any other person, and yet, feels he has barely scratched the surface of his subject. "What I want to do has no end," he writes, "since I am on the endless frontier of a branch of knowledge. I can go on as long as the years are granted to me."

Today, Juran focuses his attention on a new mission: repaying the debt he feels he owes this country for providing him great opportunity and exceptional success. The sourness and the grudge he felt toward his life as a boy have long since been replaced with an abiding gratitude and affection. Juran has established the Juran Foundation to explore the "impact of quality on society" and make his contributions in the field— and those of others—available to serve society in a positive way. "My job of contributing to the welfare of my fellow man," writes Juran, "is the great unfinished business."

John Butman
Jane Roessner

A Note from the Publisher

In 1964, McGraw-Hill published the first edition of Dr. Joseph M. Juran's *Managerial Breakthrough*. At the time, Dr. Juran's book was quickly hailed as a breakthrough book on management thinking.

Since then, of course, many thousands of books have been published by many different publishers—each book espousing a different approach or a different solution on management practices. Some have gone on to be classics, others have fallen by the wayside, replaced each year by new selections of management tomes.

One thing has remained constant, *Managerial Breakthrough*, despite many of its references and case studies from the 1950s and early 60s, continues even today to be a classic in the field of management thinking. The core principles of this book remain the same and are applicable in today's business as they were 30 years ago.

It has been said that classic books need little more than incidental updating. This is so true with *Managerial Breakthrough*. In rereading this book for the umpteenth time, we have found that Dr. Juran's messages and thinking on management from 30 years are true in today's business environment as they were when the book was first written.

In this spirit, the author and the publisher chose to retain as much as possible from the earlier edition. While we recognize that in this world of instant and constantly updated information, managers and business people expect the most current information available, the examples, references, and ideas that Dr. Juran put to paper three decades ago convey so effectively the principles that have made the whole breakthrough concept timeless.

As such, the editing and revision that was done to this new edition was incidental in that the principles and concepts from Dr. Juran's original book remain the same. Many of the historical examples continue to be relevent and effective in making Dr. Juran's point, the author and editors have made an effort to retain the character and nature of the earlier edition. To have changed this new edition extensively would have been to have changed the entire thinking of managerial breakthrough. This was not the intent of this new 30th anniversary edition.

More importantly, what has been added is the new section on quality planning. This key section covers an area that was not addressed by the author 30 years ago and in effect completes the Breakthrough trilogy—Quality Improvement, Quality Control, and now Quality Planning.

Finally, when Managerial Breakthrough was first written, men dominated the middle and upper ranks of management in business. The original edition of the book reflected that reality in the use of the masculine pronoun throughout. In the intervening years since then, women have made extraordinary gains in business and are now playing leading roles in managing organizations of all sizes and at all levels. The author and editors have attempted to change most of the original all-masculine references and pronouns to reflect the new realities of the workplace. Where they have not been changed, it was for the purpose of maintaining clarity or meaning.

1

BREAKTHROUGH AND CONTROL—A CONTRAST

The Importance of Control

Control means[1] staying on course, adherence to standard, prevention of change. Under complete control, nothing would change—we would be in a static, quiescent world.

This isn't as bad as it sounds. For a good many things, it would be wonderful to have no change. Look at some of the changes which now threaten the manager:[2]

The western zone fails this month to meet its sales quota, and by plenty.

A vital shop process starts spewing out defects, at an alarming rate.

Research overspends its budget this month, by 15 percent.

---

[1] Any communication in management soon encounters a babel of unstandardized language. In this book, the author has made a special effort to give a constant meaning to certain key words. So, as it might once have been said, "I pray, gentle reader, that thou accept my meaning while reading my book. Thereafter, by all means, return to thy native tongue."

[2] The word *manager* is used in this book in the sense of anyone who achieves results through the efforts of others. The titles of these managers are various—supervisor, foreman, department head, superintendent, manager, vice-president, president.

Two customers coldly advise that they are through enduring late deliveries, and will take their business elsewhere.[3]

These changes are all bad. As to such changes, it would be wonderful if we had Control. It would be good, not bad, if:

Sales offices meet sales quotas.

Shop processes meet quality specifications.

Departments meet expense budgets.

Factories meet delivery schedules.

So Control is by no means an evil. Some changes are bad. As to these, it is good to prevent changes, to be "static." Of course, the word "static" has a bad odor to it—it includes an implication of "no progress." Hence we do not, in such cases, use the offensive word "static." Instead we use sweet-smelling words like "orderly," "settled," "predictable."

"Prevention of change" implies the existence of an accepted standard or norm. All those words we used—quota, specification, budget, schedule—are just local dialect for the same thing, for a standard or norm. The change we are trying to prevent is a departure (in the wrong direction) from this accepted standard. Each of these departures is a disturbance which may quickly grow into a crisis that demands attention, now. In too many companies the managers are so occupied with crisis after crisis ("fire fighting") that they have no time for grand strategy. In contrast, if we can keep our operations at the accepted standard, life becomes predictable and free from unpleasant surprises. We can plan our business with confidence that the plans will be carried out.

But we can also be deluded by the spectacle of "everything under control."

The engineers report that the product performs per specification, but the customers won't buy it; a competitor has a new design which outperforms ours. The plant manager reports that he has held scrap to the "budgeted" level; yet "budgeted" scrap exceeds the company's profit. The controller reports that planned profit has been achieved, but there is no joy; a competitor's annual report shows three times our return on assets.

---

[3]Generally, the examples used in this book are chosen from industrial companies. However, in the author's experience (which has included years of service in the federal government and in the university, as well as industry), the principles apply with full force to any enterprise, whether industrial or not, whether for private profit or not.

So Control can be a cruel hoax, a built-in procedure for avoiding progress. We can become so preoccupied with *meeting* targets that we fail to challenge *the target itself.*[4] This brings us to a consideration of Breakthrough.

The Importance of Breakthrough

Breakthrough means change, a dynamic, decisive movement to new, higher[5] levels of performance.

In a truly static society, breakthrough is taboo, forbidden. There have been many such societies, and some have endured for centuries. During those centuries their members suffered or enjoyed complete predictability. They knew precisely what would be their station in life—the same as that lived out by their forebears. But this predictability was, in due course, paid for by a later generation. The price paid was the extinction of the static society through conquest or other takeover by some form of society which was on the move. This threat of extinction may well have been known to the leaders of some of these static societies. Some gambled that the threat would not become a reality until they were gone. It was well stated in Madame de Pompadour's famous letter to Louis XV of France: "After us, the deluge."

Even in twentieth-century Western civilization, there is no lack of advocates for a static society. There are those who want to retain the family farm, the locomotive fireman. There are others who want to retain "fair trade" prices, cartels, and other evasions of internal competition. (These species have their counterparts in government, in the profes-

---

[4]In naval parlance, "polishing brass while the ship is sinking."

[5]The fact that Breakthrough yields improvement does not mean that all "improvement" results solely from Breakthrough.

We have a procedure for filling customers' orders. The procedure has been so designed that, *if followed*, it fills orders in 7 working days, on the average. However, the procedure is not always followed. Periodically, someone forgets, blunders, shortcuts, gambles. Result—our actual service averages 9 days. The extra 2 days is the result of failure to follow the procedure.

We make a more determined effort to adhere to the established procedure. The blunders, short cuts, etc., are reduced. Result—our actual delivery interval drops to 7 days. This is an *improvement through better control.*

Now someone comes up with a new approach based on a new concept, i.e., new machinery, new procedures. Suddenly we have the means for providing 1-day service on 80 percent of the customer orders, and an average of 1.7 days over all orders. This is *improvement through breakthrough.*

sions, in the churches.) But the odds of holding back "the deluge" during one's lifetime have grown worse, because the tempo of change has been quickening. Even a trade, the pride and security of the worker, no longer lasts a lifetime. Our largest single labor union is the Teamsters. How many of their members drive a team of horses?

All this history is vital to the manager. The threat to the static society stems from basic human drives, the drive for more of everything—knowledge, goods, power. The resulting competition is what makes breakthrough important.

Biologists estimate that of the species that have lived at one time or other on this earth, over 98 percent are now extinct. There is no corresponding estimate as to the rate of extinction of industrial companies, products, processes, organization forms, procedures, etc. However, the mortality rate has been high and seems to be picking up in tempo.

The significance of this rate of extinction is that, as with living organisms, the products, processes, methods, etc., of industry, are only mortal. They are doomed from birth. If the company is to outlive them, it must provide for a birth rate in excess of the death rate.

It is this basic urge to outlive its mortal components which drives the company, through its managers, to find new products, processes, markets; to reduce costs, accidents, absences; to increase output, quality, profits. Only through such "good" changes can the company stay alive, strong, fresh. Failing in this, the company ages, decays, and dies.

The variety of breakthrough is as broad as human imagination. A marketing manager hires a star salesperson away from a competitor; a shop mechanic tries a new tooling idea, and it works; a scientist in the laboratory formulates a new material; a vice-president attends a conference and finds a new approach to an organization problem.

The foregoing are all cases of "aggressive" breakthrough, but there is much need for "defensive" breakthrough as well. A competitor's new product line sends a shiver through our entire sales force; now we must have something to match it. A good customer decides to make, for himself, something he has been buying from us. The government challenges the industry price structure. Three of our top scientists quit to go into business for themselves, as competitors.

Breakthrough is, then, the creation of good (or at least, necessary) changes, whereas control is the prevention of bad changes. Each is necessary for survival and health of the company. Through lack of control, the company heads for its doom slowly, in an atmosphere of constant turmoil, irritation, and abrasion. Through lack of breakthrough, though all may be serene internally, the company is headed for some swift, mortal shocks.

The Manager Must Do Both

All managerial activity is directed at either Breakthrough[6] or Control.[6] Managers are busy doing both of these things, and nothing else.

There is nothing inconsistent about a manager conducting both of these activities simultaneously. Some things should by all means be prevented from changing. Others should by all means be changed. Such is the law of life itself.

> The human biological organism devotes much energy to *preventing* change. This Control effort is applied to such things as body temperature, blood count, pulse rate, etc. (Some elaborate mechanisms exist to keep these things at a standard level.) But the human organism also devotes energy to *creating* change. This Breakthrough effort is applied to such things as learning to swim, giving up smoking, getting a job. (The mechanisms for creating such changes are mainly different from those used for control, and are likewise pretty elaborate.) But there is nothing inconsistent about the same human organism conducting both of these two very different kinds of activity simultaneously.

The company,[7] which exhibits many of the features of a living organism, likewise devotes much energy to preventing change. It must meet budgets, maintain schedules, pay its bills, distribute the mail, repair the roof. These things are done by special organizational machinery, special jobs, or even special departments,[8] called by such names as Budget Department, Production Control, Quality Control, Plant Maintenance, Internal Audit.

The company also devotes much energy to creating change. It is continually involved with new markets, new products, new plants, new ways to organize, to cut costs, to reduce waste. The company is also

---

[6]Throughout this book, the capitalized words Control and Breakthrough are used in the special meaning of an *organized sequence of activities* by which companies prevent change or achieve change, respectively. The uncapitalized forms of the words "control" and "breakthrough" are used in their dictionary meanings.

[7]Throughout this book, the word "company" will be used when referring to *any institution or corporation having a life of its own*, i.e., a corporation or partnership for profit; a service institution such as a hospital; a school; a government department. In the opinion of the author, the argument of the book applies with full force to all these institutions.

[8]The word "department" will be used generally to denote any officially recognized grouping of company activities, irrespective of the organization level or the function performed.

flushing out old things—obsolete products, processes, markets, routines. Here again, there is special organizational machinery—special jobs and even special departments, i.e., Market Research, Cost Reduction, Product Development.

The Interrelation of Breakthrough and Control

It is possible for two diverse things to be part of the same cycle of events. Day differs from night, but they are both part of one continuing cycle—the spin of the earth on its axis. The four seasons are likewise all part of one continuing cycle—the annual journey of the earth around the sun. Even life and death, symbolic of the extreme in differences, are part of one continuing cycle of birth, growth, maturity, reproduction, decay, and death.

Breakthrough and Control are also part of one continuing cycle of events. This cycle is depicted in Fig. 1.

It consists of alternating plateaus and gains in performance. The plateaus are the result of Control—prevention of change. The gains are the result of Breakthrough—creation of change. This goes on and on.[9]

Lurking behind this simple diagram are some very profound differences. Just as life by day differs remarkably from life at night, so life during Control differs remarkably from life during Breakthrough.

---

[9]Figure 1 bears out the truism—"the only constant is change." But change is not continuous—it goes by jerks. Between the jerks are the plateaus of Control.

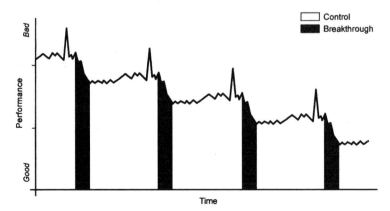

Fig. 1. Interrelation of Breakthrough and Control.

Some Differences

To study these differences we enlarge part of Fig. 1 to show one full cycle of Control and Breakthrough. The result, Fig. 2, is fundamental, and we will call it the Basic Diagram.[10]

The Basic Diagram consists of two zones:

(*a*) (left) Control Zone

(*b*) (right) Breakthrough Zone

The Control Zone of the Basic Diagram is shown in more detail in Fig. 3. It consists of some past history of performance at standard, then a sporadic flare-up, and finally, a return to the standard level of performance. The manager's role is to create the means for identifying flare-ups as they arise, discovering what causes these flare-ups, and eliminating these causes to restore the status quo.

The Breakthrough Zone in the Basic Diagram is shown in detail at the right of Fig. 2. It consists of a breakthrough to a new performance level. The manager's role is to create the means by which we (*a*) prove the need for reaching a new level and (*b*) take the steps for getting there.

---

[10]The reader is referred to Appendix B for illustration and explanation of what has come to be known as "The Juran Trilogy."

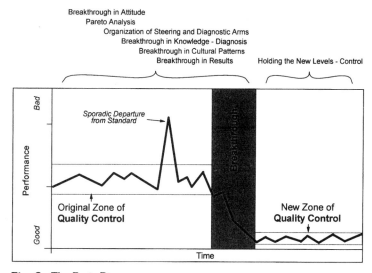

Fig. 2. The Basic Diagram.

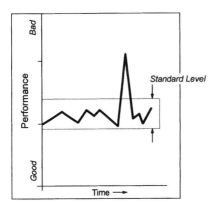

Fig. 3. The Control Zone.

These two phases, Control and Breakthrough, are performed repeat-edly by managers. Their importance is so great that managers should understand them fully: the concepts behind them; the means for carry-ing these concepts to fruition; the results achieved.

Managers are well aware that Breakthrough and Control do differ as to results. The dialects in various companies make this evident.

Breakthroughs are called drives, campaigns, programs, breakouts. Control is called fire fighting, holding the line, restoring the status quo, staying on course, getting back on target.

Managers are less precise as to the concepts which must precede these results. There is also some misconception. Time, rather than results, seems to be stressed. There is a relationship between the two, but time is an effect more than it is a cause. Generally, Control is a short-term ac-tivity, while Breakthrough is long-term. Control is a must for the short term, whereas Breakthrough is not. In the absence of Control, numerous sporadic troubles emerge and each gives immediate pain. But Break-through is a must for the long run. In the absence of Breakthrough, the rest of the world just walks away from the static company.[11]

---

[11]One executive uses the terms "action thinking" and "reflective thinking" to distin-guish the conceptual approach to Control from that used for Breakthrough. In his words: "Looking at the business of the Bell System, I know we can reach our immediate goals without a great deal of reflective thinking. But I doubt that we can build vitality for to-morrow without a lot of it, for this is the way we get deeper understanding of our prob-lems."

Quoted from Kappel, Frederick R., "Vitality in a Business Enterprise," pp. 16–17, McGraw-Hill Book Company, Inc., New York, 1960.

There is also awareness that (in most situations) *systematic* means for Breakthrough and Control are more likely to get results, and in less time, than *unsystematic* means. One company controller[12] distinguishes between "control reports" and "special reports." The former are recognized as applying to measurement of current performance against yardsticks. The latter are recognized as being of a different species—related to chronic failures, requiring exhaustive analysis and difficult solutions. Another executive[13] uses the terms "financial control" and "financial planning" to make a similar distinction. In his company's language, financial control is measurement of performance against predetermined bench marks. Financial planning involves "planning ahead in contrast to taking things as they come."

But managers generally lack awareness that the attitudes, the organization, and the methodology used to achieve Breakthrough differ remarkably from those used to achieve Control. The differences are so great that the decision of whether, at any one time, to embark on Breakthrough, or to continue on Control, is of cardinal importance. This decision hinges on managerial *attitude*. Once this decision is made, the respective sequences of steps begin to unfold, as in Table 1-1.

This is only the beginning of the total sequence of events. The respective plans for achieving Control and Breakthrough likewise exhibit important contrasts. Remember that the human organism uses, for Control, mechanisms which differ from those used for Breakthrough. In similar manner, the company uses, for Control, a cycle of events which differs from that used for Breakthrough. Some of these differences may be seen in Table 1-2.

There are other contrasts and implications to be drawn. For the moment, however, it is important to notice that:

the Control sequence is mainly one of "doing what comes naturally."

the Breakthrough sequence is studded with "special" events and obstacles.

to a high degree, Control and Breakthrough are carried out by *two different sets of people*.

These statements are not 100 percent valid, but the bigger and more complex the company, the higher the validity of the statements.

---

[12]Lillis, James F., Motivating Executive Action through Reports, *Reports to Top Management,* American Management Association, 1953.

[13]Brelsford, Ernest C., Using Charts to Present Financial Data, *Reports to Top Management,* American Management Association, 1953.

Table 1-1

Sequence of events	For Control	For Breakthrough
Managerial *attitude* is one of believing that:	The present level of performance is good enough, or if not, it cannot be improved, i.e., it is a fate, not a problem.	The present level of performance is not good enough, and something can be done about it, i.e., it is a problem, not a fate.
Managerial *objective** becomes one of:	Perpetuating performance at the present level through the Control procedure.	Achieving a better performance through the Breakthrough procedure.
Managerial *plan*† is to:	Identify and eliminate *sporadic*‡ departures from usual performance.	Identify and eliminate *chronic*‡ obstacles to better performance.

*The word "objective" as used in this book means a specific, attainable aim, so defined that it can serve as the basis of a plan of action.
†The word "plan" as used in this book means the totality of all preparations needed for carrying out an objective.
‡The concept of sporadic and chronic is evident from the Basic Diagram, Fig. 2. Sporadic departures from standard performance are of short duration. We take it for granted that we can eliminate them, since we will only be going back to where we once were. However, the chronic condition has been there for a long time, and we cannot be sure that we can root it out economically.

Implications of the Decision to Breakthrough or to Control

The foregoing differences become more obvious when we look sideways at some related fields of effort.

The military words for breakthrough are invasion, attack, offense, charge. The corresponding words for control are defense, dig in, stand fast, hold the line.

The general approach to invasion includes concepts of mobility, surprise, stratagem, maneuver. The equipment for invasion (World War II style) consisted of such things as bomber planes, parachutists, landing craft, tanks. In contrast, the conceptual approach for defense consists of entrenchment, fortification, detection. The military apparatus needed to execute these concepts (during World War II) included fighter planes, flak towers, mine fields, antitank guns.

Even the qualities of leadership differ. The invader must be capable of boldness, cunning, decisiveness, risk taking, timing. The defender emphasizes patience, alertness, suspicion, caution.

In biology, the meat eaters differ remarkably from the vegetarians. The former are built for Breakthrough, the latter for Control.

Table 1-2

Sequence of events	For Control	For Breakthrough
The facts needed are usually	Simple, showing actual performance vs. standard performance.	Complex, to permit deeper understanding of the problem than ever before.
The facts are usually collected by	"Regular" scorekeepers, i.e., accountants, inspectors, etc.	A special fact-collecting team, i.e., task force, staff specialists, etc.
Formality of fact collection is usually	Absent. Often there are not even permanent records.	Present. May require special experiments, tests, and formal reports.
The facts are usually analyzed by	The "line" people, i.e., foreman, branch manager or, frequently, non-supervisory personnel.	Technical people or specially trained analysts.
Frequency of analysis is usually	High. May require monthly, weekly, daily, or hourly review.	Low. Often is only a one-shot analysis.
Decision for action is usually by	The "line" people responsible for meeting the standard.	Upper-level supervision, since interdepartment changes are involved.
Action is usually taken by	The "line" people responsible for meeting the standard.	Departments other than those responsible for meeting the standards.

In politics, a similar contrast is found between the "outs" and the "ins." In religion, similar differences distinguish the heretics from the faithful.

Returning to company management, the differences inherent in whether to Control or to Breakthrough are equally profound. Holding present share of market is a defensive, maintenance form of action. Increasing share of market is a form of invasion which requires leadership, attitudes, and all the equipment appropriate to an invasion—research, new products, bold marketing, and the like.

In this way it is seen that the choice of Breakthrough or Control is decisive not only as to the results we want; it is decisive also as to the means. These differences in means are far more profound than managers generally realize.

In Chap. 21, under The End Points for Breakthrough and Control, we will discuss some guide lines to help the manager decide whether to Breakthrough or Control. Right now our point is that the decision is important, and that it should be made deliberately, not by default.

Universals for Breakthrough and Control

The main burden of this book is that there is one universal sequence of steps which fits all Breakthrough, and that there is another universal sequence of steps which fits all Control.

Some instances of such management universals are seen in the Training Within Industry program of World War II. One phase of this program is a four-step sequence on How to Instruct:

Step 1: Prepare the worker.

Put him at ease.
State the job and find out what he already knows about it.
Get him interested in learning the job.
Place in correct position.

Step 2: Present the operation.

Tell, show, and illustrate one important step at a time.
Stress each key point.
Instruct clearly, completely, and patiently, but no more than he can master.

Step 3: Try out performance.

Have him do the job—correct errors.
Have him explain each key point to you as he does the job again.
Make sure he understands.
Continue until you know he knows.

Step 4: Follow up.

Put him on his own. Designate the person to whom he goes for help.
Check frequently. Encourage questions.
Taper off extra coaching and close follow-up.

The significant thing is that, despite the vast variety of products, processes, operations, and people associated with World War II, these simple rules fitted *all* work situations. They were truly "universals" on how to instruct.

In like manner, the sequence of steps for Breakthrough fits *all* work situations, as does the sequence of steps for Control.

Considering the great number and variety of things which need Breakthrough or Control, to end up with only two universal sequences would seem to be a remarkable simplification. Yet it actually works out that way. The author here pleads innocent of invention. In observing many managers in many situations, he has found that each of them had invented or reinvented these sequences, and that the inventions were all alike. All the author has done is to restate these sequences in a more generalized, orderly form.[14] (Managers are, of course, too busy to write books about such things.)

What about Conventional Management Theory?

There is an extensive body of management literature which holds that the process of managing is conducted through a sequence of activities somewhat as follows:

policy[15] making
setting objectives
planning to meet objectives
organizing[16] to execute the plan
selection and training for staffing the organization
motivation of the people
appraising results

This sequence of activities is correct as far as it goes. However, it makes no distinction between two very different concepts:

1. objectives for Breakthrough
2. objectives for Control

Conventional theory does provide for distinguishing between short- and long-range planning. However, when managers discuss "How long is long?" they end in frustration. The real difficulty lies (in the author's opinion) in our putting emphasis on the calendar distinction (long vs. short) rather than on the purpose distinction (planning for Break-through vs. planning for Control). To be sure, there is a correlation be-

---

[14]There have been some interesting speculations on how ordinary arithmetic might have been invented. In some ancient community, it had long been known by the hunters that two rabbits plus three rabbits made five rabbits. The fishermen knew that two fish plus three fish made five fish. The women knew that two children plus three children made five children. Then along came some fellow who just loafed in the cave but figured out that two plus three made five, whether you were talking of rabbits, fish, children, or anything else.

[15]The word "policy," as used in this book, means a statement of principle to be used as a broad guide or limitation to managerial action.

[16]The word "organizing," as used in this book, means the division of the total work pile into logical, man-size parcels called jobs, and the coordinating of these jobs into a unified whole.

tween the purpose and the calendar; Breakthrough programs are generally long range, and Control programs short range. However, it is confusing to put the planning emphasis on the effect (the calendar) rather than on the cause (the purpose to be achieved).

It is common experience that when "Breakthrough thinking" and "Control thinking" are confounded, the pace of Breakthrough suffers seriously. Consider the example of product development.

During the nineteenth century, conventional organization practice was to make one executive, the "Works Manager," responsible both for product development and for manufacture of the product. In those days, product lines were relatively stable. As a consequence, the product development function was commonly the "Drawing Office" adjunct of the factory.

As the pace of product development quickened, the instincts of the managers responded. They recognized that product development, which is primarily devoted to Breakthrough, should not remain yoked to manufacture, which is primarily devoted to Control. The response was to create separate Product Development departments. The effect was far more profound than just redrawing lines on an organization chart. The new departments, clearly devoted to Breakthrough, changed their approach drastically. They set up research laboratories, those mysterious chambers which up to then had existed only in the universities. They even hired college graduates! They departed from precedent in many other ways.

The importance of the case lies not in the organization change; it lies rather in the recognition that there existed a confounding of "Breakthrough thinking" with "Control thinking." In this case and in others (Market Research, Industrial Engineering), the confounding was resolved through organization change. But in many cases, a solution through organization change is not feasible, so the confounding remains.

It is the conviction of the author that conventional management theory, as well as the various schools[17] of management, all stand to gain by

---

[17] An interesting and useful classification of management theories was recently made by Prof. Koontz. He identified the following approaches or "schools."
management process
empirical
human behavior
social system
decision theory
mathematical
All of these "schools" have something useful to contribute to the Breakthrough sequence or the Control sequence or both. As Prof. Koontz points out, it is only the efforts to build these things into cults which has created much confusion and antagonism. See Koontz, Harold, Making Sense of Management Theory, *Harvard Business Review,* July–August, 1962, pp. 22–46.

distinguishing clearly between objectives for Breakthrough vs. objectives for Control. Once this distinction is made, other distinctions follow as a matter of course—in planning, organizing, staffing, motivation. The end result is two parallel sequences of activity, one devoted to Breakthrough, the other devoted to Control.

These two parallel sequences originate in a common road which then forks as follows:

Policy making
Setting objectives

Objectives for Breakthrough	Objectives for Control
Breakthrough in attitudes	Choosing a unit of measure
Use of Pareto principle	Choosing a standard
Organizing for breakthrough in knowledge	Designing a sensor
	Measuring performance
Creation of Steering Arm	Interpretation of results
Creation of Diagnostic Arm	Decision making
Diagnosis	Action
Breakthrough in cultural pattern	
Transition to the new level	

The drastic differences exhibited by these two sequences make it evident that when we talk of a single sequence for managerial action, we are straining our classifications beyond the elastic limit. To be sure, whether we are creating or preventing change, we must organize, select, train, motivate, etc. But the organization forms are drastically different. The selection and training are drastically different. The motivations are drastically different. And so on. Such differences should be brought out in the open, rather than be obscured by a common label.

Does this new emphasis, on the great differences between creating and preventing change, presage a new school of management? The author believes that it does, based on the reactions of many industrial managers to the "Breakthrough Lecture."

2 BREAKTHROUGH—A PANORAMIC VIEW

The Unvarying Sequence

There is an unvarying sequence of events by which we break out of old levels of performance and into new. The details of this sequence are important, and we will discuss them in succeeding chapters. But first it is well to see the sequence as a whole, and the interrelation of the various steps. The summary which follows is in the same order as the succeeding chapters.

The Basic Diagram (Fig. 2) shows this sequence superimposed on the graph of performance.

The starting point is the *attitude* that a breakthrough is both desirable and feasible. In human organizations there is no change unless there is first an advocate of change. If someone does want a change, there is still a long, hard road before change is achieved. But the first step on that road is someone's belief that a change—a breakthrough—is desirable and feasible. That a change is desirable is mainly an act of faith or belief. Feasibility requires some digging. This leads to the second step.

The second need is to see whether a breakthrough is likely to happen if we mobilize for it—a sort of feasibility study. In most situations, this feasibility study includes an analysis to separate the really major parts of a problem from the rest—separating the "vital few" from the "useful many." The author once gave this type of study the name of the *Pareto analysis.*[1]

The Pareto analysis is a management tool of uncommon power and versatility. It finds the few needles of vital problems in a haystack of trivia. These vital few problems then become the subject of a drive for new knowledge. But creation of new knowledge does not just happen—we must organize for it. This leads to the next step.

Organization for breakthrough in knowledge is next. It requires that we appoint or create two pieces of organization machinery. One is for directing the breakthrough in knowledge, the other for doing the fact gathering and analysis. We will name them the Steering Arm and the Diagnostic Arm, respectively. For a breakthrough in knowledge, both of these arms are necessary. Neither one, by itself, is sufficient. Lacking a Diagnostic Arm, the Steering Arm becomes a debating society. Lacking a Steering Arm, the Diagnostic Arm is a ship with lots of sail and little rudder. Whether these arms are formal Committees, Departments, individuals, etc., "depends," and will be discussed in Chaps. 5 and 6.

The Steering Arm has the job of directing the acquisition and use of the new knowledge. But new knowledge requires research, which in turn requires direction, facilities, and theories. The Steering Arm, which consists of the key person or persons affected by the "vital few" matters of the Pareto analysis, meets these needs by providing:

unity of purpose
theories to be affirmed or denied
authority to conduct the factual and analytical studies
action based on the resulting new knowledge

The Diagnostic Arm does the detailed work of fact collection and analysis needed to achieve the breakthrough in new knowledge and to pave the way for action. This work generally requires time, skills, and objectivity not possessed by the Steering Arm. The Diagnostic Arm supplies the missing time, skills, and objectivity.

Diagnosis can now proceed. Under direction of the Steering Arm, the Diagnostic Arm goes out on the trail and brings back its findings. These are talked out, resulting in further directions and further detailed studies. This goes on and on until the new knowledge needed for action has been acquired. At this stage, breakthrough in knowledge has been achieved.

---

[1]See, for details, footnote, p. 48.

However, breakthrough in knowledge does not automatically create a breakthrough in performance. Experience has shown that the technical changes needed usually affect the status, habits, beliefs, etc., of the human beings involved. Anthropologists have given the name "cultural pattern" to this collection of human habits, beliefs, practices, etc.

Breakthrough in the cultural pattern is in this way an added essential step. Before the new levels of performance can be reached, we must discover the effect of the proposed changes on the cultural pattern, and find ways to deal with the resistances generated. This turns out to be a difficult, important, and fascinating problem.

Breakthrough in performance can now be achieved. This is the result we had set out to attain. But it turns out to be a squirming, elusive result. The plan for attaining it runs into numerous obstacles. Even after the result has been attained, it doesn't stay that way—there is some backsliding. All this squirming requires the firm grip of "control."

Control, during and after attainment of the new level, becomes the final step. The means for achieving Control are a separate sequence of events, and are the subject of the second half of this book.

Why an Organized Approach?

All human progress has been a series of breakthroughs, and many, perhaps most of these have not been formally organized. Yet they happened. Why, then, do we talk of an *organized* approach?

The answer is that an organized approach can greatly increase the probability that we will really get a breakthrough, and can drastically shorten the time for doing it.

The company needs breakthroughs in performance—lots of them. Whether organized or not, these breakthroughs do in fact use the steps we have traced. But the examples we will discuss in later chapters will show, again and again, that in the absence of an organized effort, the performance levels would have remained at their old levels—the very levels at which they stood during years of unorganized approaches to breakthrough.

The author realizes that few managers will accept these assertions just based on logical reasoning. In such matters, conviction comes from successful experience. The manager who has gone through a few instances in which an organized approach has outdone long-standing performance develops a conviction akin to the faith of the true believer. He or she has seen several "miracles," and he or she knows that it is now within his or her own power to create added Breakthroughs. He or she then tackles longstanding situations with full confidence that he or she possesses the tools needed to secure the new results.

We will return to this need for an organized approach (in Chap. 5). Meanwhile, let us start to examine, in detail, the nature of the Breakthrough cycle. To facilitate reference, we will reproduce at each chapter heading, the entire list of segments of this Breakthrough cycle.

3 BREAKTHROUGH IN ATTITUDES

THE PARETO PRINCIPLE
MOBILIZING FOR BREAKTHROUGH IN KNOWLEDGE
THE STEERING ARM
THE DIAGNOSTIC ARM
BREAKTHROUGH IN KNOWLEDGE—DIAGNOSIS
RESISTANCE TO CHANGE—CULTURAL PATTERNS
BREAKTHROUGH IN PERFORMANCE—ACTION
TRANSITION TO THE NEW LEVEL

Managerial and Personal Attitudes

The journey to breakthrough can be long and intricate, but the first step is refreshingly simple. It all begins because one individual feels motivated by an idea for breakthrough—any individual, any idea. An operator drops a grimy form into the suggestion box. A vice-president brings a magazine article to a staff meeting. A district manager gets a tip from a customer. A staff specialist is set afire by a speech he hears at a conference. A supervisor vows—"we'll fix this thing once and for all."

What happens to these ideas is anything but refreshingly simple. At the very start of its life, an idea of consequence must run a gauntlet of several or many people, any one of whom can dim its chances by a determined "no."

What makes someone say "no" to an idea for improvement? Is it that some managers dislike lower costs, safer plants, better quality, more prompt deliveries? Absolutely not. In the author's experience, *all* managers (and for that matter, nonmanagers) want these things. The managers, in particular, exhibit an occupational drive for new, better results.

But the manager is also a person. Like the conscientious objector, the rebel, or the heretic, he carries around some internal pressures which conflict with his duties to the organization. Usually the manager's pressures are under such control that they do not hinder his acting out his managerial role. In some cases, his personal pressures move him in the same direction as his managerial pressures, and the result is a "driver." In other cases, his internal pressures conflict with his role as a manager to so great an extent that he drags his feet.

In this way, each manager is a split personality. Two sets of forces are present:

(*a*) His or her duties as a manager

(*b*) His or her drives as a person

The distinguishing characteristic of these two roles is simple. The managerial role examines a proposition from the standpoint—"What is best for the company?" The personal role stresses—"What is best for me?"

These forces may aid or hinder each other, in varying degrees. The resulting permutations of this internal tug-of-war make up the wide assortment of visible responses to proposals for breakthrough.

This distinction between manager-role attitudes and personal attitudes is of cardinal importance. Failure to grasp it leads to accusations that a manager lacks such attitudes as cost-mindedness or quality-mindedness. (This is like accusing the American Legion of lack of patriotism.) The result is a fruitless argument and a residue of bitterness. The real need is to discover just what are the forces that prevent the manager from playing his or her natural role.

Manager-Role Attitudes

"What is best for the company?" would ideally be answered by putting together all pertinent facts and discussing them in the president's cabinet meeting. The practical situation falls far short of this ideal. The manager does not have all the facts. Neither does he or she have the experience and judgment represented by the cabinet. So the manager must interpret, as well as he or she can, what would be the likely judgment of the top people in the company.

This interpretation is strongly influenced by the manager's personal role. This means that the manager role and the personal role become intertwined. In practice this is indeed the case. But right now, to understand the manager role, let us make the assumption that the manager examines propositions solely from the standpoint "What is best for the company?" Under this assumption, what are the forces which shape his decision?

There are a number of these forces:

the company climate for Breakthrough

the past record of successes and failures in attempts at Breakthrough the extent to which the company has taken to narcotics to forget its troubles

the extent to which there is preoccupation with control

Company Climate for Breakthrough

Let's look at three contrasting cases. First is the approach used by Montgomery Ward & Company during the reign of the late, unlamented Mr. Sewell Avery.

> Avery believed that the United States would, in due course, go into a second Great Depression. His fears bordered on the pathological. He cast his vote of lack of confidence in the country's future by holding his company static while its chief competitor prospered vigorously. The efforts of Avery's subordinates to change his views resulted only in a record turnover of vice-presidents. In such a situation, no one but the company's directors had the power to act. Montgomery Ward's directors failed to act.

Next, let us look at some notes of an interview with a manager—we will call him Ray—in a company which, mercifully, will remain nameless:

> They talk progress. They say it on the bulletin boards and in the house organ. But they don't really mean it. They wouldn't open an office on the West coast. The young fellow who was pushing it decided to quit. He put himself in hock to open there. Now he's making nothing but money. They wouldn't go into Product X after all the work we put into it. Our competitors, after starting later, are making a killing. They wouldn't acquire the M company. Now it's as big as we are. Where they do move ahead, it isn't with a fresh, clean approach. They patch here, use baling wire there. Oh, you can get some things done if you fight for it. But you are on your own. No help from them. Grudging thanks if you make it, and a lot of ridicule if you don't.

Finally, consider the policy of a well-known New Jersey company. Breakthrough is not only a stated policy at the top; the entire system of setting objectives, and of planning to meet them, provides for Breakthroughs. In preparing the annual plan and associated budget, each manager, without exception (clear down to the first-line supervisor on the factory floor) is required to include a *budgeted improvement*. This is not done by writing down a percentage; it must be based on a statement of what deeds will be done, what improvement projects will be tackled, and how these projects will be worked out. The management is not satisfied with a promissory note—it asks for, and receives, a pledge of specific actions.

The foregoing represent three contrasting climates for Breakthrough. Mr. Avery was against it.

Ray's top management is apathetic. It pays lip service to Breakthrough, but doesn't really support it.

The New Jersey company's top management has a positive approach which it has succeeded in carrying clear down to the first level of supervision.

In all cases, the policy at the top had an immense influence on what happened throughout the company. This influence stemmed from two essential, separable forces:

1. The climate
2. The organized approach

Under a hostile climate, the approach becomes academic. Nothing will happen anyway.

In Ray's company, the climate was permissive at best. In addition, the absence of an organized approach put every manager on his own. Most of them just lapsed into an attitude of "Well, if that's the way they want it, I just work here." Ray was too much of a professional to live under such an attitude, hence his agony.

In the New Jersey company the climate was more than favorable, it was coupled with an organized approach which made Breakthrough mandatory.

The effect of changing climate can be dramatic. Sonnabend[1] relates a case in which there was need for improving the team approach and the self-motivation of company executives. A program was set up for doing these things. One striking result was the shift from a tendency to blame everything on top management to a tendency to be creative and constructive.

We will shortly examine the organized approach. Meanwhile we observe that, as in biology, climate is a major factor in determining whether growth will be stunted, or ordinary, or prolific. In the company, climate is created at the top. It is created not so much by the words as by the sincerity behind the words, evidenced by example and deed.

---

[1]Sonnabend, Roger P., "An Experiment in Motivation," *Management Record*, July–August, 1962, pp. 19–22.

Echoes from the Cemetery

Every company has a cemetery full of dead projects. In the proposal stage, each was warmly advocated by some enthusiast. Some projects worked out. Others did not. It turns out, in retrospect, that it is hard to predict which projects will work out well and which will come to rest in the cemetery.

Except for new product development, the mortality rate of projects has not been too well documented. For new product proposals it is known to be shocking. One study[2] devoted to new chemical products shows that:

of 540 ideas proposed
  92 were regarded as pertinent
  8 were approved for development
  1 went to market

· The mortality rate has made the manager wary of all projects, no matter how plausible. In defense he has improved his methods of review. These include:

providing objective tests such as computation of Return on Investment
broadening the base of review by securing participation of other managers
revaluing the project at logical intermediate stages

These and other methods still fall short of adequate predictability. The choice of timing is most difficult, as witness the ill-fated streamlined car which was brought out 20 years too early.[3] Quite aside from his personal zest for change, the ideal manager must be wary of wasting the company's assets.

Lacking a fully scientific approach to evaluation, we must still rely heavily on managerial judgment. Of course, this opens the way for heavy-handed intrusion by the personal-role half of the manager's split personality. But it is what we do, and must continue to do for the foreseeable future.

---

[2]Jones, Ralph W., "Management of New Products," *Journal of Industrial Engineering,* September–October, 1958, pp. 429–435.

[3]In the early 1920s, one of the first books ever written on Job Evaluation was published. It failed to sell its first printing. A decade later someone else's book on Job Evaluation was published. It sold over 100,000 copies. The latter book rode in on the wave of the collective-bargaining needs resulting from the passage of the Wagner Labor Relations Act.

Desensitizing the Manager

Industry teems with opportunities to which its managers have been blinded by preoccupation with "variances." We can see this graphically in Figs. 4 and 5. In Fig. 4 we see a performance which has generally been "under control." The peak was an exception. In time-honored fashion, all hands had rushed to the scene, and restored order. Now all that remains is a peak on the chart and a loss approximately equal to the shaded area. Everyone concerned may feel pretty good about the whole thing—the fire brigade made short work of the blaze.

Now turn to Fig. 5 and suddenly the whole perspective changes. The shaded peak turns out to be an insignificant loss. The real loss is the double-shaded area, and it is this area which is the reward for Breakthrough. How obvious! Why isn't this opportunity obvious without such charts?

The answer lies in a widespread narcotic effect of the use of "variances." The basic concept behind use of "variances" is sound, as we shall see in the chapters on Control. A variance signals a departure from plan, in the wrong direction. Something should be done about it. But the converse, i.e., that absence of a variance means all's well, "ain't necessarily so."

A factory process has for years been yielding only 90 percent good product despite periodic efforts to improve the yield. Hence, over the years, various actions have been taken to recognize the 10 percent loss as "normal."

The cost standards now take into consideration the 10 per cent normal loss. Hence the cost report sounds no alarm (shows no "variance") unless the yield falls below 90 percent.

The material order cards provide for an order factor of 110; i.e., an extra 10 percent is ordered to anticipate the normal 10 percent

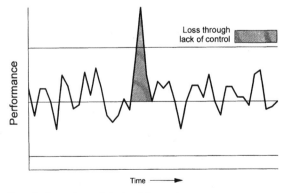

Fig. 4. Loss through lack of Control.

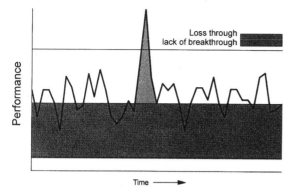

Fig. 5. Loss through lack of Breakthrough.

loss. Hence there will be no alarm signal due to shortage of material unless the yield falls below 90 percent.

The machine capacity has been made adequate to process this extra 10 percent material. Hence there will be no alarm signal due to machine bottlenecks unless the yield falls below 90 percent.

By defusing these and other alarm signals, we *desensitize* ourselves to the existence of the 90 percent. We have, with the best of intentions, learned to live with this bad-smelling mess. We no longer notice it, since we have made ourselves shockproof to the evidences. But the mess is still there. When an outsider sees it for the first time, he is shocked, since he had not been rendered shockproof.

One of the purposes of an organized approach to Breakthrough is to bring these situations back out into the open so that they can again shock people and stimulate them to action.

Preoccupation with Control

A high proportion of managers simply have no time for Breakthrough because they cannot leave the treadmill of control. They do *not* need to be convinced of the merits of Breakthrough. They *do* need respite from the never-ending emergencies and crises. Their situation is much like that of so many limited-income people who would like to make a change of other sorts—change jobs, travel abroad, start their own business, build their own home. But there is no respite from the never-ending needs for shoes, dental care, and other current crises of their growing family.

Seldom are these harassed managers able to work their way out. More usually, it requires help from upper management, with an assist from the staff people. The harassed manager can still find time for participating in the *guidance* of Breakthrough. But the remaining parts of the Breakthrough sequence must be worked out by other people.

Other Manager-Role Influences

There are still other factors which influence our ideal manager's answer to the question "What is best for the company?"

The state of executive development of the manager and his peers. The level of sophistication influences the ability to communicate with each other and to optimize company performance, rather than departmental performance.

The availability of tools for discovering the optimum. The most obvious example is the Return on Investment determination, but there are many others.

The age of the company. Older organisms show their age. They develop methodical, even ponderous ways of doing things. In theory, the company can be kept fresh and vigorous forever. In practice, this requires such highly sophisticated managing that few companies really create an in-house fountain of youth. But it can be done. Adoption of Breakthrough as a philosophy of life is one of the essentials.

The size of the company. The smaller company is inherently more sensitive to the need for change, more nimble in responding to the need. The big company must, in due course, break itself up into decentralized operating units, and the need to respond to change is one of the main reasons.

There are other factors, but it is not necessary to list them all. The point is that for every obstacle there are ways of making the best of it. The real obstacle is to mistake the problem for a fate.

Personal-Role Attitudes— The Environment

We now leave our ideal, 100 percent company-oriented manager and return to reality. The manager obviously considers "What is best for me?" We can better deal with these personal-role attitudes by separating them as between

the environmental influences, i.e., the boss, professionalism, etc.

the inherent traits of the individual, i.e., to oversimplify, is he man or mouse?

First, as to the environment.

The Boss

"What is best for the company" and "what the boss wants" are by no means the same thing.

> Every day, year in and year out, each man should ask himself, over and over again, two questions. First, "What is the name of the man I am now working for?" and having answered this definitely, then, "What does this man want me to do, right now?" Not, "What ought I to do in the interests of the company that I am working for?" Not, "What did I agree to do when I came here?" Not, "What should I do for my own best interests?" but, plainly and simply, "What does this man want me to do?"

So wrote F. W. Taylor[4] in his "Success" lecture. Taylor was not given to expression in vague terms—his writings admit of no misinterpretation.

The growth of written policy, objectives, standard practice, routines, etc., has narrowed the gap between what the company needs and what the boss wants. But there is still a gap, and the manager must deal with it.

The boss may have authoritarian tendencies. He cuts short the subordinate's participation. Consent becomes academic. Management by fiat rears its unwelcome head. Even the right result becomes distasteful because it is to be reached by the wrong means.

If such a boss is still young and healthy, the spirited subordinates tend to leave; the rest tend to become apathetic.

At the other extreme, it is the boss who is apathetic. The resulting power vacuum invites a struggle for power which no one can escape. Each individual becomes a contestant or the follower of a contestant, since the legitimate leadership has abdicated.

Professionalism

Those who have lived all their working lives in industrial companies can be deluded into believing that the sole forces motivating individuals are the pay, the hope of promotion, the fear of what the boss can do to them. Such beliefs are a logical result of generalizing from just one of the many patterns in which life is lived. Actually, there are some other, powerful motivations. One of these is inherent in the idea of a profession.

[4]Copley, Frank B., *Frederick W. Taylor*, Harper & Row, Publishers, Incorporated, New York, 1923, vol. 1, p. 131.

The true profession is based on some essential public service requiring special knowledge for its performance. People who enter this profession are specially selected, trained, and examined for this service. If they qualify, they are rewarded by a license to practice. Only the license holders may practice the true profession—they are given a monopoly which is limited only by a code of ethics.

The profession provides its members with some deep satisfactions, including:

a source of personal income and security
a basis for self-respect and the respect of others
a sense of being accepted and of "belonging"
an opportunity for "advancement in the profession"

This is a formidable list of satisfactions. It is therefore not surprising to discover that the professional, though hired by a company, still retains strong loyalties to the profession.[5] The profession demands a sense of duty, a code of conduct, a level of craftsmanship. The young professional is indoctrinated by all this, and much of this doctrine stays with him or her. The hired professional also looks to his or her "standing in the profession" as well as to his or her "standing in the company."

The manager has been taking some definite steps toward professionalism. He attends courses, seminars, and conferences with other managers. He leads meetings, writes papers, gives lectures, and otherwise acquires greater awareness that managing is a separate body of knowledge, different from anything else. The resulting knowledge and exchange of experience make the manager more objective as to his decisions, more sure-footed as to his convictions, more mobile as to job tenure.

There is an exhilaration in all this. The professional type of manager has acquired a built-in drive for doing a good job. Nowhere is this drive more evident than in its determination for Breakthrough, for better performance on all fronts. Armed with this drive, the manager simply cannot be comfortable with slovenly performance, whether of his own, of his subordinates, or even of his boss.

Other Environmental Factors

The manager has still other vested interests. He or she came from some specialty (accounting, mechanical engineering) to which he or she remains

---

[5]Many professionals regard the profession, not the company, as their true career, and move readily from one company to another. Many become self-employed.

partial. He or she has been associated with some market, product, process, to which he or she is likewise partial. He or she has lived with some department (purchasing, personnel) and does not readily accept its disappearance through decentralization. Most certainly he or she does not readily accept any proposal which will cut into his or her status, prestige, or other values. Any proposal which is a threat to the importance of his or her role is likely to be contested.

These vested interests are always more obvious when the other person has them. The generals and admirals have faced these problems to an intense degree.

> The Navy is not only an armed force—it is a society. In the forty years following the Civil War, this society had been forced to accommodate itself to a series of technological changes....These changes wrought extraordinary changes in ship design, and therefore in the concepts of how ships were to be used; that is, in fleet tactics and even in naval strategy....To these numerous innovations, producing as they did a spreading disorder throughout a service with heavy commitments to formal organization, the Navy responded with grudging pain. It is wrong to assume, as civilians frequently do, that this blind reaction to technological change springs exclusively from some causeless Bourbon distemper that invades the military mind. There is a sounder and more attractive base. The opposition, where it occurs, of the soldier and the sailor to such change, springs from the normal human instinct to protect oneself and more especially one's way of life. Military organizations are societies built around and upon the prevailing weapon systems. Intuitively and quite correctly the military man feels that a change in weapons portends a change in the arrangements of his society.[6]

Note the concept that the Navy is a "society." We will have a more detailed look at this concept when we look at "cultural patterns" in chap. 9. There we will see that the industrial worker likewise is a member of various societies and that this membership can raise havoc with proposed changes.

A negative attitude resulting from environmental factors seldom is directly traceable to its cause. The famous complaint that "the Navy is being nibbled to death" was exceptional in its directness. More usually, the negative attitude is stated on the merits of the proposal, and it may well sound plausible. Those who are advocating the proposal can easily be led on a wild goose chase by these plausible reasons when the real reason is to be found in the cultural pattern.

Let us now turn from environment to the basic human traits of the managers.

[6]Morison, Elting, "A Case Study of Innovation," *Engineering and Science*, April, 1950.

The Spectrum of Personal Attitudes

Suppose that for each "no" to an idea, we made out a coroner's report of cause of infant mortality, including precisely what was in the mind of the manager who did the deed. Analysis of these melancholy reports would show that the spectrum of personal attitudes follows the familiar bell-shaped curve (Fig. 6). For our purpose, we need only divide this curve into three sections:

1. *A little band of Innovators.* They exhibit an itch for change.
2. *A great center of Conservatives.* They are neither for nor against change. They are just for results.
3. *A little band of Inhibitors.* They are negative on ideas for change.

As we have seen, all of these people, in their managerial role, want lower costs and the rest. But they differ as to the extent of the internal pressures they carry around.

> An experiment in change[7] provides some quantitative idea of the proportions under the bell-shaped curve of attitude.
>
> A team of scientists undertook to help a village of Peruvian potato farmers improve their productivity. The scientists came up with an agricultural plan involving blight-resistant seed, fertilizers, insecticides, and even a method of financing.
>
> The scientists then discussed the plan with the village leaders, who rejected it—it wouldn't work. But it also became evident that the leaders' opposition was due to vested interests. An improvement of farm productivity by "imported" methods would under-

[7]Collier, John, and Mary Collier, "An Experiment in Applied Anthropology," *Scientific American,* January, 1957, pp. 37–45.

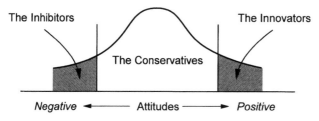

Fig. 6. Attitudes toward Breakthrough.

mine the leaders' status as agricultural experts, and thus chip away at their overall leadership status.

The scientists then went over the leaders' heads by proposing the plan to the entire village. After some heated discussion and shifts of position, a residue of 17 farmers (about 10 percent of the total) entered the project for the planting season. Some of these venturesome few were rebels; most were just so poor they had nothing to lose.

The project was a stunning success. Each of the 17 farmers harvested more than a double crop of potatoes!

The following season, 85 of the farmers (about half the village), including one of the leaders, bought the new plan. Again it was a success. In the third season, 135 of the farmers (about four-fifths of the village) were on the band wagon.

Personal Attitudes— The Inhibitors

Let's start with an actual case:

> Two industrial engineers had a good idea for a new product. They asked for, and received, the general manager's O.K. to develop it. Then they found themselves frustrated by the Product Development Department which would not supply various essential facilities and skills needed for such a project. The thing reached a crisis, forcing the general manager to transfer the project to the Product Development Department. Thereupon everything fell into place, and the project became a great success. The Product Development Department was clearly blocking a good project in order to assert their monopolistic "right" to develop new products.[8]

The Inhibitor has a whole host of such reasons for calling a halt to "progress." A monopoly on product development in an electronics plant, or on agricultural expertise in a Peruvian village is a fairly obvious reason. It is a defense of "rights" which are regarded as "vested" by long possession. Less obvious, but no less compelling, are those situations which require that we deny what we have said for a lifetime.

When the Renaissance astronomers contended that the sun, not the earth, was the center of the universe, the shock to humanity was severe.

---

[8]Ronken, H. O., and P. R. Lawrence, *Administering Changes*, Harvard University Press, Cambridge, Mass., 1952.

Men were being asked to deny the long-standing beliefs of untold generations, beliefs which their own senses had confirmed. The implication to a keen observer is obvious—only a fool is deceived by his own senses. The implication to a descendant is no less obvious. If this long-standing belief is defective, then all long-standing beliefs are suspect, and so is the stature of revered ancestors, teachers, and leaders.

Aristotle had said nothing about the planet Jupiter having satellites. Hence we had best not look through Galileo's telescope. Otherwise we might loosen some nightmare of facts to jolt our deep dream of dogma.

The manager of today is often put into a parallel position. Someone proposes that he embark on a sequence for Breakthrough to improve performance X. The manager of the activity is well acquainted with performance X—for years he has devoted time and energy to this job. A likely train of reasoning now is:

"Performance X has gone on for some years now despite our efforts to improve it. Since we are experienced, competent people, and have not been able to effect a significant change, it follows that no one can effect such a change."

This kind of reasoning can come from earnest, sensible people. But if they say it too often or too loudly, an added train of reasoning develops:

"After what I've said so often, if we now succeed in Breakthrough, won't I be the damn fool."

No less painful are those situations in which the manager's[9] beliefs are based not on the limitations of his or her senses, but rather on things which are accepted on faith from his or her predecessors—a modern form of ancestor worship. This managerial catechism is extensive. It teaches him or her that managers should have an unlimited right to run the business, that people are motivated solely by the desire to earn more money, that overhead is an evil, that operators have lost their pride of workmanship, etc. These are beliefs kept fresh by the self-sealing thought system in which so many managers operate. To violate one of them is like breaking a sacred idol, or denying the Bible.

> A company controller had for years waged war against overhead—in his mind, overhead was a disease which must be kept from spreading. He succeeded in blocking many proposals, but the company lost its leadership to competitors who went ahead with such proposals.

---

[9]It is necessary here to distinguish (a) an attitude which resists embarking on the Breakthrough cycle from (b) cultural resistance to a proposed technical change. The former is the subject of the present chapter; the latter is dealt with in Chap. 9.

To cite another example:

> A company undertaking change from a functional to a product grouping of organization experienced keen opposition from the Purchasing Manager. This was surprising because the man was due to retire in a short time anyhow. The explanation was actually that he regarded "his" department as a monument to himself, and could not bear to see it torn down.

We will, later in this chapter, discuss constructive approaches to personal attitudes. In the case of the Inhibitor, the approach must be from the flank. He or she is immune from persuasion through logical reasoning.

Personal Attitudes—
The Conservatives

The badge of the Conservative reads "Show me."

This response to ideas is outwardly constructive and friendly. It keeps things fluid. It opens the way for more facts and light. It gains more time for minds to adapt to change. It creates an atmosphere of objectivity. The trouble it creates is mainly in the mind of the impatient Innovator. He interprets "Show me" as a delaying tactic, as well as a slur on his own competence.

The Conservative's insistence on "results before change" is one of the most valuable stabilizers in the entire company structure. If we are to have continuity and cohesion, we should not give up something that works until the thing that is to replace it has been demonstrated to be workable. This concept has so much obvious value that even some cost in concurrent operation of the old and the new may be warranted.

Some years ago the author[10] drew an image of one Emil, a Conservative who had fashioned a defense against Innovators.

DEALING WITH THE "OBSTRUCTIONIST" SUPERINTENDENT

At a gathering of Quality Managers a young executive was eagerly relating how they had reduced waste in his company, how through quality control they had discovered some new things about the process, and how the production superintendent had taken action.

One of the listeners shrugged his shoulders.

---

[10]Juran, J. M., Dealing with the "Obstructionist" Superintendent, *Industrial Quality Control*, July, 1955, p. 24.

"In my company you wouldn't get to first base with that, and all because of Emil."

Emil, it turned out, was an "old-time" production superintendent. Emil was set in his ways. Nothing could make him change. And the management was just too softhearted to take Emil off the job because he had 31 years' service, and had been on his job 13 years. Emil still had six years to go for retirement. Until then, no progress was possible.

Then a curious thing happened. Another listener interrupted: "One of our superintendents is just like that—only his name is Charlie." Then followed a whole chorus of interruptions. Everyone, it seemed, knew in his own company a superintendent, a manager, or a foreman who fitted the description of Emil.

So Emil is everywhere, only his name is something else. But for those responsible for quality control, is this a fate or a problem? Is no progress possible, or is the need only to find a solution which fits Emil?

I have met Emil in many plants. From him, from his bosses, from his associates, and from his subordinates I have learned much about him and his attitudes, including his attitude toward quality.

Curiously enough, Emil would rather make good products than bad ones. He likes to have it said of him that "Emil does a good job." Emil would rather have a high rate of yield than a low rate, because then he can meet his delivery schedules easier. Emil would rather have his subordinates make high earnings than lose those earnings in rework. I have never met a production head named Emil or otherwise who preferred bad work to good work.

The Emils I have met have some other things in common. Out of a long career with the company, they can recall many pleasant memories but also some bitter ones. Here and there they have endured an uninspiring boss, a siege of unwarranted blame, or a piece of skullduggery from some industrial adventurer who tried to rush through in two months what takes a year or two to mature.

Emil looks to these experiences for much guidance to meet the problems ahead. He is getting on in years and he is slowing up. No longer does he consider it a calamity if he is passed up for promotion. But it would be a real calamity if he should be blamed for some big failure, and risk losing the status he already has.

It took Emil many years to become a superintendent. Most of those he started with are still on the machine or on the bench. In their eyes, and in his own eyes, he has arrived.

Emil is reconciled to the idea that he will probably never get to be manager. Younger employees have already passed him up in enough numbers to make this clear. The big thing, for Emil, is not to lose his job as superintendent. The young superintendents are of a different mind. The last thing they want is to remain a superintendent all their life. They can afford to gamble and take chances with new ways. But Emil is too far along in years and in service to dare to gamble.

So Emil uses the utmost caution to protect his flank. His security is not threatened one bit by the usual day-to-day fires he must put out. He has been doing that for many years, and knows how to cope with the day-to-day problems. Any threat to his security will not come from these familiar problems, but from something which is to him unfamiliar and untried.

This brings us to the heart of the problem of dealing with the "obstructionist." Emil is going to "obstruct" whatever is a threat to his security. He would not be human if he acted otherwise. The problem in dealing with Emil is "simply" to avoid a threat to Emil's security.

For some engineers this is all wrong. They are advocating something that is so logical (to them) and so valuable to the company (in their opinion). Why should this not be adopted forthwith? Why is it necessary to act out a game with Emil, to cater to his whims, to make it seem that it is really his ideas which are being put into effect?

In particular the engineers reproach their own top management. Emil, they say, should be ordered to put these new ideas into effect. Yet this suggestion by the engineers betrays shocking ignorance of the fundamental rules of organization. If top management is to hold Emil responsible for results, it must give him collateral authority to decide to act. To order him to adopt this or that new proposal would be taking away with the left hand the authority top management gave Emil with its right hand.

So there is no escape from selling Emil himself on the ideas. If the engineers could only grasp this fact! Once they put their minds to it, they could discover many devices for selling; in fact, they could borrow them intact from other heads in their own company. If they make their first job that of convincing Emil that they are no threat to his security, they have crossed the real barrier.

My own rule for judging whether Emil is going to be a problem is to discover whether Emil has (a) integrity, and (b) common sense. If these things are present, the limitations on results lie only in the sales ability of the engineers.

The Conservative, who is also most of humanity, is not the first to embark on a change—that is left to the Innovators. Until the change has been tried and proved, the Conservative holds back. Logical reasoning will, by itself, not galvanize him into action. That happens only when he sees others reaping the benefits of the change.

At times, logical reasoning dictates the path of conservatism anyhow.

In a submarine cable project, some Bell System engineers had the option of using certain new materials which gave promise of superior performance. The engineers deliberately chose the old, tried and proved, "inferior" materials. They were too ignorant of the unknown deficiencies which might, as uninvited guests, accompany the superior performance of the new materials.

The Conservative homemaker buys a new product, not on the basis that it has this or that new feature, but because more venturesome friends have bought and are satisfied. The Conservative manager buys new systems, procedures, machinery, and ideas on a similar test of proved usage.

Like the Inhibitor, the Conservative is bound by the past, but to a different degree and for different reasons.

The Inhibitor's ties with the past are based on dogma; the Conservative's ties are based on results. The Inhibitor will not tear down an old fence; to him old fences are sacred. The Conservative may tear it down, but only after he knows why it was put up.

The Inhibitor opposes the new idea because it is an alien. The Conservative opposes the new idea because he fears its unknown defects—he doesn't mind aliens, but they must be law-abiding. Proof by usage will eliminate the opposition of the Conservative, but not of the Inhibitor. To the Inhibitor, a law-abiding alien is still an alien, and therefore undesirable.

Personal Attitudes—
The Innovators

The badge of the Innovator reads "You can't stop progress."

The Innovators are a wide assortment. They include:

The explorers—those who are so stimulated by adventure that they will face the risks of the unknown.

The discontented—those who have concluded that any likely change is preferable to continuance of what they are now doing.

The specialists—their advocacy of change is greatly influenced by their urge to advance their specialty.

The staff—their full-time job (their manager role) is one of promulgating change.

These and other varieties of Innovators constitute a mixed bag. Collectively they are the yeast in the industrial cauldron. They can also be mighty irritating because, unlike the Inhibitors, the Innovators are generally an aggressive, insistent, noisy lot.

In his less exuberant moments, the Innovator can make out a pretty good case for considering Breakthrough as a way of life. Here is the way he might state his case—his version of the faith of the true believer:

"During my own lifetime I have seen a lot of Breakthroughs in products, processes, methods, and everything else. Experienced, competent people presided over all these things for years, and yet Breakthroughs were made. All this has been so widespread that it is nonsense to assume that performance X or any other performance is immune from improvement."

This line of reasoning is hard to refute.

For many years, the 4-minute mile was regarded as beyond the capability of human beings. Now, suddenly, there are many people who can run a mile in under 4 minutes. Has the human race come up with a new breed of athletes? Not at all. People have found ways to make better use of what athletic skill they have always had.

One well-known form of Innovator is the inventor. His devotion to his brain child is legendary. Yet it may not be enough to deal with entrenched attitude. Sometimes an admiring passer-by takes up the fight and becomes the real promoting force.

After examining the history of some important Breakthroughs in military hardware, one investigator[11] concluded:

1. At the outset, the idea encounters sharp resistance from officialdom.
2. In response to this resistance, promoters emerge. Often the main promoter is someone other than the inventor.
3. The proponents do their promoting (including "bootlegged" research) through informal channels.
4. Typically, one individual emerges as champion of the idea. Failing this, the idea dies.

The fierce devotion of the inventor or promoter to the invention is universal. Schon quotes Arthur K. Watson:[12]

> The disk memory unit, the heart of today's random access computer, is not the logical outcome of a decision made by IBM management. It was developed in one of our laboratories as a bootleg project—over the stern warning from management that the project had to be dropped because of budget difficulties. A handful of men ignored the warning. They broke the rules. They risked their jobs to work on a project they believed in.

The classical true believer is one who has witnessed a miracle, and through this has become willing to accept, on faith, matters which others, equally intelligent, would view with skepticism.

---

[11]Schon, Donald A., "Champions for New Inventions," *Harvard Business Review*, March–April, 1963, pp. 77–86.

[12]Address to the Eighth International Congress of Accountants, New York City, Sept. 24, 1962.

The native of the Amazon has never seen a skyscraper. He would reject an assertion by a missionary that, on the very land on which he now stands, it is possible to erect a house as high as a hundred men, in which house a thousand men can live. But any child living in a modern city would accept this assertion unhesitatingly, since he or she has witnessed such miracles.

Dramatic change in managerial performance is no less a basis for faith. The manager who has gone through a number of successful instances of purposive change acquires a faith through this experience. This faith then serves to sustain him or her when he or she considers new proposals for a walk into the unknown. This same faith tells him or her that improvement is limited only by human ingenuity, to which there is no known limit. The steam shovel can outdig a thousand laborers; the powered combine can outperform a thousand farmhands; the assembly line can outproduce a thousand mechanics.

The Innovator is capable, in short order, of rising to a high pitch of enthusiasm, or plunging to the depths of frustration. He has difficulty grasping the idea that most human beings prefer a settled, stable, predictable life rather than the excitement of the chase. He can be impatient and even contemptuous of those who do not share his priority of values. At his best, he is a refreshing, formidable source of new strength for the company. He can also be a pretty narrow character, pushing some technique for its own sake. He can argue for changes which make his department look good but at the expense of overall company economics. At his worst, he is a fanatic with his eye on the grandstand rather than on the ball—an industrial pest.

Dealing with Attitudes

This chapter opened by noting that attitudes toward Breakthrough were decisive at the very outset of the sequence of events. It will close by summarizing what can be done about negative attitudes.

All levels of the company can contribute. The list which follows has classified these contributions to indicate in what respects the various levels can help the most. But there is no clean separation.

Top management can do the most. It can:

(*a*) Clarify the company's policy toward Breakthrough.

Top management should, at one of its meetings, discuss the question "Breakthroughs or not?" The preparation and discussion should be thorough enough to permit the extensive soul searching necessary for genuine conviction that Breakthrough is an essential ingredient of modern company life. Once convinced, top management should communicate the resulting policy to all. (*Note:* If the record of top management has long been one of opposing progress, their reputation will be in line with this record. Thereafter, no amount of just talk will change this reputation. Only a long series of deeds to the contrary will be effective.)

(*b*) Set the example by living up to the stated policy.

Top management can take the initiative on some projects. It can provide active encouragement of projects proposed from below. It can set an example of praise, not ridicule, for those who succeed in achieving a long-needed Breakthrough in the very operation they have supervised.

> In one company a program of quality improvement resulted in cutting the cost of defects in one department by $250,000. At a meeting called to discuss the extension of the program to other departments, one manager snorted: "If it was possible to save so much money, doesn't that prove how poor the supervision has been?" The snorter was promptly squelched by the other managers. "If that were our attitude toward improvements, who would dare to try them?"

It is not enough to avoid ridicule of successful Breakthroughs. There should be positive encouragement. Where praise for successful Breakthrough is a sure thing, the whole level of receptivity to ideas has been raised.

(*c*) Create unity by requiring written objectives, and plans for reaching them.

Top management can require that major company and departmental objectives be identified and planned for. Such a requirement goes far to establish a sense of unity, and permits more effective mobilizing of the company's resources by concentrating on a few clearly defined objectives for Breakthrough.

(*d*) Challenge the standard as much as the variance.

A widespread weakness among top managements is to put emphasis on variances from standards which have been set by the lower levels. The emphasis should be the other way around. Top management should devote its main effort to ensuring that the goals are sound.

(*e*) Provide for improving the caliber of managers.

Top management can take the initiative in requiring increased use of modern methods for selecting, training, and motivating managers. As this caliber is raised, a sense of professionalism combines with the acquired skills to create a dynamic force for improving performance.

(*f*) Review the prevailing incentives for the presence of decay and outdated dogma.

Top management should take a fresh look to see whether the system of incentives actively encourages Breakthrough by making the rewards worth the risks. In addition, the premises behind the incentives should be challenged—do they recognize the multiple drives of the industrial manager, or do they assume that his or her sole motivation is more money?

Next, as to middle management.

Middle management obviously participates in policy formulation, setting objectives, and planning. But mainly, middle management has the job of executing the plans to meet the objectives, all within the policy framework of the company. This job bristles with skills, tools, techniques, methods.

Middle management can:

(g) Make participation in Breakthrough a part of every job description:

> In the late 1950s, a meeting of the Manufacturing Council of American Management Association found itself discussing: "Is the manufacturing manager responsible just for Control, i.e., meeting standards of cost, delivery, and quality, or is he also responsible for Breakthrough, i.e., stimulating improvement in these things?" The votes for dual responsibility, which were well in the majority, included some advocates of *budgeted Breakthrough*. But it was also significant that these men, generally presidents or vice-presidents, in their companies, included a minority who regarded Breakthrough as someone else's job.

The law of change is the law of life itself. In the biological organism, every cell is harnessed to both control and breakthrough. The more nearly the company can parallel this, the more surely is it equipped to respond to the inevitable challenges of time.

(h) Provide regular channels for the flow of ideas and actions, so that improvement projects can be identified, attacked, and brought to a conclusion.

There are a variety of ways in which management can create an organized approach for Breakthrough. (Much of this book is devoted to examining these ways.) The point here is that some regular channel must be provided—it should be mandatory, not optional.

(i) Forge the tools and instruments needed for objective valuation of projects.

There is a broad list of these—return on investment, economic order points, make or buy, etc. They are aids to decision making because they narrow the range of human judgment needed, and hence narrow the range of disagreement among the participants.

(*j*) Adopt proven ways of increasing the batting average.

The greater the record of successes in Breakthrough, the greater the confidence of the team in going after further improvements. The "proven ways" include broadening the base of participation, providing for the necessary staff support, revaluing projects at logical intermediate stages, providing for dealing with cultural resistance. We will discuss all of these later.

(*k*) Throw away the opium pipes.

Middle management should be alert to the dangers of concluding that a long-standing poor performance is "normal." This is like smoking opium. The problems are still there, but we are drugged into forgetting them. Unhappily, the problems don't forget us. Emphasis on variances is fine provided the standard is sound.

(*l*) Set the example by personal participation in the breakthrough process.

Hoffman[13] states it well: "Strangely, the boss does not ask the training director or methods analyst to explain the new production schedule or sales campaign. He does it himself. Yet, when it comes to [approach to Breakthrough] he implies his own ignorance and lack of interest by asking a staff expert to explain it for him...."

(*m*) Assign people to situations new to them.

All of us, even the Inhibitors, can be objective about jobs in which we have no vested interests to protect. Assignments to committees or to study groups are steps toward making people more objective. Assignment to a different job has often been a turning point for those afflicted with an overaccumulation of prejudice.

(*n*) Give two cheers for efforts.

What about praise for failure to Breakthrough? It shouldn't receive all three cheers. The marketplace pays off for results, not for effort. Such must also be the rule within the company. But there should be recognition of well-intentioned effort. A record of 75 percent successes in Breakthrough would be very good indeed. The inevitable failures must be dealt with sympathetically, to convey understanding of the problems facing the Innovator, and to give him or her encouragement to keep trying.

Finally, the staff departments can contribute importantly to the problem of attitude (including their own attitude). Some of the things the staff can do are:

---

[13]Hoffman, Frank O., "Improve Your Profits Day by Day," *Harvard Business Review,* July–August, 1963, pp. 59–67.

(*o*) Look behind the words of the objector to understand his situation.

The maddening part of dealing with personal attitudes is that the reasons are seldom stated in words—they must be deduced from the situation. The Inhibitor never says "This would violate my vested monopolistic rights," or "This would break one of my idols." Instead he says "This will never work." "My business is different," etc.

> In his book "Red Bread" (1930), Maurice Hindus relates the reaction of Russian collective farmers to a proposal to use mechanical incubators for hatching chicks. "Nobody has ever done it." "It is not natural." "It will just waste eggs." The proponent patiently pointed out that Americans had got amazing results with incubators. No matter. "We don't care what happened in America." "American eggs might be different." "Machines can never take the place of hens."

The Innovator's words likewise disguise his or her real reasons. He or she never says "If this works, it will make me a hero." He or she is careful to leave himself or herself out of it: "Everybody is going over to this procedure." "We wouldn't be in this fix if we were using the XYZ system."

Even the Conservative, exemplified by Emil, exhibits a facade. Emil does not say "I'm too old to gamble." He says "You gotta show me," meaning "Let someone else gamble. I'll move when it's a sure thing."

The more completely the proponent of an idea knows the very real pressures facing his or her peers, the more surely can he or she adapt the proposal to meet their inevitable responses.

(*p*) Sell the Innovators by logic, the Conservatives by results.

An idea without precedent must be sold solely by logical reasoning. Where there is precedent, the sales kit contains a record of results as well as a chain of logic.

The proponent of the unprecedented idea is well advised to limit his or her approach to the Innovators who, alone in the spectrum of personal attitude, will step boldly into the unknown.

The Conservative wants to see the results of precedent. He can be accommodated when the Innovator has taken the gamble in his own company. Alternately, he can be taken to learn about such results in another company—by visiting that company, or by talking to his opposite number at some conference.

(*q*) Leave the Inhibitor for the last.

Neither the logical reasoning of the Innovators, nor the results achieved by the Conservatives, are enough to convince the Inhibitor. He begins to think about change when he finds himself conspicuous because everyone else has changed. He still is not "convinced" but he cannot openly remain a minority of one.

(*r*) Recognize the great power inherent in the cultural pattern.

The staff specialist had better recognize it, since it contains mysterious, invisible forces which cause "resistance to change." We will study these in detail in Chap. 9.

(*s*) Aid the person on the treadmill.

The manager who is busy fire fighting *can* "find" time for fire prevention—*the staff person's time*. This joint activity is the very heart of the Breakthrough process.

4 THE PARETO PRINCIPLE

MOBILIZING FOR BREAKTHROUGH IN KNOWLEDGE
THE STEERING ARM
THE DIAGNOSTIC ARM
BREAKTHROUGH IN KNOWLEDGE—DIAGNOSIS
RESISTANCE TO CHANGE—CULTURAL PATTERNS
BREAKTHROUGH IN PERFORMANCE—ACTION
TRANSITION TO THE NEW LEVEL

Vital Few and Useful Many

A manager has an idea for Breakthrough: "Our inventory of finished goods is too big. Let's cut it." His staff meeting agrees—the attitude hurdle is cleared. So far, so good. We have moved from *whether* to cut inventories to *how* to cut inventories. Soon the question is asked, "What does our inventory consist of?" The Controller is given the job of answering this. He comes back with a table of figures, of which Table 4-1 is an extract.

We see from the Controller's figures:

1. Of the 500 catalogue items, the top 25, or 5 percent of the *items,* account for 72 percent of the *dollars.* We will call these 25 items the *vital few.*
2. The bottom 395, or 79 percent of the items, account for only 5 percent of the dollars. We will call these 395 items the *useful many.*

The implications are profound. If, by magic, we could wipe out the last 79 percent of the items completely, we would cut the total inventory by only 5 percent. In contrast, if we could reduce the inventory level of the vital few, by just one-third, the result would be a rousing 24 percent cut in the total inventory!

In other words, any real cut in inventory can come only out of the vital few.

47

Table 4-1. How Much Inventory

Catalogue description	Dollars of inventory for this item	Numerical rank of this item	Cumulative percentage of items	Dollars, cumulative, for all items	Percent of dollars, cumulative
A1 generators	$90,000	1	0.2	$90,000	9.0
A4 generators	60,000	2	0.4	150,000	15.0
QK motors	52,000	3	0.6	202,000	20.2
	—	—	—	—	—
	—	—	—	—	—
	—	—	—	—	—
4F valves	7,400	25	5.0	720,000	72.0
	—	—	—	—	—
	—	—	—	—	—
	—	—	—	—	—
K9 caps	27	105	21.0	950,000	95.0
	—	—	—	—	—
	—	—	—	—	—
	—	—	—	—	—
MT sleeves	1	500	100.0	1,000,000	100.0

To summarize what we just went through:

We started with 500 problems of reducing inventory—too many to get our arms around, so

We listed these problems in their order of importance.

This listing showed that *as a practical matter* we have only 25 problems, a number we *can* get our arms around.

The generalization of the foregoing is what the author has called the Pareto[1] principle. What we did was to:

1. Make a *written* list of all that stands "between us and making this change."
2. Arrange this list in *order of importance.*
3. Identify the *vital few* as projects to be dealt with individually.
4. Identify the *useful many* as things to be dealt with as a class.

---

[1] Vilfredo Pareto was a nineteenth-century economist whose studies included the distribution of wealth and income among the citizenry of that day. Most of the wealth was concentrated in a few hands, and the great majority of people were in poverty. The principle of separating the vital few from the useful many is mighty old, and many men, including this author, have reinvented it. However, recognition that this principle applies so widely in management, and that its use can be formalized, is fairly recent. See, in this connection, Juran, J. M., Universals in Management Planning and Controlling, *The Management Review*, November, 1954 (the terms "vital few" and "trivial many" (now known as "useful many") were probably first used here); see also Juran, J. M., Pareto, Lorenz, Cournot, Bernoulli, Juran, and Others, *Industrial Quality Control*, vol. 17, No. 4, p. 25, October, 1960, for a confession that the author has probably credited the Pareto principle to the wrong man.

Universal Assortment;
Universal Sorter

In the case just recited, a problem in inventory reduction exhibited a complex appearance—a wide assortment of obstacles to Breakthrough. The role of the Pareto principle was to sort these many obstacles into two piles, the vital few and the useful many. (Once sorted, the two piles can be dealt with by means we will examine later.)

The stunning thing is that *all* management attempts at Breakthrough face a wide assortment of obstacles, and that, on application of the Pareto principle, *all* these assortments exhibit the properties of the vital few and useful many. The fact that these managerial problems exhibit this universal property makes the Pareto principle a universal tool for analysis. Like the Training Within Industry universal on How to Instruct, the Pareto principle is a universal for sorting any conglomerate mixture into two neat piles, the vital few and the useful many.

Let's examine some cases in various management situations.

In the marketing function, any sales manager knows that customers are a mixture; a few percent of them contribute most of the sales. In the sales manager's dialect, these vital few customers are "key accounts." For example,[2] a company with 389 customers found that:

The top 10 percent of the customers accounted for 60 percent of the total dollar sales.

The bottom 80 percent of the customers accounted for 24.8 percent of the dollar sales.

Customer orders also exhibit the principle of the vital few and useful many. The same study showed that of a total of 2,753 orders:

The top 13 percent of the orders resulted in 66 percent of the sales dollars.

The bottom 68 percent of the orders resulted in only 7.1 percent of the sales dollars.

Figure 7 is an analysis of sales volume by product, and shows graphically the relationship of the vital few and useful many. There are 20 products in the line. The top 4 products account for 75 percent of the sales; the bottom 16 products account for only 25 percent of the sales.

The vital few (by other names) show up in other aspects of marketing. Analysis of sales volume of individual salesperson discloses who are

[2]Blecke, Curtis J., *National Association of Cost Accountants, N.A.C.A. Bulletin*, The Small Order Problem in Distribution Cost Control, Sec. 1, pp. 1279–1284, June, 1957.

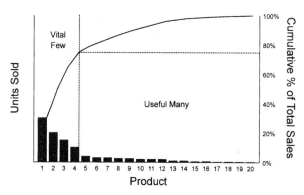

Fig. 7. Vital few and useful many in the product line.

the "star salesmen." Analysis of credit losses discloses who are the "dead-beats." Analyses of sales by territory, by marketing channel, and in still other ways, all exhibit the phenomenon.

One manager has a very simple way of dramatizing the Pareto principle. He draws the diagram[3] of Fig. 8. He explains it as follows:

"The column on the left represents our total number of dealers, and the column on the right our total volume of business. The diagonal indicates that about 80 percent of our customers give us less than 15 percent of our volume."

The *manufacturing function* is well supplied with activities which exhibit a mixture of vital few and useful many. One of the most exhaustively studied has been in connection with quality control. The "diseases" of the product, like the diseases of man, are highly concentrated

---

[3]Figure 8 is from the U.S. Department of Commerce publication "How Manufacturers Reduce Their Distribution Costs," an uncommonly practical study. Available from the Superintendent of Documents, U.S. Government Printing Office, Washington, D.C.

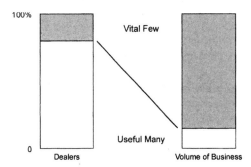

Fig. 8. A simple graph of the Pareto principle.

as to their incidence. This is so whether the diseases are classified by product, by process, by cause, by defect name, by department, by operation, by operator, or by part number. To illustrate:

In an instrument company, of 85 product diseases in one department, the worst 3 accounted for 71 percent of the losses due to defects. In a machine tool company, 2 of the 15 departments contributed over half the scrap and rework; one intricate part was the cause of 50 percent of the loss.

In meeting delivery schedules, the Pareto principle is out in full force, although the dialect is again local. To production control people, the "vital few" are the "bottlenecks." A formalized approach (PERT) for predicting bottlenecks in complex system planning has coined the term "critical path" as a label for the vital few.

Cost of manufacture likewise can use the Pareto principle.

In one company, out of 250 catalogue items of expendable tools and supplies, the top 5 items, or 2 percent, accounted for 64.9 percent of the dollar cost. The lowest 95 percent of the items accounted for only 17.2 percent of the dollar cost.

Requisitioning materials from stores is another instance. Analysis of size of requisitions in one company showed that:

the top 3 percent of the requisitions accounted for 62 percent of the value of material requisitioned.

the lowest 81 percent of the requisitions accounted for only 5.5 percent of the material requisitioned.

The same relationship holds for cost of maintenance and repairs. In one company, analysis of cost of maintenance by causes showed that:

6 percent of the causes resulted in 83 percent of all maintenance and repair charges. (In this company the lingo of the maintenance department referred to these vital few cases as "hospital jobs.")

76 percent of the causes resulted in only 8 percent of all maintenance and repair charges.

In the *personnel function* it is well known that employees are a mixture exhibiting the vital few and useful many as to absences, accidents, tardiness, alcoholism, etc.[4]

---

[4]Even as to talkativeness. A researcher counted the number of times that people spoke in a 2-hour conference of eight persons. There was a total of 70 remarks. The most talkative man spoke up 41 times, the second 21 times. Together, these "vital few" made 62 of the 70 statements, or about 90 percent of the total. The remaining six conferees, the useful many, spoke a total of 8 times, with four of these conferees maintaining silence. (From American Management Association Production Series, No. 187, p. 39, 1949.)

In the *purchasing function* it is pretty well known that a few percent of the orders account for the bulk of the money spent. This phenomenon becomes the basis for a graduated table of delegation as to whose signature is final on purchase requisitions.

But the matter does not end there. For example, a company studying some other aspects of purchasing found that:

the worst 6 percent of the vendors caused 81 percent of the late deliveries.

the worst 5 percent of the vendors caused 87 percent of the rejections for quality.

In the *technical function* the universal mixture is likewise present, though not as fully explored as in other functions. The sales potential of new products is an example. The few big projects have more sales potential than a whole host of small ones. Analysis of the work done by service laboratories has often shown that there is a shocking amount of formulation, making of samples, etc., devoted to the useful many orders.

In new product research and development there are always the vital few problems. The researcher's dialect is "critical" components, or the "state-of-the-art" components. These will take more effort than all the useful many combined.

In the *financial function*, the assortments susceptible to the Pareto principle are legion, although many are known only to the accounting fraternity. For example:

At B. F. Goodrich Company, a study of vendors' invoices showed that:

(*a*) The top 11 percent of the invoices accounted for 68 percent of the dollars recovered because of vendors' errors.

(*b*) The lowest 34 percent of the invoices accounted for only 1 percent of the dollars recovered because of vendors' errors. This relationship was used in reducing the effort of checking. The vital few invoices continued to be checked in detail. The useful many were put on a sampling basis.[5]

A similar study, with parallel results, is seen in the problem of aging of the 100,000 accounts receivable of a large department store.[6]

---

[5]Buhl, William F., "Statistical Controls Applied to Clerical and Accounting Procedures," *American Society for Quality Control Transactions*, 1955, pp. 9–26.

[6]Trueblood, R. M., and R. M. Cyert, "Statistical Sampling Applied to Aging of Accounts Receivable," *Journal of Accountancy*, March, 1954, pp. 293–298.

Cutting across all functions is the activity of *organization planning*. A basic concept here is the principle of delegation—that while there are myriads of decisions and actions to be taken, comparatively few of them need to engage the attention of top people. In the dialect of the managers, these vital few are the basis of the "exception principle."

The principle is very old. An early example is charmingly related in the Old Testament. Following the exodus of the Israelites from Egypt, their leader Moses found himself the sole judge of the disputes which arose among the people. The number of such disputes was enough to make this solitary judge a bottleneck in decision making. In consequence, the people "stood by Moses from the morning into the evening," waiting for Moses to make decisions. Moses' father-in-law, Jethro, saw this spectacle and ventured advice. (For which Jethro has become regarded by some as the first management consultant on record.)

Jethro's advice	Translated into modern management dialect
"And thou shalt teach them ordinances and laws, and show them the way wherein they must walk, and the work they must do." (Exodus 18:20)	Establish policies and standard practices, conduct job training, and prepare job descriptions.
"Moreover thou shalt provide out of all the people able men, such as fear God, men of truth, hating covetousness, and place such over them, to be rulers of thousands, and rulers of hundreds, rulers of fifties and rulers of tens." (Exodus 18:21)	Set up an organization; first-line supervisors to have 10 subordinates; second-line supervisors to have 5 subordinates, etc.; appoint those who have supervisory ability.
"And let them judge the people at all seasons; and it shall be that every great matter they shall bring unto thee, but every small matter they shall judge: so it shall be easier for thyself, and they shall bear the burden with thee." (Exodus 18:22)	Institute delegation of authority; routine problems to be decided down the line, but exceptional problems to be brought to higher authority.

We can now summarize the foregoing. The vital few are everywhere, but masquerading under a variety of aliases. In their more benevolent forms they are known by such names as key accounts or star salespeople. In their weak moments they are known as the bottlenecks, Most Wanted Criminals, critical components.

We could go on and on.[7] In preparing bids, experienced managers know that a few major components are decisive. The rest can be thrown in as a percentage. In valuing a plant, the experienced engineer singles out the major pieces of equipment and values them individually. The rest he figures as a percentage, or by studying a sample and applying the findings to all.

The useful many are also everywhere. They are the cats and dogs of the product line, the nuts and bolts of the inventory, the small customer orders, the petty cash stuff.

When We Lack the Numbers

Up to now it has been easy to rank the mixture of things in order to disclose the vital few. The ranking was easy because the things could be counted—they were in *numbers* of dollars, people, defects, orders, accidents, etc.

But lots of things can't be counted—morale, good will, friction, etc. What then?

> A company decided a Breakthrough was needed in the marketing of its product line. The key people were polled on the question "What stands between us and improved marketing of our line?" There was an avalanche of nominations—41 of them.
>
> To discover which of these 41 constituted the vital few, a ballot was created. Each of the key people was asked to rank the 41 nominations in the order of importance (as he saw it). After everyone had voted, the rankings were added up, the problem with the lowest total going to the head of the list, the second lowest total to second place, etc. The top 5 problems turned out to be:
>
> 1. Morale of the Sales Department
> 2. Time interval required to develop and make new products
> 3. How to generate new product ideas
> 4. Relation of the Sales Division to the Engineering Division
> 5. Training of salespeople
>
> This was definite enough to serve as a basis for proceeding with the next steps in the Breakthrough cycle.

---

[7]A readable example is seen in the study of the mating habits of "arena" birds. A zoologist was observing several hundred male sage grouse, all waiting at their stations during the mating season. Of 114 matings observed in a clan of males, 74 percent involved the top four males in the pecking order. It bears an uncomfortable resemblance to the award of defense contracts. (See Gilliard, E. Thomas, "The Evaluation of Bowerbirds," *Scientific American*, August, 1963.)

In broad studies, such as "How can we improve profitability," the nominations for the vital few can be quite an assortment of topics.

> A company making components for reciprocating gasoline engines was feeling the effects of the industry's trend to gas turbines. They decided to make a broad study of what to do about it, under the vague heading of "How to improve profitability."
>
> At the first meeting of the steering committee, 37 topics were nominated as candidates for the vital few. They included such things as:
>
> We need a logical successor to this product line.
>
> We are taking a big loss on small orders.
>
> Our pricing to customers is illogical.
>
> Our costs are out of line.
>
> We are not getting enough for our research money.
>
> We don't know our markets well enough.
>
> What is the most economic lot size?
>
> Our quotations are bawled up by our method of distributing burden.
>
> Despite so wide a mixture, a priority was voted and Breakthroughs were achieved. Interestingly enough, one result was to raise the profitability of the "dying" product line to a level that looked pretty good compared to all other lines.

What Good Is It?

In the experience of the author, the list of the vital few (through use of the Pareto principle) does *not* come as a complete surprise to all concerned. On the contrary, some of the problems on the list have long been notorious. To be sure, some of the projects will come as a genuine surprise. But the big accomplishments of the Pareto analysis are rather that:

1. Some notorious projects are confirmed as belonging among the vital few.
2. Some projects, previously not notorious, are identified as belonging among the vital few.
3. The useful many are identified. This is not new, but the extent is usually shocking.
4. The magnitudes are, to the extent practicable, quantified. Ordinarily, this has never before been done.

5. There is established a *meeting of the minds as to priority* of needs for Breakthrough. This is the biggest contribution of all, as it sets the stage for action.

The Pareto analysis also provides an early check on the attitude toward Breakthrough. If either the vital few or the useful many look like good candidates for change, then the original hunch is confirmed, so far. If, on the other hand, the Pareto analysis shows that none of these is economically worth tackling, that is likely the end of the matter.

Dealing with the Vital Few

Although each of the vital few is an important, unique problem, they exhibit some common characteristics as a species:

1. Each is interdepartmental in character. (There are some exceptions to this, but not many.) In industry, the really important problems are mainly interdepartmental.
2. Each is a unique problem, requiring study in depth if there is to be a solution. This study in depth cannot be made just in the executive offices—it includes much digging in the "field."

Some elaboration is in order here. So far, in sorting the vital few from the useful many, we have stayed in the office. We have worked from reports, statements, general knowledge, and such. These were good enough to *identify* the vital few. They are *not* good enough to *solve* the vital few. Solution requires that we get out into the "field," i.e., the shop floor, the branch office, the laboratory, the warehouse. Only there will we find the causes, the details, the really new knowledge we need for Breakthrough.

There are thus *two levels of analysis,* in the office and in the field. The executives, the committees, the controllers, the staff people, can make good headway in the office in identifying chronic problems. But let no one be deluded into equating a problem identified with a problem solved.

A mechanic comes up to his foreman. "Boss—I got a problem." The boss looks at it, understands it, and realizes that the mechanic cannot, by himself, solve it. So the boss says, "You sure have got a problem," and walks away.

Stupid, isn't it? Yet when we identify a problem in the office, and tell a manager, in effect, "You sure have got a problem," is it any different?

The vital few are, with few exceptions, *interdepartmental,* and beyond the capacity of any one department manager to solve single-handed.

There are, then, two needs to be met if we are to get somewhere in solution of the vital few:

1. We must meet the interdepartmental implications.
2. We must go beyond the mere identification of a problem, and into the depth needed for solution.

These needs are, for the most part, met by the Steering Arm and the Diagnostic Arm which we will discuss in later chapters.

Dealing with the Useful Many

It is not feasible to deal individually with the useful many—they must be dealt with *as a class.* In fact, one of the big opportunities for Breakthrough is to devote less individual effort to each of the useful many!

> In the early days of the safety movement, progress was made as to both the vital few and the useful many:
> The engineers developed safeguards for the notoriously hazardous operations, i.e., the vital few. Each of these safeguards was *tailor-made* to meet a specific hazard.
> The personnel specialists developed psychological campaigns to be directed at all employees. These campaigns were *not* tailor-made for specific employees; one campaign was directed at all employees, identically and simultaneously.

Another way of looking at the useful many is to regard them, collectively, as one of the vital few problems. This comes up very often. Managers speak of the "small order" problem, the petty purchase problem, the unprofitable end of the product line, etc. We will see, in Chap. 8, that these classes of the useful many constitute some very real problems, as a class, and that they lend themselves to ready diagnosis and remedy, as a class.

The Awkward Zone

The author exaggerated a bit when he said that the Pareto principle sorts things into two piles. It is really three piles. The third is a residue which falls between the vital few and the useful many. This residue might be called the "awkward zone." The inhabitants of this zone are not individually big enough to justify tailor-made analysis for each.

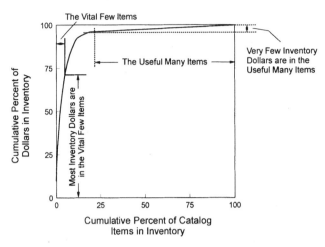

Fig. 9. The Pareto distribution.

Neither are they collectively small enough to be dealt with as one homogeneous mass.

The Production Control fraternity has worked up a dialect for these three piles—A, B, and C. The A items are the vital few inventory items which represent the bulk of the money. The C items are the useful many, but the money they represent "you could stick in your eye." The B items are the awkward zone (Fig. 9).

In Breakthrough, the first emphasis is on the vital few. Subsequently, ways are developed for dealing with the useful many. An incidental result of all this is a better understanding of what to do about the awkward zone. We will return to this in Chaps. 8 and 10.

And So on to Mobilizing for Breakthrough in Knowledge

With the sorting of the topics into the three piles, we conclude a phase—that of identifying the problems. Solution of the problems requires the two added steps we noted above:

1. An interdepartmental approach
2. A diagnosis in depth, beyond what we can do in the office

For most company situations, these steps are not automatic—they require positive assignment of people to do them. This assignment is done by Mobilizing for Breakthrough in Knowledge, our next chapter subject.

5 MOBILIZING FOR BREAKTHROUGH IN KNOWLEDGE

THE STEERING ARM
THE DIAGNOSTIC ARM
BREAKTHROUGH IN KNOWLEDGE—DIAGNOSIS
RESISTANCE TO CHANGE—CULTURAL PATTERNS
BREAKTHROUGH IN PERFORMANCE—ACTION
TRANSITION TO THE NEW LEVEL

The Timeless Quest for New Knowledge

The Pareto principle has taken us a long step down the road. Instead of being mired down in a hopeless bog of many problems, we stand firm, facing just a few specific projects. How do we go at them?

Let's get some perspective by seeing how man has done this over the centuries. How did early human beings achieve Breakthroughs? How has the manager done it without books on Breakthrough?

We can be fairly positive about the answers. Our predecessors achieved Breakthroughs by joining together three great ideas:

1. Discovery of new knowledge
2. Dissemination of this discovered knowledge to those who could use it
3. Application of the new knowledge to the solution of old problems

In modern management phraseology, these three great ideas are the *functions* of discovery, dissemination, and application. Today, these functions are as necessary to a Breakthrough as they have always been. However, the manner of conducting these functions is very different, especially in companies of any substantial size.

The Discovery Function

In common with many other animals, human beings are inquiring, observant creatures. But they are unique in the ability to ponder on these observations and to generalize from them. (The biological mechanisms by which they do all this, we leave to the psychologists and physiologists.) The result of these wonderful powers is discovery of new knowledge, an essential ingredient in Breakthrough.

Human beings' acquisition of new knowledge is derived from a variety of sources:

(a) *Accidental discovery.* Glass was probably discovered in the embers of an ancient hunter's overnight fire.

> In January, 1839, when Charles Goodyear accidentally dropped a mixture of India rubber, white lead, and sulfur on the kitchen stove, human beings took a giant step toward commercial use of rubber.

There is still much discovery by accident. A worker forgets to perform an operation. By the time he or she remembers, it is too late—the job has been shipped. He or she waits apprehensively for the backfire. Nothing happens. Slowly it dawns on him or her that the operation may be unnecessary. Next time he or she will probably omit it deliberately. If it works again, he or she has discovered new knowledge, and faces the question of whether to share it with the management.

(b) *Systematic observation and analysis.* The word *systematic* is what distinguishes this type of discovery from the accidental.

The calendars of early civilizations exhibit amazing accuracy, and testify to the winningness of early human beings to conduct patient, systematic observation.

Today's systems of records and reports exemplify the enormous use we now make of systematic observation and analysis.

(c) *Experiment.* For early human beings this wasn't easy. In most communities, the quest for survival was itself an overtime job. Lacking time, apparatus, and instruments, and living in an atmosphere of taboos and suspicions, the would-be experimenter must have endured monumental frustrations. In those times of darkness, his superstitious neighbors might question whether he were man or demon. The other members of his "profession"—the alchemists, astrologers, and the like, included quacks. It must have taken plenty of recklessness or courage to perform experiments.

In contrast, experimenting is today an accepted, thriving business. The experimenter is in demand, housed in air-conditioned splendor, and showered with amenities, not the least of which is respectability.

(d) *Imports.* (Knowledge obtained from someone else is still new to the recipient.) For primitive human beings this was a bleak source. Communities were isolated and generally disposed to guard both their privacy and their skills from outside view.

Waiting for Accidents to Happen

Despite this wide assortment of means for acquiring new knowledge, early human beings depended largely on accidental discovery. Knowledge accumulated from this source, even over many centuries, didn't amount to much by today's standards. As a consequence, accident, rather than people's determination, decided when needed knowledge would be acquired. A generation of people needing badly some specific chunk of new knowledge could not, with confidence, set out to acquire it. Mainly they would hope that some future generation would stumble on it by accident. Such frivolous, creeping progress meant that chance, not people, was master of the situation. It was no way to solve this year's problems.

All this has changed, drastically. Modern industry relies mainly on planned experiments and systematic observation, all heavily seasoned with imported knowledge. Accidental discovery plays a minor role and, though welcomed, is not relied on.

This great shift in sources of new knowledge has been made both possible and necessary by the march of science and technology ushered in by the Renaissance. That great revolution took Western civilization out of the valley of superstition and ignorance, and made possible the challenge of long-standing, unsupported beliefs through fresh thought and scientific experimentation. The resulting tools for creation of new knowledge are available to the manager. He has good use for these tools, since the Renaissance also triggered off a quickening of the pace of technological change.

Discovering on Purpose

Today's industrial pace demands that the manager, not accident, be the master of the situation. To meet competitive challenges (better yet, to take the initiative), the manager must be able to say "Let's Breakthrough here," with confidence that it will happen. Waiting for an accident to show up is today just a form of demoralizing helplessness.

Managers have recognized this need of discovery "to order," and have forged several managerial tools to help it along. These tools include:

(a) *Recognizing the needs for a discovery function.* Discovering on purpose requires selected, trained people, who have the time and objectivity to conduct purposive discovery. The discoverers also need access to the sources of facts, as well as the necessary facilities—space, equipment, assistants. For every pound of explorer reaching the top of Mount Everest, a hundred pounds of supplies are needed at the base.

(b) *Detaching the discovery function from day-to-day operations.* In the smaller companies, and even in some jobs in larger companies, the dual role of discoverer-manager gives a good account of itself. This works out best when the job embodies a high content of technical skill. James Watt, the steam engine pioneer, was also a cofounder of the firm of Boulton and Watt. In his role as discoverer, Watt used the company as a laboratory. Josiah Wedgwood similarly was creative in pottery design and processing, while at the same time running a shop in which he could apply his discoveries. At the departmental level, people like the toolroom foreman, or the head of the measurement laboratory, are well placed in a dual role. So are nonsupervisors such as the machine setter, the toolmaker, the maintenance mechanic.

> Following the voyages of discovery, the growth of transoceanic marine navigation required precise means for locating a ship's position at sea. The latitude problem was solved first, after which the problem of longitude continued to baffle the experts. Early in the eighteenth century, the British Parliament offered a reward of £20,000 for a device which could determine longitude at sea within an accuracy of half a degree.
>
> One possible solution was the perfection of a chronometer which would enable the ship at sea to know, with precision, the time at the prime meridian. This solution came not from the captains, the navigators, or other ship personnel; it came from landlubbers—the mechanics and clockmakers.

Industry has also found that its needs for discovery are not adequately met by the full-time operations person. This is true even as to his or her own job, and much more so as to things that are no one individual's job. Discovery on a broad enough scale has required creation of *full-time discoverers* with all the necessary time, facilities, etc., and a vested interest in discovery.

(c) *Creation of specialists.* Late in the nineteenth century, the "scientific management" movement came over the industrial horizon. Its leader, F. W. Taylor, identified some principles for doing work, one of which was that the methods for doing work must be based on "science, not rule of thumb." The shop foremen of that day were in no position to advance the cause of science. Hence Taylor separated the function of planning of work from that of executing the plan. A new species of specialist was born—the efficiency expert. (When this species developed notoriety, a reform movement adopted aliases—industrial engineer, methods engineer, etc.)

During the twentieth century, the movement to separate industrial diagnosis[1] from operations gained momentum. Marketing followed manufacture by creating the diagnostic service of Market Research, as well as that product diagnostician, the Product Manager. In the technical function, product research and development were separated from engineering. In Purchasing, specialisms such as Value Analysis emerged. And so it has gone on—Procedures Analyst, Quality Control Engineer, etc.

Through such specialists, managers have created discoverers rather than wait for discoverers to appear somehow. This is, again, taking the initiative rather than leaving it to chance. Many of the specialist forms in use in industry today are the result of management creation and fiat, not the result of chance interest of inquisitive free-wheelers.

Nor have the specialists been left to their own devices on how to make discoveries. An enormous body of specialized literature has emerged, and has provided for much training of the full-time specialists. Even for dual discoverer-operators, there are seminars, conferences, and other forms available to train them in work simplification, job analysis, etc.

There are also forms of training in creativity, and evidence to suggest that those who receive such training come up with more and better suggestions than those who lack such training. Harris[2] describes such a course (as conducted in General Motors Corporation) and reports on before-and-after results. Employees who took the training increased their suggestion frequency by 40+ percent, while untrained employees showed no increase.

Discovering on purpose vs. discovering by accident is seen to be a matter of organization, not a matter of science. Purposive discovery requires that individuals be put into a position where all or part of their responsibility is to make discoveries.

Whether finding new knowledge is *incidental* to one's job, or *is the job itself*, makes quite a difference. In the former case, there is no priority for acquiring new knowledge—to do so is beyond the call of duty anyhow. You are praised if you do, but you are not damned if you don't. In contrast, when one's career stands or falls on the acquisition of new knowledge, the human faculties respond with admirable vigor.

---

[1] Industry didn't start this. The early municipalities, armies, and temples employed royal commissions, field auditors, and other specialized departments to separate investigation from operations as to certain matters.

[2] Harris, R. H., The Creative Skill, *Mechanical Engineering,* October, 1962, pp. 39–41.

The Dissemination Function

To do any good, new knowledge must travel from the discoverer to the applier. In years gone by, this was very unlikely—the discoverer usually tried to keep new knowledge to himself, and the applier usually wanted nothing new.

Early industries stood savage guard over important knowledge. Methods for production of silk, long a Chinese monopoly, were so well guarded that for centuries other nations had no idea the fiber came from an insect.

In 1291, the Venetians moved their entire glass industry to their island of Murano, mainly for security reasons. It was a capital offense for a man to leave Murano to practice elsewhere. Travel of workers was closely guarded.

On the receiving end, many communities were dominated by families or organizations who wanted a static society to help retain their power. Anything new might touch off a chain reaction of newness—a revolution. Hence products, processes, customs, rituals, taboos, etc., went on and on, generation after generation. Even a man's trade lasted for generations. Those were the "good old days," so they say. Today products, processes, and customs don't go on and on. They turn over pretty fast. An individual's trade doesn't last a lifetime. (What a profound change that is!)

The pace of dissemination is well illustrated by a fascinating example:

> The first draft animal domesticated by human beings was the ox; so the first draft harness was developed to fit the thick, short neck of oxen. Later, when the horse was domesticated, the ancients put the ox harness on horses rather than to redesign a harness specially for the long, narrow neck of horses.
>
> The ancient forerunners of our industrial engineers collected comparative data on the relative pulling efficiency of horses vs. human slaves. The human slave could pull about 35 pounds. The horse, choked under heavy loads by his ox collar, could pull only about 140 pounds—about 4 slave power. The ancient time and motion study people went further in their studies. They also measured the amount of grain needed to keep horses and slaves fit for pulling loads. By coincidence, this ratio was also 4 to 1. The amount of pulling per bushel of feed being alike for man and beast, the usage was probably guided by the relative supply of these two forms of traction. The one thing the ancient time-study people did not do was to ask—"What is an ox collar doing on a horse?"
>
> Meanwhile, the Chinese had, during the early centuries A.D., come up with a new collar, specially designed to fit the horse—a true horse collar. This multiplied the pulling power of the horse by

about 4; a horse could now pull as much as 15 slaves. But it took about 600 years for this collar to find its way from China to the necks of European horses.

An interesting table of "Transmission of Certain Techniques from China to the West" is found in Charles Singer's classic *History of Technology* (Vol. II, pp. 770–771, Oxford University Press, Fairlawn, N.J., 1956). Of the 45 Chinese inventions or discoveries listed, the average time lag was about 9 centuries.[3]

Such dissemination of knowledge was glacially slow by today's standards. Short of massive movements like the Crusades, or the rise of Islam, there was very limited communication.

With the rise of the great organizations (armies, churches, states), the possibility arose of making communication more than a matter of luck. The discoverer and the user could be brought together deliberately through the machinery of organization. Moreover, the communication could be made mandatory.

The modern industrial company makes wide use of this purposive communication. Not only have we taken positive steps to increase the flow of discovery and the flow of use. We have taken positive steps to ensure that the discoverers and appliers get together on purpose, not just by accident.

One form of this linkage is to make the discoverer and applier the same person, as discussed above. Where this can be done, he doesn't fight as much with himself as he does when he is two separate people.

A second form is to give the applier some captive discoverer. The plant manager's staff now exhibits industrial engineers, quality-control engineers, and others. We noted various other such specialists in the discussion on Discovering on Purpose, above.

A third form of linkage is the committee or team approach. We create many such teams, with membership from both appliers and discoverers. Then they must meet and deal with each other.

Still other forms are in use—suggestion systems, staff coordinator, consultants, etc. The variety in use testifies to the importance and difficulty of the problem.

With all these modern forms, our dissemination is still not complete. The operator who discovers a new way may keep it to himself or herself despite the existence of a suggestion system. Customers learn much about usage of our product, but have a poor pipeline for feeding this

[3]In those days, technology flowed from the East to the West, not the other way around.

back to us. Vendors know a good deal about how our competitors do business, but we have not set out to collect such information.

So, as with the discovery function, we have a residue of unsolved problems in the dissemination function. We will shortly return to this.

The Application Function

Despite clear responsibility for results, plus implied responsibility for improving results, there should be no delusions about any eagerness on the part of managers to apply new knowledge.

Career discoverers have an obvious, vested, and even fierce interest in propagating their discoveries. Their importance in their own eyes as well as in the eyes of the community is closely related to the degree of recognition of their discoveries.

In contrast, the appliers have no such vested or fierce interest in using discoveries, especially the discoveries of others. Instead, the applier has his own set of vested interests, which include a system of beliefs, habits, status, etc., all linked to the existing order of things. Whether he applies some new discovery is a matter of balancing the benefits of this new discovery against the detriments of disturbing the existing order.

In the days when the appliers had no organizational connection with the discoverers, the decision of the appliers was final—no one could order them to accept a discovery. Such independence of action made acceptance of a discovery a pretty dubious matter. The discovery might be turned down because it was no good (in the opinion of the applier); or because, though good, the price for using it came too high in cultural disturbance; or just because the applier didn't like discoverers.

Today the applier is often a hired person or hired manager. As such, he or she faces a new ingredient in his or her decision—he or she must consider the needs of his or her company as well as his or her own needs. Not only that, the discoverer, who is often in the same company, has access to people who, if convinced, are in a position to influence the applier.

The applier, then, has also undergone much change. He or she has less freedom of choice, is under greater urge to consider the discoveries, and is driven by the pace of change to regard discoveries as a fact of life rather than as an unwelcome surprise.

A Major Fork in the Road

The foregoing has all been essential to bring us to a most important fork in the road. Granted that to achieve Breakthrough we must use the great ideas of discovery, dissemination, and application of new knowledge.

Our problem is how the company is to use these ideas in solving the vital few problems. More specifically, are we to:

(*a*) "Let nature take its course," i.e., make known that here are the projects on which we need Breakthrough, and let things happen "naturally?"

(*b*) "Mobilize specially," i.e., assign definite responsibilities for carrying out the three basic needs of discovery, dissemination, and application?

The author asserts that in most company situations the approach must be one of mobilizing specially. Before looking at the case for this, consider the case for letting things happen naturally.

Letting Nature Take Its Course

There are able, sincere managers who put the case this way:

"We have always managed to make improvements without making a big fuss about it. Compare our product line with what we made 30 years ago—there is no relation between them. Look at our factory processes. They are completely different from what we had 30 years ago. Look at our marketing. We used to sell through agents. Now we have sales offices, product managers, advertising, and all the rest. Look at our finance. We used to get along with mighty little paper. Now we have budgets, punch cards, computers. All these things happened, and it came naturally. Why do we need to go into some complicated organization deal?"

It is all too easy to give emotional answers to this question (which itself has some emotional content). An emotional response might well be: "If we're so good at cleaning up our problems naturally, how does it happen that we still have so many unsolved vital problems?" But emotionalism doesn't get too much done. A dispassionate answer has to be that if our "natural" way of solving problems will give us prompt enough answers to the vital few, we do not need to mobilize specially. But we can be trapped into an emotional answer because we do not really understand what has been our "natural" way of bringing change about.

If we look back at actual cases in our own company, we soon find out that things did *not* happen "naturally." They happened because determined people made them happen. Our company has, in miniature, gone through what the human race has gone through. Our new knowledge has come from all the usual sources—accident, methodical experiment, imports, flashes of intuition. We have exhibited all the usual difficulties of communication between discoverer and user. And our users have been subjected to all the human pressures which resist the social effects of technical change.

So there is nothing unusual about us. Our "natural" way has been the human way, with its successes, failures, delays, and all the rest. The real question posed is as follows:

Will our traditional pace of discovery, dissemination, and application solve our major problems fast enough to satisfy us? If so, there is no need to create special, organized effort to speed up the pace. If not, then some special steps are in order.

This question puts the first emphasis on results, where it should be. First we must agree on what results we need (solution or not, promptly or not). After agreeing on what results we need, it is time enough to talk of the means (regular or special, formal or informal).

There are conditions under which letting nature take its course can get admirable results, with a charming simplicity. Such, for example, is the case when the causes and remedies are all confined to one department. In such a case, the department head may well be able to do the entire job by:

(*a*) Putting on the hat of discoverer and finding the new knowledge needed

(*b*) Communicating this new knowledge to his other self—the department head

(*c*) Putting on his hat of department head and applying the new knowledge

> In a Japanese pharmaceutical company, the author heard a story from one Mr. Naka. He headed a small self-contained department making penicillin from basic materials. He also had a problem—the yields were very low, around 30 percent. But Mr. Naka was also a competent investigator. Through experimentation and analysis, he improved the process and ran the yields up to over 70 percent. As to this Breakthrough, he was a one-person gang—he directed the project, he designed the experiments, conducted them, found the answers, and applied them. "Mobilization" here was a simple matter of one adequate man being in the right place.

Breakthrough by a Small Company

The following is an elegant example of how a tiny company achieved a significant Breakthrough at a critical period of its life. First, the events which led up to the crisis.

In the late 1920s an electrician—we will call him Alec—went into business for himself. We will call his company Ace. For about 20 years he and a helper constituted the business. He kept no records of materials, time, or anything else, much. He set prices by feel or to meet competition. He did have a bookkeeping service which made essential entries for him at the end of each month.

At the end of World War II, Alec was swept into the boom of converting coal-fired furnaces into oil or gas heating. These conversions required an electrical hookup. Alec's reason for getting into this boom was simple—he had access to the materials needed for these electrical installations.

Those were the days. Business just rolled in. Alec added more and more men until he had a crew of a dozen. Alec's costs were dreadful, though he couldn't know this—he had no records. But it didn't matter. Materials were so scarce that fantastic prices could be charged. So Ace made plenty of money. It was wonderful while it lasted.

It lasted 3 years. By 1948, materials were in good supply, and competition drove prices down. Alec cut prices to meet this competition, and now began to lose money. A crisis developed in 1949.

By this time Alec had brought two young relatives into the business, both engineers. As Ace continued to lose money, Alec's ways of running the business came into disrepute, and the young fellows had their chance to wade in. They now insisted on answers to some long-standing questions.

A cardinal question was "What are our costs?" To answer this required records. For 1 month they kept careful records of the time and material on each job. Table 5-1 shows the resulting costs of labor and material, for each electrician employed.

The following big facts emerged from Table 5-1.

1. Ace had labor costs about 30 percent higher than competition, and material costs about 10 percent higher.
2. Ace's best electricians were meeting competitive costs.
3. There was a shocking variation in costs among Ace's electricians.
4. Generally, the electricians who turned in the lowest labor costs also turned in the lowest material costs (Fig. 10).

Now the managers were poised to take the first necessary step—to bring all electricians up to the level of the best. This they did by retraining the "poor" men and releasing the hopeless ones.

Having made their labor costs competitive, they set up means to keep them that way. They had determined that labor costs should not exceed one-sixth of the billing price. They set up to watch this daily.

Table 5-1 Costs for Installing Electrical Hookups

Electrician No.	$ labor	$ material	$ total
1	8.70	16.50	25.20
2	9.10	15.90	25.00
3	9.40	17.10	26.50
4	9.90	17.80	27.70
5	10.40	17.40	27.80
6	10.80	17.60	28.40
7	11.20	18.40	29.60
8	11.60	17.20	28.80
9	12.10	18.80	30.90
10	12.30	19.70	32.00
11	12.60	18.00	30.60
Average cost	10.74	17.67	28.40
Competition (estimated)	8.25	16.50	24.75

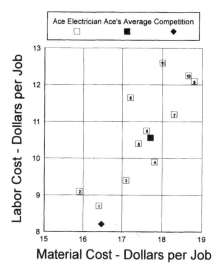

Fig. 10. Variations in cost of electrical hookups.

Next as to material cost. They had found out what could really be done, and had trained the electricians to do it. Now they saw to it that material issued[4] by the stock clerk was only 10 percent greater than job averages. Shortages were rare, and were usually met by improvisation. Pilferage was also discouraged through this control.

---

[4]The material was sent to the site by truck and timed to arrive ahead of the electrician, who supplied his own transportation from site to site.

All this was only the beginning. The knowledge of costs also disclosed that the main cause of job-to-job cost variation had been the men, *not the conditions at the site.* This threw open to question the long-standing practice of estimating each job and bidding on it. It became feasible to set a flat price for all installations for a given customer. Not only did this avoid the detailed effort of estimating, bidding, etc.; the customers[5] loved it. Business increased considerably.

Operating on a flat cost per job left Ace open to the risk of getting only the "tough jobs." To guard against this, Ace kept a plot of the costs by customer. Figure 11 shows successive averages of five jobs each for various customers. It was evident that some customers did operate solely in high-cost areas. Ace was generally able to get relief from these customers because it had the facts to back up its contentions.

And so it went with other problems. Through facts, analysis, and action, Ace cut the turnover of customers, charted its seasonal variations, improved its performance against schedule, and improved its quality.

Within 2 years of the crisis, the force of electricians had grown to 35, and a profitable operation was under firm control.

The Ace Company example is a little gem. As a case in Breakthrough, it is complete. Yet there were no frames of reference, agendas, minutes, memoranda. Two young fellows with sound instincts seized an opportunity, and whizzed through the entire Breakthrough cycle, unerringly.

---

[5] Ace sold to over 100 customers, varying from a gas company with a gas-heating monopoly in a large city, down to small dealers who sold a burner a month.

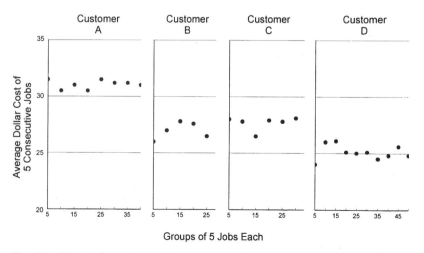

Fig. 11. Job cost for various customers.

When Nature Must Be Helped

As we move away from the very small company, or the small self-contained department, mobilization for Breakthrough in knowledge becomes increasingly more complex:

(a) The problem is interdepartmental in character and hence beyond the capacity of an unaided department head. A *team* effort is needed.

(b) The new knowledge needed cuts across several departments and is difficult to acquire, necessitating much time and skill from those who can devote themselves to such projects and to nothing else.

(c) The dissemination and application of the new knowledge again affect a multiplicity of departments, again requiring a *team* effort.

"Team" is basically a good word. It has connotations of belonging, being accepted, being appreciated, contributing to the common good. These are all universal needs.

But in the manager's experience, some sorry practices have been perpetrated under the guise of "teams." These are not isolated cases, a company here or there; they exist in profusion.

In the late 1940s the author studied, in 39 industrial companies, the status of their programs for improving their control of quality. The results were jolting. Eighteen of the companies were doing well or were on a good road. But twenty-one companies had failed or were on the road to failure.

Analysis of why these efforts had failed showed that the main cause was inadequate participation by the very line people who had the basic responsibility for results:

Companies that	developed a level of shop participation that was		
	High	Average	Low
Succeeded or progressed	9	9	0
Stalled or failed	0	2	19

In theory, all companies had a team effort, the line people and the newly created staff Quality Control Departments. In practice, many of the new staff departments were engaged in what the lawyers call a "frolic of their own."

More recently, a study of causes of success and failure in computer installation[6] has come up with strikingly parallel results.

[6]Garrity, John T., "Top Management and Computer Profits," *Harvard Business Review*, July–August, 1963, pp. 6–12, 172, 174.

Of 27 installations studied, 9 were classified as "unmistakably successful"; the remaining 18 were "marginal at best."

The areas of greatest difference between the two groups show up in...operating management's involvement....

In the high achieving companies, operating management plays a strong role every step of the way—in project selection, planning, manning, and progress review. And operating management takes major responsibility for the results.

Not so in the average company. Here technical management tends to dominate, often by default rather than by choice, while the operating management stands by as a frequently none-too-friendly onlooker.

In most companies, the vital few problems are also interdepartmental in character. Thereby they require "mobilization" in two important respects:

1. *A team effort to guide* the discovery, dissemination, and application of the new knowledge.
2. *A specific assignment of specialists* to do the detailed work associated with this team effort.

Stated in the language of the next two chapters, this mobilization consists of:

1. *A Steering Arm* to direct the discovery, dissemination, and subsequent use of new knowledge.
2. *A Diagnostic Arm* to do the detailed work of securing the new knowledge.

This form of mobilization is not some invention of the author. It is, rather, an expression of a method which innumerable managers have invented and reinvented for Breakthrough in problems of an interdepartmental character.

6 THE STEERING ARM

Personal and Impersonal Supervision

Let's take a stop watch and follow a shop foreman around. We'll record how *he* is supervised. We soon find that while he has lots of supervision, he seldom sees his boss! How then does the foreman get his orders? He gets them from *impersonal* supervision of all sorts.

Some of this impersonal supervision consists of *standing orders*—the procedures, the manuals. A personnel manual prescribes the rules for handling hirings, training, discipline, and other employee-relations problems. There are other manuals or books of routines, on purchasing, maintenance, safety, etc.

Then there are those impersonal orders which *change* from day to day. Shop orders published by some department tell the foreman what product he is to make and how much. Product specifications published by a second department tell him what qualities are to be achieved. Process specifications (published by a third department) tell him how to achieve this. Schedules (by a fourth department) tell him when. And so it goes.

Nor is this all. To a great extent the foreman is supervised by *unwritten precedent.* Somewhere in the past a practice was started. As it was repeated over and over again, it took root and became the accepted practice. Having been accepted, it is an unwritten impersonal supervisor. "That's the way we do it around here."

These forms of impersonal supervision very likely guide over 90 percent of the time of the foreman we set out to follow around.[1] Yet it all works well because he is on familiar ground. He has been doing all these things for years. In part, the daily events are repeats of previous events. In part they are variations, but still within his orbit of experience. Collectively, they are things he can take care of without going to the boss for specific directions.

This principle of impersonal supervision reaches its climax in the automated process, which requires no personal boss at all. All supervision is built into the cams of the machine, the servomechanisms of the process, the program of the computer. The laws of mechanics, chemistry, or electronics take it from there, and the thing cycles over and over again in its persistent, dogged, faithful uniformity. It does the usual thing in the usual way, no questions asked.

So, for the usual thing done in the usual way, there is little need for personal supervision, whether for the foreman, the branch manager, the chemist, or for that matter, the vice-president.

Yet these people cannot do without getting some personal supervision. For example, situations arise in which the impersonal bosses conflict with each other.

> The schedule says "This job must go out this week—the customer is faced with an emergency." But getting the job out this week means overtime and extra costs, thus violating the orders of two other impersonal bosses—the personnel manual and the cost standard.

Such cases do come up. So do cases which are not covered by the manuals or by precedent. Faced with these conflicts or these new situations, the foreman needs help in the form of a personal boss who has the last word, who can say "Never mind the cost standard—get the job out on time."

Breakthrough Usually Means a Personalized, Team Direction

By our very definition, Breakthrough is a departure from the usual, familiar way, into the unknown. The manual, the routine, the precedent

---

[1] An actual study made in a personnel department showed that:
Clerical workers spent about 2 percent of their total work time with their boss.
Supervisory personnel spent about 6 percent of their total work time with *their* boss.
See Carroll, Stephen J., Jr., Measuring the Work of a Personnel Department, *Personnel*, July–August, 1960, pp. 49–56.

are of no avail—they are intended to do the precise opposite, to keep us where we are. The impersonal supervision cannot help us in Breakthrough. Instead, we must look to *personal* supervision or direction of some sort.

We saw in Chap. 5 that achievement of Breakthrough is normally a team effort. (The cases favorable for Breakthrough by a one-person gang are special and, except in the small companies, are infrequent.)[2] Normally, the interdepartmental nature of the problem requires a team approach, which we now see must be personalized as well. The leadership must come from *a team of persons,* not from a team of manuals or routines. We will, in this chapter, examine the team approach in great detail. To conduct this examination, it is well to review the solution via the one-person gang.

Our example of the one-person gang was Mr. Naka (p. 68). Mr. Naka made his Breakthrough by combining the roles of discovery, communication, and application, all in one person.

The one-person gang is such a simple solution to the problem of Breakthrough that some programs are based on training people to be one-person gangs. Such is the case of the methods-improvement programs.[3] People are trained in a sequence as follows:

pick a job to improve.

study the job by various diagnostic tools, i.e., process chart, flow diagram, etc.

challenge everything—why do it at all, why do it this way, etc.

work out a better way, through eliminating, combining, changing sequence, improving, etc.

apply the new way, both technically and socially.

This is a universal sequence. If one person is in a position to carry it out in full, the stage is set for a solo performance by a one-person gang. This may be a nonsupervisor—a shop mechanic, an office secretary, a truck driver. It may also be the supervisor of a department (as was Mr. Naka). The solo performance is made possible because we are dealing with a localized situation. One person is in a position of having the skill to analyze plus the authority to act. Mr. Naka's department was a

---

[2] Even when a one-person gang does the entire job of discovery and dissemination and application, his thought processes must differ from those used for conduct of day-to-day activities. One author uses the terms "reflective thinking" and "action thinking" to distinguish these thought processes from each other. See Kappel, Frederick R., *Vitality in a Business Enterprise,* pp. 16–17, McGraw-Hill Book Company, Inc., New York, 1960.

[3] See, for example, Mogensen, Allan H., "Carrying Out a Methods Improvement Program," *Factory Management and Maintenance,* July, 1949, pp. 66–88.

miniature, self-contained factory. It made a finished product from basic materials. Hence solution of his problem of yields was independent of other departments, and he could and did do the job single-handedly.

Industry fairly teems with opportunities for local Breakthrough by nonsupervisors or supervisors. Much has been learned about how to train individuals to be able to make these Breakthroughs locally. But use of this learning has been confined to a minority of companies. This is a pity. Not only is there much to be gained in improved performance through local Breakthrough; there is also much to be gained in improving the caliber of the managers of tomorrow. Those who are at home in making local Breakthroughs have acquired a habit which can be invaluable when they move into broader responsibilities.

Once we are beyond the capacity of the one-person gang, we have the need for a team effort. There is wide latitude in the composition of the team, but no latitude in its *function*. The team must perform the function of *steering* the Breakthrough, which includes provision for *diagnosis*. These two essentials give rise, in most cases, to a separate Steering Arm and Diagnostic Arm.

A common intermediate form is a team composed of a department head and subordinate supervisors. As to departmental matters, this team qualifies as a Steering Arm—it can contribute unity of purpose, theories, etc. But the team is usually deficient in its ability to do the diagnostic job, for reasons we will examine in Chap. 7, The Diagnostic Arm. The team can, to a large degree, make up for this deficiency by utilizing the available staff people to do the diagnostic job, in other words, by creating a Diagnostic Arm. Here, for example, is how an oil company puts the responsibility up to its managers and supervisors:[4]

> Each manager and supervisor has full responsibility for the efficiency and profitability of his unit. If engineers, special staff groups, or methods-improvement teams exist *within* his unit, he should use them to assist all concerned, but not to relieve either himself or his subordinate supervisors of responsibility for it and the burden of attentive interest in it. If such groups exist at *higher levels*, they should become active within the manager's unit only on his request, and his superior should make clear that the *manager* is the one expected to come up with improvements. The staff specialists should make their reports and recommendations to *him*, not to someone higher up. It will be up to each manager to use such groups' findings in shaping his own actions or recommendations.

[4]Quoted from Hoffman, Frank O., "Improve Your Profits Day by Day," *Harvard Business Review,* July–August, 1963, pp. 59–67.

This need for "leadership from a team of persons" is rather widespread. In consequence, we see many such teams in industry. They go under such names as "New Products Committee," "Cost Reduction Committee," "Profit Improvement Committee," etc. They are identified with some Breakthrough effort, and they play a vital role in mobilizing the company's resources relative to that Breakthrough.

The foregoing Breakthrough-type teams are in obvious contrast to other kinds of teams which are *not* aimed at Breakthrough; such as:

the assembly line, the tabulating-room crew, the shipping gang, and other operating teams

the Grievance Committee, the Material Review Board, and other trouble-shooting teams engaged in fire fighting, breaking bottlenecks, and otherwise restoring the status quo rather than breaking into a new level of performance

These obvious contrasts are clear, and create no confusion. Yet there is much confusion from other sources, principally:

the all-purpose team which has responsibility *both* for coordinating current operations and for guiding Breakthrough. The various Management Committees, Executive Committees, Operating Committees, etc., are commonly of this type.

the ill-defined team which has so vague a charter no one really knows what it is supposed to do.

the decision-making type of team (true management by committee).

In this chapter we will define the type of team and team effort needed for guiding discovery, dissemination, and application of new knowledge; in other words, for guiding Breakthrough. To avoid the reflexes of existing terminology, let us coin the term Steering Arm to designate such a team. Our definition of Steering Arm is, then, a team engaged in guiding the discovery, dissemination, and application of new knowledge.

Everyone Wins

First, let us look at how the Steering Arm contributes to Breakthrough. It makes its contribution in two major ways.

1. The company stands to gain because the team direction supplies several ingredients which greatly increase the likelihood that Breakthrough will in fact be achieved. These ingredients are:
   (a) *Unity* of purpose.

(b) *Theories* to be tested.

(c) *Authority* for the experimenters who are to test the theories.

(d) Knowledge about the *cultural pattern.*

(e) *Action* after the results are in.

2. The team members also stand to gain, for a variety of reasons:

(a) Their "rights" in the problem are respected, adding to their personal *security.*

(b) Their *social needs* are fed by inviting them to belong to a team, as an equal.

(c) Their *ego needs* are fed by providing them an arena in which they can exhibit their knowledge, skill, and experience.

(d) Their *self-fulfillment needs* are fed by providing an opportunity for creative thought, and for identification with new results.[5]

Unity of Purpose

The outsider who has seen various companies under stress soon reaches some generalizations about the people in such companies:

they are competent, sincere, hardworking.

they are being driven by their bosses for results.

they are not getting the results, and they know it.

Lacking victories over their competitors, and unable to defend themselves from their bosses, they lash out at each other, thus making unity of purpose even harder to achieve. Lacking unity in working on the company's problems, each person does what he or she can—he or she works on those things which he or she can accomplish single-handedly. The overall result is a situation of many capable individuals, each pecking away at some part of the company's problems. These uncoordinated efforts have very little chance of getting anywhere.

A long step toward unity of purpose has been taken by the Pareto analysis (Chap. 4). That analysis has made clear that only the vital few projects are worth a lot of effort. In fact, a usual prompt result of publication of the Pareto analysis is that people are encouraged to drop their efforts to solve problems *not* on the list of the vital few.

However, the steering team is able to take another long step toward unity. It can agree—"We will concentrate on these three (or so) projects,

---

[5]This classification follows that used by Prof. Douglas McGregor in his incisive analysis, The Human Side of Enterprise, *The Management Review,* November, 1957.

and we will quit strewing our efforts over the rest." This identifies the enemy still more precisely, and sharpens the senses of the team more acutely. Now the team begins to look stronger than its enemies.

An added form of unity of purpose is to direct efforts at optimizing *company* economics and goals. Uncoordinated individual efforts are necessarily directed at departmental or individual goals. In such cases, some strange, unwelcome consequences flow from the best of intentions. The Credit Department makes a wonderful record, and ruins the sales volume. The Sales Department runs up a record volume, but too much of it is unprofitable business. The Manufacturing Department is proud of meeting the cost standards and delivery dates, but the Service Department is flooded with quality complaints.

Theories to Be Tested

All recipes for managerial progress include the ingredients "Get the facts. Analyze the facts." This is correct as far as it goes, but factual analysis is far deeper than these vague statements. What facts shall be gotten? What are we trying to prove, or disprove? Only if we go beyond the level of platitudes will "the facts" have much meaning.

There are two levels of analysis for any project:

(*a*) Analysis for *symptoms*. This is a Pareto-like analysis to identify the vital few symptoms of some general problem. This analysis is usually made "in the office" from information and reports which are a by-product of regular operation.

(*b*) Analysis for *causes*. This is different. It is a study in depth, "in the field," i.e., the factory, the warehouse, the sales district. The aim is to discover what stands between us and Breakthrough for this project.

During the late nineteenth century there was much effort to do something about yellow fever, a disease which flourished in several parts of the world, including Panama. When work began on construction of a canal across the Isthmus of Panama, yellow fever was one of the vital few problems. It required no profound analysis of "the facts" to identify yellow fever as a major problem. But getting rid of yellow fever was another matter. First there was need to answer the question—"What causes yellow fever?" When this question was put, there was no lack of answers. "Yellow fever is caused by the discharges from the sick." Or by the water. Or the jungle air. Or a bacillus. Or a mosquito. Or any of nineteen other things.

No amount of analysis of "the facts" could prove (or disprove) that the cause of yellow fever was the water, the bacillus, the mosquito, or some other of the many theories advanced. It was necessary to *create new facts*. These new facts were not some by-product of operations; they were *specially gathered to test theories*.

We will, in later chapters, discuss the process of testing out theories. But at this point we must note the need for a supply of theories to be tested. If Dr. Carlos Finlay had not theorized (in 1881) that a mosquito "causes" yellow fever, the trail might not have ended in 1901 when Dr. Walter Reed proved, through experiments on brave men, that *Stegomyia fasciata* did "cause" yellow fever.

The steering team is the main source of theories as to what stands between us and Breakthrough. Assemble a steering team and put the key question on the blackboard: What causes leaks in castings? How can we raise our share of market to 20 percent? What causes late deliveries? There will be a spate of theories—a dozen, several dozen. They cannot all be "right," or important. But the critical theory will very likely be on the list. The steering team includes the very individuals who have for years pondered on these problems. Here and there they have pursued their theories by rudimentary experiments. They have walked into the fog, though not far enough to recognize the moving shapes. They are fully equipped for theorizing, but have been unable to prove or disprove their theories because they lack the full facilities for experimenting.

Authority to Experiment

Experimentation "in the field" is a dream to the investigator, but a nightmare to the field personnel.

A foundry process was losing 20 percent of the product because of porous castings. The defects showed up after the castings had gone through a sequence of operations in various departments. To discover the relationship between causes in the foundry and effects in later operations, an extensive series of experiments was designed. These experiments required that thousands of castings be numbered and followed through the various departments, with a complete recording of data as to processing conditions.

These experiments turned out to be the key to solution of the problem—the defects were cut to 2 percent. But for many weeks the experimental castings and the experimenters were a widespread nuisance to several shop departments all trying to get their regular work done. The experimenters needed space, instruments, and other facilities. The experimental castings could be processed only under the eye of the investigators. Special records had to be kept. Special segregations, sequences, tools, and processing conditions had to be met, all requiring the time of busy supervisors.

No investigator could, on his own authority or personality, have persuaded the various shop foremen to do all this extra work. The experiments were run because the production superintendents were part of a steering team which had a mission of solving this problem.

Whether in the factory or in some other part of "the field," conduct of experiments requires priorities in assignment of workers, equipment, instruments, and other facilities. Who is to provide these priorities? Clearly, the members of the steering team who, in their regular jobs, preside over these facilities.

One of the important benefits of experimentation in the laboratory (rather than in the field) lies in the fact that the experimenters are in their own house, rather than being unwelcome guests among in-laws. Yet even here, the laboratory or pilot studies are under conditions so different from those prevailing under full-scale operation that a further round of experiments is necessary for debugging.

The foregoing should all be kept in mind by the manager who leaves it to some staff specialist to "try this out." The trial may enmesh a whole series of departments, each the industrial castle of some human supervisor who has a keen awareness of his "rights." It is asking a great deal to put on the unaided staff specialist the burden of enlisting extensive support for an experiment which *he* feels may be useful, but which is an irritating interference in the eyes of the individuals who have to endure the consequences.

Nor is the answer to "order" people to let the diagnostician conduct "his" experiment. There are a hundred ways of making the experiment not worth doing. Delays, misunderstandings, "throwing the book," acting dumb—it has been developed into a fine art. The crux of it is whether the experiment is "his" or "ours." Let it be "our" experiment, and it is amazing how the signal lights all suddenly flash "go."

So widespread is the need for experimentation that it must be regarded as a vital link in the chain of industrial Breakthrough. Those who can grant or withhold the authority to experiment can advance or retard progress so decisively that the steering team is not complete without them.

Knowledge of the Cultural Pattern

Industrial developments of the twentieth century have made clear that in industry, as well as anywhere else, human beings evolve a pattern of beliefs, habits, practices, etc.—a "culture." This pattern is so important to the members of the culture that they may be unwilling to change it, even in the face of "incentives" offered by persons who are outside the culture. As we will see in Chap. 9, "resistance to change" is mainly a resistance to the social effect of technical changes. This fact makes it important to be able to predict precisely what will be this social effect.

Generally, the staff specialists, the diagnosticians, do a sorry job of dealing with the cultural pattern. Many of them are not even aware of its existence. Thereby they create added problems through blind insistence that change be judged on technical merits alone. Those staff specialists who are aware of the existence of cultural patterns are still unable to predict just what cultural disturbances the proposed technical changes will generate.

The list of contributions of the Steering Arm includes the identification of just what impact the proposed changes will have on the cultural pattern. The Steering Arm members, who live in the culture, or are neighbors of those who do, can be of great aid in making this prediction. Where the impact of the change is on nonsupervisors, any prediction by supervisors still leaves much to be desired. These two groups live in cultures so different in outlook that each has great difficulty grasping the motivations of the other. Despite this, the Steering Arm still has a contribution to make.

Action on the New Knowledge

When the time comes to take action, it will be taken by the members of the Steering Arm. They command the departments which can change the specification, change the procedure, design a new package, reassign duties, etc.

They take this action in their regular capacity as supervisors, not in their capacity as members of the Steering Arm. They have never forgotten their "rights" to run "their" departments. However, by having been consulted, by participating, and by all the other useful devices afforded through being a part of the Steering Arm, the action they now take is their own—not something rammed down their throat by outsiders.

Veterans of many an industrial battle usually feel that here we have the greatest benefit conferred by a Steering Arm. The member is no longer in the situation of being asked to accommodate himself to changes worked out by someone else. He has participated fully, and they are *his* changes.

The Steering Arm Contributions to Its Members

Beyond the foregoing contributions to the company's needs for Breakthrough, the Steering Arm contributes importantly to the well-being of its members in their capacity as persons. The word "importantly" is used here in its literal sense. As persons, the members of the Steering Arm exhibit all the needs of normal human beings—the need to be secure, to be accepted, to be respected, to be listened to, to contribute, to undergo new experiences, to be creative, to achieve "self-fulfillment." As it turns out, membership on a creative team satisfies many of these essential needs. To be specific:

(a) *Safety and security.* The human being has exhibited an historical drive for mastery over his or her own fate. This drive is in several ways aided by membership on a Steering Arm. Of prime importance is the matter of rights in the job.

All human history teaches that repetitive performance of the same act establishes rights in the performance of that act, whether this is "squatting" on vacant real estate, eating at the same table in the company dining room, or closing the President's news conference with "Thank you, Mr. President." (Rights such as these gradually become private "property rights.") Recognition of these rights is a form of *security* equivalent to "seniority" in the nonsupervisory levels, or to "ownership" in the world outside of the company. The United States Constitution provides: "No person shall...be deprived of...property, without due process of law; nor shall private property be taken for public use without just compensation." The manager's "rights" in his conduct of "his" department are reaffirmed by inviting him to join the team which might bring about changes.

Aside from the defense of his rights against encroachment by other managers,[6] there is the matter of mysterious "natural" forces. Industrial worker, no less than his cave-dwelling ancestors, is forever faced with such forces. They have capacity for good or evil, and there is no telling why they switch from one to the other. Our ancestor depended on rain

---

[6] And against the arbitrariness of his own boss. The drive toward industrial unionism was in part directed toward freedom from arbitrariness of the boss.

for crops. If it failed mysteriously, the crop failed. Today we have huge areas in which we raise immense crops without depending on the rain.

Today's mysterious industrial forces are of other sorts. Customers can bring welcome prosperity or disastrous layoffs. A process can turn out beautiful product one day, junk the next. Living with such forces is as comfortable as living in earthquake country. We lack mastery over that part of our fate. Breakthrough is one of the means for increasing this mastery, and membership on the Steering Arm provides the member with a handhold on one of the wheels of destiny.

(b) *Social needs*. A basic human need is to belong—to be accepted as an equal, to be heard, to receive from, and to contribute to the team. For the most part, industrial problems are team problems. There is no solution on the basis of "You do your job and I'll do mine" when the job is joint. To be denied participation is to be excluded, shut out, rejected.

Participation is, of course, quite different from consent. Participation requires emotional as well as mental involvement. It requires originality and creativeness. It forces the participant to assume part of the responsibility for what happens. Consent, in the absence of participation, requires little of all this and is correspondingly sterile in the satisfactions it provides.

Our debates (on participation or not) often miss the main point. The enthusiasts for participation equate it with democracy. "If we need it outside the company, we need it inside." The opponents of participation follow the authoritarian line—"The crew can't run the ship." What is overlooked is the fact that Breakthrough and Control are vastly different in their needs for participation. Breakthrough, with its high content of creativity, must have a high degree of participation. Control properly involves a high degree of authoritarianism and hence a lower degree of participation.

(c) *Ego needs*. These are the needs for self-respect, either through possession of knowledge, skills, etc., or through demonstrated competence in one's undertakings; the needs include also the respect of others, and the status derived from such respect. These ego needs have a continuing appetite, and must be fed month after month by new deeds, new appreciation, new recognition. The series of adventures presented by a program of Breakthrough is an admirable source of fuel to feed the insatiable appetite of our ego needs.

(d) *Self-fulfillment needs*. This is Prof. McGregor's term for the needs of individuals to be creative, to continue self-development, to achieve potentialities. Here again, the very nature of Breakthrough provides opportunities and demands for creativity. Many a deep breath of satisfaction has been drawn by those who have advanced the art through hurling themselves at long-standing problems. Some of us have occasion to visit many companies and are given a tour of the "sights" of such an industrial community. With remarkable regularity, the guides on such a tour point out those practices in which "we are now the best in the industry." More tangibly, Breakthrough helps to meet the self-fulfillment needs of individuals by giving them a living laboratory in which to test their theories, by giving them a share of credit for results achieved by the team, by letting them share in the status which is earned by association with such results, by building up their own morale through the infectious confidence of membership on a winning team.

From another viewpoint, Breakthrough activities provide an in-house school for executive development. Creation and introduction of change are in the postgraduate curriculum of courses in executive development. Yet the most vivid cases are to be found not in the books or the simulation exercises; they abound right in the company.

The foregoing is a formidable list of contributions to the well-being of steering team members in their capacity as persons. This is not to say that these needs can feed on a diet of Breakthrough alone. However, it does happen to be the case that participation in Breakthrough helps materially.

Activating the Steering Arm

Before a Steering Arm can become effective, several steps have been taken somehow:

(a) Leadership for creating the Steering Arm
(b) Definition of a charter
(c) Appointment of the members
(d) Agreement on the internal machinery of the Steering Arm

All this may sound formidable, but it is in fact what is gone through, often without realizing it. To elaborate:

(a) *The creator.* The Steering Arm doesn't suddenly come to life, but its creator does. The creator may be any one of several who sees the need and who follows the Talmudic precept, "When you see the need for a leader, be thou that leader." Such a person gets in touch with several peers: "Let's get around the table and talk about it." The creator may also be the one who has the broad responsibility for the results which would be achieved by Breakthrough. The approach is to bring together those who have something to contribute, to outline the problem, and to give them the responsibility for coming to grips with it. Either way, the resulting Steering Arm can become effective.

Both of these ways—spontaneous leadership and "legitimate" leadership—can result in effective Steering Arms. Legitimate leadership is
preferable, since it does not depend on the lucky rise of spontaneous
leadership, and since the resulting Steering Arm cannot be attacked on
the ground that it lacks official sanction. But where legitimate leadership does not do its job, the leadership must be spontaneous, or nothing
will happen.

(b) *The charter.* The Steering Arm should have a fairly clear definition
of scope (our overseas friends call this a "frame of reference"). If the creator has not defined this scope, the Steering Arm should draft its own
scope. Where the Steering Arm has been appointed by higher authority,
this draft should then be approved by the appointing authority.

A company facing a competitive challenge to its long-standing
quality leadership undertook a positive program to do something
about it. It created a Steering Arm in the form of a Quality Improvement Committee. The approved charter was as follows:

Identify the specific needs for quality improvement, whether
for quality leadership, field complaints, inspection procedures,
quality controls or cost reduction.
Direct and make the necessary arrangements to secure the facts
and analyses needed as a basis for proposals for improvement.
Prepare specific recommendations for improvement.
Follow up to insure that agreed-on actions are put into effect.
The Committee should devote itself to long-range, continuing,
chronic quality problems for which the company does not have
ready solutions. The Committee should not become involved with
"day-to-day fire fighting" problems.

In contrast with this Steering Arm for Breakthrough in a specialty is
another with a charter to study the basic organization of the company.
In this case the President's letter states the background as well:

I am convinced the time has arrived for us to make a fundamental study of the organization of our company.
We have for years operated with an organization pattern fea-
turing functional departments in Sales, Production, Engineering,
etc. This has made for expertness in handling these functions, but
has also made it difficult to secure coordinated action as to given
products or markets or as to other inter-departmental matters.
Presumably the difficulty of coordination will increase as the company grows larger and larger. This problem of coordination for
specific products or markets has in turn generated numerous suggestions that we change our organization structure by creating a
number of product groups each headed by a general manager who

would command the marketing, engineering, production and possibly other functions associated with that group. There have been informal discussions of this plan or organization, but we have never gone into it deeply enough to see the full implications.

I am convinced that we would take unnecessary risks were we now to make organization changes in this direction without seeing a fairly complete blueprint in advance. But I am also convinced that we can and should prepare this blueprint.

Aside from the possibility of improving our operation through a drastic change in organization form, there may well be opportunities for improvement through re-organizing within our present functional framework, i.e., eliminating functions, combining functions, rearranging. It appears, then, that we have a job of preparing two blueprints: one on what we would be getting into if we made a drastic revision in our organization; the other, a revision within our present functional organization framework.

I believe we can make use of the Operations Research approach in tackling this job. To this end, I am designating a new Committee on Organization, with responsibilities as shown on the attached Frame of Reference. It will be the job of the Committee to develop these two plans of organization and to work up recommendations as to which course we should follow.

The Committee members will be: _____. _____ will serve as Chairman. _____ (head of Operations Research Section) will serve as Secretary. Dr. _____ will be available to the Committee as consultant.

I am asking the Committee to render its final report by June 30, so that whatever course we adopt, we still have time to agree on who will occupy the various posts, on the budgeting approach and on other matters needed to make the revised organization effective by next January 1.

——————, President

FRAME OF REFERENCE FOR THE COMMITTEE ON ORGANIZATION

The Committee has the responsibility for designing two organization plans. One of these plans is to utilize the principle of setting up managers for various logical subdivisions of the business. In this connection, the Committee should determine:

(1) Whether such subdivisions should be by product, or by market, or by some combination of these.

(2) How many such subdivisions should be created.

(3) Which of the present functional departments should be divided among the subdivisions, and to what extent.

(4) What new posts should be created, and what present posts should be abolished, combined, split, etc.

The other plan is to retain the present principle of functional organization for the company. In this connection, the Committee should determine:

(1) What new duties should be created, what present duties should be abolished, what duties should be combined, split, etc.
(2) As a result of (1), what new posts should be created, what present posts should be abolished, what posts should be combined, split, etc.

The Committee's report should include, for each plan, all information regarded by the Committee as appropriate for a study such as this, and should in any event contain:

(1) Proposed organization charts showing such detail as is needed to make clear the effect of the changes. These charts should be restricted to showing posts and should *not* name the individuals to be assigned to the posts.
(2) Tables showing the effect on the present organization chart, i.e., which posts remain unchanged, which are changed, which are abolished, and what new posts are created, with reasons for all changes.
(3) An estimate of the effect on the company budget as to (*a*) salary costs and (*b*) other costs.
(4) A discussion of the benefits and detriments of going to either of the new organization setups, with quantitative estimates where possible.
(5) A proposed procedure for making each of the proposed organizations effective, including:
   (*a*) A timetable showing what steps should be taken and in what sequence.
   (*b*) Such training, rotation, or transition steps as might be appropriate.
(6) A recommendation to the President on which organization form to adopt and why.

The Committee should *not* prepare any recommendations as to which individuals are to fill what posts.

On matters of great importance, the time spent in preparing a formal Frame of Reference is amply justified. Not only does it provide clear directions to the Steering Arm; it establishes the legitimacy of their resulting requests for data and other assistance from the rest of the organization.

There are many companies in which the executives scorn such formality. Sometimes the climate of collaboration is so good that formality can largely be dispensed with. More usually, the executives are simply unaware of the needs for clarification and especially for "legitimacy." The human drive for "rights" pervades all companies, even those with good climate, and especially those with poor climate of collaboration. When security is not provided by a system of law and order, people must provide it for themselves by taking the law into their own hands.

A Steering Arm can have either a continuing life, i.e., the New Products Committee, or a life for this project, i.e., the Committee on Organization described above. Either way it has the same general responsibilities, the same method of approach.

(c) *The membership.* The guiding principle is that the membership of the Steering Arm should be coextensive with the nature of the problem. Recall the contributions of the Steering Arm: unity of purpose, theories to be tested, authority to experiment, knowledge of the cultural pattern, action on the new knowledge. An individual appointed to the Steering Arm should be able to make these contributions to the problems at hand.

A common mistake is to appoint, to each Steering Arm, people of high rank because they carry great weight in the company. This is good when the problem requires it, i.e., the above study of the company's organization structure, or a study of the company's approach to new products. However, high rank is a detriment when the problem is closer to the firing line, i.e., improving deliveries from the warehouse, or quality in the machine shop, or productivity of the clerical staff. For such problems the various vice-presidents are normally too far removed to make useful contributions. In addition, there is the risk that the middle managers who *could* make the most useful contributions are bypassed and frustrated.

The most important guess to make is "Who will be called on to introduce the changes essential to effectuate the breakthrough in results?" If we can guess this correctly, we have identified the most important individuals to put on the Steering Team.

> A hospital faced with a severe problem in morale of nurses created a task force to find an answer. The morale problem was found to have its origin in stresses due to simultaneous and conflicting demands on the nurses' time. From there the trail led to the way in which hospital activities were scheduled by the various departments. The schedules had been uncoordinated, resulting in impossible demands on the nurses during certain hours of the day. The remedy was "obviously" to change the scheduled activities of some of the departments. However, it had not been foreseen that a problem in morale of nurses might have its origin in the scheduling of departmental activities. Hence the department heads involved had not participated in the study from the outset. This lack of participation affected their willingness to change their practices, and it took a long time to convince them.

It is, of course, not always predictable at the outset just where the trail will lead. A study to improve customer service may lead to changes in product design, in marketing organization, in manufacturing processes, etc. But while these things are not predictable at the outset, they become evident as matters proceed. If it turns out that important action may be required of some nonmember, it is most desirable that that individual be brought into the deliberations once this does become evident.

> At Kaiser Steel Corporation, projects for improving process yields are tackled by various Steering Arms, each consisting of:
>
> the mill superintendent, who serves as chair
>
> the division metallurgist responsible for the operation under study
>
> the supervisor of the Statistical Control and Yield Section, who serves as secretary. (This section has general diagnostic functions.)[7]

There are still other forms. S. C. Johnson & Son, Inc., uses "sponsors" as shepherds to guide a new product idea through the development stage.[8] Here the Steering Arm is a small *ad hoc* committee. Beyond the development stage and on to commercialization, a broader "product committee," with the "sponsors" as a nucleus, becomes the Steering Arm, again on an *ad hoc* basis.

As we saw in the case of Mr. Naka (p. 68), there are situations in which the Steering Arm can be a one-person gang. The criterion, as always, goes back to the basic need for "guiding the discovery, dissemination, and application of new knowledge." If the situation is such that one person is able to do all this, there is no point in burdening him or her with others.[9]

(d) *The internal machinery.* Industrial experience has demonstrated conclusively that a group of people embarking on a continuing joint adventure needs a set of team rules. The Steering Arm is no exception to this. The vast body of experience we have had with "problem-solving committees" or other such team efforts suggests how the internal machinery of the Steering Arm should function.[10] The elements of this include:

1. Definition of the *scope* of the activity. This should be reduced to writing in a charter or a frame of reference as discussed above.

---

[7]Curry, James A., "Searching for Assignable Causes in an Integrated Steel Plant," *American Society for Quality Control Transactions,* 1956, pp. 89–98.

[8]Johnson, Samuel C., and Conrad Jones, "How to Organize for New Products," *Harvard Business Review,* May–June, 1957, p. 56.

[9]In this connection, a deathless remark by Charles F. Kettering is in point. When someone commented on Lindbergh's historic solo flight across the Atlantic—"Isn't it wonderful, and to think he did it alone," Mr. Kettering responded, "It would have been still more wonderful if he had done it with a committee."

[10]For an excellent analysis, see "Problem Solving Conferences," National Industrial Conference Board, Studies in Personnel Policy, No. 176.

2. Duties of the *chairman*, which include calling the meetings, keeping the discussion on the track, seeing that there is a clear conclusion for each topic discussed.

3. Duties of the *secretary*, which include preparation of an agenda, and keeping and issuing minutes. Normally, the secretary is a part of the Diagnostic Arm (see Chap. 7).

4. Duties of *members*. These are to participate, to contribute data, theories, assistance.

5. The *agenda*. This should be prepared as guided by the Committee's priorities, and distributed in advance of the meeting, so that members are alerted and can come prepared. It is most helpful to attach to the agenda the results of the analysis conducted since the last meeting.

6. The *minutes*. These should summarize the Committee's deliberations, show clear disposition of the various topics discussed, whether concluded or carried over, and who is to take what action. In this way, the minutes serve also as a basis for follow-up.

Perhaps the greatest departure from conventional committee activity lies in the need to create a continuing atmosphere of challenge to long-standing opinions, beliefs, practices. At the outset, these challenges will not be welcomed. Yet as theories and beliefs are tested, affirmed, discarded or modified, the Committee will gradually acquire the habit pattern of distinguishing clearly between fact and opinion.[11]

The Task Force

The amount of "discovery, dissemination, and application of new knowledge" needed by companies, even of moderate size, goes beyond the capacity of any one Steering Arm. What then? Does this require a whole network of Steering Arms?

To a degree it does, and there is nothing wrong with this. Breakthrough in customer service from the warehouse can go on while other Steering Arms are working on the cost system, the plant layout, and the make-or-buy policy. Given worthwhile projects, we can go at them up to the digestive capacity of those who must conduct full-time jobs while they sit part time as members of one or more Steering Arms.

---

[11] In his participation as an "outside member" of various Steering Arms, the author has observed that many, having acquired this habit pattern in the committee meetings, have carried it into their noncommittee work as well.

When the total Breakthrough needed goes beyond this capacity, and cannot wait, a new approach is required. One form of this is the Task Force.

> The Iredell company decided to make a fundamental review of its approach to marketing. The size of the study was immense. The company had numerous profit centers, generally product based. Most of these had histories as independent companies and still retained separate field sales forces, methods of promotion, tradition, etc. It was clear that a really fundamental study would require the full time of a dozen competent people for a couple of years, supplemented by data, advice, etc., from the operating divisions.
>
> Iredell decided to create a Task Force to do the job. A dozen competent individuals, mainly operating executives, were in fact detached from their jobs and assigned full time to the Task Force. They received aid from the operating divisions and the company's staff services. It took them 3 years, and the result was a drastic change in the approach to marketing.

The Task Force is in common use. More usually, it is concerned with straight operating missions (military operations, producing a new moving picture, a new product development, etc.). But the Task Force concept is usable in Breakthrough, and is a good organization form when the work to be done is well beyond the capacity of part-time activity by busy managers.

What Happens in the Absence of a Steering Arm?

We have talked mainly about providing a steering team as part of the sequence of a new effort for Breakthrough. Before leaving the subject, let us note that a lot of damage is being done through failure to provide a steering team in various continuing Breakthrough activities. These failures usually are called failures of "coordination," which is a good one-word label for the contributions of the Steering Arm.

A widespread example is the problem of new product development. As product obsolescence has quickened, it has become necessary to step up the birth rate of new products to keep pace with the quickening death rate. It has also been recognized that those engaged in new product development should devote themselves fully to this, without being forever drawn into day-to-day fire drills. Accordingly, departments of Research and Development (Diagnostic Arms, in the lingo of this book) have been created to give them freedom to concentrate on new product development. So far, so good.

But new product Breakthrough is an activity of far greater scope than the scientific or engineering achievements. Market research must precede scientific research—before you develop a product, find out how many you could sell if you had it. For every hundred new product ideas thrown into the hopper, only two or three come out alive. These surviving infants have a voracious appetite for company funds. The cost of production prototypes is several times the cost of the "breadboard" models and is, in turn, dwarfed by the cost of preparing for production and marketing, especially for consumer products.

It would seem obvious that such fateful steps should be taken only with careful coordination. Yet in many companies, no specific provision is made for such coordination, other than the regular hierarchy of supervision.

The symptoms of absence of a Steering Arm are familiar, and have been recited over and over again. For example:[12]

> We started our organization planning with the conventional staff approach—and therein lies the tale. Working with all the divisions we defined philosophy, precepts, approach, techniques, chart and job description formats, organization manuals, and so forth—the usual tools familiar to you all. Some informed outsiders have been kind enough to rate this material as pretty good. The effort was strongly supported by the President which was, of course, essential.
>
> But in spite of the generally recognized need and the logic and completeness of the approach, there was great apathy. There was noticeable resistance in some spots. Many organizations were analyzed. Some were reorganized, on paper at least, but with little real dollars and cents results where it was needed the most.

When the urge for Breakthrough is great, the absence of a Steering Arm creates a vacuum of leadership. The resulting scramble will fill the vacuum, but not necessarily in a way which will do the company any good.

One series of would-be leaders comes from the various staff departments who possess the diagnostic skills we will examine in the next chapter. These skills, though necessary, are not sufficient to achieve Breakthrough in the absence of a Steering Arm. The staff specialists are unable, by themselves, to supply unity of purpose, theories, authority to experiment, knowledge of the cultural pattern, and action for remedy.

[12]McNair, Malcolm P., Jr., The Task Force Approach to Getting Monetary Results from Organization Improvement Counselling, *Advanced Management*, December, 1958, pp. 9–12.

Yet this inability is not enough to stop an enthusiastic staff specialist from advocating his specialty as a cure for the situation at hand. The result can easily be a program of remedy before diagnosis or, more accurately, without diagnosis.

> The temptation to start with remedies instead of diagnosis is so common that it merits separate discussion. The peril exists because many people are engaged in "hard sell" of remedies, but few are engaged in hard sell of diagnosis. The stock-in-trade of staff departments, consultants, vendors, and others consists to an important extent of prefabricated remedies: profit sharing, training programs, job evaluation, statistical quality control, integrated data processing, etc. The difference in the number and intensity of those selling remedies and those selling diagnosis is great enough to be a widespread cause for by-passing diagnosis.[13]

The record on this point is really damaging. Legions of Industrial Engineering departments have failed their companies. Their tools, invented in the days of great gangs of unskilled labor, were designed to reduce the cost of such labor. When factories mechanized, the unskilled labor force shrank, but the Industrial Engineers continued to concentrate on this vanishing problem, while a host of new problems—plant maintenance, material handling, data processing—emerged and demanded solution. Left to themselves, the engineers were guided by the nature of their prefabricated techniques, not by the company's needs.

A similar road was followed by the Statistical Quality Control people. They literally plastered the factory walls with Shewhart charts while the company's main quality troubles—unrealistic specifications, vendor relations, clear definition of responsibility, unwise economics, vague standards, etc.—went on and on. And so for the Operations Researchers, the Brainstormers, the Motivation Researchers, etc. There is nothing ill-intentioned or evil about it. It is just in the nature of things. Tool-oriented people approach problems with so heavy a bias that they should not be given the sole responsibility of choosing where they are to direct their efforts.

A second would-be leader is top management itself. When an aggressive top manager is sucked into a middle management need for Breakthrough, the effect can be costly because *there is no adequate challenge to the big boss' views.* Members of a Steering Arm can and do challenge each other, vigorously. But a middle manager is in no such situation respecting the Big Boss.

To the middle managers, one of the most unwelcome forms of top-management invasion is the bringing in of a drove of outside consul-

---

[13]Juran, J. M., "Industrial Diagnostics," *The Management Review,* June, 1957.

tants for a broad-scale survey. These consultants then swarm over the place, interviewing managers and acquiring ideas and data, all under a correct, cool relationship. The resulting report is seldom used, since the managers are united against something in which they have not really participated. In this way, the loss may be limited to the fee paid. But where top management orders the consultants' recommendations made effective, the consequences may be devastating.

Many another well-intentioned top manager adopts or imports a remedy because it has been well sold, because it seems to him to fit the case, because it is the talk of the town, or even because his competitor has it. These remedies are, of course, effective for certain ailments. But the ailments are often not on the manager's list, if he but knew it.

Even more damage can be done when top management has some private theory (or fixation) which is imposed to the exclusion of all else.

> One executive is convinced that the real need is for everyone to work harder, to put in longer hours, to take shorter vacations. A second feels that the only real contributors to the company's welfare are the operator at the machine and the salesman with the order pad; all else is fluff. A third feels that this business of organization, planning, and controlling is fine, *but* if you just get good men on the key jobs everything will work itself out. A fourth concentrates on whatever comes to his attention from personal observation—lights not turned out, long coffee breaks, company facilities used for personal mail, etc. And the list could be extended to include still other species.
>
> These are all cases in which preoccupation with a private nostrum is a roadblock to open-minded diagnosis. Under such conditions, lower-level managers must, among themselves, generate informal leadership for diagnosis purposes. Otherwise, a realistic approach to the company's problems may never be attained.[14]

A third form of leadership which moves into the vacuum of power is the "clique." This is one version of the informal organization which prevails wherever human beings are thrown into association. The clique is oriented to the needs of its members, which may or may not conflict with the needs of the company. The example of the product development department blocking the industrial engineers (p. 33) is a case in point.

The nature of cliques is a subject of its own.[15] Our interest is merely that when there is no Steering Arm, the guidance of Breakthrough may

[14]Juran, *op. cit.*

[15]See, for example, Odiorne, George S., "The Clique—A Frontier in Personnel Management," *Personnel*, September–October, 1957, pp. 38–44.

gravitate to a clique. Usually it is a misfortune, and sometimes a calamity. Either way, it is no fault of the clique, only of the managers who abdicated their responsibility.

Irrespective of which force moves into the vacuum of leadership, the damage is compounded. The effort wasted going down blind alleys also diverts attention from the main road. In addition, failure to solve the problem tends to harden beliefs that the problem is insoluble, thus creating a negative attitude toward reopening the matter.

The manager who is pondering on alternatives for leadership in a Breakthrough project should look back at the needs met by the Steering Arm: unity of purpose, theories to be tested, authority to experiment, knowledge of the cultural pattern, and action on the new knowledge. These purposes must be met somehow, and the measure of Breakthrough leadership is the extent to which these purposes are met.

We now turn to the Diagnostic Arm, which is the main source of grist for the Steering Arm.

7 THE DIAGNOSTIC ARM

Why a Diagnostic Arm?

In creating the Steering Arm, we have made some valuable contributions to Breakthrough. Why is this not sufficient to give us results? Why do we need still another arm of organization? The answer becomes evident when we look back at Table 1-2 (p. 11), which compares the kind of facts and analysis needed for Breakthrough with those needed for holding the status quo.

It is evident that, for Breakthrough, the legwork of fact collection and analysis is a considerable chore, requiring:

(a) Time
(b) Diagnostic skills
(c) Objectivity

As we will see shortly, the people in the Steering Arm are normally unable to contribute these requirements. They lack the time, are normally not trained in the necessary diagnostic skills, and normally lack complete objectivity; i.e., they have an involuntary bias because of their vested interest in the existing order. Accordingly, if these things (time, diagnostic skills, and objectivity) are essential to Breakthrough, they must be contributed by someone else. That someone else is the Diagnostic Arm.

Lacking these facilities of time, special skills, and objectivity, a Steering Arm can only set the stage. It can establish unity of purpose, and it can theorize about what stands between it and Breakthrough. Extensive progress beyond this "debating society" stage depends on getting the theories tested. This the Steering Arm cannot do without aid from the diagnosticians.

Examples of Diagnostic Arms

There is nothing new about the Diagnostic Arms. Throughout all recorded history, managers (kings, priests, merchants) have used investigators of all sorts. Some of these investigators were explorers (Marco Polo, Christopher Columbus); others were military spies;[1] still others were inventors (Archimedes).

In modern industry the need for Diagnostic Arms is very extensive. These needs are not limited to temporary task forces; some needs are of a continuing character and hence require a permanent Diagnostic Arm. For example:

Breakthrough needed	Usual name of Diagnostic Arm
New markets	Market Research
New processes	Process Research
Cost reductions in manufacture	Industrial Engineering
Improvement of product quality	Quality Control Engineering
New Products	Product Research and Development

Later in this chapter, we will examine some of the implications of the existence of so many Diagnostic Arms. Meanwhile, let us see in some detail how the Diagnostic Arm contributes to Breakthrough.

Time to Diagnose

The time for diagnosis, and especially for experimentation, can be prodigious. But only the trained experimenters are aware of the kind and duration of time needed. (The untrained experimenter takes many short cuts and sometimes gets away with it.)

[1]Joseph to his brethren: "Ye are spies; to see the nakedness of the land ye are come." Genesis 42:9.

The need for time spans a wide array of activities. The need extends
to the original design of experiment; getting acceptance of this design
by the Steering Arm; acquiring the necessary instruments and materials; creating the field conditions required by the design of experiment;
informing everyone along the line of march; designing the data sheets;
conducting a dry run to see whether all is in readiness. And all this is
just preparation.

Then comes the data collection. Where this is done under operating
conditions, much checking and monitoring are needed to ensure that
the design of experiment is actually being carried out. A log of operating conditions may be necessary. This data collection may be short—
hours or minutes—or it may go on for months.

A third major segment of time is data analysis and presentation. Even
the more obvious cases of analysis require the drudgery of "reduction
of data," i.e., converting a myriad of tiny pieces of information into a
grand mosaic of meaning. More intricate cases of analysis may require
a search for relationships hidden in the data, using sophisticated techniques such as analysis of variance or multiple regression.

Time is needed both in the worker-hour sense and in the calendar
sense. The worker-hours needed vary considerably from one case to another, perhaps a range of 10,000 to 1. The calendar time over which these
man-hours are spread is more nearly uniform, perhaps a range of only
100 or 10 to 1.

The need is often for uninterrupted time. Particularly in data collection, and to a degree in the entire experimentation process, the diagnostician must be in a position to devote full time to the experiment.
When several pots are boiling he must be there to watch them, which
means freedom from the need to participate in fire drills. This need for
continuity is by itself usually enough to rule out part-time experimenters, especially line supervisors who have a day-to-day treadmill to
walk and who must be on call to numerous subordinates and peers.

A final aspect of time is mobility. The diagnostician must follow the trail
wherever it leads—to the various shop departments, the offices, the warehouses, the customers' premises, the vendors' plants. Such mobility is generally denied to the line supervisor, since the work of his or her department is built on the premise that he or she will be around most of the time.

The Nature of Diagnostic Skills

Diagnosis ranges widely in depth and complexity. A company president can, from the profit statements published in *The Wall St. Journal*,
discover in minutes that the profitability of his company compares
poorly with that of his competitors. Discovering *why* they are different

may take a few months of the time of a trained investigator. Taking the steps needed to bring his company up to the level of his competitors may take years of cut and try. Here is an actual case.

> The president of the Squires Company noticed from published financial statements that his principal competitor, Melcher Company, was "on the move." For a period of 2 or 3 years, this competitor's profitability rose and rose until it reached a level double that of Squires'. The president assigned a skilled diagnostician to discover how Melcher managed its business.
>
> The diagnostician studied the file of Melcher's annual reports, house organs, promotional material, and the like. In addition, he interviewed former Melcher employees currently in the employ of Squires. From all this "legitimate industrial espionage," he was able to identify, with remarkable clarity, the business policies, methods, and results of Melcher, and to contrast these with those of Squires.
>
> The report of the diagnostician became the subject of much soul searching in Squires, because the policies and practices of the two companies differed drastically. This soul searching in turn resulted in profound changes in Squires' ways of doing business. These changes were in the nature of cut and try extending over a period of years.

Diagnosis may be limited to review of existing data (analysis) or it may be extended to creation of new data (experimentation). Both of these activities range across the spectrum from utter simplicity to unbelievable intricacy. Anybody can handle the former and only the professionals should tackle the latter.

Analysis of Prior Operations

Breakthrough in knowledge is not tied to new experiments. The past activities of people are also in the nature of experiments, and analysis of these past activities can be a most fruitful source of "new" knowledge.

> The Mohr textile company was failing to delivery samples of its new designs in time for display at the industry's semiannual "show." A fierce controversy broke out as to the cause of this failure. The departments primarily involved were (a) the Product Design Department, which had responsibility for creating new designs in its laboratory, and (b) the Manufacturing Engineering Department, which was responsible for getting the factory ready to produce.

Under Mohr's approach to new products, Product Design prepared designs, and developed materials and processes in its laboratory, all under a tight security system to minimize the risk of piracy of design. A high-level company committee reviewed progress from time to time, and agreed on which products to take to market. Once agreement was reached, Manufacturing Engineering was brought into the picture to ready the factory for manufacture.

The center of the controversy was Product Design's contention that Manufacturing Engineering was too slow in doing its job. The charges and countercharges reached the president, who found himself unable to get objective answers from men so emotionally worked up. Lacking the time to get into the details personally, the president turned to his consultant.

The consultant's approach was to find out, *from existing information*, what had happened to the time. He studied, in detail, the life cycle of 10 new product developments. He found that, on the average, Manufacturing Engineering took 5 months to get the factory ready to produce. But he also found that it took on the average 24 months from the time a new product idea was propounded until Manufacturing Engineering was brought into the picture.

This finding put a new light on the controversy. If Mohr were to shorten its total 29-month cycle from product idea to "ready to manufacture," the main opportunities were in the 24-month interval, not the 5-month interval. The company found an answer by "clearing" a manufacturing engineer for security once a new product showed promise (which was well below the 24-month average).

The significance of the case rests in the fact that the entire analysis was conducted on history, with no need for experiments.

Creating New Data

Breakthrough in knowledge may at times be achieved entirely from analysis of information already in existence. But often enough this information is inadequate, and new information must be created. This concept is a difficult hurdle for some.

In the "line" it is current operations which count. Any information is a by-product. But in the development laboratory, or the field market research studies, the "operations" exist solely for the purpose of creating information.

Steering Arm members should be sensitized to the existence of this difference. There will be numerous occasions when thorough analysis of available information is still not adequate to Breakthrough in knowledge. New data are needed, and it may be necessary to set up special studies or experiments to generate these data.

In time, Steering Arm members come to accept this need, and it is a pleasure to watch them arrive at this state. People whose long-standing views are challenged—"How do you know that?" "Has that ever really been proved?"—are resentful at the challenge. But a few months later they hedge their statements around "This is what I believe, but I don't recall that it has really been proved." This circumspect attitude is accompanied by a more receptive attitude toward suggestions for creating new data.

> A company making tools and hardware for builders sent its analysts out to the building sites to record the problems as actually encountered by the builders—time spent on various operations, material wastage, unit costs, etc. The study exploded many prior theories of what the customers needed.

Experimental Skills

The irrepressible curiosity of human beings gives rise to a vast amount of experimentation. Through experimentation the child discovers how to ride a bicycle, blow bubbles, catch a baseball, and do a thousand other feats. The child who becomes a manager brings with him or her a lifetime of experimentation, and he or she does not hesitate to try his or her hand at experimenting in managerial problems as well. But there is a big difference.

In the world of the child, the relationship between cause and effect is usually obvious, then and there. In the world of the manager, the time interval between cause and effect is seldom measured in minutes—it stretches into weeks, months, years. The variables are numerous, so that it is not really evident which of the many possible causes provoked the result. And the amount at stake increases enormously. In consequence of all this, industrial experimentation requires far more sophisticated approaches than the manager is even aware of. (None of this prevents the amateur experimenters from tackling jobs which the professionals approach with trepidation.)

Experimental skills embrace several related skills, as follows:

Design of experiment
Collection of data
Analysis of data
Interpretation of results

Design of Experiment

The most important aspect of any experiment is whether, if carried out, it will really test the theory under study. This aspect is what the statisticians call "design of experiment."

> The experiments designed to test the effectiveness of the Salk vaccine for poliomyelitis were probably the most extensive ever conducted on human beings. Polio was, even at its worst, a rare disease. Hence comparison of vaccinated vs. unvaccinated persons required a large "sample" in order to get "significant" numbers for comparison. Actually, arrangements were made to bring over a million human beings into the sample. Yet the entire experiment came close to being a colossal failure because of a built-in bias in one of the proposed designs for experiment. Under this design, the incidence of polio among vaccinated children would be compared with the incidence among unvaccinated children. But hidden in this design was a serious potential bias. Before a child could be vaccinated, permission had to be secured from his parents. This need for permission brought in the variables of parents' education, religious convictions, economic status, etc., all of which had potential effects on the incidence of polio among unvaccinated children.
>
> A different approach was proposed to eliminate these possible biases, through the use of "dummy" shots (placebos). In other words, children whose parents granted permission for vaccination were to be given either the real vaccine or a placebo, but no one, not the children, or the parents, or even the medical people giving the "shots," would know which was which. The shots were to be coded, and only the people at headquarters would have the code book.
>
> Happily, the placebo form of experiment was adopted, and the results were accepted as free from bias.

Inherent bias is not the only consideration in design of experiment. An experiment design which is free from bias can get into trouble on other counts.

(a) *The precision of measurement* may be too coarse in relation to the thing under study.

> The naked human eye is unable to see microbes. Only after the invention of the microscope was it possible to prove that tiny organisms caused many diseases.

In like manner the manager may be unable to "see" some things until more precise instruments are developed. If the merchandiser uses a single mark-up percentage, an expensive refrigerator will carry the same dollar mark-up as 100 neckties. (The rise of the discount house was in part based on awareness that such a mark-up pattern was unrealistic.) To pave the way for deeper understanding, more precise allocation of the overhead charges is necessary.

(b) The sample size may be so small that the results are *"statistically nonsignificant."*

The following two cases have much in common:

(1) A crap shooter coins a new expression—"Come on, you cute, cunning cubes!" He is rewarded by making his point. He tries the experiment a second time. Again he wins. And a third time. What does it prove?

(2) A sales manager has designed a new sales kit and pitch for her sales force. The thing is put on test, and makes a sale four times in the first ten calls. The old average is only two sales in ten calls. What does it prove?

The statistician would sniff at both of these results. Either could have happened by luck. Neither is "significant" in the dialect of the statistician.

How big a sample *do* we need? The skilled analyst has specific answers for this, and his answers may avoid a precipitate decision, may cut the cost of sampling, or may affirm a hunch decision.

(c) *The cost* of experimenting becomes forbidding.

The amateur's attempts to evade the pitfalls of the diagnostic world take various forms—increasing the size of sample, holding everything constant but one variable, and the like. Generally these run up the costs of experimentation, sometimes enormously.

In contrast, the professional has found ways to throw a bridge high above the morass of detail. Are there many bothersome uncontrolled variables? If convenient, he holds them constant; if not, he "randomizes" them so that they are not bunched enough to distort results. Is there too wide a range for the suspected variables? He does his experimenting at a few selected values on the scale of measurement. Is the number of experiments forbidding? He designs Latin squares and other elegant means for experimenting on several variables simultaneously, with incredible reductions in cost of experimentation.

Collection of Data

Our Steering Arm may have concluded—let's conduct a market study on consumer reaction to our product. Can we turn this job over to the nearest sensible person and forget it? Let's try it, and see what happens.

Our sensible person soon finds himself or herself in another world. Is he or she to measure consumer preferences for our product vs. others? If so, it is necessary to give the consumers pairs of samples, in a statistically designed submission to avoid bias (the consumer panel must be representative of our consumers generally, they must not know which product is which, there must be no hint of answers desired, etc.). But our sensible person has other possible roads—is he or she to measure whether consumers like our product or not? This is different from "preference," and involves a different set of statistical tests—rating tests rather than preference tests. Nor is this all. What should we submit to the consumers—our regular product, special samples, an assortment across the range, etc.? It all depends on the precise purpose of the test.

The conduct of the test likewise has pitfalls. Those who carry out the details of the plan may take short cuts, mix up the samples, the sequence. The supervision of these details must include participation by the diagnostician who understands which parts of the structure are so vulnerable that loving care is needed.

Analysis of Data

Normally "data" consist of numerous, even myriads, of tiny facts. One of 1,292 housewifes interviewed answers one of 42 questions by saying "three." This one of the 8,139 castings machined today was so porous that it was set aside as scrap.

Each of these tiny facts has little value to the manager. Collectively, they may cause him to take some drastic action. But the facts cannot be judged collectively until the myriads of tiny facts, each unimportant, have been boiled down to a few big facts, each very important. This boil-down is called reduction of data.

Where the data are extensive, this boil-down requires knowledge of the statistical measures for central tendency, dispersion, correlation, etc. It requires knowledge of the mathematical processes by which these measures are computed. It requires knowledge of the clerical procedures and tools available for mathematical computation. And these days, it requires understanding of the potential inherent in modern technology.

Interpretation of Results

Probably the most hilarious blunders in the world of diagnosis are made in interpreting results.

A scientist trained a flea to jump on the command "jump." Then
the scientist conducted some experiments on the flea. He removed
the flea's front legs. On the command "jump," the flea jumped, but
not as far as before. Removal of the middle legs cut the distance further. Finally, the scientist removed the remaining two legs and
commanded "jump." The flea did not move. Over and over again
came the command "jump," and still no movement.

Then the scientist solemnly recorded his conclusion: "Removal of
a flea's legs impairs his hearing."

For many centuries, patient observers in many lands had looked up at
the heavens and mapped the course of celestial bodies. Calendars of
amazing precision were worked out, at a time when people believed
that a flat earth rested on the backs of four huge turtles. Yet the spatial
arrangement of the celestial bodies eluded these same people until a few
centuries ago. Only as analysts could derive laws, principles, or relationships from the observed phenomena could this mechanical arrangement be proved.

In some situations, the data yield their conclusions readily. In such
cases the amateur is as good as the professional. But increasingly, we go
into studies which tackle multiple variables—improving yields of a
manufacturing process, revising the approach to marketing, reconsider-
ing the economics of make or buy, discovering the optimum number of
warehouses. These questions are anything but simple. Even when the
data are all in, the job of extracting their meaning from them is complex.
The extraction process requires familiarity with strange things—analysis of variance, multiple regression, confidence levels, etc. It is no place
for the amateur.

Objectivity

For 25 years, Horace lived a methodical life. Every night he
wound his alarm clock to wake him the next morning. It was a severe shock to discover, after 25 years, that his clock was actually an
8-day clock.

All of us have an involuntary bias due to our vested interest in the existing order. When *we* discover we have unwittingly wound the 8-day
clock daily, our normal reaction is "I could kick myself." When *someone
else* discovers this, our reaction is compounded because our embarrass-
ment is there for all to see.

We will leave to the life scientists the details of why we feel pain when we are discovered to have lived a mistake. The cultural anthropologists point out that some of our long-standing beliefs are derived from people who were most important to us in our formative years, the family members, the teachers. If some of what they told us is now suspect, what can we trust? And what if we have passed these beliefs on to the next generation? Will it mean that their confidence in us is undermined?

In the company we have some related feelings to combat. We have learned some things from bosses we respect; we have taught them to subordinates who respect us. Moreover, our reputation for being right stands to be chipped away, or so it seems.

The Steering Arm member is, during nonsteering hours, a member of some specific department, and exhibits all the loyalties of a team member. With singular unanimity, Production supervisors line up against Sales supervisors on questions of schedule changes. Witness how the Army, Navy, and Air Force officers so unanimously support those weapon systems which *their* branch would operate.

Whatever the causes, the biases are there. The extent of this is such as to jeopardize objectivity seriously. When we test our product against that of our competitor, we take risks if the individual who developed our product is also responsible for the tests. If our experiments may lead to an action which Production has long resisted, we take risks if Production alone is to conduct those experiments.

The Negative Side

So far in this chapter we have tended to show that the diagnostician is rather an indispensable sort. Yet the record shows his past as a highly checkered career. Not only that, today's seminars, conferences, and literature, no less than the talk in the corridors, make it clear that the diagnostician has a long way to go before he or she is as fully accepted, say, as the employment interviewer or the purchasing agent. What causes this gulf between the opportunity and the reality?

There are many reasons—the line people, the boss, the comparative youth of industrial staff activities. These matters we will discuss in their turn. Right now we are concerned with the diagnostician's contributions to his own troubles. Fundamentally, these originate in the fact that the diagnostician is technique-oriented while trying to be of service to managers who are results-oriented. But this problem is compounded by two others—the diagnosticians as a "profession" and the diagnostician as a person.

Orientation—Results vs. Techniques

The manager's prime need is to get results. His or her status and career are bound up with the extent to which he or she can get results. The kinds of techniques or tools used to get results are secondary to the manager. So is the question of use of science vs. art.

In theory, the staff specialist is there to help the manager get results. In practice, the specialist has a severe bias toward his specialty. His "professional" identification is bound up with this specialty—he has studied it, has given courses in it, belongs to a society devoted to it, has written papers on it, is a member of committees, etc. It is a world from which he derives important satisfactions and to which he exhibits a loyalty akin to patriotism.

The basic, obvious rule, often violated, is that the energy of the diagnosticians should be directed at solution of problems, not at pursuit of techniques. This requires that the problems be identified first. The nature of the problems is then decisive as to the kind of specialists needed, and further as to the role which will be played by the specialists. This sequence holds, whether we are dealing with specific projects or with a continuing specialist department.

As an example of the former, here is the definition of duties for the Diagnostic Arm (called the Quality Analysis Group) created to serve the Quality Improvement Committee described on p. 88, Chap. 6:

> The purpose of this group is mainly to serve the Quality Improvement Committee. The Group head will act as secretary of the Committee and as liaison between the Group and the Committee. The specific duties of the Quality Analysis Group are:
>
> Design of experiments to study problem areas identified by the Committee
>
> Direction, conduct, and coordination of experiments authorized by the Committee
>
> Collection, analysis, and presentation of data
>
> Preparation of the Committee's agenda and minutes

Applied to a continuing specialist department, the basic rule is the same, though the application differs.

The objectives, plans, and budgets of permanent diagnostic departments should be reviewed and discussed *with the departments served* so that they participate in setting objectives, etc., before there is a final approval. Such participation aids greatly in arriving at a realistic budget.

Diagnostic departments should issue periodic reports of progress, and copies of these reports should go to the departments they serve.

"Staffing-level evaluations" of members of diagnostic departments should include participation by the departments served.

Unless these and related forms of guidance are used, it is difficult for the Diagnostic Arm to adopt realistic budgets and directions. Lack of participation by the departments served makes the diagnostician an "outsider" in those departments.

Lacking a meeting of the minds on objectives and plans, the diagnostic departments, in their frustration, may do a whole series of ridiculous things—ridiculous to those who are not faced with the frustrations. The outward evidences are familiar enough.

They refine techniques without having applications for them.[2] They design courses of study in their specialty and urge mandatory attendance by all. They paper the walls with charts and propaganda. And they begin to engage in antisocial acts—negative positions on everything, being conspicuous at meetings, rudeness, sarcasm. All this invites retribution, and the stage is set for tragedy.

> During the 1940s the author studied the progress of new programs of quality control in 39 different companies. Over half the programs were in serious trouble. The frustrations and antisocial acts were unmistakably present.

Finally, there is the fact that diagnostic specialties are mortal. The two most usual causes of death are:

the specialty becomes obsolete because of new technology.

the specialty becomes so well standardized that it can be turned over to the regular operating people.

Managers should be especially alert to identify extinct specialties. The specialists hang on, for obvious human reasons.

When the company has no history or (what is worse) a sorry history of staff department activity, the role of the diagnostician will not be understood. An attempt to introduce a staff department as such will meet with great resistance.

> In one backward industry (processing walnuts) the approach to reducing costs and increasing production was to create study groups of supervisors from the production departments. These

---

[2] And are accused of inventing wonder drugs when the diseases haven't been invented yet.

people were then trained in use of Industrial Engineering techniques appropriate to their operations. This approach turned out to be a stunning success. It also paved the way for establishing a system of cost measurement. Finally, it produced the climate necessary for introduction of an Industrial Engineering department which would develop standards for cost control.[3]

The Diagnostic "Profession"

The profession, like the Union, the New York Yankees, or other human aggregation, has a life and a drive of its own. In the case of the company's diagnosticians, there are in fact a number of aggregations, many known as staff departments. These face the biological problems of birth, growth, maturity, and (hopefully) immortality. None of this is easy, since there are perils of all sorts, including competing staff departments.

> For example, many companies use a review procedure to find potential cost reductions before putting new designs into production. However, for purchased parts or components, such a review procedure has not been so prevalent. To plug this gap there was evolved the activity known as "Value Analysis." A new category of staff specialist was created—the Value Analysis Engineer. A new Steering Arm in the form of a Value Analysis Committee was organized to guide the work. So far, so good. But all this has invaded the claimed territory of the Manufacturing Planning Department (or some other department) who state their arguments in depth:
>
> we are already doing this.
>
> we aren't doing this but we should have been doing it.
>
> we shouldn't have been doing it, but if it is to be done, we should enlarge our scope, not set up a new department.

Some of this proliferation of Diagnostic Arms is justified by the number and variety of needs for Breakthrough. Some of it is harder to justify, though easy to explain. The upper management has concluded that an existing staff department has lost its capacity for imaginative, original thinking. Hence a new, promising activity is not turned over to this plodder. Instead, a new department is set up for the purpose. In time, the new department will probably swallow up the old. Meanwhile, both departments coexist, but not peacefully.

---

[3]Buffington, A. L., "Productivity in Food Processing," *The Journal of Industrial Engineering*, September–October, 1958, pp. 346–347.

The existence of competing staff activities has necessarily sharpened competitive abilities. In particular, the diagnosticians have learned a few things about merchandising. They look sideways at the "soap is soap" fraternity and suspect that packaging, promotion, and advertising are the real determinants of share of market. So with cigarettes, cosmetics, beer, and much else. Why not do some merchandising of diagnosis?

> An example of skillful merchandising is "Work Simplification." Mr. Allen H. Mogensen, who popularized the term, did so with techniques which were useful as well as colorful. He made extensive use of "before and after" movies of operations. He stressed widespread participation and training, more than did most of his contemporaries. He constantly looked for new and better showmanship. In addition, he was personally a dynamic, persuasive salesman. A hundred other individuals had comparable technical competence, but none was so thoroughly sold on his own product, so eager to talk about it, and so able to infect others with his enthusiasm.

The true professions (medicine, law, engineering, etc.) enforce a fairly strict code which prohibits colorful merchandising. The diagnostic "professions" have not yet reached this state of being subject to real sanctions if they violate such a code. Hence there are no restraints on the enthusiastic or the greedy. Neither are there any restraints on charlatans who have the greed without the professional skills.

Some sorry spectacles have resulted. In the heyday of piece-rate systems for factory employees, literally dozens of payment formulas emerged, each the patent of some would-be-successful consultant. The idea of the brand name has taken firm root and is going strong. The separation of planning from execution masquerades under a dozen names (Operations Research, Industrial Engineering, Sales Planning, Profit Planning, Operations Analysis, etc.).

All this makes it difficult for the manager to distinguish the genuine from the imitation. No less difficult is the problem of the devoted professionals when they are charged with "guilt by association."

The Care and Feeding of Diagnosticians

Who is this diagnostician, who plays such a useful role provided he or she does not write the script?

Generally, he or she is a young, ambitious, career-minded individual, long on technical training, short on practical experience, positively green as to human relations problems. Often, he or she thinks of his or her career as bifurcated, consisting first of his technical specialty and later of management. His or her company generally encourages this thinking—the diagnosticians are one of the important sources of supply for developing the managers of tomorrow.

In the scale of human needs,[4] his or her emphasis is on social needs, ego needs, needs for self-fulfillment. He or she does have some problems as to physiological and safety needs, but hardly to the extent exhibited by the nontechnical people in the company. In consequence, the schemes of incentives developed in the nineteenth century for factory laborers are not particularly applicable to him or her. (There is even a serious question whether these schemes are applicable to today's factory employees.)

If the conventional carrot and stick do not apply to these diagnosticians, what does apply? There seems to be general agreement that the company should provide the professional with:

a competitive salary and fringe benefits

a comfortable, well-equipped workplace—attractive quarters, adequate equipment, a well-stocked library, a flow of technical literature

a degree of stability, so that the company's diagnostic forces are not built up and reduced like so much product inventory

opportunity to progress in the profession—to maintain membership in professional societies; to publish papers; to attend exhibitions, conventions; to sit on committees

an atmosphere of support for professional work—company technical publications; awards for technical achievements; competent, inspiring technical leadership; personal interest of top management

opportunity for progress in the company, assignment to a variety of challenging problems; participation in committee work; association with upper-level colleagues and with managers; an atmosphere of mobility in job rotation and promotion

opportunity for self-development; in-house programs of technical and managerial training; access to local universities, libraries; periodic attendance at distant courses, seminars

treatment as an individual—opportunity to inquire, to discuss, to complain; to be appraised as an individual; to communicate with others

"freedom" in his or her work. On examination, this freedom is seen to be composed of several freedoms, some obvious, some controversial:

(a) Freedom from routine chores. There should be adequate support by technicians, clerical people, etc.

[4]See p. 79.

(*b*) Freedom from detailed supervision. It is irritating if not insulting for the professional to be watched at every step of a process in which he or she is presumably the expert.

(*c*) Freedom to plan his or her work, to choose the method. Now it begins to be controversial. The author would prefer to see this as freedom to nominate the method, with doubts being resolved in favor of the professional.

(*d*) Freedom to choose the project. This is the real controversy. The advocates put this freedom on the ground of the need for creativity. "Only the free mind can be creative." Much of this is nonsense. Unlimited freedom is synonymous with lack of purpose. Only as freedom is limited (whether by others or by oneself) can energies be directed at specifics. So there must be a choice of project. If the professional chooses it, he or she may go down a road attractive to him or her, but at the end of it he usually finds he or she has lost something he or she needs badly—the feeling of making a contribution to the team.

Some companies have taken this (freedom to choose the project) seriously. They are willing to set aside a percentage of the professional's time to let him pursue projects of his own choosing, using company facilities. The record on this is not yet conclusive.

But there is no lack of opportunity for creativity on projects chosen by a Steering Arm. From extensive experience in many company situations, the author can say flatly that the diagnosticians associated with such projects were stimulated to creativity far more than when they were on their own.

What Diagnostic Arm for Top Management?

This is a special case, in several respects:

there is no widely recognized, accepted category of specialists in top management problems such as we find in market research, production control, etc.

the problems are so broad and intricate that any diagnosis in depth seems forbiddingly long and costly.

any determined opposition to use of diagnosticians now comes from Very Important People—people who are general managers, officers, and even directors of the company.

The result has been a very limited use of a true Diagnostic Arm at these levels. The Organization Department of the Standard Oil Company of California included a charter for such diagnosis.[5] So did the widely publicized Control Section of Koppers Company.[6]

Other companies have used staff groups for such diagnosis under the name of Business Research[7] or Operations Research.[8] Actually, a goodly number of companies created departments of Operations Research when that term was enjoying a good press. However, the work of most of these departments soon settled down into specialties such as the inventory control–production control complex.

Some top managements solve the problem by the use of outside consultants. Sonnabend reports use of this method in trying to raise the level of performance in his company. The consultants interviewed various managers, analyzed the information, and fed the results back to the managers when the latter met as a Steering Arm.[9]

Use of outside consultants solves some problems. They certainly have the time, and often the skills and objectivity, to contribute importantly to useful diagnosis. But these outsiders bring in a bias of their own. This bias is inherent in the outside consulting company's formula of selling manpower at a price of about three times their labor costs. The income of the partners (who own the management consulting companies) comes mainly from the profit made by selling this manpower, and only incidentally from the fees earned by the partners in their personal capacity as consultants. The urge to sell this manpower, and to keep it sold, is so strong that it can bring out the worst in people who would otherwise prefer to live by high professional standards.

If There Is No Diagnostic Arm

Lacking a Diagnostic Arm, there will be no diagnosis unless other means can take over. These other means are often deceptively ineffective.

[5]Hall, George Lawrence, "The Management Guide," Standard Oil Company of California, 1948.

[6]Walker, George M., "The Control Section: A New Aid to Management," *Modern Management*, October, 1949.

[7]Dockson, Robert R., "Business Research as a Tool of Management," American Management Association, General Management Series, No. 156, pp. 27–34.

[8]Swan, A. W., "Running an Operations Research Department in an Industrial Organization," *The Journal of Industrial Engineering*, September–October, 1957, pp. 269–274.

[9]Sonnabend, Roger P., "An Experiment in Motivation," *Management Record*, July–August, 1962, pp. 19–22.

A problem in customer service is the subject of earnest discussion by the managers of the X company. The main points have been made as follows:

> MANUFACTURING MANAGER: About half the orders in the house are classified as "Rush." There's no such thing as "Rush" when Sales puts that many in the "Rush" category.
>
> SALES MANAGER: Our people have been so disappointed by the regular delivery service that they have to use "Rush" to get the customers taken care of.
>
> GENERAL MANAGER: Well, what can we do about it?

The stage is now set for sweeping the whole thing under the rug. Each manager may agree to "bring this up with my fellows at our next staff meeting," and makes a note to that effect. They may designate a subcommittee to look into it and see what can be done. But all this may miss the realities.

The realities are that two of the nine sales districts account for three-quarters of the "Rush" orders; that of the average 7 weeks to fill an order, over half is due to a bottleneck in one shop process, a bottleneck to which the general manager had unwittingly contributed when he vetoed that appropriation; that it is feasible, by design standardization, to reduce the "tailor-made" part of the time interval by two-thirds, etc.

The makeshift efforts at diagnosis may still turn up these vital facts, but the odds are against it.

And On to Diagnosis

With the availability of the Steering Arm and the Diagnostic Arm we have mobilized for new knowledge. The process of using these two Arms for securing the new Knowledge we will call Diagnosis, which is the subject of the next chapter.

8 BREAKTHROUGH IN KNOWLEDGE—DIAGNOSIS

The Purpose of Diagnosis

So far we have taken three positive steps in the Breakthrough process:

1. Change in attitude, from why do anything at all about this, to let's do something about it.
2. Economic analysis to identify the few projects which need study in depth.
3. Organization for diagnosis.

In this chapter we will discuss diagnosis itself, its purpose, its methodology, its limitations.

Historians have documented the remedies tried on King Charles II by his physicians:

> ...a pint of blood was extracted from his right arm, and a half-pint from his left shoulder, followed by an emetic, two physics, and an enema comprising fifteen substances; the royal head was then shaved and a blister raised; then a sneezing powder, more emetics and bleeding, soothing potions, a plaster of pitch and pigeon dung on his feet, potions containing ten different substances, chiefly herbs, finally forty drops of extract of human skull, and the application of bezoar stone; after which His Majesty died.

Medicine has come a long way since 1685—in many countries. In contrast, there are still large parts of the earth in which primitive "remedies" are still the rule.

The contrasts in management medicine are no less remarkable. The stage is set when it becomes evident that a serious ailment will not remedy itself. Now the urge is to do "something"—anything plausible. Product line A hasn't been selling very well. Someone in authority decides that a new salesperson bonus plan is needed. If he but knew it, the real need is modernizing of the product line. But he doesn't know it. The new incentive plan is as useful as Charles II's bezoar stone. So is the adoption of a foreman training program to remedy poor labor relations, when the real problem is a slippery plant manager.

The end purpose of diagnosis is to create *a mosaic of knowledge* sufficiently complete to serve as a guide to management decision and action.[1] The mosaic is made up of bits of data, fact, proof. It need not be complete; when most of the pieces are in place, the picture can be recognized. The mosaic may even include some wrong pieces or pieces out of place, but there is a limit to this. The greater the extent of pieces out of place, the greater the risk of a wrong decision or action.

Specifically, the Steering Arm is trying to answer the question "What stands between us and attainment of X?" (X may be more sales, higher morale, less waste, product leadership, etc.)

The Steering Arm undertakes to achieve the purposes of diagnosis by:

1. Creating an atmosphere of academic freedom—the steering group must regard itself as a forum for search of truth.
2. Securing a supply of facts, beliefs, theories, etc., as a kind of raw material to work on.
3. Extracting available knowledge from this supply.
4. Identifying the need for further knowledge.
5. Creating new knowledge to meet this further need.
6. Arriving at a course of action.

Academic Freedom

This term, so well understood in the university, has no exact parallel in the company. It is the freedom to think as one wishes, and to express those thoughts freely, even if it is known that these thoughts will be unpopular.

---

[1]This excludes "basic research" in which the purpose is to push back the frontiers of human knowledge, not to solve a specific problem. In Diagnosis for Breakthrough, the purpose is to help solve a problem. Any advancement of human knowledge is incidental.

In feudal England, so the story goes, there were seated around the fire at the inn an assortment of travelers: pilgrims, merchants, a couple of knights, and an Earl. The discussion turned to horses, and the question arose—How many teeth does a horse have? There were several views—26, 28, 32, 36. Then the Earl spoke. "My belief is that the horse has 28 teeth." Whereupon one of the knights said, "My lord, since you are the highest ranking person here, that concludes the matter."

At this point one of the merchants meekly made a suggestion. "Since we have some horses hard by, would it not be prudent to open the mouth of one, and count his teeth?"

The merchant was promptly squelched. How did he dare to question the words of an Earl?

Publicly challenging the views of a senior in rank is only one form of living dangerously in the company. Another section of the code of conduct requires that we recognize the special rights and status of the other person on matters involving "his" or "her" job—we will respect his or her property and he will respect ours. When the manager of the western zone makes a dubious assertion about "his" zone, the code requires that we do not challenge him. In turn, he will not challenge our assertions about "our" job.

This "treading with care" is proper as to orders or commands. We should not tell the other person how to run "his" or "her" job, nor should he or she tell us how to run "ours," if we are to avoid chaos. But in the Steering Arm we are concerned about the flow of ideas, not orders. Orders should be channeled strictly; ideas should flow freely, without boundaries.

Finally, there is the matter of nonconformity. It takes courage to advance unpopular beliefs. Yet the successful theory is usually a minority view—it must be, because of many theories advanced, only a few can be valid.

Academic freedom makes its contribution by requiring that the pursuit of truth take precedence over all other considerations. It provides freedom from the reprisals which an institution so commonly imposes on its members—reprisals for challenging the views of others, whether the boss, or the vested interests, or the majority. It makes nonconformity tolerable if not respectable. It encourages challenges, not only to logic and facts, but to long-standing premises as well. As a final, exhilarating by-product, academic freedom provides the Steering Arm members with a welcome bit of participation in man's timeless quest for truth.

Securing a Supply of Theories

A Steering Arm is in session. The chairman puts the question "What stands between us and attainment of X?" Each member's assertions are listed on a blackboard, *without challenge*. After every member has had a turn, there is a call for seconds. Finally, the ideas are all on the board, and discussion can proceed. At this point let us have what the motion-picture people call a flashback. Where did all these assertions come from?

Some are directly the result of the experience, observation, and experimentation (deliberate and accidental) of the members of the Steering Arm. Other assertions have come up through the suggestion system, down from bosses, and in all directions from associates.

A further source of theories is the "check list." Someone—a journalist, consultant, staff specialist—has compiled a list "38 ways to cut material-handling costs," "How 12 companies increased their share of market." Such lists are of special value in reawakening interest in ideas to which Steering Arm members may have become shockproof over the years.

The members also derived some theories from the experience of other companies which have been faced with the attainment of X. These other companies may be competitors or not.

> The manager of a furniture company conducted his production operations in a five-story factory in Jamestown, N.Y. He had a problem of how to progress the product from one operation to the next. On completion of an operation (say, rough-cut 600 legs for dressers), how could the fact of this completion be communicated to the proper people so that the cut legs could be moved to the next station (perhaps on another floor) for further processing?
>
> The manager found his answer on his vacation. He was at a large airport and visited the control tower. Here he observed the tower directing a wide assortment of activity, in the air, on the ground, in the offices. Suddenly it flashed on him that the air-traffic problem was like his own traffic problem, and that the control-tower idea could be fundamental to both. The ability of the control tower to regulate traffic was based on several principles:
>
> 1. The control tower had possession of all schedules, regulations, priorities, etc.
> 2. Two-way communication existed between the control tower and all else.
> 3. All hands were required to report their actions to the control tower.
> 4. The control tower had a monopoly on orders regulating movement.
>
> On his return from vacation, the manager set up a "control tower" in his factory—a little office on the mezzanine. The control tower received the master schedules and had copies of all sequences of operations. A couple of dozen telephones were strewn around the factory to make it convenient for operators to call the

control tower to advise that they had finished this or that operation. The control tower noted this on a progress sheet, and issued a new assignment to the operator, subsequently using the "bull horn" to notify the operator to move the product to the next station.

The manager of the furniture company achieved an intellectual triumph in finding a set of traffic-control principles common to an airport and a furniture factory. It is this presence of common principles which makes it possible for managers to attend seminars, conferences, and courses and to learn from each other despite wide diversity in their company products, processes, and operations.

One of the most fruitful sources of theories is the competitor's method of operation.

A widely prevalent problem in multiproduct-line companies is what to do about a product line which is losing money and would require much investment to do otherwise. In such cases it is of the utmost importance to discover how much profit competitors make on this product line, since the road forks sharply:

(*a*) If the industry generally has become unprofitable, the result will be spin-offs and acquisitions to cut the number of companies in the business.

(*b*) If the industry generally is profitable, then some competitors are doing quite well, and it becomes useful to find out how they do it.

Learning something about competitors brings up the ugly word "espionage." Journalists and editors are so intrigued with the cloak-and-dagger potentialities of this word that much nonsense has been written about gathering industrial intelligence. Actually, over 80 per cent of the potentially useful information about competitors can be secured from published information (the published annual reports of the company, the published house organ, published promotion material of the company, published reports and stories from financial and business journals) plus interviews with ex-employees, vendors to the industry, common customers, trade-association officials, trade-publication editors, consultants, etc. (These interviews are properly limited to discussion of business practices.) The failures to learn how successful competitors succeed are the result of lack of organized effort to make use of legitimate information, rather than of lack of piracy of formulas and such.[2]

---

[2]On certain technical matters, it appears that more can be learned from studying how birds navigate, porpoises swim, and bats use radar than by studying human competitors.

For a general discussion of approaches, see Furash, Edward E., "Industrial Espionage," *Harvard Business Review*, November–December, 1959.

(At this point our flashback fades out.)

With a list of theories on the board, discussion can proceed. In due course the list will be shaken down. Also some new and revised theories will emerge. The Diagnostic Arm, especially, as it conducts the detailed studies and analyses, will come up with new theories.

In passing now to the various stages of discussion and analysis, let us note the special role played by that much-maligned person, the theorist. The company, no less than humanity, advances solidly to new levels of performance on the steppingstones of tested ideas. A supply of ideas or theories for test is vital for such advances. When we reach dead end as to ideas for Breakthrough, the theorist comes to our rescue. A willingness to get his or her neck out and a willingness to be wrong most of the time (the wrong theories greatly outnumbered the right theories) entitle the theorist to respect and sympathy along with the abuse normally inflicted.[3]

Extracting Available Knowledge

The list of assertions on the Steering Arm's blackboard can now be used to develop the mosaic of knowledge:

1. Within the assertions are contained a number of facts, proofs, truths, which can be extracted and made part of the mosaic,
2. The resulting incomplete mosaic can then be used as a basis for management decisions and actions, or
3. Steps can be taken to complete the mosaic through creation of added bits of knowledge.

Extracting knowledge from the list of assertions is not so simple. It turns out that some formidable obstacles stand between the Steering Arm and the mosaic:

The semantic jungle.   The very words used in making assertions do not convey a common meaning.

The protective plumage.   Some assertions are just beliefs, opinions, or theories. But they are so cunningly disguised to look like facts, truths, and proofs that it is very difficult to distinguish one group from the other.

Conditioned reflexes.   A situation in which certain words have become fighting words, so that rational discussion is not possible.

---

[3] For an example of theorizing by playing the role of the customer, see Busch, Gerald A., "Prudent-manager Forecasting," *Harvard Business Review*, May–June, 1961, pp. 57–64.

The desire for peace. Some problems are so annoying that we would like to hide them. Perhaps they would go away.

Axiomatic beliefs. We have come to accept some beliefs as beyond challenge. Yet they are the basic cause of our problem.

Let us first look at a few of these obstacles in more detail. Then we will consider how the Steering Arm deals with conflicting views among its own members.

The Semantic Jungle

In discussing the merits of an assertion, the first question is "What do you mean?"

It is well known that communications, the unspoken as well as the words and phrases, have different meanings in different localities. This applies to industrial localities as well—not only different companies, but also different plants, zones, and districts in the same company. It applies even as to different departments in one company location.

> A steering team met to set standards for blemishes on lenses, prisms, and other components of optical apparatus. The term "beauty defects" had for years been used in the company as a short-hand name for scratches, pits, bubbles, and other such visible flaws. As the team talked, it turned out that beauty defects, like blood, were of several types:
>
> Type A: interferes with customer usage, i.e., scratch in the focal plane of a microscope
>
> Type B: no real interference with usage but naturally visible to the customers, i.e., scratch on the big end of binoculars
>
> Type C: no interference with usage and visible to the customer only unnaturally, i.e., looking through a rifle sight from the back end
>
> Type D: no interference with usage and not visible to the customer unless he introduces added optical elements to aid the naked eye.
>
> Until these types are defined, any one man literally did not know what the other fellow was talking about.

The company's semantic troubles are more widespread than is generally realized. Three executives are talking about "decentralization." One has in mind a geographical dispersion of operations. Another is thinking of delegation of authority from the president to the vice-presidents. A third is thinking about reorganizing the company from a functional to a profit-center form.

Even when we are dealing with things which can be counted, we can run into semantic troubles.

> At a general manager's staff meeting, there were four answers to the question "How many motors did we get out yesterday?"
>
> The production manager had a count of the number assembled; the quality manager, of the number tested; the sales manager, of the number packed; the controller, of the number invoiced.

The key to a semantic riddle is the question "What do you mean by beauty defects?" Or "decentralization?" Usually a meeting of the minds can be reached, whereupon constructive discussion can proceed. However, there are also cases in which there can be no meeting of the minds, because the words have become the masters instead of the servants.

Protective Plumage

The words used by a person have both a dictionary meaning and an intended meaning. Sometimes these coincide; often they do not. Behind the protective plumage of the spoken words are some realities which face the speaker. The Steering Arm members have the job of discovering these realities. Only in this way can there be progress in Breakthrough.

Behind the protective plumage are a wide variety of realities. We will consider only a few usual examples—reflexes, axioms, confused logic.

Whatever the realities, the removal of the protective plumage exposes someone to a sort of shameful nakedness. It may long have been the practice to put matters to rest by such statements as:

The customer would never agree to anything like that.
That would never work—plastics are brittle.
That shouldn't make any difference.
My people would never do a thing like that.
That's what sells the product.

Those who have long done business based on such assertions are upset when they are subjected to questions such as:

How do you know that?
Isn't that just untested long-standing belief?
Could we see the facts on which you base that?

There is no escape from such challenges. Tact is essential, so that there will be no drying up of the flow of assertions. The unavoidable irritation can be minimized by constant strengthening of the concept of academic freedom.

Reflexes

When a word becomes so firmly attached to a deep-seated belief that no separation is possible, we can no longer get a meeting of the minds by definition alone. So long as the "trigger" word or phrase continues to be used, the deep-seated reflexes preclude rational discussion. Such words are easy to recognize when they involve other people:

Algérie Française, Solidarity Forever, Apartheid. These are labels for a hardened pattern of beliefs.

> The word "nonproductive" is used in a variety of meanings. Under one of these meanings, "nonproductive" is a synonym for evil.
>
> To some managers it is the outward appearances that are decisive. The operator at the machine is "producing." But all those other guys—they just batten on what the "real producers" put out. There have been enough such managers, and enough accountants as accessories, to twist the meaning of the words into unrecognizable shapes. The differences in historical origin[4] once made it necessary to distinguish "production" workers from others. These others were called "nonproduction" workers, and hence "nonproductive" in a special meaning of that term. But this special meaning came to be ignored in myriads of cases. The word "nonproductive" came to be used in its dictionary meaning, which equates a "nonproductive" worker with a parasite, an idler, a no-good bum. All this persists in the face of overwhelming evidence that many companies with high overheads have flourished mightily.[5]

The Steering Arm may find it necessary to coin new words to bypass the reflexes.

---

[4] The modern manufacturing company has its roots in two older species, the merchant and the craftsman. The successors of the craftsman, performing fabricating operations on the product, are the "productive" people, paid by the hour or the piece, wearing blue collars. The successors of the merchant, conducting the activities of buying, bookkeeping, selling, and warehousing, are the overhead people, paid by salary, and wearing white collars.

[5] Derived from Juran, J. M., "Overhead Control: Sharp Tools for Managing a Dull Concept," American Management Association Special Conference on Managing Corporate Overhead, 1962.

The early industrial engineers adopted the term "efficiency" to describe their sphere of interest. They held themselves out as "efficiency experts." When unqualified people rushed in to take advantage of the esteem in which efficiency experts were held, the term became a target for ridicule. The industrial engineers had to abandon the term as a "kiss of death."

Other words have met similar fates: usurer, tyrant, commissar.[6]

Words become obsolete, just as do other human institutions. (Try reading Chaucer in the original Old English text.) Once a word gets a bad reputation, it is hard to hit the comeback trail.[7] The usurers, tyrants, and commissars gave up trying to convince the public that the good members of their species outnumbered the bad.[8] It was easier to change the name of the species.

There is also great risk in using an unchanging word to describe a changing pattern of human activity. The word "weapons" or "ordnance" has been an unchanging generic term for describing military hardware. Yet the hardware described by this unchanging term has undergone unbelievable changes. Wars have been lost because defense ministers clung to outdated weapons. They had "weapons" or "ordnance," but for the wrong war.

The Steering Arm faced with an insoluble problem in attitude should step back from the scene and draw a deep breath. They should look for critical words which have changed their meaning, have developed multiple meanings, have become worn out, or have become so charged with emotion that they preclude rational discussion. When the attitude problem is centered on such a key word, it may be necessary to bypass the word altogether.

Tabling the Trouble

Cartoonists have had a field day with the committee which "tables the matter." Industrial man does a lot of this. Sometimes it works. Someone is transferred; so someone else inherits the problem. We go out of that

---

[6]*The New York Times* reported on July 29, 1963 (p. 22), that the South African government has dropped the word "apartheid" and now prefers the term "separate development."

[7]Today's young man calls his girl "sweetie pie" or some other species of pastry. Centuries ago he called her his "tart."

[8]When a few neighborhood dogs take to biting children, the community rises up and muzzles or exterminates the lot, the many nonbiters as well as the few biters.

line of business; so we no longer have that problem. Some restless person doesn't know it can't be solved; so he or she solves it.

The Steering Arm must be alert to identify the subtle forms of tabling a trouble. For example:

> A Steering Arm was studying why the company's new products so often got into serious trouble in manufacture and marketing. It became evident that the planners for manufacture and for marketing had not had enough time, enough information, enough testing. Now one of the members spoke up—"Communications, again." Everyone nodded. The problem was "diagnosed" by finding a one-word label to describe the mess.

This type of diagnosis is widespread. One situation is labeled "politics," another is labeled "people," others are labeled "planning," "organization," etc. A complicated situation is covered over by a simple-sounding label. Everyone seems relieved, as though the problem is solved when it is covered up or labeled. But what has really been accomplished?

Not much, really. There may be a form of relief in giving something a name, "butter fingers" for the fumbling shortstop, or "bonehead" for his confused teammate. These labels may be descriptive, even colorful or amusing. But as far as diagnosis is concerned, we have made hardly any headway. If the result is only that all agree this is a fine label, then we have simply evaded diagnosis. We have swept the mess under the rug, put an approved label on it, and gone on to other things. But the mess is still there.

Tabling the trouble may be the right thing to do. But it should be done deliberately, not unconsciously.

Axiomatic Beliefs

A most difficult hurdle for a Steering Arm is beliefs which have come to be accepted as axiomatic.[9]

> A Steering Arm was considering a pricing problem faced by the Pelletier company. Pelletier had long sold its products to independent wholesalers at price A. The wholesalers, in turn, had resold to retailers at a higher price B. In earning the price differential (B mi-

---

[9] An axiom is a self-evident truth, so obvious that no proof is required.

nus A), the wholesalers had performed various services of selling, warehousing, breaking bulk, billing, etc.

Then a great change gradually overtook the industry. Some retailers grew very large, through development of superstores or chains of stores. Their purchases of the products became so considerable that they saw no point in paying the higher price B, since they had little need for the wholesalers' services. Accordingly, these retailers had come to Pelletier offering to buy directly from the manufacturer at the lower price A, and pointing out that their purchases exceeded those of many wholesalers.

Some Steering Arm members opposed making such an arrangement with the retailers. In part their opposition was due to fear of alienating the wholesalers. But most of the opposition came from the axiomatic belief that "retailers must pay the retail price." It was as though the occupation printed on the customer's business letterhead was decisive as to pricing.

Unfortunately, the retailers were declining to cooperate. They were creating new sources of manufacture, with the result that the entire social structure of the industry was crumbling away.

In a well-seasoned article, Levitt[10] has pointed out that many industries are in trouble because managers mistook the business they were in. Railroad executives considered that they were in the "railroad business," not the transportation business. Because this belief bordered on the axiomatic, they lost their business to other forms of transportation. In like manner, the "movie industry" clung to a declining form of entertainment while other forms flourished. And so for other examples.

The axiomatic belief is the embodiment of that waggish statement: The trouble isn't in what we don't know; the trouble is that *some of the things we know aren't so.*

Resolving Conflicts in Diagnosis

An admirable formula for getting a Steering Arm off dead center appears in the following case, taken from a classic paper:[11]

---

[10]Levitt, Theodore, "Marketing Myopia," *Harvard Business Review*, July–August, 1960, pp. 45–56.

[11]Coonley, Howard, and P. G. Agnew, "The Role of Standards in the System of Free Enterprise," American Standards Association.

Years ago the gas industry proposed to the American Standards Association that there should be national specifications for cast-iron pipe. When the manufacturers were approached they said that it would be useless to talk with the engineers of consumer companies who were impracticable theorists. The engineers in turn said that it was hopeless to try to cooperate with the manufacturers who had been working off inferior pipe on them for a dozen years and whose willingness to live up to specifications they doubted. It was a year before it seemed safe to invite them to sit down in the same room to talk things over. After much talk they agreed to develop new specifications cooperatively. A wise and experienced engineer agreed to take the chairmanship of the technical committee, but only upon three conditions:

1. They must agree to agree upon what they did agree upon and what they did not agree upon. That is, they must first agree upon the exact point at which the road began to fork. This was done, and agreement was reached upon what the moot questions were, one of which was the accuracy of a certain formula.
2. They must agree upon why they disagreed upon these moot questions. After long discussion they decided that there were insufficient known facts to give the answer, and hence one person's opinion was as good as another's.
3. They must decide upon what they were going to do about it. The final result was that the manufacturers raised some $70,000, which was expended in large part under the general direction of the engineers, and the necessary facts were obtained. With the facts at hand, the controversies disappeared.

Awareness of the variety of obstacles discussed earlier in this chapter can be helpful in guiding the Steering Arm to find what are the areas of agreement, what are the areas of disagreement, and where is the exact fork in the road. All this is in the nature of fitting genuine pieces into the mosaic of knowledge, and discarding the false pieces. What is still missing must then be supplied by experiment.

The foregoing sequence is not usually followed in settling differences. The usual human tendency is to get into a discussion of "who is right." But this should be the very last consideration. Prior to this should be the consideration of what is right, and even preceding this is the first question of all, namely, what is important.[12]

---

[12] For a more scholarly analysis, see Schmidt, Warren H., and Robert Tannenbaum, "Management of Differences," *Harvard Business Review*, November–December, 1960. They point out that differences may arise over facts, methods, goals, or values, and that reasons for these differences may be due to information, perception, or role of the conflicting parties.

An office manager was under attack for using too cumbersome a procedure for processing customers' orders. But he knew every detail of the procedure and defended it all as "necessary." All this was on the basis of "who is right."

Then someone worked up information to show that, of the total time elapsed between receipt of a customer's order and shipping the goods, only 8 per cent was consumed in physical handling of the goods. The remaining 92 per cent was in the order-processing procedure. This fact pierced the shockproof armor. Now the office manager turned his attention to the really important problem.

The Trail of Experimentation

It is difficult to write about experimentation without waxing eloquent. Some historic feats of experimentation arouse admiration akin to that stirred by a great work of art.

Observation of the honeybee has disclosed an amazing system of communication. A bee discovers food. It returns to the hive and "tells" the other bees, in various ways, all about the discovery. More specifically,[13]

The bee signals	By
The distance of the food from the hive	A choice of several dances (coarse measure) plus the speed of the dance (fine measure).
The direction of the food from the hive	The center line of the dance movement. The bee has a built-in compass (the eye) and a chronometer for navigation with respect to the sun. In communicating to the hive, the bee translates direction relative to the sun into direction relative to gravity.
The quality of the food	The vigor and length of the dance.

Since bees don't talk to humans, von Frisch had to design experiments to learn all this. And he did, elegantly.

The trail of experimentation starts with the Steering Arm's list of assertions. But let no one be deluded. Some of these assertions are based on prior experimentation, either deliberate or involuntary (substitution of materials, forgotten operations).

---

[13]See, for example, Frisch, Karl von, "The Language of the Bees," *Scientific American,* August, 1948.

This prior experimentation is a decided help in formulating theories but is a decided nuisance in other ways. To the amateur experimenter, a half-baked experiment still yields a superb product. In consequence, it is common for members of the Steering Arm to regard this or that theory as "proved" by past experiment. In such instances, the job of *disproving* invalid theories may be as time-consuming and as essential as the job of proving the valid theories.

If there were full objectivity on the part of the Steering Arm members, the disproving of invalid theories would be no problem. But the biases are there. These people have acted on their half-baked experiments, or have prevented others from acting to the contrary, or have made strong statements based on these invalid theories. All this has gone on for years. A proved new theory sweeps all these past actions and statements into the dustbin and with it part of the reputation of the individual who was wrong for years. Human beings do not stand idly by while this goes on; they resist damage to their reputation, and in any event, they need time to adapt. To require that time be taken to test and specifically disprove the invalid theories is one form of resistance, which takes the trail of experimentation down dead ends just to prove they are dead ends. In the words of Thomas Henry Huxley, "The great tragedy of Science—the slaying of a beautiful hypothesis by an ugly fact."

Attainment of X may require that we first attain A, B, and C, none of which would have seemed to have much to do with X. Edison's invention of the electric lamp is a case in point.

Edison was a one-man Steering Arm, as well as being, simultaneously, head of a Diagnostic Arm—one of the first industrial product development laboratories.

In his capacity as a one-man Steering Arm, Edison recognized a social need for electric lighting. The electric-arc lamp was already in use. However, the arc light was so brilliant that its use was confined to large areas, i.e., street lighting. Small areas—homes, stores, offices—were still lighted by gas or by oil lamps.

Other investigators also were aware of this social need. But they soon dismissed the problem as economically impracticable. Their reasoning stemmed from what appeared to be the inevitability of Ohm's law. Arc lighting was low-voltage high-current lighting. High currents required heavy copper wires to avoid overheating and risk of fires. When these investigators calculated, by Ohm's law, the amount of copper needed to feed such currents to the homes and businesses of large cities, the answer was startling— *there wasn't that much copper on earth*. The second level of the problem, economic feasibility, looked like the end of the trail.

Edison found a way out, in theory, turning Ohm's law in his favor to do it. Instead of using 10 volts, why not use a higher voltage, say 100 volts? By Ohm's law, ten times the voltage would mean only 1 per cent of the current, hence 1 per cent of the copper, and presto, the world's copper supply was easily adequate and economic.

With this Breakthrough at the economic level, the problem became one of technology. The road soon branched into technical needs:

1. Design of a high-voltage generator
2. Design of a lamp which could work at high voltages and low current

One of the lamp designs made use of the principle of incandescence in a vacuum. Edison's laboratory[14] found that there was added need to:

(*a*) Develop a degree of vacuum never before attained. No vacuum pump then in existence would do; so a new pump would have to be invented.

(*b*) Find a material which would become incandescent yet not burn up. This search led Edison to the carbon filament.

It is seen that the trail of meeting a social need—lighting by electricity—led, finally, to the solution of three technical problems:

Design of a high-voltage generator

Design of a high-vacuum pump

Design of a lamp filament

Optimizing Company Economics

Examples of pursuit of personal or departmental goals to the detriment of the company are legion. The Steering Arm, through its broad base of thought and its access to the tools of diagnosis, is in a good position to optimize the company's performance. The Steering Arm then finds itself heavily involved in:

(*a*) The formulas, "models," or other diagnostic tools for computing the optimum

---

[14]In the minds of some historians, Edison's major contribution to industrial civilization was *not* his personal inventions, but his *creation of a laboratory,* manned with a team of scientists and engineers, who could, collectively, solve complex problems in technology.

(*b*) The costs, quantities, and other numbers which must be worked up to get useful answers from the formulas.

For example, the size of the finished-goods inventory influences many departments and three sets of company costs:

the cost of "carrying" the inventory (interest, taxes, insurance, storage, obsolescence, etc.)

the cost of selling the product (it rises sharply when there are shortages)

the cost of making the product (more or fewer machine setups, changing the production rate, controlling, expediting, etc.)

The company's interests are best served when the sum of these three sets of costs is a minimum.

If the Steering Arm can identify the proper ingredients in this formula or "model," and set up the means for using it, an interdepartmental solution has been reached which is optimum for the company. Failing this, the various departments continue their individual pulling and hauling.

There are already available some general use "models" for optimizing company economics—the Return on Investment formulas, the Break-even Chart, Economic Lot formulas, etc. The Steering Arm should become informed as to those tools which are appropriate for its problems. This it can do by drawing on its diagnosticians and on the various staff specialists in the company.

Formula or not, there are still pitfalls. No Steering Arm should be deluded into believing that because something is reduced to numbers, it has become precise.

Consider a problem in Return on Investment. The diagnostician proposes use of some formula, and this is accepted. But the matter does not end there. Lurking behind the neat figures are some very cloudy assumptions. Two of the more usual traps are:

1. *The traffic-estimating trap.* Many projects are in a form such that the expenditure is relatively constant (a new machine, process, computer, etc.). However, the return depends on the amount of "traffic"; i.e., there is a saving per unit sold, made, processed, bought, etc. Hence the return depends absolutely on the estimate of future traffic. Because we are dealing with the future, this estimate is some person's judgment. If the advocate of the project is the sole estimator, look out!

2. *The efficiency trap.* It is usual for the proponent of a project to assume that it will attain its optimum efficiency (which it will not). Moreover, he or she compares the costs (under this optimum efficiency) with

costs of the present method under its actual level of efficiency (which could be improved). His or her figures, therefore, include a saving which could be made solely by bringing the present process up to its optimum level of efficiency. To cite an earlier example:[15]

It is 1948; method A is in use; the annual cost is $100,000. An engineer proposes a change to method B to reduce the annual cost to $75,000. (The charges for making the change are only $6,000; so it looks like a good return on the investment.) The executive approves the change.

It is 1951. Method B has been in effect for more than 2 years. The annual cost is now $88,000 (not as low as the $75,000 anticipated, but a good reduction from $100,000 just the same). Now comes a second engineer. He proposes a change to method C, to reduce the annual cost from $88,000 to $74,000. (The cost of making the change will be only $5,000.)

The executive studies the proposition, and suddenly starts. The proposed method C is nothing more than the original method A!

The moral, and another universal:

"One of the choices for action is better use of the existing setup."

Frequently, a Steering Arm discovers that there is need to expand greatly the amount of diagnostic effort; i.e., an investment in diagnosticians will yield a big return.

In a metal-products company, losses due to defectives ran to about 20 per cent of the cost of production. A Steering Arm found, in year 2, that the original Diagnostic Arm would have to be enlarged considerably in order to conduct the numerous experiments needed. How the added costs subsequently looked is shown in Table 8-1.

Clearly, the company had, over a 3-year period, invested $150,000 in diagnosis costs over and above the level prevailing in year 2. What did they get for this investment? The answer is to be found in the scrap bill, which appears in Table 8-2.

It is seen that, over the same 3-year period, the cumulative reduction in the scrap bill was about $1.5 million, in this case a fantastic return on the investment.

---

[15]From Juran, J. M., "Universals in Management Planning and Controlling", *The Management Review*, November, 1954.

Table 8-1. Cost of Diagnosis

Year	Costs of diagnosis ($000)		Increase of total costs over year 2 ($000)	
	Salaries	Total	Annual	Cumulative
2	14.7	14.9	—	—
3	55.6	55.6	40.7	40.7
4	59.3	74.1	59.2	99.9
5	58.2	64.7	49.8	149.7

Table 8-2. Returns From Diagnosis

Year	Per cent scrap	Actual dollars scrap (000)	Scrap at year 1 levels ($000)	Decrease in scrap from year 1 levels ($000)	
				Annual	Cumulative
1	24.6	1,290	1,290	—	—
2	25.6	1,354	1,354	—	—
3	18.9	841	1,120	279	279
4	13.2	658	1,245	587	866
5	11.7	573	1,225	652	1,518

The Mighty Spectrum

Variety is everywhere. From the immense galaxies of space down to the minute atoms of the hundred-odd known elements, there are wide variations in size, length of life, activity, etc. The biological world exhibits exquisite variety in form, size, structure, function, etc. This universal urge for variety spills over into human affairs, and thereby into the affairs of the company, and of the manager.

Outside of the company, the spectrum of variety poses some perplexing problems:

the school children include the gifted, the ordinary, and the dull. Shall we give the same lessons to all, or shall we tailor-make the lessons?

the incomes of people range from very high to meager. Shall we impose uniform or graduated taxes?

Inside the company, variety is also everywhere. But while the manager may contemplate the wonders of the spectrum, he must also face the realities.

An actuary in the Fateful insurance company discovered that the automobile accident rate varied noticeably with the occupation of the driver. Some important occupations had an accident rate less than half that of the average of all occupations. The company management turned down his proposals to change its uniform premium system to one which charged different premiums based on occupation. The actuary resigned and set up his own company to sell insurance only to people in the low-accident occupations. His company is a resounding success.

The idea that the spectrum can be a hatching ground for new companies may seem farfetched. Actually, it has hatched out entire industries. Consider how misuse of the spectrum by the department store helped give birth to its mortal enemy, the discount house.

In department store cost accounting, it is fairly simple to departmentalize the cost of goods purchased, and the direct costs of selling (salesperson's salaries). Still other costs can be allocated with modest effort, i.e., rent chargeable due to floor space occupied. But there remain some important costs, i.e., the services of receiving, transport, shipping, credit, accounting, advertising, etc., which require real effort to allocate correctly to the various selling departments. The general practice had been not to make this real effort. Instead, these service costs were allocated to the selling departments in proportion to departmental sales.

The practice of spreading these service charges uniformly (per dollar of sales) across the entire spectrum of products was at its worst in the "big ticket" sales. The home appliance department was charged as much for selling one expensive refrigerator as was the haberdashery department for selling 100 neckties.

In addition, there was the spectrum of customer usage of services—availability of a showroom, demonstration of the product, buying on credit, etc. Customers who benefited little from these services were charged as much as those who benefited greatly.

The inventors of the discount house turned these misuses of the spectrum to good account. They adopted realistic pricing as well as reducing or eliminating services which many people could do without.

Other success stories have been written by discovering and filling a gap in the spectrum.

American Motors Corporation had noted that imported cars ranged in overall length from 136 to 177 inches, while domestic cars fell in the range from 202 to 229 inches. The gap in the spectrum was a major factor in American Motors' decision, in 1954, to concentrate on the "compact" car which it put out in overall length ranging from 149 to 200 inches.[16]

Many companies have suffered devastating losses because of incomplete planning of mass-produced products. (The planning error is multiplied by the large number of units inherent in mass production, hence the great size of the loss.)

To avoid recurrence of such losses, managers resort to a detailed planning routine. This routine takes each new product through a series of planning departments: Product Design, Manufacturing Planning, Production Control, Industrial Engineering, Purchasing, Quality Control, and still others. Generally, all this is justified because of the great amounts at stake and because the cost of planning is amortized over many units of product.

For small-quantity production, the economics of this routine are quite different. With so few units of product, the potential losses due to poor planning are not so serious, while the unit cost of complete planning rises sharply. Even worse may be the channeling of scarce specialist time away from the projects which really need it.

This contrast would seem to be obvious. Yet it is common enough to find companies with a spectrum of products, from mass-produced to jobbing, all of which are subjected to the same elaborate procedure. The "logical" reasons which bring this about are:

unawareness of the costs except in a vague way

the jurisdictional urge of the various planning departments to retain their hold of the entire spectrum

the very real difficulty of administering a "spectrum of procedures" short of creating separate all-purpose departments for the low-volume products

a willingness to use company funds to cut the risk of personal criticism[17]

The cardinal question to be answered on problems of the spectrum is "Tailor-make, or standard?"

The ability of the Steering Arm to deal with the spectrum is, in the first instance, dependent on separating the contents of the spectrum:

[16]Chapin, Roy D., Jr., "The American Motors Success Story," *The Management Review*, November, 1956, pp. 9–16.

[17]Government departments have been notoriously addicted to using the same elaborate procedures for trivial matters as for important matters. But the politicians and the public press have contributed to this attitude by making headlines out of any government error, however small. So it is "logical" for the government employee to spend $10 of public money to avoid $1 worth of personal criticism.

mass production and jobbing; high risk and low risk; vital few and trivial many; special and standard; etc.

Secondly, the need is to identify (*a*) the efforts being devoted to the
separate parts of the spectrum, and (*b*) the results achieved. This takes
some doing. Seldom are the costs and other measures readily available—they must be coaxed out, dug out, blasted out. See "Those Pesky
Costs," below.

Finally, the need is to come up with separate plans of action for the
various segments of the spectrum. We will look at this in some detail in
Chap. 10.

Pareto Again

The Pareto principle of "vital few and useful many," so helpful in the
economic analyses of Chap. 4, reappears in many problems in diagnosis.
The fact is that the roads to action for the "vital few" are different from
the roads followed for the "useful many." The vital few require highly
individualized, tailor-made action, and hence individualized diagnosis.
The useful many require mass action, and hence diagnosis as a class.

> In one company the timetable was congested because an over-
> worked manager required that all purchase requisitions come to
> him for signature. No amount of talk about "principles of delega-
> tion" could change this. Then someone analyzed the purchase req-
> uisitions. He found that the top 4 per cent of the requisitions repre-
> sented 90 per cent of the money. This information convinced the
> manager that he could shed 96 per cent of the paper and still keep
> a personal grip on 90 per cent of the money. He bought the pro-
> posal, not on any theoretical principle, but on just common sense.

The Pareto principle appears again during analysis of what goes on in
a complex process:

> When United Steel Companies in Sheffield, England, looked for
> the causes of defective steel rails, there were over 80 suspects. A
> complex statistical analysis showed that 3 of these suspects ac-
> counted for half the defects. This was proved out; i.e., "When they
> attended to these factors, the defectives were sure enough reduced
> by 50 per cent."[18]

---

[18]Private communication, A. W. Swan to the author.

We saw in Chap. 4 that every activity in the company exhibits the operation of the Pareto principle.[19] The usefulness of the principle is hard to overstate. It should be one of the main tools in the kit of the Steering Arm.

Those Pesky Costs

Knowledge of the costs is always helpful, and often decisive, in arriving at a course of action. However, the costs are frequently not readily available from the regular accounting summaries. It is tempting in such cases to drop the subject—the books aren't kept that way; it would require setting up new accounts; it would be too expensive to get the information, etc.

In debating whether to get the cost information, the steering team should keep in mind:

1. The need is not to get continuing information—a one-shot study will do.
2. The information can often be acquired by estimates without using the accounting system at all.
3. The precision of the estimates need be only that precision needed for decision making. Whether the estimate shows $100,000 or $80,000, or $120,000 (say for waste), the management decision (on doing something or nothing) is identical.
4. While digging into such detail may be distasteful to the managers, it is not distasteful to the diagnosticians.

In any situation where knowledge of costs is important, but the costs are not known, all concerned should brace themselves for some possible shocks. *Unknown costs are usually too high.*

A very common form of unknown costs is that of the "useful many." Here the cardinal need is to find the "cost of one cycle of activity." The need is readily seen in clerical work, though it extends to all forms of the useful many.

The bulk of the clerical work in most companies stems from two sources: (1) filling customers' orders and (2) making purchases. Each of these sources pours out a series of repetitive cycles of activity, involving sequential participation by various departments. Such a cycle of activity costs money, and this cost can be determined. Moreover, this cost

[19] Very likely, the Pareto principle is a special case of the Spectrum (or vice versa).

should be determined, since useful decisions on dealing with the useful many cannot be made without knowledge of these costs.

The purchase-order cycle has been created to deal with the critical and important items of purchase. These purchases justify a formal, orderly purchasing routine, complete with written requisitions, written approvals, competitive bids, multiple copies of papers, invoices, vouchers, checks, and the rest. The minimum cost of processing one such cycle of activity can easily run to several dollars.

But this means that for many purchases, the cost of processing the papers exceeds the value of the goods purchased. This situation actually prevails in many companies. It prevails because:

1. The same routine is used both for important purchases and for trivia.
2. The irritations and costs do not come to the attention of top management, since any one instance is too trivial to find its way to the top.
3. In the absence of easy means of bringing matters to a head, the situation goes on and on.

On the customer-order side, a similar situation prevails. The customer order goes through credit verification, editing, stock selection, packing, shipping, invoicing, accounting, etc. Collectively, this procedure can run to several dollars a cycle. This is easily justified on large orders. It is a shocking waste on the useful many orders.

The key fact is the cost of one cycle of activity. At this point it is all too easy to give up. How can one determine the cost of a cycle which is performed in so many departments? "We don't keep the books that way."

It isn't easy, since it requires a special study. It is necessary to go to *each* of the participating departments and make two counts:

(*a*) How many invoices, requisitions, accounts receivable (or whatever) does the department process?

(*b*) How many people, staff-hours, dollars (or whatever) are used to process these papers?

This type of study can give us the process cost at each step in the cycle. Collectively, these permit us to price out the cost of one cycle, which is the key cost figure.

Table 8-3 is an example of such an allocation of distribution costs.

Table 8-4 shows the resulting costs, expenses, and profit by size of order.*

---

*Tables 8-3 and 8-4 are from Sevin, Charles H. "How Manufacturers Reduce Their Distribution Costs," p. 59. U.S. Dept. of Commerce. Available from Superintendent of Documents, U.S. Government Printing Office, Washington, D.C.

Table 8-3. Method of Allocating Costs

Functional costs	Bases of allocation	Cost per unit
Order taking:		
Personal calls	Number of personal calls	97.5 cents per call
Phone solicitation	Number of phone calls	23.8 cents per call
Packing and shipping:		
Boxes and packing	Actual according to cost of box used	
Loading in cars	Hundredweight loaded	4.3 cents per hundred-weight
Delivery:		
Freight	Actual by orders	
Drayage	Actual by orders	
Sales bookkeeping:		
Billing and analysis	Number of items	3.0 cents per item
Posting, etc.	Number of sales invoices	12.0 cents per invoice
Credits and collections:		
Personal calls	Number of calls	10.8 cents per call
Statements and office	Number of customers' accounts	17.7 cents per account
Bad debts	Per cent of sales (on sliding scale)	From 2 to 0.1 per cent
General overhead	Number of units sold	8.7 cents per unit

The matter is not limited to paperwork. In many businesses, a customer order requires a special setup—making a pattern, setting up a machine, matching a color. These activities require the time of specialists. It is not uncommon to find that these preparatory steps cost in the range of $10 to $25 per order.

For an order of $1,000 or so, this preparation poses no problem. But the useful many come in to plague us. Many customers want just one unit on the order, or only 10 pounds of paint. Under standard pricing, the billing may be only $25 despite the fact that the pattern costs $20, or that the laboratory cost to match the color is $20.

There are other unknown costs. A particularly deceptive form is the "iceberg" variety, where the subsurface costs greatly exceed the visible costs.

The obvious cost of carrying inventory is the interest on the money. The subsurface costs—storage, handling, deterioration, obsolescence, etc.—are several times as great.

A piece of equipment is damaged in a fork truck. The replacement part costs $100; the loss due to equipment down time is far greater.

Table 8-4. Results of Cost Analysis by Size of Order

Size of order, units of product	Income margin	Expense	Profit
Less than 25 units	$0.05	$0.14	($0.09)
25 to 50 units	0.04	0.06	(0.02)
50 to 100 units	$0.03\,^1/_2$	$0.03\,^3/_4$	$(0.00\,^1/_4)$
100 to 200 units	$0.03\,^1/_4$	$0.02\,^1/_4$	$0.01\,^1/_4$
200 to 500 units	0.03	$0.01\,^1/_2$	$0.01\,^1/_2$
500 to 1,000 units	0.03	$0.01\,^1/_4$	$0.01\,^3/_4$
Averages, entire business	0.03	$0.01\,^3/_4$	$0.01\,^1/_4$

( )=loss.

Some Steering Arm members become militant at disclosures of un-known costs, and attack the accounting system for failing to bring these out into the open. Such attacks are regularly repulsed. Industry's ac-counting procedures have been set up primarily to measure results, not to identify opportunities. (Even as to measuring results, the accountant has problems.) The Steering Arm should accept the need for digging into costs as a necessary, constructive part of its job.

Diagnosis of Organizational Problems

We have seen (p. 88) that a Steering Arm can take on a project of reor-ganization of a company. Nor does it have to be done on the basis of "I think...." The Frame of Reference (p. 89) required the Steering Arm to work out alternative forms "on paper," estimate the costs, and prejudge the benefits and deficiencies before making their recommendations.

Organizational and jurisdictional problems show up in middle man-agement as well.

Three departments were contending for command of the com-pany metallurgical laboratory:

the Foundry Department, on the ground that regulation of the foundry processes involved much service from the laboratory, and that the foundry should have control of this service

the Engineering Department, on the ground that their develop-ment work in metallurgy required laboratory services which needed professional direction the Quality Control Department, on the ground that the laboratory tests were the basis for numerous decisions on material and product acceptance, clearly a quality control responsibility

A study was made of the time allocation of the laboratory, which showed that it rendered:

Service	Per cent of time
Foundry	15
Engineering	10
Quality Control	75

This analysis was decisive in leaving the laboratory in the Quality Control Department.

At the bottom of the company, still other needs are encountered, and appropriate diagnoses can be worked out.

One company undertook to define, with precision, the authority[20] of its foremen.[21] It listed all the needs for action faced by the foreman. These were then classified as to:

full authority—no obligation to ask the boss beforehand or to tell him afterward

authority with obligation to inform—no obligation to ask the boss beforehand, but must tell the boss afterward

limited authority—must ask the boss beforehand

As before, the Steering Arm has available to it a variety of prefabricated tools for analysis:

the organization chart to depict the flow of commands and responses

the job description to define duties and responsibilities of a post

"activity analysis" to define who does what for an activity which cuts across a variety of posts

[20] A good rule in organization analysis is that no meeting of the minds is really reached until we talk of *specific actions or decisions*. We can talk of who is responsible for budgets, or inventory, or quality, but little is settled. It is only when we get down to the action words—measure, compute, prepare, check, endorse, recommend, approve—that we can make clear who is to do what.

[21] "Every Foreman Knows Exactly What His Responsibilities Are," *Factory Management and Maintenance*, September, 1951.

Management Improvement or Employee Improvement?

Still another essential need in diagnosis is to clarify whether a given improvement in performance is to come from the management or from the employees.

Improvements can come from both sources. Consider the needs in increasing sales, improving productivity, improving quality. Management can provide better product lines, more efficient machinery, better measuring instruments. The employees can provide more time on the job, less holding back, fewer blunders. But we can also identify some of the really basic principles in this relationship:

1. The few really big changes must come from the management—a new product which leap-frogs all competition, a new process which can outproduce its predecessor 4 to 1, a new machine which holds tolerances beyond all previous experience. Here each of a comparatively few individuals makes a big contribution.
2. The many small changes must come from the employees. Here each of a large number of individuals makes a small contribution.
3. Before an employee can do his or her job at all, he or she must be provided, with the three indispensables:
    (*a*) Knowledge of what he is supposed to do—the specification, quota, routine, procedure, etc.
    (*b*) Knowledge of how well he or she is doing it—the amount of sales, production, waste.
    (*c*) Means for changing his or her performance if he or she is failing to meet his or her goals.
    Unless *all* of these three essentials have been provided, management has not finished its job. The employee cannot then be held responsible for meeting his or her goals; i.e., the job is not employee-controllable and hence is management-controllable.[22]
4. Once the employee has been provided with these three essentials, the job is truly employee-controllable. But will the employee deliver a superior, average, or inferior performance? This depends on his or her state of mind. But management is not helpless here. It can conduct programs (drives, campaigns) to intensify the attention to the matter at hand (cost-mindedness, quality-mindedness, etc.).

---

[22]We will return to these three indispensables later in this book—they are also the indispensables for control, whether by the employee or by the manager.

Diagnostic Tools

The Steering Arm has no need to invent diagnostic tools other than for unique situations. Generations of managers and specialists have devoted energy and ingenuity to invention of such tools. By now, quite a battery of prefabricated tools is available for use in a wide variety of problems in diagnosis.

A number of company departments are mainly used as diagnostic tools for upper management, i.e., Market Research, Product Research, Operations Research. The various company laboratories are in part diagnostic tools for technical matters. Some multipurpose departments are in part diagnostic tools, i.e., Cost Accounting, Quality Control, Production Control. The Diagnostic Arm is strictly a diagnostic tool.

Then there are the vast arrays of special-purpose management tools. Every management function has its own, and there are some that cut across various functions. Table 8-5 illustrates some of these.

It is unlikely that any one Steering Arm will encounter a problem in diagnosis for which there exist no prior diagnostic tools.

The Steering Arm members should not rely solely on their personal knowledge of the availability of diagnostic tools. They should, through the company's specialists, draw on all resources in the company, and on outside services as well—the literature, seminars, conferences, libraries, industrial journalists, consultants. These resources not only are able to help identify prefabricated tools; they can also supply knowledge of pitfalls and causes of prior failures.

Running the Machinery of Diagnosis

Diagnosis for Breakthrough typically extends over a period of months. During this calendar time, the Steering Arm members are mainly tend-

Table 8-5. Some Diagnostic Tools

The function of:	Makes extensive use of:
Marketing	Distribution cost analysis
Finance	Break-even chart; Return on Investment formula
Personnel	Organization chart, job specification, activity analysis, morale survey
Manufacture	Time study, motion study, process chart, Gantt chart, Economic Lot Formula, Shewhart chart

ing their regular duties, while the Diagnostic Arm is conducting the detailed data collection, analysis, etc. These two patterns of activity are stitched together by a series of joint meetings. During any one of these meetings the time is occupied mainly by:

> presentation, by the Diagnostic Arm, of the results of study conducted since the prior meeting
>
> discussion of these results
>
> agreement on what needs to be done, and by whom, before the next meeting

Any single meeting of the Steering Arm is in the nature of a problem-solving conference. As such, it should be conducted with use of the rules of conference procedure. These are well documented.[23]

However, since Breakthrough problems commonly require a few calendar months for diagnosis, there is an added need for planning and continuity. Let us follow through an example.

The Nestor company undertook a study of the profitability of the X product family, consisting of several product lines of large units sold to industrial customers. The units were mostly fabricated at the factory, but there was added fabrication during installation on the customer's site. A Steering Arm (a committee) of managers was assigned to study this problem, with the aid of a skilled diagnostician whom we will call Mr. Ring.

At its first meeting (in December) the Committee proposed an extensive list of topics for study. These were grouped, for convenience, into 26 topical groups. The problem group ranked second for priority was concerned mainly with fundamental economics, and included the specific problem:

> A procedure should be worked out to facilitate decisions on shop make vs. buy, including working up the cost comparison, burden absorption, freight charges, etc.

This is the problem we will trace through to solution, using the committee agendas and minutes.

The minutes of the second meeting (in January of the following year) include the following:

---

[23]The excellent references include: "A Guide to Successful Conference Leadership," *Personnel,* May, 1948 (this is a digest of Standard Oil Co. of New Jersey's course in conference leadership); "Problem-solving Conferences," National Industrial Conference Board, Studies in Personnel Policy, No. 176.

5. *Make or Buy.* It was concluded that the Committee needs clear decisions on how "Make or Buy" decisions are being reached. Mr. Ring is to prepare information showing:

1. Who now makes the decisions on whether to "Make or Buy"?
2. On what basis are these decisions being made?
3. At what time in the progression of events are these decisions being made?

This is to include the decisions on "Self-erect vs. Subcontract."

There was a general belief that, collectively, the "Make or Buy" decisions are very important to the profitability of the X product line from several standpoints, i.e., the estimates, which regulate success in bidding; the costs which regulate profit; and the engineering which affects many things including the timetable.

It was felt that there might be some value in tabulating competitor practice on "Make or Buy," as well as looking into the question of a variable practice depending on geographical location.

Because recent company profits have exceeded estimates, the question was raised—"Are our `Make or Buy' decisions made on inflated shop estimates?"

Ring dug into the procedures and data. His agenda of Mar. 7, 1958, presented four pages of findings which can be summarized as follows:

A. Work is subcontracted if:
  1. Our shops lack the facilities to do it.
  2. Our shops have the facilities but have a higher cost than the subcontract price.
  3. Our shops have the facilities but are operating at full capacity and could not meet the timetable.
B. As to decision making:
  1. There is a well-established channel for decision making.
  2. The qualitative considerations for decision making are clear.
  3. The quantitative considerations for decision making are:
    (a) Clear as to plant capacity.
    (b) Not clear as to cost of making vs. cost of buying.

As an example of B (3(b), Ring showed, for a given design of box:

	Cost to make	Cost to buy
Labor	$275	
Burden at 115 per cent	317	
Price		$450
Total	$592	$450

On such figures we have generally assumed that the boxes should be bought, at a savings of $142 each.

However, this does not take into account the fact that the fixed portion of the burden goes on even if the job is subcontracted. With this in mind, the figures become:

	Cost to make	Cost to buy
Labor	$275	
Variable burden	171	
Fixed burden	146	$146
Price		450
	$592	$596

The effect of unabsorbed burden is greater than we have realized.

When the steering team discussed the foregoing, they identified four different stages of use of the sticky cost comparison, with a question at each stage.

1. When cost estimates are being made to serve as a basis for preparing a bid, should the cost estimate of shop-make be on the basis of standard burden (for capacity operation) or actual burden (for below-capacity operation)?

2. When bids are prepared, should the basis of the bidding be the cost of make, or of buy, or the lower of the two?

3. Once a bid has been successful, should the decision of whether to make or buy (placing orders for the physical goods) be influenced by the factor of unabsorbed burden?

4. When accounting is done on the finished job, and actual cost exceeds estimated cost due to unabsorbed burden, should the excess be charged to:

(a) All product lines

(b) Only the product lines using the slack facility

(c) A separate idle plant account

(d) Something else?

Ring was sent back for still more information pertinent to all this, especially the effect on other products of low sales in product X.

It is seen that what started as a simple-sounding thing has mushroomed into many questions. The questions had always been there but had been obscured by the Semantic Jungle.

At a subsequent meeting in April, conclusions began to be reached.

The team agreed to use standard burden for preparing shop estimates for bidding purposes, since burden rates had been established on the basis of long-range levels of operations. (This conclusion confirmed existing practice.)

As to preparing bids, the team agree to use the "buy" price if it were lower than the "make" cost (on the basis that competitors had access to the same "buy" price); what to do if the "make" cost were lower than the "buy" price was deferred.

As to placing orders for physical make or buy, some new questions arose, including disposing of the facilities altogether, and going completely to a buy basis. This created another assignment to Ring—What would happen to long-range profits if we did dispose of the facilities?

The accounting question was deferred—it had "political" overtones, since it affected the profit performance of some of the men on the team.

By the June meeting, Ring had studied still other costs which were in fact incurred when a job was subcontracted rather than shop-made, i.e., cost such as procurement, inspection, and material handling. He found that these came to 5 per cent of the fabrication portion of the subcontractor's price. At the team meeting, all agreed that this 5 per cent must be added to the contractor's price to make the comparison valid.

When the Committee returned to the question of preparation of bids, in the case where cost to make was less than the subcontract price (adjusted by 5 per cent) there was an end to unanimity. All members except the Finance Manager felt that the bid should be based on the lower of these two figures. (The split recommendation went to the General Manager, who went along with the majority.)

Next, the team tackled the problem of establishing a new procedure which could be used by the regular departments, day after day, for reaching decisions on whether to self-make or subcontract. Ring was asked to:

(a) Draft a form which would facilitate making the cost comparison

(b) Make the rounds of all departments to ensure that the form took account of all costs

(c) Work up a recommended procedure for use of the form

The accounting question was also disposed of, but not settled. The company's auditors were making a study of accounting procedures; so the team concluded to wait until the auditors had made their report.

By the August meeting, Ring had designed the cost-comparison form and made the rounds with it. The cost-comparison portion was as shown in Fig. 12.

The steering team concluded that the Chief Estimator was in the best position to execute these forms since he was in the middle of these data anyhow.

The steering team concluded that the Production Manager's decision should be final on make vs. buy if he followed the minimum cost as de-

Cost Comparison

	Item	Cost to Self Make	Cost to Subcontract
A	Plate shop labor		
B	Plate shop variable burden (0.6 x Std. Burden Rate x A)		
C	Plate shop fixed burden (0.4 x Std. Burden Rate x A)		
D	Machine shop labor		
E	Machine shop variable burden (0.6 x Std. Burden Rate x D)		
F	Machine shop fixed burden (0.4 x Std. Burden Rate x D)		
G	Other shop labor		
H	Other shop variable burden (0.6 x Std. Burden Rate x G)		
I	Other shop fixed burden (0.4 x Std. Burden Rate x G)		
J	Freight and trucking		
K	Material		
L	Subcontractor's fabrication price		
M	Additional cost to subcontract (0.05 x L)		
N	Duty		
O			
P			
Q			
R			
	TOTALS		

Fig. 12. Make or buy cost comparison.

termined by the cost comparison. Otherwise, he would have to go to the upper management for an exception.

By now (September) the original purpose of going into the "make or buy" question had been largely met. But the act of turning this stone over had disclosed some unexpected sights. The team now went after these as well. They directed Ring to put together information to compare:

(a) Subcontractors' estimates at the time of bid preparation,

(b) Subcontractors' estimates at the time of make vs. buy decision, and

(c) Actual subcontractor charges

The improved grip on the make or buy decision resulted in a further look at "Can we, through standardization, set the stage for lower costs and greater self-fabricate?"

The final appearance of the make or buy topic was at the October meeting. A final draft for shop procedures was agreed on, and the topic was removed from the agenda.[24]

The solution of this make or buy problem took place over a series of eight meetings extending over ten calendar months. Make or buy was only one of many topics considered. For example, the September meeting considered the following topics:

---

[24]Not quite. The success of the make or buy study inspired the team to study the question of self-install or subcontracting the installation.

make or buy

cost-control system for product family X

why bids for new business have been unsuccessful

should field erection be done by self-erection or by subcontracting

economics of the company's construction depot

duties of the company's field representative

review of self-erection costs to test out some theories on why they had varied

improving shop estimating

comparison of product design vs. that of competitors (the question was whether the company was making Cadillacs to sell at Chevrolet prices)

organization of the company, especially as to the engineering responsibilities

progress on a cost-reduction program

As the Diagnostic Arm, Ring contributed importantly to the very real progress made. His agendas ran to as many as 38 pages of data, charts, analyses, flow diagrams, etc. He went into all nooks and crannies of the company to collect all this, and through him the Steering Arm visited these same nooks and crannies. His summaries gave perspectives that the team members would have missed purely in their departmental capacities.

Diagnosis of Social Effects of Technical Changes

Diagnosis is not complete unless we have learned what will be the "social effects" of the changes we are leading up to.

For the sake of giving this subject the space it deserves, the entire next chapter is devoted to it. This sequence is *not* with any idea that, after diagnosis is complete, we can begin thinking about the social effects. Absolutely not. What will be discussed in the next chapter should be thought out as part of the work of diagnosis.

Patterns of Action

As the mosaic of knowledge approaches completeness, ideas for action emerge with it. At times the action is anything but obvious, and a flash of ingenuity is necessary. The diagnosis may also have made clear the need for actions which at one time would have seemed ridiculous, i.e.,

turn down customers' orders for business
fill an order but don't charge for it
pay a claim without verifying the validity

Chapter 10 is devoted to the action patterns which result from diagnosis.

9 RESISTANCE TO CHANGE—CULTURAL PATTERNS

Technical Change and Social Change

The entire purpose of the Breakthrough sequence is change, beneficial change. This change has its effect in two ways:

1. The effect on the machines, products, processes, things. We will call this the *technical change.*
2. The effect on the people associated with these things. We will call this the *social change.*

There is no such thing as a technical change without a social effect. *Any* proposed technical change automatically is proposing some social changes as well. These social changes are a form of threat to the status, habits, beliefs, etc., of the people involved—the sales force, the pattern shop, the billing clerks. They have a "way of life" which is important to them, and which they will defend against invasion.

The social change is such a big trouble maker that those involved in Breakthrough should understand thoroughly the nature of social change.

In the early factory days of few machines, materials handling was done by human laborers. The most important single operation was picking things up and putting them down. Periodically, things were dropped, feet were injured, toes were smashed.

Then someone invented the safety shoe which provided a "hard hat" for toes. Industrial companies propagandized these shoes, and subsidized the price to make it easy for men to buy them. Many men did buy them, but few men wore them. That was puzzling.

The trail led to the wives. The shoes not only looked unwieldy; they marked a man as a factory laborer—a badge of low caste. When the safety shoe was redesigned to look like a dress shoe, the usage rate rose sharply.

In this "simple" instance, it can be assumed that the technical change had been well executed. The right kind of material was used; it withstood the impacts as measured in the test lab and as proved on the factory floor. There had been some diagnosis beyond this—the need for a price subsidy and the need for a propaganda campaign were recognized. But the diagnosis fell short of discovering the effect of the shoes as a negative status symbol.

This same instance also opens the door just a crack to let us see that human reaction to change is not some simple animal irritation. The reaction is very complex. It stems from the myriads of habits and beliefs which the human being derives from the numerous groups and circles, i.e., "societies," of which he or she is a part. To understand all this requires a journey into the nature of human motivation. This brings us to the work of the behavioral scientists, since the real experts in human motivation are these scientists, *not* the managers. Unfortunately, the behavioral scientists have not translated their findings fully into the manager's dialect. We must, therefore, get just a bit acquainted with the dialect of these scientists. A basic element of that dialect is the anthropologist's concept of "culture."

If any reader is now tempted to skip a few pages because of the ivory tower–sounding word "culture," the author respectfully suggests "Don't skip." The concept of culture is fundamental to "resistance to change," and hence is of the utmost importance to the manager.

The Concept of Culture

"Culture" is a body of learned behavior, a collection of beliefs, habits, practices, and traditions, shared by a group of people (a society) and successively learned by new members who enter the society. So says the anthropologist.[1]

This definition is important to us, for a very good reason. Anthropologists have by now studied numerous "cultures."[2] From these studies they have observed some consistent effects when technical changes are introduced into societies. The conclusions from these studies are valid as applied to any human society, industrial or otherwise. If our district offices, factories, warehouses, etc., meet the definition of a "culture," then the great body of study of cultures is applicable to these industrial societies as well.

Culture, then, is just a shorthand description, a label, for the fabric of human habits, beliefs, traditions, etc. It is a fabric, not a kettle full of bits and pieces. The elements of the culture are so interwoven that disturbance of one element has effects on many others.

> The chemical laboratory has become congested, and an addition is built, robbing the company parking lot in the process. The displaced cars must find parking space on the overcrowded public streets. Employees have to leave home earlier to find a place to park. Their spouses and children have to adapt themselves to this new routine. New car pools are formed, creating some fresh social groupings, tearing others apart. Wide waves of disturbance begin to spread from so innocent a beginning as the need to relieve congestion in the chemical laboratory.

Among the ingredients of a culture is the scale of values—what is important, what is not. Cultures differ remarkably in what they consider important, and many tragedies have resulted from ignorance of these differences.

> Following the mutiny of the crew of the *Bounty*, the mutineers, along with a number of Polynesian men and women, fled from Tahiti to Pitcairn Island. When the white men decided to divide the land of this island among themselves, a bloody little war broke out, resulting in virtual extermination of all the men. The white men

---

[1]Mead, Margaret, Editor, "Cultural Patterns and Technical Change," UNESCO, Paris, 1951; also published by Mentor Books, New American Library of World Literature, Inc., New York, 1955.

[2]The classic book, which is fascinating as well as rewarding, is Benedict, Ruth, "Patterns of Culture," Mentor Books, New American Library of World Literature, Inc., New York, 1946. Originally published by Houghton Mifflin Company, Boston, 1934.

had not realized that, to the Polynesian, deprivation of rights in land was the worst possible humiliation.

There is general awareness that cultural differences are pronounced as between races, religions, nations. But there are also sharp differences within industry.

In that delightful musical "How to Succeed in Business without Really Trying," one incident concerns the multiple candidacy for the post of head of the mail room. The man who is to make the decision announces that he will judge the candidates solely on merit. Thereupon "the nephew" (of the president's wife) screams that this is "unfair." Whereupon the audience roars.

But the nephew had a valid point. Nepotism is a widespread basis for promotion. In many countries, including the United States, there are "family businesses" where it is regarded as ethical and proper that the important posts be staffed by family members. In contrast are the many companies in which nepotism is taboo—there are written rules forbidding anyone to report to a relative.

Can promotion based on merit, and promotion based on nepotism both be "right"? Yes they can.[3] The fact that something is "different" does not make it "wrong." Societies differ greatly in their approaches to religion, housing, taxes, political organization, etc. Who is to say what is right or wrong? The need is for peaceful coexistence, in the dictionary meaning of those words.

The manager may well ask "How is it that we now must talk of cultural pattern? We have been managing industry for years, and have made many changes affecting the lives of people, all without using the words 'cultural pattern'." The answer is that we have for years "solved" these problems by violence or oppression, and now must use more enlightened ways. Historically, we have encountered monumental difficulty in making changes.

The eighteenth century English hand sawyers who repeatedly destroyed water-powered sawmills had their counterparts in the nineteenth century Luddites who broke up textile machinery. In similar vein, American teamsters smashed the first pipelines emerging from the Pennsylvania oil fields. Their factory counterparts bitterly resisted the introduction of the Taylor system into the shops.

---

[3] There are nine and sixty ways of constructing tribal lays,
And every single one of them is right.
Rudyard Kipling

When members of a twentieth century company are faced with a threat to something they regard as important, their reaction can be antisocial, anticompany (or so it seems to the other fellow). In the case on p. 33, the Product Development Department defied a decision of the General Manager in order to enforce their "monopoly rights."

Note that this willingness to sabotage[4] a new product, on a theory of rule or ruin, came from the highbrows, the scientists, the Ph.D.s, the very flower of our industrial civilization. We are apt to associate cultural patterns with native tribes in New Guinea, or the South Sea Islands, since such have been the favorite laboratories of the cultural anthropologists. The point is that *all* societies, without exception, exhibit recognizable cultural patterns. Hence *the cultural pattern is a universal*; i.e., it is found wherever human beings are found. The Product Development Department was, in a sense, proving it was composed of human beings.

The sabotage of a company project is but one of a long catalogue of outward evidences of resistance to an unacceptable change. When the members of the culture are in power, they can (and do) deal summarily with the advocate of change—ridicule, burning at the stake, or just throwing the bum out. But when the advocate of change is in power (the boss) or just sits near the throne (the staff), the member of the culture is in a quandary. To reject the change is to invite reprisals; to accept the change is to destroy something important (to him or her).

The fact that the violence and machine smashing took place in days when those in command had overwhelming political and economic power to back them up only shows how intense the forces of resistance can be. Today those in command of the companies no longer have such overwhelming power. The resistances can no longer be trampled on—they must be dealt with by more enlightened means. It is this need for enlightenment which forces us to look for a deeper understanding of "resistance to change."

The Bee Crashing into the Window

It is a sobering experience to see a bee hurling itself at a window, over and over again, until it reaches the bee's equivalent of exhaustion. The fool insect is trying to fly through a solid wall!

---

[4]The word sabotage itself is derived from "sabot," the wooden shoe which French spinners kicked into the threads of the textile machines to force stoppages.

Those who have not been sensitized to the existence of the cultural pattern have much in common with the bee at the window. Here is a proposal, technically sound and economically useful. Yet nothing happens. Resistance consists of a mysterious roadblock here, a fool argument there, a wild-goose chase yonder. The advocate of the change may well conclude that there are enemies around, and he or she may get personal about it. But all too often he is trying to walk through a solid wall. The wall is invisible to him or her because he has never been sensitized to see anything in that part of the spectrum.

In the famous Hawthorne experiments,[5] some engineers set out to study the effect of illumination on productivity of factory operators. To create a laboratory, they walled off part of a factory department, taking care to make the working conditions "identical" with those in the big room, i.e., the regular factory department.

The experiments became hopelessly confused. Productivity in the "laboratory" rose and rose, whether illumination waxed or waned. The baffled engineers turned to the behavioral scientists for explanations. They found out. To the engineers and managers, the working conditions (technical) were the same in the "laboratory" as in the factory. But to the employees, the working conditions (social) were radically different.

In the big room, the employees were forbidden to talk to each other—conversation was regarded as a drag on productivity; in the "laboratory" they could talk to their heart's content, and did. In the big room, they were subjected to a long catalogue of petty disciplines; not so in the "laboratory." In the big room, they were nobody; people who walked down the center aisle knew only that these nameless operators assembled telephone relays. But in the "laboratory" these nameless operators suddenly acquired status; engineers and managers addressed them by name, asked them how Jimmy's cold was getting on, explained the project, and otherwise treated them as members of the team. The engineers never dreamed that these "little" things might have more effect on productivity than something as important (to an engineer) as lighting. To the operators, these social matters were of great importance. Lighting—bah! They could (and did) assemble relays in light too dim for reading a newspaper.

What was happening was, of course, a meeting of two cultures. To the engineers, the right to talk, the freedom from petty disciplines, the status of being known by name, etc., were all commonplace. These needs

---

[5]Roethlisberger, F. J., and W. J. Dickson, "Management and the Worker," Harvard University Press, Cambridge, Mass., 1939.

were already being met, and the engineers, having taken them for granted, were immersed in other matters. But for the shop workers these needs were not being met, and hence were high on the scale of values. In consequence, the engineers, having been brought up in one culture, could not grasp the importance of these "rights" to members of another culture.

This leads us to a cardinal rule for advocates of change:

You must be aware that *you are dealing with a pattern of human habits, beliefs, and traditions which may differ from yours* and which may therefore view this change in a way totally different from your view.

As Seen by the Members of the Culture

Every culture has its own system of motivation, status, values, rights, "way of life." Any proposed change is a potential threat to parts of this system, and is therefore examined carefully to judge its social effects.

This examination is conducted against the list of human needs as emphasized in the culture. Some of these are highly individual in character: the animal needs; economic security; freedom from arbitrary action of the boss; still other forms of security.

The member of the culture also exhibits some needs which are of a collective nature. He or she looks to his or her fellows to help him or her meet these—the need to belong, to be accepted, to be listened to, to be respected. Because these are essential human needs, the member will exhibit conduct which appears to be contrary to his or her self-interest. He or she does so in the interest of the group.

> The Hawthorne experiments[6] found that group pieceworkers were governed by a group code of conduct which included:
>
> maximum output standards
>
> minimum output standards
>
> rules about "squealing" to supervisors
>
> forms of punishment
>
> rules of status, rules for exchanging jobs, etc.
>
> This group code of conduct *took precedence over the company rules.*

Some proposed technical changes are obvious in their likely social effect. They threaten to abolish a whole segment of human activity. A

[6]Roethlisberger and Dickson, *op. cit.*

bridge which will make the ferry boats obsolete will have some devastating effects. So will the automated process or the computer.

But most of the effects are far more subtle.

> Hundreds of companies have been taken by surprise in a sequence of events as follows:
>
> the management works out a new arrangement with one group of people—the piecework operators, the commission salespeople, or whomever.
>
> this new arrangement is satisfactory to the people directly involved.
>
> now some people "not even involved" enter the picture. They point out (for example) that there has always been a difference in pay between production and maintenance workers; the proposed change will close the traditional gap, and something will have to be done for the maintenance people to retain the old relationship.
>
> The first reaction of the managers is "it's none of your business." But it turns out that, by the iron rule of status in the culture, it *is* their business, and they make it stick.

The social values are so important to members of the culture that it is most desirable they genuinely accept the changes (meaning they have been satisfied on the social effects). Failing this, the consequences can be severe.

Sometimes human ingenuity finds a way out. There is outward acceptance but inward rejection. There is "lip service," to use an ancient term.

But the advocates of change are also ingenious. They contrive schemes of check and audit, to ensure that acceptance is real. The result can be serious strains and frustrations for the members of the culture. There may arise a whole series of unwelcome consequences:

> general belligerence, verbal attacks, anger. The King's messenger is beaten up, new machinery is sabotaged, the time-study person's notebook disappears.
>
> immature, even childish behavior. If we can't outvote the president, let's circulate bawdy jokes about him.
>
> return to former practices, less satisfactory though they are.
>
> unsupportable statements. Galileo's telescope is a fake—stars are painted on the lenses.
>
> substitute outlets for energies—alcohol, gambling.
>
> flight from reality—blaming others, chronic bad health.

All this may seem to depict the frustrations of unacceptable change as a pretty grim business. This is the intention. We need only to look sideways at the integration problems of the South (and the North), or the furor over fluoridation of water, or the matter of prayers in the public schools, to realize that twentieth century man retains some firm ideas about longstanding beliefs and habits. The resulting frustrations can be widespread enough to arouse organized resistance. They can bring on frustrations which border on mental-health problems.

We can now state a second basic rule for advocates of change:

You should, as part of your diagnosis, *discover just what will be the social effects of your proposed technical changes.* Which beliefs will be denied, which habits will require change, which attitudes will be challenged. The more precisely you can predict all this, the better able you will be to prepare your case for dealing with the inevitable resistances.

What Acceptance of Change Involves

Logical explanation alone (by the advocate of change) is not the answer. The logic is from the viewpoint of the advocate, and thus is logical only as viewed from *his or her* culture.

Criticism of the existing order is regarded as an unpardonable sin. It is an attack on long-standing beliefs and thus on the believer and (sometimes even worse) on those who taught him or her those beliefs. A staff specialist who attacks an existing culture can make himself personally obnoxious to a point that the merits of his proposals are obscured by his personal unacceptability.

The acceptance of change in this way involves:

1. *Unlearning* old habits, attitudes, beliefs. This is a painful process at best. It can sometimes be made easier by going into the history of the belief to establish that, though originally well founded, it has become obsolete by the march of events.

> In the problem of pricing for "wholesalers" and "retailers" (p. 130) it proved helpful to all concerned to reconstruct the history which led up to the pricing structure. This history actually verified the logic of the original decision, while showing that the conditions which had made the decision so logical were no longer in effect.

2. *Learning* the new. This is encouraged by "consistent, prompt attachment of some form of satisfaction." The forms of satisfaction are fa-

miliar enough—praise, approval, increased status, sense of participation, material reward.[7]

Stress is laid on the satisfaction of learning a new skill, of belonging to a particular social group. Moreover, the learning must be by actual doing, by experiencing, by "living through a long series of situations in which the new behavior is made highly satisfying—without exception if possible—and the old not satisfying."

The idea of positive training programs has gained great impetus from the profound trends toward automating the factories and the offices. The unions have begun to accept the idea that the trade or skill now can have a life span shorter than the human life span. And the managers have begun to accept the idea that the company has a positive responsibility for training when programs of change are involved.

Principles to Be Observed

Today's physicians avoid reference to the fact that their profession was, until a few centuries ago, cojoined with that of the barbers. Today's managers have comparable skeletons in the ancestral closet, so far as introducing change is concerned.

In the centuries of slavery, barbarism, and other forms of absolute domination, changes were rammed down the throats of the many by the few.[8] The cultural pattern of the many was unknown, or ignored, or even trampled upon.

In the political enlightenment of the more recent past, governors have become increasingly more responsive to the voices of the governed. This wave of enlightenment has swept over industry as well. In consequence, industrial managers now devote much study to considering the impact of proposed changes on the people who will be affected.

---

[7]The anthropologist tells us that there are societies in which thrift, hard work, and knowing where your next meal is coming from are not regarded as virtues. The author, reared in Western society, once found it hard to believe this. But having since seen such a society, he understands.

> He was driving on the Fijian island of Viti Levu. He passed miles of breadfruit trees, banana trees, coconut trees, taro root, and marine life. It was clear that the Fijian knew exactly where his next meal was coming from.

The same reasoning pervades companies which have yet to feel the cold winds of adversity or the bite of competition. Here is a student's report:

> The Phillipsburg Company has shown only a limited interest in controls of any sort, probably because the organization was built around a series of monopolies and has always enjoyed a fairly healthy financial position. At the present time management seems prepared to dump money into research with only casual regard for the results. The system of controls as it now exists depends upon the opinion of the director rather than upon facts.

[8]For example, bricks without straw. (Exodus 5.)

Managers' problems of introducing change are not limited to dealings with their underlings. Managers are ever trying to introduce new products to their markets, new arrangements with their vendors, new images to the public, etc. The economic power may rest in the proponents of change, but it can also be the other way around. In any event, some "outsider" is trying to introduce change into a going culture. To do so, he is well advised to be able to predict where the sparks will fly.

But how does one go at it to consider the impact of proposed changes on a cultural pattern? Here again, industry can get help from the behavioral scientists. The cultural anthropologists have studied this problem in a variety of human societies, and have come up with a set of principles which should be observed by staff specialists or other proponents of change. The present author has restated these principles in industrial language and has exemplified them through incidents in which he has been an observer or an active participant.

As worded, these principles and examples put the staff specialist in the role of advocate of change and the line supervisor in the role of a member of the culture faced with absorbing a change. However, the principles are regarded as applying universally, irrespective of who is the advocate of change and which is the culture threatened; e.g., the labor union advocating change is faced with a cultural pattern of industrial managers.

1. *The staff specialists who propose change must understand that the premises on which they base their proposals are merely products of the culture in which the expert happened to be reared. They are not necessarily universal truths.*

A foreman retires and there is need to appoint a new foreman. The superintendent offers the job to a qualified worker and is shocked when the promotion is declined. In the same way, a scientist may prefer the laboratory to the directorship; a professor may prefer the classroom to the deanship. It is stupid to accuse such people of "no ambition" because they elect to follow a way of life which is preferable to them.

2. *The culture of the line supervisor serves him or her well by providing him with precedent, practices, and explanations. These things, however unenlightened, have the advantage of predictability and thus assure, to some degree, peace of mind. The more the staff specialist recognizes the real values this culture has for the line supervisor (instead of disparaging it as "ignorance," "stubbornness," "too-old-to-learn," etc.) the better will he or she be able to prepare his or her case.*

An accountant worked up a financial report to improve control of the inventory of copper rod. The rolling-mill superintendent never read the report. Instead, he continued to rely on two stripes painted on the wall of the storage shed. Years ago he had given the foreman orders to keep the pile of stored rod high enough to cover the lower stripe, but not so high as to cover the upper one. By this method, he was able to review the inventory situation at a glance on his daily trip through the shop. The system had never failed, and the varying price of copper had never bothered him. Had the accountant translated his report into suggested changes in the height of the paint stripes, he might have gotten somewhere.

3. *The staff specialist should examine proposals from the viewpoint of the line supervisor, since that is what the latter is bound to do anyhow.*

A manufacturing engineer, under pressure to reduce manufacturing costs, concluded, after studying competitors' products, that his or her own company's specifications were needlessly tight and thus not competitive. He or she then proposed to the manufacturing vice-president that a joint study be undertaken by the manufacturing, sales, and engineering departments to confirm or deny this conclusion. Despite the engineer's evidence, the manufacturing vice-president rejected the idea because manufacturing performance was currently under fire from the president. The manufacturing vice-president felt that before he or she could make such a proposal (which could be construed as muddying the water) he or she would first have to solve some of the more purely manufacturing troubles.

4. *The staff specialist must avoid the temptation to deal with a localized problem through a sweeping master plan which goes far beyond immediate needs. If he urges the sweeping plan, he or she risks rejection of the entire proposal, including the solution to the localized problem as well.*

A procedures analyst was assigned the job of working up a plan for delegating approval of purchase orders. The company was ready for such a plan, and the analyst put together a good one. However, he or she succumbed to the temptation of extending it to cover the delegation of authority for approval of capital expenditure projects also. The climate was not right for securing action on the latter. As a result, his or her plan for purchase orders lost out too.

5. *Unless the line supervisor is genuinely convinced that the change should be made, he or she is likely to return to his or her old ways rather than endure the tensions of frustrations brought about by the change.*

A staff quality-control engineer succeeded in convening a meeting of company executives to hear him out. He put on an entertaining, convincing display, using pinball machinery, dice games, charts, etc., and aroused a highly favorable reaction among the executives. The plant superintendent honestly didn't understand what the engineer was driving at. However, he was unwilling to get in the way of anything which had so favorably impressed top management. The engineer went to work but, swept away by his own enthusiasm, he spent his energies devising numerous charts which had little relation to the actual problems faced by the shop. The shop faced many real quality troubles which required diagnosis and solution through a variety of remedies. The engineer had only one remedy and was trying to apply it to all the company's troubles. Within 2 years, the charts had fallen into disuse, and the whole program was discredited. All that was left was widespread confusion and irritation in the shop.

Rules of the Road

The spectacle we have presented thus far may be summarized as follows:

> the advocate of change is interested solely in introducing a technical change.
>
> he or she is generally unaware that his or her proposals do pose a threat of social changes to members of the culture affected.
>
> he or she is specially unaware of just what are these threatened social changes.
>
> he or she is also unaware of how seriously these threatened social changes are regarded by the members of the culture.
>
> hence he or she is baffled by the mysterious resistances to his or her proposed technical changes.

We now turn to the specific recommendations for what to do about cultural resistance. These recommendations are in the nature of rules of the road for the Steering and Diagnostic Arms.

Two of these recommendations are so basic that they are listed under separate headings, i.e., Participation, Timing. The rest are lumped together under the heading "Other Recommendations."

Participation

The anthropologist states it this way:

Secure the active participation of those who will be affected, both in the planning and in the execution of the change.

Until the twentieth century, industry provided little participation either in planning or in execution. Staff specialists made their studies in isolation if not in secrecy. Their proposals were sent "up the line" as high as possible so that they would become unquestioned edicts by the time they hit the action levels.

These practices brought reprisals in the form of lack of cooperation or even active opposition in future studies. Data were withheld; studies were distorted; rumors were started to gang up on the specialists. So the specialists learned to change their ways. Instead of bypassing the action level (by sending their proposals far up the line) they brought them to the action level. "I've made this study, and would like to get your criticism before proposing it."

Even this concession falls short—it is participation in the execution but not in the planning of the change, and hence is already late in the day. As we saw in Chap. 6, participation in the planning is of the highest importance, for a wide variety of vital reasons.

Some experimental evidence is available to measure the effect of prior participation. Lawrence reports a marked contrast between a no-participation group and three other groups in which participation was substantial. The former was characterized by a drop in efficiency, with associated increases in hostility, turnover, and grievances. The latter resulted in increases in efficiencies, with no accompanying hostility or quits.[9]

An incidental effect of participation is that of informing the people in the culture and conveying an understanding of the nature of the change. Lacking such understanding, the grapevine takes over and may create needless shocks and difficulties.

Participation serves mainly to bring out, at the very outset, the objections that are bound to come out anyhow. If these objections are faced when proposals are still in a fluid state, the solutions are easier to find, and the personal relations are less abrasive. Participation is very likely the most useful single tool in dealing with the resistance of the cultural pattern.

Timing

Time is in several ways a factor in dealing with the cultural pattern. Several of the recommendations of the anthropologist relate to the time dimension.

(a) *Provide sufficient time for the mental changes to take place.*

This vital rule is violated often and needlessly. There are numerous ways of applying it. For example, in suggesting changes, propose distant effective dates to allow time for all to become familiar with the idea before being subject to the change itself. If a proposed change is rejected, let some time pass before bringing the subject up again.

---

[9]Lawrence, Paul R., "How to Deal with Resistance to Change," *Harvard Business Review,* May–June, 1954.

The importance of *time as an ingredient of change* is well known to the chemist, the politician, and many others. The industrial staff needs to grasp this principle firmly.[10]

(b) *Start small and keep it fluid.*

To protect both the staff and line person, the unexpected should be provided for. Change should be introduced slowly and gradually, so that, if necessary, the original plan may be modified as experience dictates.

Industry uses this principle extensively. The pilot plant, the test town, the trial period are all means of trying out on a small scale, and of learning at little risk, before taking the big plunge.

(c) *No surprises.*

One of the main reasons why a culture develops is that it makes life predictable. It is true that even an established culture includes patterns of change, e.g., progression from apprentice to journeyman, the annual model, periodic collective bargaining. But the type and pace of these changes are also predictable in the established culture.

It is the unexpected change—the one that defies explanation—which breeds chaos and drives the individual to find a way to relieve his tension.

(d) *Choose the right time.*

The "right" time is influenced by the number of changes already in progress (there is a limit to the digestive capacity); by the record of prior successes or failures; by the rhythm of good or bad feeling between the cultures involved. The planning should specifically consider the timing.

Other Recommendations

These are listed in the order usually encountered in the progression of a change rather than in the probable order of importance.

1. *The planning should include participation not only by the advocates and by those who will be affected; the planning should also include third parties who can supply balance and objectivity.*

As yet, industry has made little use of this idea.

2. *Strip off all technical cultural baggage not strictly needed for introducing the change.*

---

[10] The process of mental change is not like shifting a mechanical lever, throwing an electrical switch, or activating a chemical reaction. It is more like a biological process, in which a series of events must take place, each waiting patiently until its prerequisite has been completed.

An analogy may be that of the incubation of the chick. It takes 21 days from the time the egg is laid until the chick hatches. But suppose we try to speed up the process by applying heat, so we light a bunsen burner under the egg. Result—one hard-boiled egg.

There have been numerous violations of this principle in industry. An accountant assigned to work up a company training course in cost control may want to "lay a foundation" of general and cost accounting. Personnel people have urged courses in psychology as essential supervisory training background for a company venture into employee testing. The recent insistence of many quality-control specialists on supervisory training courses in statistics, and the current emphasis by operations research specialists on mathematical tools, are of the same order. The situation was well summed up by one harassed supervisor: "If education is that painful, I prefer to remain ignorant."

3. *Work with the recognized leadership of the culture.*

> A dramatic example was the decision of the American government to conduct the military occupation of Japan by retaining the Emperor in nominal authority. The long-standing tradition of obedience to the Emperor was in this way utilized to make effective the orders of the occupation forces.[11]

Applied to industrial situations, this recommendation says, in effect, only the members of the culture understand the habits of the culture. Sometimes industry has misused this by pitting members of the culture against each other, i.e., the pace setters of the Efficiency Experts. But where a respected member of the culture has been genuinely convinced on going ahead with the change, he or she can be of great aid to the proponents.

The leadership of the culture is sometimes referred to as the "informal organization." It goes farther than this. The person who is to present the proposals to the culture should also be acceptable to them. Otherwise, his or her personal make-up may hinder rather than aid the contact between the cultures.

4. *Treat the people with dignity.*

The classic example in industrial history is the Hawthorne experiments.[12] The shorthand of describing the changes as seen by the relay assemblers was that they were being treated with dignity.

5. *Reduce the impact of changes by weaving them into an existing broader pattern of behavior, or by letting them ride in on the back of some acceptable change.*

A company was in customer trouble because of broken delivery promises. When the staff people recommended a more centralized production control function, the departmental production control people

---

[11] This was hardly original. Cortes used the same device during the conquest of Mexico, as did Pizarro during the conquest of Peru. And they were not the first, either.

[12] Roethlisberger and Dickson, *op. cit.*

argued against the change. Seeing trouble ahead, the staff people made it their business to include in their plan remedies for some long-standing needs of the production control department, such as increased clerical assistance, improved paperwork, and mechanical aids. That did it.

6. *Put yourself in the other person's place.*

Any individual derives his or her attitude toward change from *his or her own* point of view, not from the view of the proponent of change.

An American visiting in England proposed to a British firm of silversmiths that they explore getting around the American import duty on finished silverware by bringing American-owned silver into England, performing their operations, and shipping the finished goods back duty-free. The immediate reaction of the British firm was to reject the idea. The rejection had nothing to do with import technicalities; it was based on the fact that in England a silversmith company that worked on silver it did not own occupied a much lower social status than a company that owned the silver it fabricated. (A similar caste distinction prevailed in American industry generally, as between prime contractor and subcontractor, or between manufacturing companies and manufacturing service companies.)

It is when the proponent of change runs into seeming blind opposition (you gotta have north light; the blue grinding wheels cut better; we tried plastic handles years ago and they didn't work, etc.) that he or she must move most cautiously. "Blind opposition" is how it looks to the staff person. It may only mean that the staff person has failed to grasp the situation as viewed by the line.

7. *Make use of the wide variety of methods available for dealing with resistance to change.*

There are many ways of overcoming resistance to change. You may:

(a) Try persuasion to secure change. Much depends here on the extent of prior participation and on the extent to which the individual is *treated with dignity.*

In one company, an important executive was in the habit of using new ideas, especially those suggested by employees, as a basis for taunting supervisors with the question, "How is it that you didn't think of this during all these years?" The result was a "freeze" by supervisors to all proposals for change, employee suggestions or otherwise.

Then someone went to work on the important executive and convinced him that he was doing a lot of damage. He revised his policy and began to "accentuate the positive," holding up as good examples those supervisors who showed improvements through change. Within a year, the supervisory freeze had fully thawed out.

(*b*) Change the environment in a way which makes it easy for the individual to change his or her point of view.

Company X contemplated putting up a new hosiery mill in a Southern community. Conditions were generally favorable. However, the past record of industrial companies in the community had been unenlightened. In consequence, factory work was low in the social scale, and candidates for factory work contained a high percentage of undesirables.

The company not only put up a modern air-conditioned factory building; they provided a handsome recreation room and permitted employees to use it out of hours for social events. Because this recreation room was the best facility of its kind in the area, it became an important social center in the community. The employees of Company X, far from being under the social stigma of factory workers, were looked up to because of the high standing which the company had earned in the community. As a result, Company X enjoyed a wide choice of candidates for employment.

(*c*) Remedy the causes of the line person's resistance.

The example of the safety shoes (p. 155) is in point here. But it is also important to distinguish between the asserted reasons and the real reasons for the resistance. The words used may only be the most convenient way of saying "I haven't thought this through yet."

(*d*) Create a social climate which favors the new habits.

A familiar example is the stimulation of patriotic feeling during a war. In industry, it may be observed when group incentives replace individual incentives. The machinist no longer stands by waiting for the crane operator to finish; he or she is now willing to help the crane operator who, for his or her part, is now less likely to enforce jurisdictional boundaries. A similar situation develops between functional divisions when a company decentralizes into product divisions. A new spirit of collaboration arises because the social climate demands it.

This social climate includes specific recognition, e.g., service pins, which bestow dignity and status on career employees. The awards for safety, housekeeping, etc., fall into the same category.

8. *Forget it.*

We do not know what is a good batting average for proposed changes, but it is well under 100 percent. Abandonment or shelving of a project is always an alternative. Even when there is no cultural resistance, the project reviews should include abandonment as an alternative.

The really stupid thing to do is to make an issue of overcoming the cultural resistance. This loses sight of the merits of the project. The real project becomes one of "winning." The situation begins to meet the classic definition of fanaticism—"redoubling your efforts when the original objective has been forgotten."

Out of the Morass

The foregoing has been a long list of principles, rules of the road, and recommendations, enough to fit most situations. But many managers will get only limited comfort from the list. In dealing with cultural patterns we are at our worst, hampered as we are by our limited basic knowledge and by our own emotional involvement.

We now leave the morass to set foot on the more solid ground of taking action.

10 BREAKTHROUGH IN PERFORMANCE—ACTION

TRANSITION TO THE NEW LEVEL

Action by Whom?

All responsibility for decisions, actions, and results rests on individual supervisors. The committee system makes no change in this responsibility.

So commences one company's Standard Practice Instruction on committees.

The emphasis is well placed. During Steering Arm deliberations, little attention is paid to whether a member is talking in his capacity as

(*a*) a member of the Steering Arm, or

(*b*) a foreman, district manager, engineer, or whatever his or her regular job is

When the time comes to take action, this distinction becomes vital. Unless a company prefers chaos, it will make it clear that *responsibility for action is individual*. The Steering Arm may deliberate, theorize, discuss, and recommend as much as it will, but action should be by the members in their *individual* capacity. If the Steering Arm issues orders, the chain of command breaks down and no one knows who is his or her boss.

How then does the Steering Arm get things done? By convincing members and nonmembers that they should act in their individual capacity. This the Steering Arm does through its deliberations, through its minutes, its recommendations.

It may seem to be stressing a minor distinction to say that the Steering Arm members are acting in their individual capacity. But the distinction is major. No manager will sit back while a committee issues orders to his department. If he or she does, he or she ceases to be the manager.

The Steering Arm does have an important hand in developing a *plan* for follow-through. We will examine this plan shortly.

Solution Distinguished from Diagnosis

The diagnostic process aims at clarifying problems, testing theories, discovering causes. Finding a solution or remedy[1] is something else. When standard solutions are applied, the diagnostic process and the solving process can overlap extensively, and no one cares. But when a unique solution is needed, the distinction becomes quite important.

> We prove that yellow fever is transmitted by the sting of a mosquito. Now what? Shall we shield the human beings? Shall we develop a form of immunity? Shall we eradicate the mosquito? Any of these solutions is a huge undertaking, with extensive need for ingenuity as well as resources.

The need for solution through a stroke of ingenuity was brilliantly analyzed by one of the most profound management thinkers[2] of our century. Consider one of her cases.

> A cooperative of dairy farmers used a common platform for unloading their cans at the creamery. The platform could not accommodate all the farmers simultaneously, so some had to wait while others unloaded. The conflict was on which group of farmers should have precedence in unloading first—the hill farmers or the valley farmers.

Under the title of "Constructive Conflict," she defined three ways of resolving differences.

---

[1] Generally, "remedy" is a defensive act in response to an attack or threat. Solution is a more general answer to problems, whether offensive or defensive.

[2] Follett, Mary Parker, in H. C. Metcalf and L. Urwick (editors), "Dynamic Administration," Harper & Row, Publishers, Incorporated, New York, 1941.

1. *Domination.* Here one of the farmer groups would have scored a victory, and the other a defeat. But the conflict would not be over—the defeated group would keep the matter alive.
2. *Compromise,* i.e., the hill farmers are first one week and the valley farmers are first the next week. Here neither group is really satisfied.
3. *Integration.* A way was found to rearrange the platform so that both groups could unload simultaneously.

The essence of the true solution, integration, is that a brand-new approach, an invention, was worked out so that the conflict really disappeared. This is the ideal solution, and it requires an invention.

Consider a widespread problem in restaurants. Normally, the waitress starts by writing the customer's order down on an order blank. Now, the need is to transmit the order to the chef. When this is done verbally, a whole series of problems arises:

the chef's memory is taxed by so many orders.

the chef resents the personal orders and personal pressure of the waitress, who is "below him" in the restaurant pecking order.

the multiple orders create confusion as to priority.

the use of verbal orders denies the opportunity for tracing errors.

This list of problems is largely wiped out by use of a simple mechanical gadget, the "spindle." It is a drum to which the written orders can be clipped, in the same sequence as received from the customer. At one stroke, the problems of memory, priority, and responsibility for errors disappear. In addition, the orders to the chef are depersonalized—he or she no longer is ordered about by lower-caste employees.[3]

In this chapter we will examine the approach to solution and action in several classes of company problems:

action on the spectrum
action on the vital few
action on the useful many
action on state of mind

Whatever the class of problem, the need for ingenuity is paramount. Anything short of this can be illusory. That pleasant-sounding "let's

---

[3] For a delightful elaboration, see Porter, Elias H., "The Parable of the Spindle," *Harvard Business Review,* May–June, 1962, pp. 58–66.

agree to disagree" is especially illusory. It is decorous, and it may be painless, but it is also dead end.

Action on the Spectrum

The early drives to improve industrial safety soon identified *a spectrum of improvement*. There were individual processes which were very hazardous. There was also a general lack of safety-mindedness. The solution was to separate the components of the spectrum and to apply appropriate action to each:

> for the hazardous operations, the engineers designed and installed safeguards, each *tailor-made* for the particular operation.
>
> for the employee body generally, the personnel specialists devised psychological campaigns to improve safety-mindedness. There was nothing tailor-made about such campaigns—the identical treatment was given to all employees.

The spectrum of improvement is everywhere:

> cost of selling can be cut by a few big changes such as revising the channels of distribution; also by small changes from each of many people— better control of free samples, of expense accounts, of timetables.
>
> employee morale can be influenced by a big change such as adoption of a pension system; also by improving the attitude of each of many supervisors.
>
> quality can be improved by redesigning the product to eliminate basic faults; also by more care and fewer blunders by the numerous operators, handlers, etc.

Generally, the big changes are interdivisional in nature, requiring extensive staff work and high executive approval. In contrast, the small changes are generally the result of training and motivating the people down the line. See "Improving Mindedness," below.

Whether the spectrum is concerned with safety, or cost, or morale, or quality, or a thousand other matters, the basic question is the same: shall we deal with the components of the spectrum on a tailor-made basis or on a standardized basis?

The former consists of a case-by-case study and solution. The latter consists of a sweeping formula applied to many cases. Consider an example of a *spectrum of decision making*.

> At the end of World War II the American armed forces numbered about 10 million people. To demobilize these people required

10 million decisions on priority. Had these decisions been left to the subjective judgment of the officers, a chaotic result would have ensued. Instead, a point system was adopted—so many points for length of service, for dependents, for medals, etc. The point system made possible an automatic determination of priority for the vast majority of cases. (An individual's total points rendered a priority rating with respect to all other individuals.) Provision was made for appeal of hardship cases, which were then given individual study.

An emerging way of dealing with the spectrum of decision making is the model or formula. Formulas for Return on Investment, Economic Lot Size, Linear Programming, etc., can be structured to operate over a wide range of situations. The tables of delegation are to the same effect. There are pitfalls in all this:

the fact that some important intangibles cannot be reduced to numbers; e.g., what is the return on investment of the proposed employee cafeteria? the risk of being drugged by the authoritative appearance of the numbers when the assumptions underneath are arbitrary.

Throughout this book we have seen other cases of the presence of the spectrum—the size of customers' orders; the size of purchase orders; the amount of inventory; the degree of mass production vs. jobbing production. In these cases (and in other cases the reader can cite) the first need is likewise to determine whether the components of the spectrum should be given tailor-made or standard treatment. Breakup of the spectrum is often the answer.

A warehouse stocks many products. Some are in constant demand; others are slow movers. The engineers rearrange the warehouse so that picking the fast movers is automated; the slow movers continue to be manually picked. Result, a considerable improvement in service, accompanied by a cost reduction.

There are some other things which can be done about the spectrum. One is to cut down its excesses. This is not a matter of corking up creativity, but of providing the counterforces which will challenge the uneconomic excesses of variety. A most familiar example of a counterforce is standardization.

Department stores have been generally aware of the risks of excess variety. They have also generally adapted their merchandising techniques accordingly. "Thick on the best, thin on the rest." This rather gentle approach has been given a touch of the ruthless by the

Discount House, which cuts much further into the spectrum of variety. According to one study,[4] Macy's, a New York department store, at one time carried 139 styles of men's white dress shirts; Korvette, a discount house, carried 39. Macy's carried 19 sizes of flat sheets and 22 sizes of fitted sheets. Korvette carried 6 and 4, respectively. The Discounter's motto is stated as "Thick on the best, to hell with the rest."

The potentialities of standardization become most evident under the grim stresses of war. A hard look is taken at variety, and the results are amazing. The varieties of paint brushes are cut from 480 to 138; bed mattresses and springs from 78 to 4. In two airplanes of comparable weight, one is designed to use 601 kinds of bolts; the other, 73 kinds of bolts.

The forces of standardization do not eliminate variety—they do establish a better equilibrium between the cost and the value of variety. For the surviving variety, the need remains to determine whether the pattern of action is to be uniform or is to vary along the residual spectrum. The cost studies we met in Chap. 8 (Diagnosis) are essential to this determination. The tendency of the sales manager to widen the product line should be subject to:

full knowledge of the cost of carrying the tag end of the line

realistic spread of overheads, *not* per dollar of sales or direct cost, but based on the effort actually devoted by the overhead departments

Action on the Vital Few

The significant fact is that action is tailor-made for each of the vital few. Here are several items headlined in a program of damage control:[5]

One railroad gate was broken thirty times in one year. The gate was relocated, and there has been no damage since.

Materials-handling devices struck and damaged guard railings at the tops of seven shears thirty-eight times in one year. By using solid plate guards instead of railings, and by rounding off corners, the number of catch points was greatly reduced and damage was cut by 50 per cent.

[4]Silberman, Charles E., "The Revolutionists of Retailing," April, 1962. Courtesy of *Fortune* Magazine.

[5]Bird, Frank E., "Cost Improvement through Damage Control," *The Management Review*, March, 1962, pp. 26–30.

In 1960, 1,600 spindles on hand grinders had to be replaced. Analysis showed that at least 25 per cent of these replacements were caused by the unsafe practice of striking the locking nut to loosen it when removing the wheel. All grinders are now provided with a special band wrench; improvement in spindle quality and design also reduced breakage.

Such mechanical "fixes" are by now commonplace in our industrial civilization. This is so much the case that rivalries as to technical proficiency can obscure the different purposes of technical activity.

In the Dorf Company, the Process Development Department became increasingly bitter because "their" processes were changed by the Manufacturing Department. The developers were simply mistaken. In the laboratory, their approach properly emphasized technical feasibility. In the factory, the proper emphasis was manufacturing economics, quite a different matter.

A similar principle is used when we redesign a product for mass production. The redesigners are a breed of engineers different from the product developers, since again the emphasis turns to manufacturing economics from the original technical feasibility.

Preoccupation with the past is a serious drag on originality of action. The tendency is to take action by refining the past rather than by redesigning for the future; by grafting some change on to an existing system without rethinking the system. Putting the ox collar on the horse (p. 65) was an example. The early automobile inventors started with the available carriages and modified them to use an engine and transmission, instead of a horse. The basic redesigns came later.

The early silversmiths used a gravity-operated press to stamp the floral designs into sterling flatware. To obtain adequate striking force it was necessary to raise the stamp high in the air, manually, by pulleys. Even so, numerous restrikes were necessary. The resulting multiple impacts shortened the life of the dies, and introduced defects, but there was no other way, short of laborious hand engraving.

When electricity came along, the silversmiths harnessed an electric motor to the pulleys, and eliminated the tedious chore of hand raising the die. But they retained the gravity drop and its deficiencies (low die life, restrikes, inaccuracy, etc.). Had they gone to a fully powered short-stroke press, they would have secured far more benefit from use of electric power.

Such problems of action are by no means confined to technical matters. They extend to all functions in the company.

> The Payson company successfully marketed a cosmetic product (we will call it MELL) after many other companies had failed. Sales rose rapidly, and Payson had virtually all of the market.
>
> When important competitors began to invade the market, sales of MELL fell as to per cent share of market. Payson's top management was in a state of alarm. There was much talk of refining the past—more promotion, changes in the product, etc. But they also set out to discover why customers would switch from MELL to some other product. They learned, through market research, that on such cosmetic products, customers could be persuaded to experiment.
>
> Payson turned this bad news to good account by putting out a new product (we will call it PELL) to compete with its own MELL (see Fig. 13). PELL took sales away from all else on the market, including MELL. Payson's share of the market rose thereby.

The need for ingenuity, for freedom from the shackles of the past, is just as great in defensive Breakthrough as in aggressive Breakthrough. To be sure, the shackles are strong (the habits and beliefs more than the investment). Our industrial history teems with instances in which a new business idea by competitors has been fought, not by finding a better business idea, but by open warfare. It is a delaying action at best, and utter nonsense in the long run.

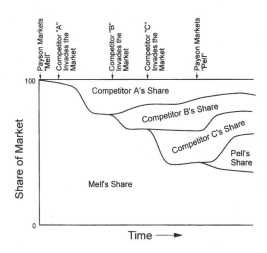

Fig. 13. An ingenious solution.

Action on the Useful Many

One aspect of the spectrum is an enormous industrial problem—how to deal with the myriads of things which individually are not important enough to command individual attention. These myriads of things we had labeled the "useful many," and we had sort of left them to their fate back in Chap. 4.

We now return to these useful many, for a most important reason: *Industry is wasting a lot of money on the useful many.* This waste is commonly the result of using, for the useful many, procedures which can be justified only for the important few.

Let's look at a series of cases:

Unprofitable products.[6] In one company, 19 of the 39 products in the line produced only 3 per cent of the total sales. When 18 of these 19 were eliminated, cost of selling was cut by 45 per cent and volume of sales was increased by 366 per cent, all in a few years.

Unprofitable customers.[7] In one company, 41 per cent of the customers, bringing in only 7 per cent of the sales, were found to be unprofitable. Over several years, most of these customers were dropped. During this period, sales increased 76 per cent, selling costs were cut in half, and a new loss of 2.9 per cent on sales was converted into a net profit of 15 per cent.

The following news item appeared in *The New York Times* on May 12, 1962:

Bank Here Drops the Small Saver

The Lafayette National Bank of Brooklyn announced yesterday that it would quit paying interest on savings accounts of less than $500, starting July 1.

[6]These and other good cases are contained in an excellent pamphlet, "How Manufacturers Reduce Their Distribution Costs," U.S. Department of Commerce, Economic Series No. 72, Superintendent of Documents, Washington, D.C.

Incidental note: When the author wrote to the Superintendent of Documents, a small excess in money was returned to him as coupons, with the following note evidencing a full grasp of the principle of the useful many:

COUPON INFORMATION

Because of the cost of writing Government checks for small sums, it is the policy of this Office to make all refunds of less than $1.00 in the form of special coupons having a face value of 5 cents each, which may be used as the equivalent of cash in making future purchases of publications sold by the Division of Public Documents. These coupons are good until used, and have been found highly satisfactory by thousands of users of Government publications each year. However, if you do not anticipate purchasing publications in the future, these coupons will be promptly redeemed upon request.

Superintendent of Documents

[7]"How Manufacturers Reduce Their Distribution Costs," *op. cit.*

The announcement of the change in the bank's policy was made in newspaper advertisements that advised depositors of less than $500 to transfer their funds "to a savings institution of your choice."

An executive of the bank said that the decision was based on an analysis that found small accounts to be "highly unprofitable."

Charles Kitlitz, executive vice president, said that 60 per cent of the bank's time and savings deposits were affected. But, he noted, each account involved "very small sums." Two-thirds were accounts of less than $100, he said.

Unprofitable orders.[8] A company discovered that most of the orders received from 57 per cent of its customers were unprofitable—they were small orders, accounting for only 2.7 per cent of the total sales. As a corollary, more than 90 per cent of the sales effort was being spent on less than 10 per cent the sales. The unprofitable business was dropped.

In the foregoing cases, the useful many were dropped. The companies had no provisions for handling them economically. But there are other solutions.

One of these solutions is to create a separate economic procedure to handle the useful many exclusively. The sandwich line at the cafeteria, the express checkout counter at the supermarket, and the vending machine for standard products are good examples. They provide fast, inexpensive service for small sales without clogging up the channels of personal service for larger sales.

Some entire businesses and even industries have been set up to deal with the useful many. The original 5- and 10-cent store was an example. The vending-machine industry is a more recent example.

It is when the useful many are present in the same house with important matters that the problem is at its worst.[9] The important matters require procedures adequate to meet their needs, and underscore this requirement by a dramatic catastrophe or two. These procedures then are used for the useful many, with an undramatic and hidden loss.

It is possible for the useful many to live in the same house with the vital few, but the respective procedures must be different. A well-studied example has been the ABC system for inventory control.

Let us take a specific example. In the B-36 bomber armament turret system, major or "A" items are only 2 per cent in number but ac-

---

[8] "How Manufacturers Reduce Their Distribution Costs," *op, cit.*

[9] It seldom starts out that way. The company starts on a simpler mixture. But the drive for growth brings variety along with size.

count for 92 per cent of the cost, while the small "C" items make up 92 per cent of the items but amount to only 4 per cent of the cost. Here the area for effective controls and economies is fairly obvious.

The very numerous but inexpensive "C" items must be handled economically, even stingily, for they probably make up three-quarters of the number of items or records handled by the buyers, order clerks, record clerks, stockkeepers, inspectors, etc. Since a large and safe protective stock can be carried quite economically, detailed analysis of order quantities and schedules can be dropped. You might first order six months' or a year's supply, seal up an adequate amount for an order point quantity, and keep no receipts, withdrawals, or other clerical records for this 75 per cent of your stock items until the day the stockkeeper must break the seal on the order quantity package and send the attached notice to the office. One of our Canadian plants, which established this routine for its "C" items, found that it cut stock postings on one line alone from 17,000 to 1,500 per year and reduced its personnel by one-half.[10]

The above case is based on erecting a procedure fence to separate the useful many from the rest. There are other ways. The fence may be physical—a separate department is set up to handle small orders, which then do not travel the long, elaborate routine of the important orders. The fence may be personal—a petty-cash buyer is set up to handle small purchases without extensive paperwork.

The small-order problem has been studied exhaustively.[11] Aside from turning down this business, companies:

try to reduce the cost of handling small orders

charge the customer at least part of the extra cost

try to change the customer's buying habits

Some of the solutions arrived at for the useful many seem nonsensical on principle, though they are well founded on cost studies. There is, for example, the case of not charging customers for goods shipped:

> If you were to place an order for under $0.50 with a well-known Canadian company, you would receive the goods plus a form letter as follows: "We have sent you the goods you have ordered. Please accept these with our compliments, as it does not pay us to bill cus-

---

[10]Dickie, H. Ford, "Key Considerations in Inventory Management," American Management Association, Manufacturing Series, No. 207, pp. 10–15, 1953.

[11]See, for a research study, "Small Orders: Problems and Solutions," National Industrial Conference Board Studies in Business Policy, No. 94, 1960. See also, "How Manufacturers Reduce Their Distribution Costs," *op. cit.*

tomers for small amounts. In turn, may we ask that your future small orders be placed with your local dealer."

In like manner, some companies will pay small claims without checking their validity. The cost of the investigation is many times the loss due to paying invalid claims.

Actually, the "principles" violated in this chapter:

turning down business
not charging for goods
paying unverified claims

are valid only as applied to important matters. For these important matters, the costs are amortized by the benefits. At the level of the useful many this is no longer the case. The "principle" was not really valid over the entire spectrum.

To summarize the action pattern on the useful many:

the useful many must be dealt with *en masse*—individual treatment is a waste.

the procedural approach for dealing with the useful many must be specially designed for economy and simplicity. If an economical, simple procedure violates some "principle" it is likely that the principle is invalid in the range of the useful many.

when the useful many live in the same house with the important matters, all solutions require a separate treatment for the useful many to avoid waste.

Increasing "Mindedness"

A common form of action is a "drive" to increase "mindedness," i.e., safety-mindedness, cost-mindedness, quality-mindedness, etc. There are lots of such drives. Most of them are duds. Some are stunning successes. There is a good explanation for this contrast.

A drive on "mindedness" assumes that the people involved have been provided by management with all the essentials of industrial responsibility:

(*a*) They know what they are supposed to do (about safety, or cost, or quality, etc.)

(*b*) They know what they are in fact doing.

(*c*) They have in their power the means to change what they are doing; i.e., they have the goggles, tools, instruments, etc.

Having these three essentials (goes the assumption behind the "drive"), all that stands between these people and high safety, cost, or quality, is the will to make use of them. It is this will which is inadequate (runs the assumption). Hence the drive is needed to step up the attention devoted to the subject in question.

The success or failure of a drive hinges on whether this key assumption is well founded. If the management has not provided *all* of these three essentials, the drive is doomed to failure. It may even backfire by subjecting the management to ridicule. If, however, the assumption is well-founded, then a drive may be fruitful. Here it is necessary to follow a well-worn trail:

1. Set up a steering group to organize the drive. In addition to line supervision, this group should include (*a*) Personnel, since they preside over so many channels of company communication, (*b*) the score-keepers (Safety, Accounting, Inspection, etc.) associated with the subject matter, and (*c*) Advertising, since the methods for selling something internally have much in common with selling something to customers.

2. Convince the people of the importance of safety, cost, quality, or whatever. The poster campaigns, slogan contests, give-aways, etc., generally do a superb job of convincing people that this subject is important to them.

3. Show everyone how to contribute to safety, etc. This cannot be done by sweeping slogans. *It must be tailor-made for each "different" department, perhaps for each individual.* There must be enough of this detail to answer the question of the people—"Granted that safety is important to me. But I just work here. What can I do about it?"

4. Solicit people's ideas, to give a sense of participation as well as to benefit from these ideas.

5. Establish goals for improvement, and a scoreboard to follow progress. Lacking these things, no one has any idea of whether the drive is doing anything useful.

6. Follow through to hold the new levels. See that new techniques get into the written procedures. Train new people and retrain the old in use of these new ways.

At its worst, the drive is a form of management threshing about from one crisis to another. Each drive swings the pendulum wildly to another extreme, resulting in a new unbalance, and requiring a new drive. This can go on and on.

At its best, the drive is a short cut to putting people in a state of self-supervision and self-motivation. The state is well described by the term "law of the situation," a phrase coined by Mary Parker Follett[12] to summarize the basic impersonal forces—competition, price cuts, product obsolescence, recessions, etc. These impersonal forces are pushing everyone around—the president, the managers, the supervisors, the rank and file. The company has no choice. It must obey these impersonal forces much as it must obey a law, hence the term "law of the situation." Under this concept there are no bosses or bossed, since all are subordinate to the law.

> Consider, for example, the "organization" of the people concerned with traffic in a large city. Many categories of people are involved—pedestrians, cyclists (especially in Europe), motorists, policemen, magistrates. There is much activity. Yet to an astonishing degree, people remain on the proper side of the road, obey the signals, avoid collisions, all without a supervisory hierarchy. The "boss" (the traffic laws) is impersonal, and all are subordinate to these laws.

Plan for Follow-through

We have now moved through a sequence of activities (and chapter headings). This sequence started with changing of attitudes toward Breakthrough and has taken us to the action stage. The intervening steps were a planned approach[13] toward Breakthrough. Two problems now remain:

1. Seeing to it that the action is taken. This is the transition stage to the new level of performance. This we will discuss in Chap. 11.
2. Seeing to it that the new level of performance does not slip back. This is "Control," and we will discuss it in the second half of this book.

[12]In Metcalf, Henry C., and L. Urwick (editors), "Dynamic Administration," pp. 58–64, Harper & Row, Publishers, Incorporated, New York, 1941.

[13]The management literature makes a somewhat different division of the subject of planning, as follows: forecasting, breakdown of the objectives, organization (assignment of responsibilities), selection and training of people, provision of facilities, a timetable, provision for measuring results, and provision for revising plans.

11 TRANSITION TO THE NEW LEVEL

The Nature of Transition

Taking action is not a matter of throwing a switch so that today we are on one level, and tomorrow on another. It is a whole series of events. These must be taken in proper sequence, with ratchets dropped in along the way to prevent slipping back. The series of events includes:

designing for dissemination. Thus far, only the Steering Arm has been completely informed. Now it becomes necessary to bring numerous people into the act. This requires that tools and procedures be designed for wide use.

training in use of the tools and procedures.

providing for continuity. Very likely the old must remain available until the new is debugged.

following progress to see that the planned sequence of events stays on course, and to deal with unforeseen obstacles.

disengaging the Steering Arm when the regular organization has acquired a firm grip.

Turn-key Transition

A move to a new house would be ever so much easier were it furnished, cleaned up, and ready for living before the people move in. You just drive up and turn the key. The Steering Arm can help provide such a "turnkey" transition by working out an agreed, ready-to-operate procedure.

The make or buy example is a case in point. The Steering Arm made a good contribution by thinking the problem through. Then they made the transition easy by providing a prefabricated procedure (Fig. 12) for evaluating make or buy instances and for approvals. It was a turn-key job, and the new tenants moved in pretty smoothly.

A related example is the method used by chain drugstores to conduct their "promotions" of merchandise. All is geared to the calendar (Fig. 14). The store manager's calendar dictates when to change displays, when to reduce stock of suntan lotion, when to amplify stocks of sporting goods. September is return-to-school month; so school supplies are promoted from Sept. 1 to 15. The month's calendar also provides for special bonuses (of various percentages) for extra sales of branded razor blades, weight-reducing plans, headache powders, etc. Such a calendar not only informs and motivates the store managers; even before this it is the basis of coordinating the work of the competing specialists at headquarters.

The job to be done is to "package" the principles and concepts developed by the Steering Arm in such a way that the many people who did

Fig. 14. The calendar as a prefabricated plan.

not sit in on the meetings can nevertheless make daily use of these principles and concepts. The "package" may consist of a form to be executed, a check list for count down, a table of numbers, a formula, a manual. The package may deal with matters of make or buy, return on investment, economic lot size, quality control sampling.

Each package is a unique project, affecting various departments, and demanding use of special staff skills. But the problems of transition are identical. In all cases there is the need to design the new procedure, to test it, to plan the transition, to train the people, and to patrol or audit the resulting changes.

Training

The steering team has devoted hours of discussion, over months of calendar time, to arrive at a new way of doing things. It is all too easy to forget that others in the company have not had the advantage of this depth of deliberation, over so long a period of time. In consequence, the value of the findings of the steering team may be lost through inadequate indoctrination of those who are to make these findings effective.

For introducing a broad change which is to affect the many, a training manual serves many useful purposes. It forces the Steering Arm to simplify its approach by reducing any complexities to simple tools and procedures.

In the 1920s there surged up a wave of interest in the economics of lot sizes, inventory order points, and related matters. Formulas proliferated to a point that the American Society of Mechanical Engineers sponsored a study to clear up the confusion. The result was the formula

$$Q = \sqrt{\frac{FPY_a}{c'i\left[kP - Y_a\left(\frac{1 - 1/n}{2}\right)\right] + c'iY_a\frac{Kp}{a'} + vB[P - Y_a(1 - 1/n)]}}$$

The idea that the factory order clerks of that day would use such a formula was simply fantastic. The whole movement died down and was not really revived until a generation later.

The conceptual approach in training must be geared to the nature of the change. Substituting formulas for rule of thumb requires ingenuity in devising special forms, tables, slide rules, nomograms, and other devices for painless use.[1]

A basic change in managerial approach can require some elaborate training.

> Hutson, a large company in the container business, undertook a broad change to "direct costing." It also broadened its concepts of the role of the supervisor in profit planning. To help introduce this change, training books were printed up to show, step by step, how the new concepts were to work. Formal training programs were used to convey the approach to all levels of supervision.

Judicious use of artwork is of great aid. Flow diagrams are most helpful to show departmental personnel the interdepartmental scheme. Cartoons reduce the tensions which have sometimes built up (Fig. 15). They help to liven up the material as exemplified by the classic cartoon Fig. 15—reminiscent of Dickens' era.

When the need is to broaden the company's base of diagnosis, analysis, or special skills, a training program becomes a must. In a sense, we become engaged in training "one-person gangs" who combine the func-

[1]The alternative, of giving courses in higher mathematics to the rank and file, has been tried many times, with uniformly disastrous results.

Let's see! *It takes so long to do this and so long to do that, we have to stop so long here, so long there, etc., etc.*

A delivery promise is a date for the Shipping Department to meet.

The rest of us have to start weeks ahead in order to get the job through the mill on time.

No single foreman can make a delivery promise, he can only vouch for how long it will take him to do his job, after he gets material. No material, no work!

Someone has to know how much work is involved in a new order, how long it takes for each operation, and how long it takes to move material between operations, in order to figure out when the first operation must begin.

How long do you think it would take us to get a delivery promise to New York if every foreman had to be contacted?

We can't wait that long! Someone has to make a schedule which CAN be met; let us know what each of us is expected to do, and, we all HAVE TO BACK HIM UP!

WE GOTTA MAKE THE SCHEDULE!!

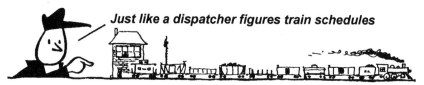

Just like a dispatcher figures train schedules

Fig. 15. Livening up the training manual.

tions of the Steering Arm and the Diagnostic Arm in one person. The programs of "Work Simplification" were of this nature.

The opportunities in such programs are exciting in the highest. They are a form of helping technology and know-how flow downhill. Few needs in industry are so acute.

> When the author was a youngster in industry, the Measurement Laboratory was a place which commanded profound respect. You took the specimen there and waited in silence while the person in the white coat took the wraps off the instrument, made the measurement, and prepared the report. Today, those mystic instruments—the optical projector, the Rockwell hardness tester, the air gage, etc., are in common use all over the factory floor. The instruments have been simplified and employees have become more sophisticated.

Irreversible and Reversible Changes

In the process of transition, some irreversible steps have been taken. The old machine, the old tool, are gone. There is no going back to them. They have been sold for junk. There is an iron finality to such irreversible changes.

Other changes possess no such iron finality. The changes in human procedures, in duties, responsibilities, organization charts, etc., may turn out to be just so much paper. Unless these changes are made effective, the transition is only partial. It may even be nonsensical, since we may find ourselves trying to operate the new facilities with procedures designed for the old.

An important signal on reversible changes is given by management itself—Does it, by example, show it means business?

> Look at two experiences in use of Return on Investment. Both companies concluded that ROI should be the basis of decisions on capital expenditures. Both companies devised forms to facilitate the calculations. Both announced the new party line: from now on, this is the road we will follow. At this point, their paths diverged.
>
> Company A set up training meetings in which the procedures and the reasons behind them were explained. Employees were required to work out examples and to discuss their significance. The first person who tried to bypass the procedure was told "I won't even listen to you until you put your figures together." The procedure took hold.

Company B did none of this, and the stage was set for a failure. The really decisive move came when one manager, impatient with the new procedure, went to his superior and sold his project without the figures. The flimsy wall had been breached, and other unsold managers gleefully poured through the opening. The procedure was dead.

Retaining reversibility is not pure evil. If the old ways are discarded before the new is proved, chaos can move in. Numerous programs of electronic data processing have fallen into this trap. The manual records were abolished before the new system was debugged. Result—no management reports, foul-ups in production control, inventory management, customer service, etc. When continuity is essential, the old should be retained until the new is firmly in the saddle.

The Audit

When a change is reversible, there are many reasons which tempt an individual to go back to the old ways. When many people are involved, it is inevitable that some will try a reversal. Their reasons may be meritorious or misguided, or just testing to see what happens.

In many reversals nothing happens because no one in authority realizes that the change has been reversed. As one person "gets away" with it, another tries it. The number increases, and the time goes on, until the original change has disappeared without a trace.

The need here is to plug an instrument into the situation to detect these reversals. If no mechanical instrument is available, a human instrument must be used. In factory processes this individual is known as a patrol inspector. In office procedures he or she is the auditor. His or her job is to examine the practices, to see if they conform to the procedures, and to report on the departures.

This patrol or audit need not be a frequent thing. Procedures change slowly, and audits at a frequency of monthly or so will detect anything really serious. As the new procedures become rooted, the audit can be reduced in frequency.

Enter Control

Up to this point, our discussion of the Breakthrough cycle has made no reference to Control. Now it is timely to establish a connection.

We defined Control as staying on course, adherence to standard, prevention of change. But a plan for Breakthrough, to be successful, requires that we adhere to the plan, which in turn requires that we *keep the plan on course,* meet the targets or goals of the plan, prevent outside forces from damaging the plan.

So, even during the execution of a plan of change, we find it necessary to use the tools of Control to keep the program of change on course. Once the changes have been made effective, the tools of Control are again needed, this time to hold the gains achieved.

Control, then, is not synonymous with preventing a change from past history. It is more nearly synonymous with *preventing a change from planned performance.* Where the plan is to follow past history (as it often is), Control becomes the means of preventing a departure from history. But if the plan is to break with history, Control becomes the means of keeping this break on course.

Staying on course, then, applies to both:

(*a*) Adhering to a plan for creating change.

(*b*) Adhering to a plan for preventing change.

Some authorities use the single word "control" to designate both forms of staying on course. We probably need new wording to distinguish these two, such as:

(*a*) Aggressive control, the means by which we adhere to a plan for creating change.

(*b*) Defensive control, the means by which we adhere to a plan for preventing change.

The similarities between aggressive control and defensive control are so great that this book deals with both simultaneously. Chapters 12 through 20 are devoted to Control, whether aggressive or defensive.

Exit the Steering Arm

Unless the Steering Arm is meant to have a continuing association with the subject matter (e.g., New Products Committee), means must be provided for letting go of projects once Breakthrough has been achieved. The baton should be released when it is clear that the next person has a firm grip on it.

There is a value in formalizing this change-over. The minutes of the Steering Arm should show that the item has been dropped from the agenda. Other usual signals are the formal approval of a new procedure, the delivery of a new tool, the issuance of a new organization chart, etc.

And So on to Control

Once the new performance levels have been reached, we have done with Breakthrough and with transition. The job now is to hold the new level, to prevent change. The next nine chapters are devoted to this job.

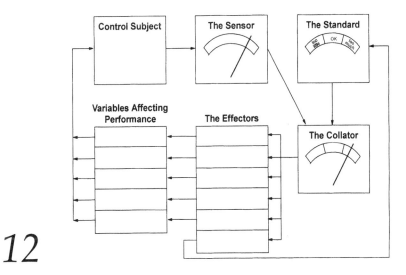

12

CONTROL—A PANORAMIC VIEW

What Is So Important about Control?

The opening chapter of this book discussed the importance of "Control" and included a definition of Control—"staying on course, adhering to standards, prevention of change."

The great importance of Control lies in the fact that there are literally millions of things for which we must stay on course, adhere to standards, prevent change.

The Apex company, a maker of automotive replacement parts, employs 350 employees, with sales in the $5 to 10 million range annually. Look at the numbers of things which must be controlled.

First as to customer relations. Apex has 3,000 customers with whom it maintains contact on about a dozen fronts—catalogues, prices, credit, etc. Result, about 36,000 things to control.

Second, as to customer orders. There are 20,000 of these annually, averaging about 5 "lines" each. About 100,000 things must go through the steps of selection and billing. The 20,000 orders require assembly, packing, shipping, credit, accounts receivable. A total of about 300,000 things to control.

Next, as to accounting. 25,000 checks are written annually. Half of these go to pay the 350 employees their salary or their earnings on the 3,000 active piecework standards, after deducting a variety of taxes and adding a variety of fringes. Other checks are written to pay the 300 vendors for the 5,000 purchase orders issued annually. Costs are collected from 17,000 time cards, 6,000 job orders, and 20,000 material requisitions. A total of 21 burden centers aids in preparing statements based on 450 fixed asset accounts and 150 general ledger accounts. About $1/2$ *million* bits of information must be kept under control.

We are only warming up. Let us turn to control of quality in this small company. For any manufacturing company "quality" is something to be controlled—it is one of the main reasons the customers buy the product. How many subcontrols lie behind the control of quality?

Apex makes or buys about 1,000 different parts, components, or materials. Each of these involves about 10 qualities to be met. However, the total number of such pieces of product made and shipped runs to 170 *million* (Apex is a mass-production shop). So there are about *1.7 billion* individual qualities to be controlled.

In our discussion of Apex, we have omitted hundreds of thousands of things requiring control, i.e., the inventory controls, the production timetables, the process controls, the cost system, the budgeting system, the personnel program, the purchasing function, the engineering function. We have not reckoned with all the changes which pour in on Apex daily. Customers change their needs, resulting in cancellations, rescheduling, overtime; engineers change the designs, with a resulting flurry of activity in tools, processes, work standards, gages; new legislation results in different taxes, rules for doing business; competitor action requires changes in prices, channels of sale, methods of promotion.

There is no need to labor the point. Even the small company has an immense number of things to regulate. Failure to regulate these inevitably causes pain—to the customers, the employees, the vendors, the tax collectors, the owners, the company itself.

Now let us take a second look at Apex. The supervisory hierarchy consists of:

1	president
3	vice-presidents
29	managers and supervisors
33	total

These 33 bosses, with the 300 or so nonbosses, have the problem of regulating myriads of things each year. They do a good job of it— Apex is a successful company. How do they do it?

The Unvarying Control
Cycle—The Feedback[1] Loop

Apex does this immense amount of regulation through one basic device—
the feedback loop. This is no new invention—it is billions of years old.

> Apex, with 350 employees and a few billion things to regulate, is
> dwarfed by one biological organism. The human being, for exam-
> ple, has about a *million billion* living cells. Each of these cells is a
> chemical factory more complex than the entire Du Pont Company;
> so it has plenty to control. In spite of this unbelievable complexity,
> this vast collection of cells acts as one unified organism. This or-
> ganism does its amazing job of digesting food, replacing dead cells,
> maintaining the blood counts, etc., by employing an incredible ar-
> ray of feedback loops.[2]

In the biological organism, each of these feedback loops is associated
with some control subject important to the organism, e.g., body temperature.

For each of these control subjects, the organism has evolved a full set
of devices out of which it builds a closed loop. These devices are:

1. A sensing device (sensor or receptor) for detecting or measuring
   what is going on. The resulting information is transmitted to

2. A control center (collator) which compares what is going on to some
   concept of standard. The control center then issues orders to

3. A motor device (effector) which takes action to bring results into line
   with standard.

For example—the organism backs into a hot radiator. Heat-sensitive
receptors detect the temperature, and signal this to a "local" control center. The center analyzes the information, concludes that "this is quite
different from standard," and issues orders to various muscles, "Let's
get out of here."[3]

The human race, a comparative newcomer on earth, has reinvented
the feedback loop and now makes wide use of it. This usage is wide-

---

[1] Feedback—the giving (feeding back) of information about the control subject to some
analysis mechanism which then uses the information for decision making.

[2] If the readers would understand "control" in depth, let them study the nervous system
of biological organisms.

[3] Happily, all this takes place in less time than is required to explain it.

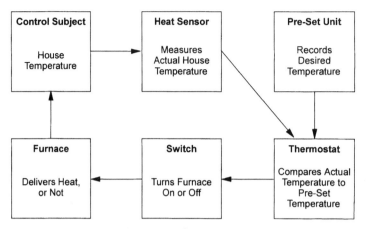

Fig. 16. Feedback loop for control of temperature.

spread among engineers with their controllers, regulators, and servo-mechanisms.

A useful way to see the feedback loop is in block-diagram form. Figure 16 shows this diagram applied to regulating the house temperature. A heat sensor measures actual temperature and feeds the information to a thermostat which compares actual temperature to the preset value. If the difference is greater than tolerance, action is taken to start the furnace.

Of course, our interest lies in managerial control. Here we find that the manager likewise has reinvented the feedback loop and makes extensive use of it. The manager's feedback loop exhibits an unvarying sequence of events which is logically cut up into eight steps.[4] During this chapter we will look briefly at each of these steps and at their interrelationship. In Chaps. 13 through 20 we will examine these steps in detail. The sequence is as follows:

1. *Choose the "control subjects."* This is a choice of what we intend to regulate, i.e., the level of sales, accidents, quality complaints, expenses, etc. For any chosen control subject, we create the remaining series of activities of the control cycle.

---

[4]It may seem to some readers that it is slicing things pretty fine to cut the control cycle up into so many pieces. The reason is simple. Other than in very small companies, these steps are all taken by different people or even different departments in the same company.

2. *Define a unit of measure.* Experience shows that we communicate poorly with each other if we talk of keeping levels of sales "high," accidents "low," quality "good," etc. These adjectives mean different things to different people, and the result is confusion, irritation, and animosity. By creating units of measure, we can describe these levels in numbers instead of adjectives. Our communication then improves sharply, and the attention shifts from debates on the meaning of adjectives to the real job at hand.

3. *Establish a standard* level of performance in terms of the unit of measure. As we shall see, we are not limited to history in choosing a standard. The standard may come from engineering studies, from competitors, from plans for Breakthrough. Whatever the source, the standard becomes the level we are trying to hold.

4. *Create sensory devices* for measuring actual performance in terms of the unit of measure. Sensory devices may be mechanical instruments, sales reports, cash-register tapes, copies of shipping papers, etc. Whatever form they take, they are able to read actual performance in terms of the unit of measure.

5. *Mobilize for measurement.* Create the organizational and mechanical machinery for using the sensory devices to measure and report actual performance. This organizational machinery may be very simple (a shop inspector to read an instrument) or quite complex (a cost accounting department).

6. *Compare actual performance with standard.* This comparison goes on at all levels of the company. The shop operator compares his gage reading with the blueprint tolerance. The district sales manager compares his or her sales with forecast. The plant manager compares his shipments against schedule. The Board of Directors compares the month's actual profit against budgeted profit.

7. *Decide on action needed* in view of the difference between actual and standard performance. The range of decision is wide. Do nothing at all. Investigate further. Change the target. Revise the process. Get rid of the district manager.

8. *Take the action.* This may be as simple as twisting a knurled knob on a machine, or as complex as revising a major business procedure.

In this sequence of events, steps 1 through 5 are preparatory. They set the stage for the repetitive regulation which is to follow. Steps 6 through 8 are repetitive—they cycle over and over again.

This fundamental sequence is followed in every instance of managerial Control.

Figure 17 shows the diagram as applied to control of expenses.

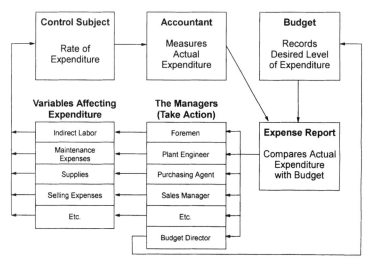

Fig. 17. Feedback loop for control of expenses.

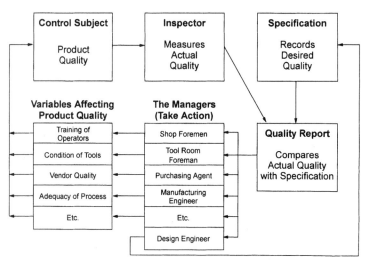

Fig. 18. Feedback loop for control of quality.

Figure 18 shows the corresponding control of quality.

Figure 19 shows the corresponding control of deliveries against schedule.

These diagrams remind one of a Shakespearean play being given in New York, Paris, Moscow, and Tokyo. The actors are different; the languages are different; but the same play is being acted out!

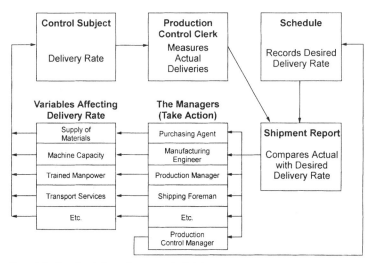

Fig. 19. Feedback loop for control of deliveries.

The essential identity of these feedback loops can be depicted by labeling the loop with generalized terms, as in Fig. 20. This universal nature of the feedback loop is the basis of the oft-repeated conclusion: *If you know how to control, you can control anything.*[5]

The Control Pyramid

If the foregoing is indeed the universal cycle for control, how can a little company possibly go through this cycle billions of times per year? It does so by adopting some ingenious short cuts:

1. The company designs its procedures and processes to be nearly *foolproof* and to do repetitive acts with high precision. This makes it possible to run the process for a long time without provision for intermittent regulation.

---

[5]If we were dealing with one control cycle, one feedback loop, our story would be delightfully simple. It would also be of little practical value. The industrial complex involves myriads of feedback loops. The same sensor feeds data to a wide variety of usage stations, each of which receives data from a wide variety of sensors. Meeting a standard is not a simple either/or; it is a problem of balance against meeting many other, related standards.

So in talking of the single control cycle we are talking only of the isolated, laboratory model. We derive much philosophic and academic knowledge from studying this pure model. But the real world of control teems with complexity, errors, short cuts, departures from theory.

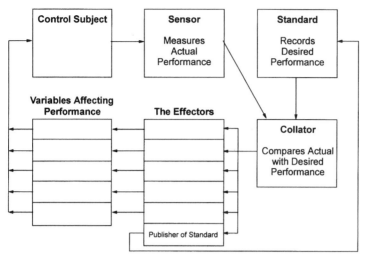

Fig. 20. Feedback loop for control of anything.

An Apex stamping tool knocks out 100,000 good pieces without stopping. A street traffic signal cycles "stop" and "go" for months on end. A gasoline engine purrs through its four-cycle routine millions of times.

2. The company makes extensive use of *automatic control*. Here the feedback loop operates without human participation. (The automatic control for regulating house temperature is an example.) Human effort is needed only in the programming and in the periodic maintenance of the hardware.

In part, these automatic controls are cost-reduction devices. But in part they must be used because no human being can equal their performance. In such things as automatic process control, missile flight guidance, and sophisticated production controls, the human beings are not sufficiently swift, accurate, and reliable to be able to do the job. Some Asian countries which have bought factories (such as an oil refinery) actually wanted to eliminate the automatic controls and substitute the less costly (to them) manpower which abounds there. But it couldn't be done—the factory couldn't be operated at all unless the automatic controls went with it.

At this point, we might view the number of things to be controlled as a broad-based five-layered pyramid (Fig. 21). The two bottom layers have already been taken care of through foolproofing and through automatic control. Through these means the number of things to be con-

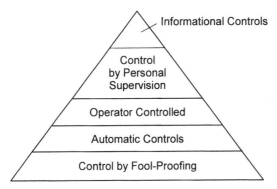

Fig. 21. The Control pyramid.

trolled has been cut down to size so that human regulation can take it from there. The human regulation now takes several forms.

3. The company does most of the human regulation through *operator*[6] *control* right at the firing line. The operator, the clerk, the salesperson, are provided with simple means for self-regulation.

> The Apex shop operator has: a specification; gages to tell him whether he is meeting specification; levers for regulating the process based on the gage readings. Here the operator himself closes the feedback loop.

4. The company superimposes a layer of *personal supervision* on top of the operator control at the firing line. This supervision is done by direct observation. The supervisor (foreman, inspector, auditor) closes a separate feedback loop.

5. The company arranges to provide the managers with summarized reports on important topics. This *informational control* is at the peak of the five-layered pyramid. Here the manager himself or herself closes the feedback loop.

> The Apex executives get their information on quality mainly from summarized reports on:
>
> customer quality complaints, returns, and claims
>
> quality of product compared to competitors
>
> cost of inspection and test
>
> cost of scrap, rework, other quality failures

---

[6]The word "operator" is used here in the sense of any nonsupervisor who is assigned to regulate some process.

The five layers are seen to be quite different in their design for control and in the manner of closing the feedback loop. (The informational control exercised by the manager is particularly intricate, as we shall see in due course.)

Delegation through Self-Control

What we have traced is a kind of plan of *delegation*. Despite the enormous number of things to be controlled, the great bulk is done with little human intervention. The residue is then pyramided so that the manager is left with only a reasonable number of things to regulate.

In making this delegation we have again borrowed from biology.

The biological organisms, while making use of an incredible number of control mechanisms, "delegate" the operation of these way down in the organization scale. The great majority of control in these organisms is "autonomic," i.e., it takes place without conscious acts by the General Headquarters (GHQ) of the organism. Digestion of food, keeping up the blood count, building cells for maintenance, etc., all take place in profusion. But the organism doesn't need to do any conscious thinking about these things—they take place autonomically.

The Control cycle is then not merely a neat means for holding a performance on an even keel. It is also a device (*the* device) for "self-supervision," "management by objectives," "impersonal supervision." All these terms add up to relieving the boss of the need for conscious supervision of most of the myriads of humble activities so necessary to keep things going. The boss who grumbles about the effort invested in setting up controls should keep in mind the dividends he or she gets in freedom from all that repetitive detail. In like manner, the subordinate who regards Control as a form of restraint (which, to a degree, it certainly is) should keep in mind that, in accepting regulation by the Control cycle, he avoids much personal, subjective regulation by the boss. It is a good trade, often enough.

This delegation is not done by the simple process of telling someone "You control these." Delegation is meaningless unless we have first created the conditions prerequisite to "self-control." To make it possible for individuals to exercise self-control we must provide the means for:

1. Knowing what are their objectives
2. Knowing whether they are meeting their objectives
3. Changing their performance in the event they are not meeting their objectives

All of these conditions must be met, *without exception.* Only then can we properly hold an individual "responsible" for meeting his or her objectives.

Once these conditions are met, self-control can be turned over to anyone or anything: a general manager; a functional manager; a supervisor; a nonsupervisor; an inanimate mechanism. The sequence of events by which any of these persons (or nonpersons) achieves control is, of course, the feedback loop.

The elegance of the self-control principle has resulted in a proliferation of plans to put managers, supervisors, and nonsupervisors in a state of self-control. This has been overdone; e.g., people have been told "You are responsible for profit" (or volume or whatever) when a lot of the responsibility is fictional. But let's look at some cases at various levels. We will start at the top and work our way down.

The general manager. This individual is put in charge of a profit center or division of the company. He has broad responsibility over design, manufacture, and marketing of the product, including command of the respective departments. He also commands some but not all of the supporting services. He does not have the full latitude that is enjoyed by the head of an independent company, but he has a lot to say. When we tell the general manager "You are responsible for profit," we are more right than wrong. When we go a step further and tell him "We will make your bonus depend on this profit," we are on sound ground.

The product manager. This person is a planner and coordinator for a particular product or market. He or she has the main voice as to some matters—the content of the product line, through what channels it should be sold, how it should be promoted and priced. He or she is decisive as to the sales forecast and the profit budget. He or she has the right and duty to sound the alarm when an impasse looms ahead. However, he or she does not command the technical departments, the manufacturing departments, or the field sales forces. When we tell him or her "You are responsible for profit," we are more wrong than right. He or she *is* responsible for the profit planning, for some of the ingredients of profit performance, for coordinating, and for needling. Whether a profit results from all this depends on many things beyond him or her, so many that to hold him or her "responsible" is usually unrealistic, and sometime ludicrous. Paying him or her based on this profit is another matter. Even if he or she is not "responsible," it may be a good thing to make his or her bonus (and for that matter, the bonus of the others) depend on the profit.

The functional manager. Now we are getting away from a broad control over profit, and into the narrower control of functional performance, costs, and expenses. We can, of course, talk about putting every indi-

vidual "in business for himself." We can even set up the figures to look
like a profit-and-loss statement. But no one else is fooled. The self-control is based on meeting goals for delivery, sales volume, quality, cost,
etc. Whether the company profits from this depends on other factors:
were the goals set sensibly; are there checks and balances to see that departmental success does not spell company failure, etc.

The supervisor. Now we are almost exclusively in the realm of performance standards on a narrow base. Yet creating the conditions for self-
control is far from simple

> The Madison company makes electron tubes under conditions of
> savage industry competition. To control costs, standards are estab-
> lished for material, labor, and overhead usage in each production
> department. The foreman is held "responsible" for meeting these
> standards.
>
> Now look at the problem of controlling material usage. In an elec-
> tron-tube plant this is notoriously difficult. A handful of these tiny,
> insignificant-looking parts is actually very costly. They are easy to
> spoil, lose, ignore, or hide. Yet they must be processed by many
> people who have consecutive custody over them.
>
> To set the conditions of self-control, each person who receives
> custody must "buy" the goods by writing out and signing a "check"
> (requisition). Later he "sells" to the next processor. These "checks,"
> along with a *weekly* physical inventory[7] do establish conditions of
> self-control and result in excellent regulation over material usage.

The self-control principle is the most fundamental of all, since every
person in the company is affected, from the president to the messenger.
In particular, the three indispensable conditions for self-control should be
grasped fully. Until these three conditions have all been met, the boss has
not finished his or her job. The boss may tell the subordinate "Now you
are responsible." But the response may be "You are the boss, so I agree."

Personal Supervision

When the conditions for self-control have been established, the published
specifications, schedules, quotas, and standards become so many impersonal bosses. "Management by objective" now has meaning. The personal
boss, now in the background, has been freed from many routine actions
and decisions. Small wonder that standardization has been described as

---

[7]Helter-skelter parts are counted by weight. Others are kept in self-counting trays.

the "liberator" that relegates the solved problems to the field of routine, leaving the creative faculties free to tackle the unsolved problems.

But the managers do not make their delegation absolute. They exercise control over what they have delegated. Part of this they do by "informational control" (see below). And part of his control is through personal supervision. Through personal supervision, managers provides themselves with:

1. Assurance that the self-control is in fact being carried out
2. Direct observation of some matters which must not go wrong

Not only do the managers appoint supervisors, inspectors, and auditors to exercise this personal supervision; the managers do some of it themselves. The sales manager personally calls on the key accounts. The plant manager personally checks on shortages of vital materials. The research chief personally is on hand when critical tests are being made.

It is out of the question for personal supervision to recheck every one of the myriads of things regulated through self-control. Instead, this is done on a sampling basis. Even this sampling is weighted so that the vital few get more attention than the useful many.

Some managers carry personal supervision well beyond its limit. This is the "one-person show." For a small company this can be very effective while the one person lasts. (After him, the deluge). For the large company, even when the one person lives, serious troubles develop. The biggest company afloat could sink if we tried to operate on the basis of personal supervision alone. It almost happened to the Ford Motor Company during the final years of the life of Mr. Henry Ford.

Informational Control

Control by human beings is as old as recorded history. The Egyptian tombs show various individuals—supervisors, accountants, inspectors—in the act of conducting various control actions—stimulating laggards, keeping books, checking flatness of stone blocks.

The process of control has come a long way since those days. The Industrial Revolution ushered in some important innovations in the control process, including elaboration of the use of *information systems*. For example, compare these two mechanical systems:

1. Watt's flyball governor (1787) controlled the speed of a steam engine without the use of a separate information system. As the engine speeded up, the flyballs swung out in a wider arc because of greater cen-

trifugal force. In turn, the mechanical linkage to the steam valve cut the steam supply to slow down the engine. Here *the sensor took direct corrective action.*

2. Jacquard's loom (1801) made use of a train of punched cards as a separate information system—a program. *These cards did no work*—they gave the orders to the mechanisms of the loom as to which warp threads should be raised and which should remain below the weft.

What has happened in the twentieth century is the deeper recognition of the *theory of control.* The understanding of this theory has made it possible to build a whole host of new systems of control based on the intermediary of information. *The sensor creates information, not action.*

Contract two managerial systems:

1. In an Egyptian textile mill found in the tomb of Meketre (1900 B.C.), eleven people, working in a small room, conduct all the operations needed to convert flax into linen. Three workers prepare flax, three spin, two warp, two weave. The eleventh person, sitting in the corner, is the boss. He can see all that goes on, and can issue orders to all hands. There is no need for data, forms, reports. Here the boss, *the sensor, creates action, not information.* (In all likelihood no one in the room knew how to read or write anyhow.)

2. Figure 22 is a page depicting a reporting system prepared by skilled analysts working from various statistical data. The report goes to the company's Board of Directors, people who have no time to see the operations at first hand. Here, *the sensor creates information, not action.*

With the growth of size and complexity of companies, the more primitive forms of control are no longer adequate for coordination—for "orchestrating" the various activities of the company into a harmonious whole. To meet this inadequacy, industry has already gone far down the road of information systems. But use of an information system is a drastic departure from the simple, intimate, personal observation type of control. The information system brings in a whole new assortment of people, forms, rules, timetables, formality. It is as different from personal observation as instrument flying is from seat-of-the pants flying (the analogy is quite in point).

Control Before, During, and After the Fact

We are readily spurred to action by a fire, an aching tooth, a spate of employee quits, a price slash by a competitor. Our senses detect these

Proposal Times by Group

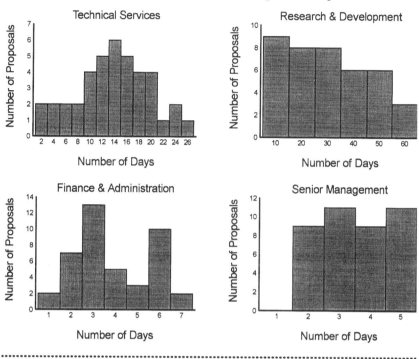

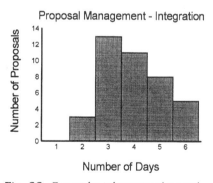

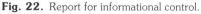

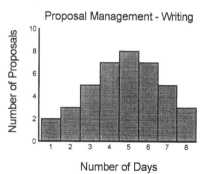

Fig. 22. Report for informational control.

things easily, and we know we are in for trouble. So we move in and control—after the fact.

Yet all these sudden actions were the culmination of a slow build-up of prior events. If we had used the principle of the ounce of prevention, we would be using control before the fact, and would head off these catastrophes.

Some control before the fact requires that we have sensors which "lead" events; i.e., a rising temperature predicts a fire; a rising cost curve predicts losses; a rising birth rate predicts more baby carriages, schools. We will look at this approach in Chap. 16.

Other control before the fact is a matter of taking preventive action when the means are known.

> In the Ace example (p. 70), material usage was controlled before the fact. Notorious wasters of material had been retrained or eliminated. Thereafter, only that amount of material actually needed to install the hookup was shipped to the job.

In like manner we do not extend credit beyond the proved capacity to pay; we estimate the load before we build the bridge; we prohibit smoking in designated areas; we survey a prospective vendor's plant before making him a critical source of supply; we estimate sales potential before we invade a market.

Generally, managers have a range of choice as to whether to control before, during, or after the fact. But the more lead time they want, the more effort they must put in. To control before the fact requires much analysis, setting of objectives, and detailed planning. Control during the fact usually requires skillful delegation plus investment in the means needed to put the people on the scene of action in a state of self-control. Control after the fact requires the least prior investment but is often the most costly.

But managers are not unified on where to put the emphasis. Traditions in the Accounting Department or the Inspection Department may be strongly oriented to after-the-fact reporting. "You're giving us ancient history" is a frequent criticism of these reports. Many operating managers emphasize control during the fact. Others, abetted by the staff planners, emphasize control before the fact. And it is easy enough to go overboard on controls.

The real crime is not in a mistake in judgment. The real crime is failure to face the question: "Shall we, in this case, control before, during, or after the fact?" When this question is faced squarely, the managers usually come up with realistic answers.

Technical Addendum

Our panoramic view of Control has omitted most of the technical material which is proliferating and which is the source of so much fascination to the enthusiasts. For the curious, the author has prepared a brief technical addendum which appears as Appendix A in the back of this book. This addendum is not "required" reading for the practitioner.

Now Back to Earth

In this chapter we have been up in the clouds to look down for our panoramic view. Now we bring our aircraft back for a landing and set out to examine, in detail, the various steps in the Control cycle. The next chapter is devoted to the first of these steps—choosing the Control subject.

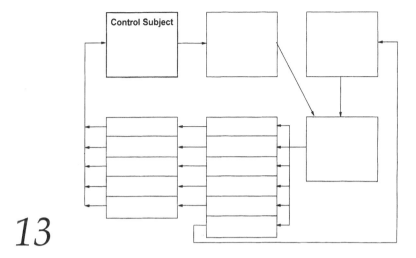

13

CHOOSING THE CONTROL SUBJECT

Control Is Specific

Controlling, or keeping things on course, is not something we do in the abstract. Control is applied to specific subjects—the diameter of the shaft, labor turnover in the warehouse, the cost of the 2A pump. Each of these subjects of control (we will call them control subjects) becomes the hub around which a feedback loop is constructed.

Since the control subject is the hub, it follows that: *If a control subject is worthless, the whole control procedure built around that control subject is likewise worthless.*

In this chapter we will examine how the manager:

identifies the control subjects

fractionates the great number of control subjects into the layers of Fig. 21

clears the way for setting up the feedback loops appropriate to these layers of control subjects

Evolution of Control Subjects

In human history, the birth of a control subject is usually a time of disaster.

When European settlers first moved into North America, a number of them suffered skin rashes from contact with the poison ivy plant, which was then unknown in Europe. Once the cause of the skin rashes was discovered and publicized, ivy poisoning became a control subject for the community.

The human being in the industrial environment similarly evolves control subjects through disasters.

> Some shop process runs berserk, and floods the factory with rejects. The trouble is traced to its lair—the temperature of a chemical bath fell so low that the chemical reaction was incomplete. At the inquest, several people of importance vow that "I'll see to it that this one will never happen again." So bath temperature becomes a control subject.

In most companies, the list of control subjects is mainly an accumulation of responses to such catastrophic failures. In this sense, the list is the result of experience—bitter experience. The company has learned, the hard way, that these things are important. Hence let's keep an eye on them.

A Positive Approach

Managers are well advised to approach the choice of control subjects as a problem in its own right.

> During the earliest years of the Management Course of American Management Association (1952–1953), the author gave case problems on controls to a good many "classes" of managers. For each problem, a company was described, and the particular official who was to make use of the controls (Marketing Manager, President, etc.) was identified. The problem was then stated as follows:

> Prepare, for this official in this company, a list of not more than 10 of the principal control subjects which he should be controlling. For each of these control subjects, determine the proper unit of measure, the type of standard to be used for comparison, the source of information, the frequency of comparison, and the mailing list. For ease in preparation and in presentation, tabulate your results something like this:

Control subject	Units of measure	Type of standard	Source of information	Frequency of comparison	Mailing list

> Use the following abbreviations:
> *Type of standard:* H for historical; E for engineered; M for market; P for planned.

Source of information: F for formal report; V for verbal report; O for personal observation.
Frequency of comparison: D for daily; W for weekly, M for monthly; Q for quarterly; A for annual; I for irregular.

The problems were a big hit. The participants had only 45 minutes to work up an "Executive instrument panel" for a company they had never studied before. A typical response was "If we can do this so well for a strange company, why can't we do better for our own company?"

Very likely a main reason for the contrast was in the fact that, in the case problem, the question of the executive instrument panel was being faced as a problem in its own right, whereas "in our own company" it was always incidental to something else.

Informational control enmeshes so many managers that a collective approach to choice of control subjects is needed. It is well to assign staff personnel to do some preparatory work of securing, from each manager affected, a list of what are his or her nominations for control subjects. These lists can then be summarized to become the basis of group discussion. This has the usual advantage of a participative approach: a broader base of ideas, a more thorough discussion, and a more genuine acceptance of the resulting controls.

Getting Rid of the Barnacles

The evolutionary approach to control subjects makes no provision for clearing out those control subjects which have outlived their usefulness. In many companies these barnacles hang on because it is no one's job to scrape them off.

The "positive" approach does provide a way out. Once a study group has worked up a list of essential control subjects, everything not on that list can be challenged. Now the burden of proof is on the person who wants to hold onto it, rather than on the person who wants to challenge it. It makes quite a difference.

Lacking a positive approach, the removal of dead control subjects is an exasperating chore. Of the dozen people who are asked to dispense with the information, there are always one or two who find reasons for playing safe.

During World War II investigators engaged in streamlining the Navy reporting system were surprised to find a long-standing report on the number of American flags lost through burials at sea. They traced the thing back and found the reason. Years ago, an admiral was defending his budget estimates before a Congressional committee. When the budget item for flags came up for review, a Congressman asked about flags lost through burials at sea. The admiral was stumped. No one had ever asked that question before. He vowed he'd never be stumped again.

In some companies the accumulation has become so burdensome that heroic measures are necessary. Reports are arbitrarily cut off to see who misses them. All reports are exhibited in the company cafeteria, and executives initial those they must have. Hardly scientific, but indicative of how tenacious the individual control subjects can become.

Fractionating the Control Subjects

By now we have a great body of experience to guide us in allocating the control subjects to the five layers of the control pyramid (Fig. 21). First, as to the controls through *foolproofing* and *automation.* The conditions favoring these include:

> highly repetitive activities (data processing, cigarette vending, injection molding) which, because of their great numbers, can amortize the cost of the engineering effort
>
> standardized conditions permitting direct responses of effector to sensor without need for human judgment
>
> a state of the art which permits designing the control hardware for high reliability and very gradual wear-out

Such considerations require that the manager base his decisions on the engineering feasibility and the investment economics of the situation. In turn, the manager must see that the engineers, accountants, and operating people conduct such studies of feasibility and economics as are needed for managerial decision.

Next, as to *operator control.* Conditions favorable for operator[1] control include:

> a familiar, stable work environment, with low likelihood of unforeseen obstacles;
>
> an organization of work which permits individuals or stable teams to finish their assignments with little need for coordination with out-

---

[1]Here again, "operator" is used in the special sense of any nonsupervisor who is assigned to regulate some process.

siders (The individual or team must be supplied with: knowledge of what needs to be done; knowledge of what is being done; means for regulating.)

established, proved procedures

completed indoctrination and training

requirement for judgment limited to the local situation

effect of failure of performance generally obvious and localized; loss due to failures generally minor

A study of these conditions makes it clear that the manager has much leeway here. He or she is the main voice in deciding how work is to be organized, whether environments should be stabilized, procedures established, training given.

Conditions favorable for control through *personal supervision* include:

a changing work environment, with frequent entry of new situations, i.e., new products, seasonal fluctuations

an organization of work which requires coordinating the work of a variety of jobs

fluidity in procedures, i.e., change-overs, revisions

continuing need for indoctrination and training

a high content of human relations problems, i.e., discipline, personality clashes

a high degree of contact with departmental "outsiders," i.e., staff specialists, the union, other supervisors

effect of failures of performance not immediate or local; cost of failures substantial

individual performance not readily measurable

situations which carry risk of fraud or other violations

The conditions requiring use of *informational controls* include:

matters of company performance as distinguished from departmental performance

organization of work requiring coordination among departments. The most important example is the common organization of company departments by function (marketing, manufacture, engineering, finance)

matters requiring review by a multiplicity of people (boards, committees, layers of managers)

managers located at a distance from their responsibility, whether because of geography or because of the number of organization levels matters requiring information from a variety of sources, or from sources outside of the company

matters requiring extensive analysis of information

matters involving great risks or heavy expenditures

matters involving relations with noncompany groups (customers, vendors, government, shareholders, the union)

The size of the company is a major factor in the results of the fractionating process. The manager universally needs a more sophisticated instrument panel for a larger responsibility. The respective control panels of the motorcycle, the automobile, the locomotive, the liner, and the intercontinental aircraft are a case in point.

> A study[2] of the personnel forms used in companies showed that large companies used eleven basic forms; small companies managed with two (the employment application and the employee record).

Some severe problems are created when a company's growth takes place under the long tenure of a single individual or team. The growth is imperceptible week to week; so there is no dramatic change from automobile to locomotive. Over a decade or two the cumulative differences are dramatic enough. But the insiders have not been aware of this, and so have not changed their control patterns to suit. The resulting underdelegation severely restricts action on all fronts.

Let the Imagination Roam

In pondering on what should be the control subjects, managers should not shackle themselves to the well known or even to the possible.

> In the early days of aviation, a frequent cause of accidents was an aircraft smashing into the side of a mountain, in the fog. Prevention of this disaster required some means of signaling "mountain ahead" in a fog. But publicizing the need stimulated many minds. In due course, means were found for detecting "mountain ahead."

There are many such examples. We need to "control" such nebulous things as morale, customer goodwill, corporate image. We can make no

[2]Knox, Frank M., "A Guide to Personnel Record Keeping," *Personnel,* November, 1942, pp. 542–561.

headway on these things unless we identify them as control subjects. Never mind that we do not know how to measure them. Identify them as control subjects and all else will follow, crudely at first, but with increasing effectiveness.

> In a drugstore, the soda fountain was an important source of sales as well as a magnet for traffic. Hence soda-fountain performance was a logical control subject, whether we can measure it or not.
> Now turn to a very complex kind of service—telephone service. No two telephone exchanges are alike. They differ in type of clientele, proportion of long-distance calls, proportion of manual vs. automatic, etc. Yet "telephone service" is a must as a control subject— that's what the company sells.
> (Actually, the method of measuring soda-fountain performance and telephone service is discussed in the next chapter.)

The opportunities for imaginative approaches are limitless. In some companies, entire major functions are poorly controlled, i.e., Research, Development, Engineering, Advertising, Maintenance, diagnostic functions generally. This goes on despite proved solutions that have been adopted successfully in other companies.

Assertions such as "you can't control creativity," "you can't measure staff work," etc., should be rejected out of hand.[3] The problem is to finish the sentence: "The job of product development (or whatever) has been satisfactorily done when…" See in this connection, Standards for a Function, p. 270.

Controls based on profits made are common. Controls based on profits lost (through failure to act) are rare. Here is another opportunity for imagination.

> In the Wales Company a problem under study was the control of delivery to customers through rush orders and expediting. An assertion of the sales manager was that, lacking these controls, the company would lose business because customers placed orders with competitors. This assertion was challenged; so a sample of 25 back orders was analyzed to see how often customers really placed orders with competitors. The study mostly bore out the sales manager's contention. One result was that "sales lost because of delivery failure" became a control subject.

---

[3]The same comment is made about controlling "honesty." But over the centuries, the banks and merchants have learned a good deal about controlling honesty.

Some Negative Approaches

> The conference room is hushed. It is evident that the Old Man is about to launch another "drive."
>
> "Look at this overtime. We're losing our shirts. It's been going up and up. Sure, we gotta give service, but we're letting the salespeople walk all over us. I've been after it for weeks and nothing has happened. From now on, no overtime unless I give the go-ahead. I want to approve all overtime requests. I want a daily report on how much..."

So a drive is on its way. Overtime has become a control subject on the vice-president's instrument panel. Previously it had been only on the foreman's list, and very lightly there.

The drive will work. Overtime will be cut drastically. But the conditions which brought about the overtime will not be eliminated—not in any short time. The facilities which were turned down a year and a half ago—we still don't have them. The inventory which had fallen month after month—that will not be built up in any short time.

In a few months the lengthening list of late deliveries and back orders will strengthen the hand of Sales to a point that a new drive is started— let's clean up the backlog.

It makes for an exciting, fast-paced, exhausting life. Employees chase first this will-o'the-wisp, then that one, then another. There is never any rest because there is no end of crises.

The crime in "management by drives" is not the drive itself. When the house is on fire all hands must operate the pumps. The crime is in enduring the conditions which make the drive inevitable.

The wear and tear on all concerned is shocking. Employees are accused of lacking cost–mindedness or quality-mindedness or safety-mindedness, or all of these, serially. Yet they lack nothing of the sort. What has happened is that the management has not evolved a plan for optimizing performance. Lacking such a plan, the employees in the departments respond to departmental and local pressures. They do what the situation calls for, *as they see it.*

The drive is seldom a Breakthrough to new levels of performance. Rather it results in a performance which was always attainable through a normal level of control effort. The drive involves no new discoveries, no Breakthrough in knowledge. The drive may lead to a "better" level than normal control could have attained. But it reaches this level by overswinging the pendulum to the other side. The overcorrection will later have to be brought back, likely in still another drive.

Another good way *not* to choose control subjects is to leave matters to unguided staff enthusiasts.

In the decade 1945–1955 the movement known as Statistical Quality Control went on such an unguided mission. They papered the factory walls with control charts[4] and otherwise conducted a technique-oriented activity. In due course, the excesses were cut back, but not before a good deal of dissent, frustration, and antagonism had developed.

A surprising amount of "control" work is done not for the purpose of regulating the company's affairs, but for the personal defense of this or that employee.

The manager of the X company is conducting a drive to improve customer service. This drive is bringing out into the open the cases of unusually poor service. As these are investigated, a brisk discussion takes place—who held up the order?

Actually, each order goes down a long line of march through a series of departments, waiting its turn in each until it is processed. At the end of the line, no one really knows just where any particular order was held up—it could have been any of half a dozen departments.

Now, with the heat on, the department heads run for cover. Each sets up to clock each order in and out. This is done not in a search for facts which will help arrive at an optimum company solution; it is done in a spirit of defense—to provide facts which will help prove that we didn't do it—it must have been someone else.

The likely need in such cases is a Breakthrough study to look for some basic improvements in procedure. The emphasis on defense may very well obscure the need for a basic study.

Some Guides to Choice of Control Subjects

A good deal of thought has been devoted to identifying the informational controls needed by the manager. Numerous check lists have been published of control subjects for various functions.[5] These lists have educational value. Managers embarking on a review of their control setup

---

[4]The ingenious, useful chart invented by Dr. W. A. Shewhart. See Fig. 42.

[5]This list is too long to be reproduced here. For a bibliography of almost 400 books and papers on the subject, see Wasserman, Paul, "Measurement and Evaluation of Organizational Performance," Graduate School of Business and Public Administration, Cornell University, Ithaca, N.Y., 1959.

are well advised to consult the literature to broaden the base of their own thinking. However, there is no such thing as a list which fits without extensive alteration. There are drastic differences among industries and among companies. Even a single company, during its lifetime, requires a changing list of control subjects.

> The control subjects for the health of a human being change drastically as he journeys through life. During his embryonic state, the health and diet of his mother are decisive. As an infant, he is helpless—unable to communicate, to forage, to know danger, to escape from it. So he must be watched lest he die by falling, by smothering, by being alone in a burning house. As an active youngster, he has a cavalier attitude toward broken legs, teeth, sanitation. As an adolescent, he may be trapped into narcotics, alcohol, debauchery. Beyond that he faces problems of overweight, overwork, until the health problems of old age descend on him. This variable list is, of course, superimposed on a continuing list of perils—open flames, sharp knives, high places, belligerent associates.

The company, in like manner, faces a changing list of control subjects as it evolves from a one-person enterprise to an industrial giant. We will consider, briefly, the major categories of control subjects in the company:

the economic climate
the financial performance
the nonfinancial performance
departmental performance
relations with outsiders

The Economic Climate

A major control subject is the forecast of sales, i.e., the future.

Some of the most critical expenditures—plant construction, machinery, inventory build-up—contain a long inherent time lag between the decision to spend and the fruits of the expenditure. During this time lag, the march of events may deny the company the benefits of the expenditure. We must make the decision (to spend or not to spend) now. A year or two from now, we will find out whether it was a good decision. How can we control the future?

We can't. We can do some sound predicting because certain events (contract awards) lead other events (construction). When we lack such "leading" indicators, we must "estimate." Even when we use the crystal ball, there are ways to cut our risks and to provide against adverse trends.

The manager can:

(*a*) Broaden the base of the estimate. Use the salespeople as a field intelligence force. Use statistical market forecasts. (Few companies use as much as 10 per cent of the available material.) Use a jury of executive opinion rather than relying on one individual's opinion.[6]

(*b*) Keep a close watch of how actual events unfold themselves vs. the forecast, and be prepared to act on the differences.

(*c*) Have an alley to run to. Be prepared with plans beforehand for dealing with various actual levels of activity, rather than going into hasty crash programs.

Edmunds[7] lists some of the factors to be considered in making major operating decisions in an automobile company:

Production by make
Future production schedules
Option and accessory installation
Production vs. orders and schedules
Industry new-car sales
Sales by make and market penetration
Sales by state or district
Age distribution of cars on the road
Registration vs. competition
Depreciation rates of cars
Truck sales by weight group
Used-car sales

New- and used-car stocks
New-car stocks by body style and district
Used-car prices
New-car prices
Commodity prices
Wage movements
Automobile credit terms
General monetary conditions
Economic conditions
Economic factors related to car sales

Other industries would have different factors, but the factors are there.

[6]See, generally, "Forecasting Sales," National Industrial Conference Board, Studies in Business Policy, No. 106, 1963.

[7]Edmunds, Stahrl, "The Reach of an Executive," *Harvard Business Review,* January–February, 1959, p. 89.

Financial Performance

The most important single measure of financial performance is return on investment.[8] No other measure so fully integrates the financial facts and so uniquely provides the manager with means for choosing alternative courses of action.

Beyond return on investment there are numerous measures—profit, sales, various financial ratios. The literature on these measures is extensive.[9] In addition, the approaches used by some specific companies have been well documented.[10]

In some industries the trade associations have supplied leadership for uniform accounting systems and meaningful ratios.

It should be realized that financial statements are *not* essential to day-to-day conduct of a business. The control subjects needed for day-to-day affairs are a layer or two farther down in the Control pyramid (Fig. 21). But the financial measures are essential to broad evaluation, setting objectives, and planning.

Profit as a control subject is vital enough to warrant a breakdown by product line, market, or other logical subdivision. The urge to apply this useful concept has resulted in some overextension. Profit-center concepts have been applied to service centers, and many managers have been led astray by the resulting "facts."

> Some companies have tried to set the research department up as a profit center. The department is charged with its costs; it is also credited with savings from process improvements, profits on patents, a percentage of profit from new products, etc.
>
> There is obvious value in knowing such facts. Moreover, the concept of comparing results achieved with costs incurred is eminently sound, over the long run. But trying to relate them to each other in *annual* "profit" statements is largely meaningless. The "income" results from the work of earlier years and is in any event the composite result of the work of numerous departments.

---

[8] For a more precise definition, see the Du Pont formula, Fig. 23.

[9] Wasserman, *op. cit.*

[10] See, for an excellent set of cases, *"Reports to Top Management,"* American Management Association, 1953. The participating companies were Burroughs, Carrier, Koppers, Thompson Products, and Ford Motor Company.

See also other American Management Association publications: "How the Du Pont Organization Appraises Its Performance," Financial Management Series, No. 94, 1950; "A Program of Financial Planning and Controls (The Monsanto Chemical Company)," Financial Management Series, No. 103, 1953.

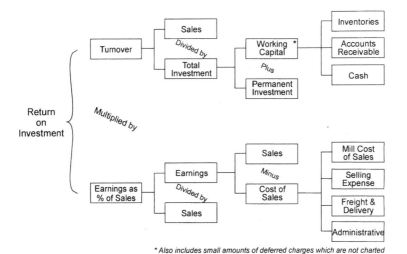

Fig. 23. The Du Pont formula for return on investment.

Nonfinancial Performance

Here we are concerned with what is commonly referred to as "statistics" rather than financial measures. Control subjects such as share of market, productivity, and quality leadership are universally on company lists. But there are also numerous subjects which are special to specific industries or companies.

> In a public utility, the dominant consideration is how to give service. Since these utilities are often monopolies, cost control is a special problem. The costs are not challenged by direct competition, and the utility has the very great difficulty of creating some form of self-competition. (This difficulty must be colossal in the communistic countries. It is bad enough in our local and federal governments.)

The emphasis in control subjects on nonfinancial performances should be on those matters that are cardinal.

> The performance of a winery is largely limited by the availability of its unique and romantic raw material—wine grapes. The crop is highly seasonal, and the yield varies from year to year. In consequence, the size and character of the crop become essential control subjects. The other materials—sugar, bottles, and supplies must also be "controlled," but they are secondary in importance to the basic raw material.

A postgraduate example of a nonfinancial control subject is performance on new product development.

Development work (development of new materials, machines, processes, products) is notoriously difficult to measure. The end result can be evaluated, but only years later. Hence it is the *progress* which must be controlled so that we do not just continue to pour money down a bottomless pit. The companies which do much development work have this problem on a large scale.

The late Morehead Patterson[11] once told the author how he was driven to adopt an organized control on experimental engineering projects.

> Early in Mr. Patterson's industrial career he determined that he would try to make and sell things no one else made—he had no interest in "slugging it out" on a basis of competition in cost cutting, price cutting, etc. This policy of dealing with proprietary products meant large expenditures for research and development, and he accepted this as a fact of life. But he found by experience that the hands on the reins of expenditure were very limp.

> An engineer would get a vote of $25,000 to investigate some interesting idea. He would disappear for a few months. Then he would reappear, tell of his findings to date, and want another $25,000 to investigate the new problems which the study had uncovered. This happened so often that we had to find a better way. Our search for a better way led to the Stage[12] System.

The Stage system as devised by AMF provided an orderly basis for:

1. Preparing project objectives, including specifications, schedules, and cost estimates
2. Preparing plans for meeting these objectives, i.e., manpower, schedules, budgets, organization
3. Evaluating actual performance against objectives
4. Periodic review of the economics of the subject

Under the AMF system, any engineering project was regarded as consisting of a series of stages, such as:

---

[11] Then Chairman of the Board and President, American Machine & Foundry Company (was AMF).

[12] The stage is defined as "a measure of progression in the evolution of an experimental engineering subject."

1. Engineering analysis
2. Engineering exploration
3. Prototype design
4. Prototype construction
5. Prototype test
6. Pilot production model design
7. Pilot production model construction
8. Pilot production model test
9. Preparation for manufacture

Each stage is defined in some detail. For example, stage 5, Prototype test, is defined as follows:

> Prototype testing in shop under simulated operating conditions and/or in the field under actual operating conditions. Includes:
> 1. Establishment of standard test specifications.
> 2. Installation and operation of prototype.
> 3. Compilation and evaluation of test data.
> 4. Minor alterations as required to conduct tests.
> 5. Preparation of a report to include:
>   (a) Evaluation of test results and comparison with specifications.
>   (b) Recommended design changes.
>   (c) Recommended specifications for pilot production models.
>   (d) Revised tentative tooling and manufacturing estimates.
>   (e) Recommended future action, including appropriation request, if any, for stage 6.

Having defined the stages, AMF provided for review of progress by an Advisory Committee of executives from Engineering, Sales, Manufacture, and Finance. This committee makes several reviews during the progression of a project, normally[13] after stages 1, 2, 5, 6, and 8. The review includes a decision either to scrap the project or to vote funds for further progression. (In each instance, the preceding stage has provided a report for the committee, which report evaluates progress to date, and recommends future action.)

The interrelation of a stage system and a review and appropriate system is shown graphically (Fig. 24) in the scheme used by Kaiser Aluminum and Chemical Corporation.[14]

---

[13]The real beginning of a project is not an engineering study, but a "curbstone" market study to see "if you had it, what good would it do you."

[14]Tietjen, Karl H., "Organizing the Product-planning Function," American Management Association, 1963.

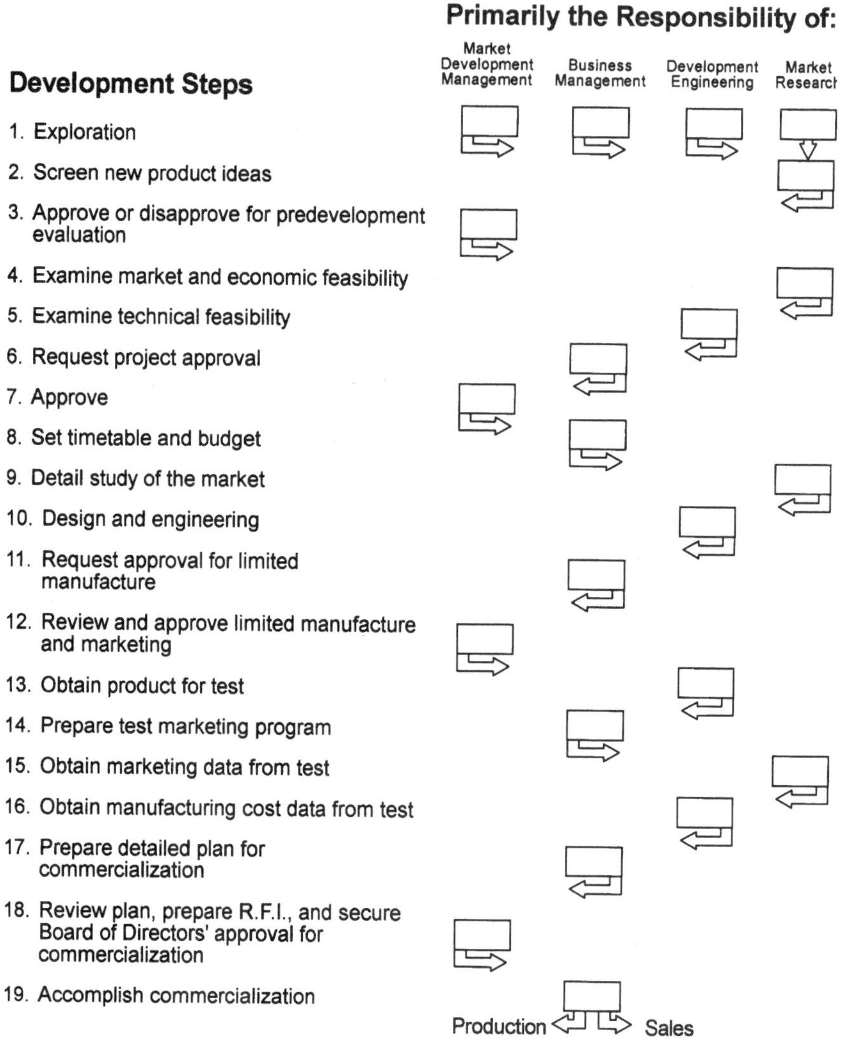

Primarily the Responsibility of:

Development Steps	Market Development Management	Business Management	Development Engineering	Market Research
1. Exploration	→	→	↻	↓
2. Screen new product ideas				←
3. Approve or disapprove for predevelopment evaluation	→			
4. Examine market and economic feasibility				←
5. Examine technical feasibility			←	
6. Request project approval		←		
7. Approve	→			
8. Set timetable and budget		→		
9. Detail study of the market				←
10. Design and engineering			←	
11. Request approval for limited manufacture		←		
12. Review and approve limited manufacture and marketing	→			
13. Obtain product for test			←	
14. Prepare test marketing program		→		
15. Obtain marketing data from test				←
16. Obtain manufacturing cost data from test			←	
17. Prepare detailed plan for commercialization		←		
18. Review plan, prepare R.F.I., and secure Board of Directors' approval for commercialization	→			
19. Accomplish commercialization	Production ← → Sales			

Fig. 24. The Kaiser stage system.

Departmental Performance

The larger the company, the greater the need for managing the various departments by specific objectives. These objectives then become control subjects.

As before, there are guides in the literature.[15] But departmental control subjects must be tailor-made. The people on the scene are the real experts. When they put their minds to it, they can come up with answers to very complex situations such as the telephone exchange (p. 250). They also come up with the numerous prosaic and intriguing measures—staff-hours per Btu, pounds of steam per proof gallon, etc.

When a large company studied the control subjects applicable to the salespeople's job they came up with a list well beyond the conventional "volume and selling expenses":

sales volume
controllable selling expense
realization (product mix, pricing)
credit and collections
attention to market conditions
application of product knowledge
work organization
conditions at reseller outlets
attitude of customers
attitude of public
contributions to company policy
routine details

Relations with Outsiders

The control subjects here are concerned with the company's status respecting customers, shareholders, the public, vendors, the union, etc.

Generally, this body of control subjects is the least well developed as to units of measure, standards, and sensory devices. In later chapters some case examples will deal with some of these topics. It will be seen that we must rely heavily on special surveys and on the tools developed by the behavioral scientists. None of this should discourage the manager. The admonition to "let the imagination roam" includes the problem of relations with outsiders.

---

[15]Wasserman, op. cit.

Precise Definition

Choice of a control subject establishes the need for a feedback loop. But design of the loop can proceed only to the extent of completeness of the definition of the control subject.

A common control subject is Return on Investment. Yet when a company determines to set goals and measure performance, a whole host of questions arise. What goes into "investment?" Do we count working capital? Shall we distinguish between owned capital and borrowed capital? Also, what constitutes return? Are capital gains or losses to be counted? Until we set out the detailed definitions (see the Du Pont examples in Fig. 23), we do not have a meeting of the minds.

The need for precise definition recurs so regularly that the manager should accept the need as an essential part of Control. To try to wave it aside as quibbling is to show an unawareness of the basic human problem of communication.

The costs of building maintenance are under attack. The general manager asks for information about the "size of the maintenance force." At a conference, three managers bring in three different answers:

The head of the maintenance department counted the "number of bodies" on the job.

The personnel manager counted the number of personnel folders under "building maintenance."

The Controller added up hours worked last week on "building maintenance" accounts and divided by forty.

We saw in the motor case (p. 125), that even counting physical units of product is tricky; the answer depends on where along the line of march we count them.

And so it goes. "Sales" is a number with a wide fringe around it—returns, credits, allowances, price changes. "Cost" is worse because there are so many cost systems, all far more complex than the layman's idea of cost, i.e., 50 cents for a candy bar.

Consider the differences between absorption costing (the conventional method) and direct costing (Table 13-1).

The building blocks used to create these two systems are identical. The same accounts, based on the same units of measure, are used to collect the little pools of cost and expense. What differs is the conceptual

Table 13-1. Contrasts in Costing Methods

Problem of	How handled under	
	Absorption costing	Direct costing
Basic division of costs and expenses	By nature of expense, i.e., materials, wages	By relation to business volume, i.e., fixed or variable
Manufacturing costs for products made and sold	Charged to products sold during that period	Fixed costs charged to the period in which incurred; variable costs charged to products at the time of sale
Manufacturing costs for products made but not sold	Charged to inventory, for later treatment	Fixed costs charged to the period in which incurred; variable costs charged to products at the time of sale
Nonmanufacturing expenses	Deducted from the gross margin for the period in which incurred	Fixed expenses charged to the period in which incurred; variable expenses charged to products at the time of sale

approach and the resulting network of canals through which the trickles of cost are collected for summary purposes.

Another essential piece of detail is that of *time*. Is the feedback loop to be closed continuously or only intermittently; if the latter, how often— hourly, annually, every tenth piece?

It is generally realized that the automated processes and the people on the firing line must regulate things event by event. Supervisors do their regulation daily or weekly. Middle management stretches this out to weekly or monthly. Top management generally makes its reviews monthly and even less frequently.

Many companies have gone to a formal adoption of a graduated scale of frequency. The reporting system recognizes who is to see what, and when. There is much value in such formality, since it permits an orderly plan for data collection, summaries, scheduling of due dates, and multiple use of the same basic information.

Koppers Company,[16] during the presidency of General Somervell, went to a rigid timetable for controls. The cardinal dates were the monthly

[16]Reports to Top Management, *op. cit.*

meetings of the Board of Directors. Working back from these dates, a timetable was set up to show the due dates for information from the operating decisions and corporate staff departments. In turn, the divisional offices set up due dates for the next tier of information (see Fig. 34).

What Is "Controllable"?

There is wide acceptance of the idea that people should be held responsible only for those results they can do something about. Recognition of this principle has resulted in separation of the controllable from all else. The foreman is "responsible" for staff-hours per ton, but not for the rent. Accordingly, the departmental budget puts rent and things like rent into the group of accounts at the lower half of the page. The foreman is called to explain only what happened to the controllables.

For example, one company divided shop costs as between controllable and noncontrollable as shown in Table 13-2.

Once this distinction was made, historical data were developed and budgets (standards) established for the controllable costs. Subsequent measurement was on the same basis.

There are, of course, borderline areas, and these must be talked out— is there enough controllability to put the thing in the upper half of the sheet? Yet experience has shown that these borderline cases do not create the major headaches as to controllability. To illustrate:

> The Ross-Bentley Company made and marketed a multiple product line. This was done through a functional organizational setup— Vice-presidents for Sales, Finance, Manufacture, Purchasing, Per-

Table 13-2. Classification of Costs

Controllable	Noncontrollable
Waiting time	Department inspectors
Employee activities	Production service engineers
Training	Stores
Overtime	Planning clerks
Setup and adjust	Tool and die crib attendance
Small tools and gages	Premiums
Repairs and maintenance	Indirect administration
Salvage labor	Salvage
Scrap	Scrap
Supplies	Labor and material not in standard
Direct administration	Rearrangement

sonnel, Engineering, etc. These officers overemphasized their respective functions, at an underemphasis on coordination by product. To improve product coordination, the company created several Product Managers, each with responsibility for planning, coordinating, and controlling activities relative to their respective product lines. The job description for the Product Manager included the sentence—"He or she is responsible for the profit performance of his or her product line."

To the upper management, the setting up of the new post was no great change. Other companies had done it with success, hence why not we? But the move was regarded by the middle managers as a very great change. All functional departments exhibited resistance to having an outsider invade "their" responsibilities as to planning, budgeting, cost control, new product decisions, etc. To make matters worse, those picked to be Product Managers were former salespeople, with very little experience in functions other than Sales, and (what is worse) with very little training in business management. This underestimate of the experience and training needed was consistent with top management's underestimate of the need for changing the atmosphere.

Top management could and did go through all the motions of measuring profit for each product line, comparing the actual profit with budgeted profit, and holding the Product Manager "responsible" for the difference. But it was of no avail. Conditions had not been created which made profit controllable by the Product Manager.

Tools for Simplification

Ingenious methods have been worked out for depicting a multiplicity of control subjects. A widespread example is the table of delegation or "limits of approvals." This table is constructed by defining:

(a) A ranking of jobs or job holders as to their right to approve various actions

(b) A ranking of actions as to their importance for approval purposes

Figure 25 is an example of such a table of delegation as applied to personnel actions.

The table of delegation, whether written or just "understood," solves another vital problem in Control—that of *legitimacy*. The human need for a "government of laws, not people," does not stop at the factory gate—it follows the human beings right into the gate.

Approvals Required	*All changes above Grade 14		Grades 11 thru 14		Non-overtime & Supervisory Employees Grades 1 thru 10			Overtime Paid Employees Grades 1 thru 10			
	President	General Mgr.	President	General Mgr.	President	General Mgr.	Works Mgr.	President	General Mgr.	Works Mgr. Office	Works Mgr. Shop
President	X										
General Manager		X									
Staff Department Head	X	X	X	X							
Department Head					X	X					
Division Head (Superintendents)							X	X	X	X	
Sectional Supervisor											X

* Staff department head initiates—President or General Manager approves.
Requests for transfers are initiated only by the supervisor receiving the employee.
Rate changes effective only at the beginning of payroll periods after approval of requests.

Fig. 25. Table of delegation for personnel actions.

Another basic tool for simplification is the Pareto principle. Various functions use different names to designate the selective emphasis which utilizes the Pareto principle.

The salespeople have "key accounts" among their customers. These get more frequent calls, preferential treatment.

The production control fraternity identifies "bottlenecks," which then get special treatment.

The inventory control specialist has defined three classes of importance, and identified them as A, B, and C. The C's get short shrift, while the A's get individual, tailor-made attention.

The quality control people recognize that the various bits of the specification are not equally important. They classify the quality characteristics as "critical," major, and minor. These classes then receive different levels of attention.

This selective process is forced by the sheer weight of numbers. All human beings, when faced with an overwhelming task, use selective emphasis to cut it down to size. But who should make the selection? Clearly, unless the management does the selecting, the nonsupervisor must, by default, make the selection. His selection will, of necessity, be based on *his* perspective and on the pressures that beset *him*.

The lesson for management is clear. If there is need for selective emphasis, the manager should face squarely the question—shall I do the selecting, or shall I delegate it? Failing a clear decision, the selection will be made at the bottom, not because the manager really wants it that way, but because he or she defaulted.

An example of management selection is seen in the Du Pont Company's control of plant maintenance work.[17]

> In the Du Pont Company plan, serially numbered work orders are issued for jobs involving more than 4 labor hours or $40 in material. The work order is the nucleus of maintenance control, and is the basis for equipment records, job analysis, work scheduling, and work measurement.
>
> However, much maintenance work is highly repetitive—cleaning, oiling, adjusting. These jobs lend themselves to control by methods long used for repetitive work. They are covered by an unnumbered patrol order system. They are the "useful many," since patrol orders account for 50 per cent of the total orders but only 10 per cent of the total staff-hours.
>
> Other control subjects for maintenance work include the backlog of work, the preventive maintenance program, the provision of spare parts for each piece of equipment, the procedures used for overhaul.

On to Units of Measure

With the choice of control subjects, we are ready to build, around each of them, the entire cycle of control activities. Basic to all of these activities is the unit of measure. The next chapter is logically devoted to the role of the unit of measure in the control cycle.

---

[17]Jessen, Jesse G., "Maintenance Cost Control," American Society of Mechanical Engineers Paper No. 57A287.

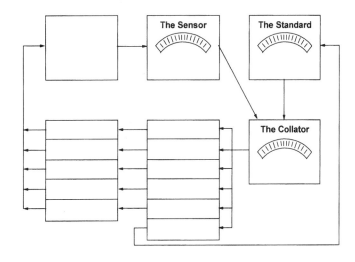

14

THE UNIT OF MEASURE

Numbers, of Course

Once the human race had invented counting, it learned to make wide use of numbers as a means of precise communication.

> When the author was on a lecture trip in Australia, he learned that the Aborigines there had invented a unique unit of measure for temperature. On a winter night in the bush country, the Aborigine, away from his home fire, and lacking warm clothing, would sleep among his huddled dogs. A four-dog night was one for the record books.[1]

We will waste little time arguing that it is better to express standards and performance in terms of numbers rather than adjectives. Our century is fully aware that measurement has been a basic contributor to the march of science. Our managers have all gone through the frustration of debating how high are "high" costs, how poor is "poor" quality. They know that once we set up units of measure, the debate shifts from the meaning of adjectives to doing the job at hand, which is as it should be.

Yet there is a curious roadblock. In those cases where we have not yet worked out a unit of measure, most managers exhibit a tendency to stay

---

[1]The American will talk of a two-blanket night.

on the dead center of debating the meaning of adjectives, rather than driving ahead to develop a unit of measure. As we will see in this chapter, developing a unit of measure is normally no great trick once we put our minds to it. Yet often enough, we seem to prefer the problem to the solution. Think of how many staff-hours are spent debating the spelling of a word when a dictionary is on a nearby shelf.

Units of Measures and Sensors

A clear distinction must be drawn between the jobs of:

(a) defining a unit of measure
(b) designing an instrument (sensor) to do the measuring

Consider the problem of measuring the effect of advertising. The units of measure are easy. They consist of such measures as:

number of new prospects per $1,000 of advertising

added sales per $1,000 of advertising

added profits per $1,000 advertising

Measurement is something else. The real problem here is to identify which prospects, sales, and profits resulted from the advertising.

In some instances—certain direct mailings, newspaper advertisements, television messages, magazine coupons—cause and effect can be related with reasonable assurance. But other forms—trade shows, outdoor advertising, and the very costly institutional advertising—are superimposed on a variety of marketing efforts, and cover a broad mixture of products and markets. These broader forms of advertising have to date defied analysis of cause vs. effect.

When someone proposes the creation of a new unit of measure, the temptation is to look sideways to see if the sensor is already in existence. This is pertinent, but it is certainly not decisive. The correct sequence is to first decide on the unit of measure and then to find the sensor. If there is no sensor, then the manager should throw down a challenge to the inventors to invent a new sensor.

Whose Language?

The fact that the most vital management controls are based on dollars has influenced some managers to conclude that other controls—middle management and supervisory—should also be based on dollars. This view, though widespread, is fallacious.

The arguments for emphasis on dollars are plausible enough:

the middle and lower managers can make better decisions if they understand the significance of those decisions in dollars.

it is logical and consistent to conduct all measurement in the same units, from the bottom to the top.

These valid arguments run head-on into the fact that, at the bottom of the Control pyramid (Fig. 21), the decisions, actions, and controls involve deeds and things, not dollars. The system of deeds is concerned with how many letters, or packages, or tons or cubic centimeters do we need to get out. How many staff-hours do we need for this? How many feet of shelf space, carload lots, reams, ton-miles? The language of deeds is the language of physical things—time, mass, space.

These two schools of thought are brought together in a simple formula:

At the top, the talk must be of dollars. At the bottom, the talk must be of things. The middle manager must do both. He must talk in dollars to the individual at the top; in things, to the individual at the bottom.

There is abundant recognition of this principle. The company financial statements are in the language of dollars. The sales forecasts and results are in both dollars and units. But the production schedules, order points, and materials requisitions are all in units.

The Pyramid of Units of Measure

The pyramid of control subjects is paralleled by a pyramid of units of measure.

At the base are the humble bits of measurement—ounces, inches, gallons. These have a long, venerable history. (Their predecessors, i.e., shekels, cubits, kotyles, were used to conduct business in the temple warehouse, the marketplace, the cottage shop.) At the base, these measures are used for decision making in event-by-event affairs. Their use as "data," i.e., grist for managerial control, is incidental.

As we move up in the control pyramid, we use these data in summary form to express measures for a day, a week, a district, a department. We also relate one measure to another to give us numerous ratios and indexes. In addition, we create measures which have nothing at all to do with day-to-day affairs but which are useful for managerial control. The company's balance sheet and profit statement are of no use to the rank and file in their day-to-day work.

A good many tools of the statistician's trade are used to process the basic data for the upper part of the control pyramid. Three of these tools deserve special mention:

Summaries. These express, in a single number, the composite effect of many numbers. The summary may be a straight addition of like things. It may be a new term coined to add up unlike things; i.e., "fringe benefits" becomes the sum of vacation pay, holiday pay, pensions, etc.

Ratios. These units of measure relate two or more numbers to each other. The "current ratio" is the current assets divided by current liabilities; the accident rate is the number of lost-time accidents divided by the million staff-hours of exposure.

Indexes. Generally these are samples of a larger mass of data, and reflect, within statistical limits, the mass form which they are selected. The Bureau of Labor Statistics maintains an Index of Consumer Prices based on compositing the price fluctuations of a sample of consumer products. The National Industrial Conference Board maintains an Index of Cost of Living. A common measure of stock prices is the Dow-Jones Index. This is a sample of 65 stocks out of the thousands traded. The prices of these 65 stocks are weighted to put all of them on a common footing of total value.

The index is a tool of uncommon versatility. A plan of delegation, of action, of legislation can be geared to the fluctuations of an index.

> To aid in control of forest fires, a "Burning Index" has been evolved. This integrates the factors which influence the risk of fire: number of consecutive days without rain, temperature, wind velocity, humidity. A formula is used to compute the Burning Index. Legislation regulating smoking, camping, etc., is then enacted in terms of the Burning Index.

In like manner, wages are geared to the cost-of-living index, or farm subsidies are geared to the "parity" index.

One industrial equivalent of legislation is the budget. The variable budget is a form of legislation geared to an index which measures company or departmental activity.

> The Adams Division of Le Tourneau-Westinghouse Company developed an index of activity[2] of the Personnel Department by:

---

[2]Jackson, W. C., "The Personnel Activity Index: A New Budgeting Tool," *Personnel*, January–February, 1961, pp. 47–52.

1. Identifying five subactivities, i.e., hirings, separations, transfers, rate changes, first-aid cases.
2. Establishing a measure for each activity. For all activities, the measure was the number of cases (hires, separations, etc.), divided by the average employment.
3. Establishing a weight for each activity. These weights were based on the relative work required to process each. The weights adopted were 6, 2, 2, 1, and 1, respectively.

The resulting weighted index was tested against past history and proved to be a useful budgeting tool.

Beyond the numerous summaries, ratios, and indexes, there are various special measures. A sophisticated example is the Break-even graph (Fig. 26), which charts the rise in costs and the rise in income over a range of sales volume. The graph makes clear the point at which the product line breaks even, and clarifies other relationships as well. The Break-even graph is used primarily at the top of the pyramid; it has no value in conducting day-to-day operations.

A Unit of Work Should...

Work measurement was a problem to the pyramid builders long before it occupied the attention of modern managers. By now criteria have been evolved to test units of measure for work.

A record center in the Army Adjutant General's office is a paper-processing "factory," keeping records on millions of people as a basis for recruitment, assignment, release, etc. An effort to improve performance of this office soon showed the need for units of mea-

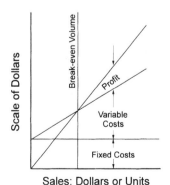

Fig. 26. The Break-even chart.

sure for the work done. The staff and line people got together and concluded, among other things, that the work of the office must be broken down into *units of work*. They concluded that a unit of work should:

> *Be countable*—a letter, a file drawer full.
>
> *Express output*, i.e., volume of work completed, such as a letter prepared, or a "case" processed.
>
> *Reflect work effort*; i.e., if license applications are processed with a high percentage of rejections, the number of applications processed is a better measure of work effort than the number of licenses issued.
>
> *Have consistency*; i.e., the work unit should have the same meaning throughout the entire organization.[3]

To this list might well be added the requirement that a unit of work should be:

Stated in the language of those doing the work.

Because work units are related to physical things, they are not additive between processes unless a system of common equivalents is set up. Laying 100 bricks cannot be added to pouring a yard of concrete unless both have been reduced to staff-hour equivalents.

The plant maintenance activities for a telephone company are related to some natural units which, based on past maintenance effort, are equated into work units as follows:

Natural units	Equated work units
100 poles	1.5
1 sheath-mile of cable	4.6
100 wire-miles of wire	14.5

The physical plant for each company division can be expressed in terms of the total natural units. These are used to compute the equated work units for each division, and this latter number becomes the denominator of an index. The numerator is the staff-hours actually used for plant maintenance. The index thus becomes staff-hours per equated work unit.[4]

---

[3]"A Work Measurement System," Executive Office of the President, Bureau of the Budget, Government Printing Office, Washington, D.C., 1950.

[4]Norris, F. E., "Performance Appraisal by Calculation," American Management Association *Management Report 37*, pp. 126–134, 1959.

In many industries the units of work are related to the unit of sale, for obvious practical reasons. In the real estate business, most units of measure are geared to the square foot of floor space, which is the sales unit. In other industries the unit may be:

per base box (tin plate)

per case (many food packs)

per gross (textile products)

per ton (the metals industry)

In its most complex form, the unit of work appears as the "output" in measures of productivity.[5]

Measuring Lack

Consider the subjects of morale, safety, integrity.

We have no direct means of plugging in an instrument and measuring these things as we measure sales, expenses, profit. But we can measure the *lack* of morale, safety, integrity. We do this by identifying the evidence of such lack, and then relating these evidences of lack to some measure of opportunity for lack.

Safety is a familiar example. An evidence of lack of safety is an accident, and we can count the number of accidents.[6] So far so good.

As soon as we try to use accident statistics, we encounter cries of "unfair." We shouldn't compare this year's number of accidents with last year's—we have more people now and hence more opportunity for accident. So we find a way to get around this. We create an artificial chunk of *opportunity* for accidents—a million staff-hours of exposure. Our "measure" now becomes a ratio—the number of lost-time accidents per million staff-hours of exposure.

This form of ratio is in wide use. Labor turnover, customer complaints, strikes, absenteeism, and many others are in the form:

$$\text{Ratio} = \frac{\text{number of occurrences}}{\text{opportunity for occurrences}}$$

Auditors and inspectors are generally judging lack of conformance to specification. Applied to multiple checks, they express their findings in

[5]See, generally, "Measuring Company Productivity," National Industrial Conference Board, Studies in Business Economics, No. 74, 1961.

[6]Which is not as simple as it sounds. See Precise Definition on p. 246.

per cent errors or per cent defective. More elaborate systems recognize differences in seriousness of errors through weights or demerits.[7]

Less well developed are measures of sales lost, production lost, profits lost, etc., due to some failure. Such measures of "lack of" nevertheless have value, and might well be researched further.

Precise Definition

In Chap. 13 we saw the need for precise definition of the control subject. We find an extension of this in units of measure. Consider the problem of counting accidents.

> Jane, Jean, and Joan are walking, arm in arm, along the freshly waxed office floor—very slippery. Then it happens. Jane slips and goes down, taking Jean with her. (Joan manages to keep her footing.) Jane bounds back up, unhurt. However, Jean is out for a week with a sprained ankle. Now, out of all that, what was the accident?

Our practice is clear. There was one "lost-time" accident, and five staff-days were lost. Jane's accident did not result in lost time; so we don't count it. Joan's near accident is likewise not counted. The cause of, or the opportunity for, the accident—the slippery floor—is not counted, though it is considered in the subsequent analysis.

The decision to count only accidents which cause "lost time" is arbitrary. But some such decision must be made if the resulting data are to have uniform meaning. So "accident" must be defined.

In like manner, "absences" turn out to be quite an assortment. There are "controllable" absences which include: unreported, unexcused, and excused; temporary leave; tardiness; early departure. Then there are the uncontrollables: compensable absence; temporary layoff; sick leave.[8]

As in definition of control subject, the managers have a responsibility for seeing that adequate precision is attained. If the manager avoids these questions, they must, by default, be settled in the lower levels. The resulting units of measure might not be to the manager's liking, were he or she aware of the details.

---

[7]See Juran, J. M., "Quality Control Handbook," 2d ed., pp. 8–8 to 8–14. McGraw-Hill Book Company, Inc., New York, 1962.

[8]Seatter, W. C., "More Effective Control of Absenteeism," *Personnel*, September–October, 1961, pp. 16–29.

Indexes for Abstractions

A concept such as "morale" commences as an abstraction. Managers say "I can't measure it but I can feel it." Then as the subject is confronted, some recognizable shapes emerge from the fog.

As to a single element of morale, it is easy to secure answers. A common form is the multiple-choice question.

> In this company, promotions are:
>
> Almost always made on merit ☐
> Usually made on merit ☐
> Made on merit as often as not ☐
> Seldom made on merit ☐
> Almost never made on merit ☐

> The answers checked can be counted, and weighted by an arbitrary score, such as 5, 4, 3, 2, and 1. The resulting average score is an index of attitude with respect to the company's promotion practice.

In like manner, sounding can be taken as to other topics regarded as a part of morale.

Nationwide Insurance Company undertook employee-attitude surveys on a wide range of questions.[9] Analysis of the results showed that there were 13 areas (or "factors," "dimensions") through which the abstraction "morale" can be more precisely defined. The company concluded that "...morale must be defined as the product of distinct, multiple and variously valued employee satisfactions." Several of these satisfactions were:

intrinsic job satisfaction (degree to which the worker likes performing his job)

working conditions

satisfaction with co-workers (primarily how well the worker gets along with those in his or her unit)

satisfaction with the administrative ability of supervisors

---

[9]Reported in Habbe, Stephen, "The Use of a Morale Index," *Management Record*, October, 1959, pp. 322–323. For technical detail, see Roach, Darrell E., *Personnel Psychology*, autumn, 1958.

As to such surveys generally, see "Experience with Employee Attitude Surveys," National Industrial Conference Board, Studies in Personnel Policy, No. 115; also "Following Up Attitude Survey Findings," National Industrial Conference Board, Studies in Personnel Policy, No. 181.

satisfaction with the consideration of supervisors
satisfaction with the work load and pressure

An example on a broad scale is the General Electric Company's Employee Relations Index (ERI).[10] Here the investigators adopted eight "indicators" of the state of employee relations: absences; disciplinary suspensions; work stoppages; separations; dispensary visits; grievances; suggestions; insurance plan participation. These indicators are combined into an index by a mathematical equation so devised that an average plant will "rate" 100, and that half the plants will "rate" between 87 and 113. Note that the General Electric ERI is in part based on positive indicators (suggestions), and in part on "lack of" indicators (work stoppages).

Combining the results of a multiplicity of such elements of morale into an index requires that they be weighted. General Electric's weighting was based on a statistical analysis by multiple regression. More usually the weighting is based on subjective estimates, with all the attendant risks.

The literature exhibits numerous instances in which investigators have devised ways of dealing with abstractions. For example:

The thing being measured	Unit of measure
Effectiveness of industrial communications*	Score in an examination based on memoranda, instructions, etc., previously issued by the boss's office
Effectiveness of conferences†	Subjective rating of incidents which take place in the conference (requires presence of an observer as an instrument)

*See Funk, Harry B., and Robert C. Becker, "Measuring the Effectiveness of Industrial Communications," *Personnel*, November, 1952, pp. 237–240.

†Harrison, Richard S., "Conference Timed-Analysis," *Personnel*, November, 1952, pp. 241–252.

Performance Rating

Performance of managers, supervisors, and nonsupervisors is a widespread control subject. The units of measure devised to express this performance are in part based on units of work and other quantitative measures. But in part, especially in the managerial levels, we are driven to

[10]Merrihue, Willard V., and Raymond A. Katzell, "ERI—Yardstick of Employee Relations," *Harvard Business Review*, November–December, 1955, pp. 91–99.

qualitative or "verifiable" approaches to "measuring" performance.[11] For such "measures" we make use of human beings as "instruments." Their results are called ratings, appraisals, evaluations. Whatever we call them, they are highly subjective, and they cause us much grief. We use them because the alternative of doing without any measures is worse.

The ratings are important to the companies because the manager is the most important variable in performance achieved. And the ratings are important to the manager. His or her job security, bonuses, pay raises, advancement, and other aspirations are geared in large part to these ratings. So are the aspirations of his or her family.

There is much we can do to reduce the effect of bias and other forms of human fallibility in these ratings. We can:

define carefully the activity under appraisal

define standards against which to appraise

train raters in the meaning of the standards and in the exercise of judgment

use multiple raters to reduce the extremes inherent in individuals (the principle of the jury system)

Statisticians have had a field day converting ratings into numbers. They ask the raters to put a check mark along a graphic scale (Fig. 27). Then the location of the check mark is measured. The resulting numbers become the grist for the statistical mill.

---

[11] For a further discussion, see Standards for a Function, p. 270.

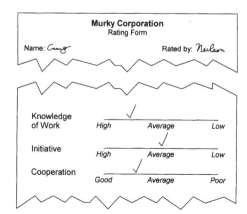

Fig. 27. Graphic scale rating form.

Alternately, the rater is asked to choose one of a graduated series of stated degrees of performance, such as:

Extremely industrious
Above average in industriousness
Average in industriousness
Below average in industriousness
Not industrious at all

A third approach is through choice of descriptive phrases, such as:

One of the hardest workers in the group
A hard worker
Works as hard as the next person, but no harder
Doesn't apply himself as well as he might
One of the laziest members of the group

The rater may also be provided with a "forced choice" of various statements about the ratee. The rater must mark which of the statements is the most descriptive and (sometimes) which is the least descriptive, of the ratee. For example:

Most	Least	
A	A	Does not get the facts necessary for making decisions.
B	B	Receives constructive criticism well.
C	C	Can definitely be promoted whenever the opportunity affords itself.
D	D	Makes too many personnel changes.
E	E	Is ready to give credit to others for good work done.

Most	Least	
A	A	Leans over backward in accepting points of view of subordinates.
B	B	Quick to size up a situation.
C	C	Coordinates the activities of all the various parts of the work.
D	D	Has little knowledge of the work of other departments.
E	E	Will take some time for him or her to prove his or her worth.

Still other methods are available. There is the "critical incident" method. In this method, the rater must adopt, as part of his or her day-to-day operation, the practice of listing various incidents which have occurred and which reflect either good job performance or poor job performance. Subsequently, at the time of rating, this list of incidents helps him or her to arrive at a better appraisal.

There is also the "field review" method. The supervisor does not make the actual rating, but does provide the information on which it is based, and must approve the final result. In this method, a skilled specialist (from the Personnel Department) discusses each employee with the supervisor, asking appropriate questions and eliciting essential information. The specialist then drafts a rating which he brings to the supervisor for revision and approval.

All these methods make use of prefabricated rating forms which then are processed through the statistical mill.

Telephone Service and Soda Fountains

There is no such things as a performance which cannot be appraised. The very purpose of a performance is to accomplish some result. If this result can be defined, the performance can be expressed in similar terms.

A drugstore chain appraises the performance of drugstore managers respecting various activities in the store: personnel relations; stock control; procedures; displays; fountain; public relations; executive ability. (All this is over and above the measurable operating results.) For example, fountain performance is reviewed using the following criteria:

1. Fountain neat and clean at all times
2. Clean floor, mirrors, menus, equipment, counter, tables
3. Keeps all glasses, dishes, and utensils spotlessly clean
4. Keeps inside floor clean and clear of rubbish and litter
5. Keeps all garbage and rubbish containers clean
6. Keeps all utensils and equipment in good usable order
7. Proper lighting maintained
8. Keeps all personal property and unnecessary equipment away from fountain

At the other end of the scale is a complex problem such as a telephone exchange. Here is a public utility—a complex service. It installs a telephone for you, keeps it in repair, provides telephone service, collects your money. The managers of the telephone company have long regarded "telephone service" as a control subject.

As the telephone company managers thought about it, they began to evolve and try out various measures. They learned that an installation which gave trouble within 30 days was usually due to faulty installation. They could count these. They could count the appointments made but not kept by installers. They found other measures of installation performance.

Turning to service in handling calls, they established 20 seconds as the dividing line for calls handled promptly. They could count these, by sampling if need be. They could count the calls improperly handled, the subscriber trouble reports, and the cause classifications. These measures could then be combined, by a weighting system, into a total measure.

Creation of a system of measurement for so complex a service required much discussion among line and staff people, and much trial of alternatives. (Steering Arm and Diagnostic Arm again.) But with so much at stake (thousands of telephone exchanges are measured by such a plan) it was well to use the evolutionary process.

The Fringe around the Numbers

In enumerating the varieties of unit of measure, we have traversed a spectrum of precision. The hard units—tons, inches, minutes—are highly reproducible and hence highly objective. There is a fringe or error even around such measurements, but the error is small relative to the thing being measured.

From these direct measures we have gone downhill in the spectrum to the indirect measures. We measure the lack of something and then manipulate the numbers statistically. These manipulations introduce assumptions of varying validity and hence becloud your results.

Farther down the spectrum are the subjective "I think this" form of "measure"—the ratings, appraisals, and such. When we try to reduce these ratings to numbers, we can readily get lost in the statistical jungle and forget the long fringe of error around each number.

Finally, we enter the twilight zone of pseudomeasurement. Here some forecaster (the market analyst, a manager, a consultant, an astrologer) predicts a number. Now the fringe is greater than the object, but we often forget this in the intricacies of the resulting statistical manipulation. Indeed, efforts are made to help us forget it by dressing these shabby numbers up so that they look quite respectable.

The manager has a duty of objectivity—of using the numbers. But if he values results, he will remain on the alert to the length of the fringe around the numbers. The length of the fringe affects his choice of standard, his tolerance as to subsequent performance, and the action he takes when there is a variance.

Now to Use the Common Language

With the availability of a unit of measure, we have a common language. This language serves us throughout the rest of the Control cycle—setting standards, measuring, interpreting, etc.

We will take these steps in turn, starting with the standard, the subject of the next chapter.

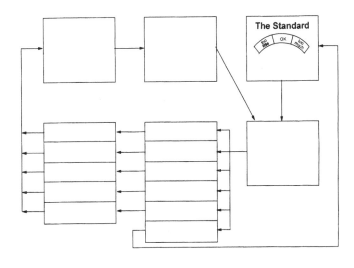

15

THE STANDARD

Need for a Standard

Without a standard there is no logical basis for making a decision or taking action. Tell a manager "Your inventory is a million dollars." He will ask "Is that good or bad?"

The standard was invented billions of years ago, and exists in profusion in all biological organisms. Biological control and actions are based on responses to those stimuli which are a departure from standard.

The human race reinvented the concept of standards. Primitive human beings had to judge whether fruits, fish, vegetables, or meat were fit to eat. They had to evolve standards for communication (language, writing), for trade, for defense. They were prolific in evolving standards (rituals, taboos) for stabilizing their culture.

The manager has likewise reinvented standards. Knowledge of performance is not enough; he must have a basis for comparison before he can decide or act.

The concept of a standard is not limited to numbered quantities—budgeted profit, scheduled deliveries, specified carbon content. Neither is it limited to "things." The concept of standards extends to business practice as well—the routines, methods, procedures. Dalcher[1] has summed up the purposes served by these "administrative" standards:

[1]Dalcher, L. M., "The Role of Administrative Standards in Business and Industry," American Standards Association, 1951.

to coordinate the work of several departments all working on the same problem

to promote consistency in handling repeated functions

to convert solved problems into routine procedures which make the solution a matter of record

to provide a guide for all who face these problems for the future

Static Societies

If anyone doubts the effectiveness of a control system in preventing change, let him or her study the old societies to see how for centuries on end they remained static.

In 1568, a Spanish expedition under Alvaro de Mendana discovered what we call today the Solomon Islands. The treasurer of the expedition, one Gomez Catoíra, wrote a detailed account of the native customs and language as part of his report to the Council of the Indies.

The report must have been stimulating, because additional expeditions, one after another, set sail for the Solomons, without finding them. The map makers kept shifting the Solomons to the shrinking unexplored places on the map. Finally they gave up—the discovery must have been a fake.

But it wasn't. In 1768, Bougainville rediscovered the Solomons. A century later, a restudy was made of the native customs and language. The *lack* of contrast was amazing. In every respect, custom, language, right down to the "pettiest detail in their dress," the mode of life was like that which Gomez Catoíra recorded so meticulously three hundred years before.

How did such societies remain so static for so long? By a clear system of standards, rigidly enforced. The community evolved standards for what one should do (rituals) and for what one should not do (taboos). People learned these things from infancy—it had never been different. The forces of belief and superstition, as well as the overwhelming presence of the community, saw to it that there was strict compliance with the standards.

The Dialect of Standards

Standards are all over, though they masquerade under a variety of aliases.

In the market, the standard for "How much should I sell?" is called a "quota."

In the laboratory, the standard for "How much should it measure?" is called a "specification."

In the office, the standard for "How much should I spend?" is called a "budget."

On the shop floor, the standard for "When should I deliver?" is called a "schedule."

And so on—target, piece rate, goal, aim, intent. The dialect varies, but the meaning is the same.[2]

Sometimes a single term is adopted to represent any standard. In one company, the term "program" was used to represent any target, whether for earnings, sales, inventories, etc.[3]

Standards Should Be...

By now there has been extensive experience in use of standards as a tool for managing. Out of this experience has come a recognized set of tests or criteria for good standards. Standards should be:

Attainable: Ordinary or "normal" individuals, applying themselves with reasonable effort, should be able to meet the standards under the conditions which are expected to prevail.

Economic: The cost of setting and administering standards should be low in relation to the activity covered by the standards.

Applicable: They should fit the conditions under which they are to be used. If these conditions vary, the standards should contain built-in flexibility to meet these variables.

Consistent: They should help to unify communication and operations throughout all functions of the company. They should also be consistent in time, so that planning for tomorrow is done in the light of knowledge gained to date.

All-inclusive: They should cover all interrelated activities. Failing this, standards will be met at the expense of those activities for which standards have not been set.

Understandable: They should be expressed in simple, clear terms, which admit of no misinterpretation or vagueness. The instructions for use should be specific and complete.

Stable: They should have a long enough life to provide predictability and to amortize the effort of preparing them.

Maintainable: They should be so designed that elements can be added, changed, and brought up to date without redoing the entire structure.

[2]The general definition of American Standards Association reads: "A standard is an agreement by authority, custom or general consent to a rule or model to be followed."

[3]The former Soviet Union appeared to use the word "norm" as a general use term for standard.

Legitimate: They should be officially approved.

Equitable: The standards should be accepted, as a fair basis for comparison, by the people who have the job of meeting the standards.

History as a Standard

By a wide margin, the most usual standard is historical. We compare April sales, shipments, accidents, scrap, etc., with March, or with April a year ago. There is much merit, and much deficiency, in historical standards.

The merit lies in their appeal to practical people. A person who is told "You did it once; why can't you do it again?" has no real answer. The historical standard meets many of the criteria of a good standard. It is attainable, since it has already been attained. It is applicable, since it has already been applied. It is stable, since it asks for no change. It is "equitable" in the eyes of the individual who is asked to meet it.

With all this, the historical standard can be fatally defective. The risk is that a poor performance may be perpetuated. Our sales may be as good as last year and the year before, but the industry is growing 15 per cent year after year. Our per cent scrap may be 10 per cent this year against 10 per cent last year. But we could economically get to 2 per cent if we really went for it. So our preoccupation with history may blind us to our opportunities.

A form of improvement standard based on improving on history was used successfully by the manufacturing vice-president of a carpet company. At the time of annual planning he would study the month-by-month performance charts of his plants and shops for costs, productivity, yields, etc. He would identify *the three best consecutive months.* Then he would put it to his managers as follows: "Here is a level you actually held for a quarter of a year. How about making that your target for the year ahead?" This proposition was difficult to debate. Where the manager could point to special conditions prevailing during the 3-month period, the talk soon led to an agreement to see to it that those special conditions became regular.

The scheme was quite effective. Not only were the improvement standards generally accepted; the entire approach tended to sharpen the analysis to discover why several months in a row could be better than history.

The Engineered Standard

The engineered standard is directed at what performance *should be,* rather than at the historical *has been.* The measure of what performance "should be" is obviously valuable. It does away with the gnawing suspicion that history is blinding us to the real possibilities.

Engineered standards are widespread in the shops, mainly in material usage, quality, process yields, and labor staff-hours. Generally they are based on close study of actual operations, plus analysis of the data to separate out the irregular and avoidable. The resulting standards are a composite of actual performance, seasoned with engineering judgment.

There are stirrings among the engineers to break out of the traditional labor and material standards into broader fields. The techniques of so-called "Operations Research" (and its numerous aliases) are being used to create models for discovering the optimum levels of inventory, profit, prices, etc. However, as yet, we have not found reliable ways to set engineered standards for some of the most critical performances on the list—what should be our share of market, whom should we promote to be general manager, what should be our level of morale.

The engineered standard also has limitations. One is the economics of setting standards. There must be enough repetition, or similarity, to provide for economic amortization of the engineering effort.

The main limitation of the engineered standard lies in its failure to meet the criteria that standards shall be attainable, applicable, and equitable. Obviously, the engineer feels that these criteria have been met. But the line worker who is faced with meeting the standards often says not. Lurking behind these stated objections may be the real objection of the line worker—he has not participated in, or consented to, the standard.

A well-worn battleground has been that of "precision" of engineered standards.

> A time-study engineer observes a shop operation with a stop watch. He is well skilled in the techniques of recording what was the actual time taken. He is also skilled in identifying the abnormal events which require separate analysis. But sooner or later he is faced with converting how long the operation *did take* into how long it *should take*; this conversion is at the very heart of the distinction between historical standards and engineered standards. How does he make this conversion? He makes it by using an estimate based on "engineering judgment," meaning he says "I think...."

It does not follow that the conversion of "did take" to "should take" would be identical if several engineers made the estimate for conversion independently, or even if the same engineer did it more than once. The engineers know the error of estimate is there, and they have conducted some experiments to measure how big it is. But they have avoided publicizing such studies.

A good rule to keep in mind is that the accuracy of such estimates depends on the number of observers, not on the number of observations. The bias is in the observers. By broadening the number of observers, the chance of extreme bias is reduced. (An ancient application of this principle is the jury as used in trials at law.)

The engineer feels pretty strongly about the importance of expertness in setting standards. He can get so wrapped up in his techniques, laws, and principles that he accepts them as axiomatic. A classic example is the conviction of Frederick W. Taylor, "the father of scientific management," that the determination of work standards and wages should be left to the expert:[4]

> Certain types of laws are too complex for the person of average experience to decide upon. Laws concerning divorce, marriage, assault, etc., the average man can pass upon because they are based upon facts of average experience. Other laws, based upon unusual experience, must be worked out by experts. Such are laws determining wages. The task which a good man in a trade can perform and the wage he should receive for performing that task are matters which can be determined by expert investigation and should be so determined. They are not subjects for collective bargaining any more than the determination of the hour at which the sun will rise tomorrow.

We will come back to this problem under the headings of Participation in Setting Standards, and Consent in Setting Standards.

Companies with a well-developed set of engineered standards have an impressive list of uses for them.

> A major maker of electron tubes has engineered standards which apply to direct and indirect material, direct and indirect labor, and those overheads varying directly with manufacturing activity. Through these standards, the company controls 70 per cent of the factory costs. Other costs are controlled by historical standards woven into budgets.
>
> Moreover, the standards are in enough detail that it is possible to establish standard costs for electron tubes before they are ever set up for manufacture. This predictive ability is invaluable in cost estimating, bidding, and planning, as well as in control of actual performance.

Examples of the engineered standard include the formulas for economic lot size, order points, inventory levels, etc. The starting principle

[4]Copley, Frank B., "Frederick W. Taylor, Father of Scientific Management," Vol. II, p. 420, Harper & Row, Publishers, Incorporated, New York, 1923.

here is that company economics, not departmental economics, are to be optimized.

In the inventory example, it is common to see several principal departments debating departmental viewpoints.

Finance points out the cost of carrying inventory—the interest charges, write-offs for obsolescence, physical storage.

Sales points out the cost of lean inventories—poor customer service, back orders, extensive expediting and correspondence.

Manufacture points out the cost of turning the factory spigot on and off—overtime costs, employee turnover costs, excess setup costs.

Actually, none of these views should prevail. Each is only one input to the "model" which will determine the levels which optimize company economics.

The Market Standard

The market standard is the performance of the other person, usually our competitor. The market standard is influential, if not decisive, in the prices we pay for wages, salaries, materials, and services. It imposes limits on our selling prices, our product quality, our speed of delivery, our credit terms, and much else.

Directors, investors, and managers compare the company's return on investment, sales, growth, and other financial measures with those of competitors.

Market standards are used to interpret the tests conducted to measure intelligence, dexterity, aptitudes, etc. Morale indexes are interpreted by reference to indexes of other companies.

Market standards are also used to interpret our accident rate, our employee turnover, and various other personnel statistics.

Some knowledge of the market standard is thrust on us. A customer says to our sales people—"I can get it at the same price from your competitor, and he'll throw in the attachments." A prospective employee balks at our starting salary—he or she has a better offer already. The labor union is alert for differentials between companies.

Other knowledge is volunteered by vendors (we sold your competitor three machines like this); by people we hired from our competitors; by consultants.

Still other information on the market is there, but we must take active steps to get it. A fantastic amount of information[5] is available from:

---

[5]The likelihood is that most companies avail themselves of less than 10 per cent of the available useful information.

government sources: various censuses; Statistical Abstracts; Survey of
Current Business; files of the Securities and Exchange Commission

financial publications: Moody's; Standard and Poor's; Dun & Brad-
street; *The Wall Street Journal; Barron's*

trade information: *Thomas's Register; MacRae's Blue Book; Sales Management's Survey of Buying Power;* studies by Trade Associations

published company information: annual reports to stockholders; house
organs; news releases; promotion literature; catalogues

Industry is a long way from making the most of the possibilities inherent in market standards. Some of the most critical decisions—life or
death for a division; broad policy on decentralization—can be aided by
digging into market data.

> Most companies have a multiplicity of product lines. Some of
> these lines are profitable, others are marginal, still others are run-
> ning at a loss. Decision as to what to do about the weak lines in-
> volves successive forks in the road:
>
> 1. Is the entire industry in which this line competes sick or
>   healthy? If sick, it is inevitable that the number of competitors
>   will shrink—there will be a "shake-out," i.e., every company
>   in the industry faces the grim decision of "double or nothing."
> 2. If the industry is healthy, some of the companies must be do-
>   ing fine. What is it they do which gets results so much better
>   than ours?
>
> Either way, information on how the competitors (the market) are
> doing is of the utmost help in reaching a decision.
>
> In the Squires case (p. 101), the study of the competitor Melcher
> disclosed his policies, practices, methods, with amazing clarity, in
> all functions: finance, research, marketing, manufacture, etc. Table
> 15-1 shows some of the policy which was deduced, and how.

Few companies undertake such studies in depth; most have only a
surface acquaintance with the ways used by successful competitors.

For some kinds of expenditures (advertising; research and development) there is no short-range measure of effectiveness. In such cases
studies of how much of the sales dollar goes for advertising or research,
in various industries, become an important basis for decision. The market percentage establishes a presumption. The burden of proof is on
anyone who wants to depart from this market percentage.

In some construction companies, the competitive bids of prospective
subcontractors constitute a market of another sort. Some contractors

Table 15-1. Deduction of Policies

Deduced policy	Deduced from
To expand mainly by development from within. (After two decades of expansion mainly through acquisition, the company had reversed its policy.)	The public record of acquisitions and spin-offs
To lease or lease back, rather than to own many of its facilities	Published accounts of long-term liability for leases, plus published information on new facilities. (Even the rentals per square foot became evident.)
To centralize manufacturing facilities.	Over a span of years involving a 70 per cent increase in sales dollars, there was an actual reduction in the number of manufacturing plants.
To decentralize distribution facilities.	During this same span of years, the number of distribution facilities rose by 45 per cent.

make their own estimates as a check on the notoriously wild bidding of subcontractors.

An official of Dow Chemical Company[6] stated it this way:

> To justify even the preliminary authorization, which may be for hundreds of thousands of dollars, we make an estimate of the total cost as a basis for economic evaluation of the project. Later, at the same time the contractors submit their bids, our estimating group submits its estimate of the cost, based on the same site visit, drawings, and specifications. We use this estimate as a check on the bids. If our estimate is much lower than the bids, we look for misunderstandings on the scope of the work, too much risk money in the bids, or a misinterpretation of some sort.

Figure 28 depicts the company's analysis of the competitive bidding on various proposals. The average bid is a form of market standard.

Interdivisional pricing presents a further need for a market standard. For some varieties of goods, transfers between profit centers should be

[6]Ross, J. E., "A Program for Controlling Construction Costs," American Society of Mechanical Engineers Paper 56-PET-10, 1956.

[7]See, for example, Dearden, John, "Interdivision Pricing," *Harvard Business Review*, January–February, 1960, pp. 117–125.

Fig. 28. Competing bids provide market standard.

at the market price if company economics, rather than departmental economics, are to be optimized. Without knowledge of the market price, a whole family of management decisions may be incorrectly based.[7]

Sometimes a "market" is provided by multiple operating units within the same company. A chain of stores stands to learn much by:

discovering from reports where are the best performances

discovering from study on the firing line how the best stores differ in method of operation from the rest

applying this knowledge to bring all stores up to the level of the best

This principle of comparing multiple units within the same company has wide application—multiple factories, offices, warehouses, departments, and even individual operators within one department.

A company making shotguns has long been plagued with defect X. About 10 per cent of the guns had to be dismantled and re-assembled because of this defect, a long, costly repair.

A total of 22 operators was engaged in assembling these shotguns. When someone studied the score of the operators as to their ability to avoid defect X, an amazing result emerged. Over a 6-month period, the five "worst" operators had 14 times as many rejections for defect X as the five "best" operators. This was a persistent difference, month after month.

The comparison left no doubt that some operators had found a way to avoid defect X. If this "secret knowledge" could be discovered by the management, it could be disseminated to all assemblers, so that all could come up to the level of the best.

And that is precisely what happened.[8]

There is much to be said for the practice of publishing "scores" of various divisions in a form of competition. The competitive urge (of individuals reared to watch the scoreboard) stimulates analysis of why the scores differ. Some energy is spent in arguing with the scorekeeper, but much is spent in constructive pursuits.

The Dutch made use of this principle while operating sugar mills in the East Indies during the 18th and 19th centuries. Data were worked up to compare, for the numerous mills, the usage of manpower, materials, and services required per unit of finished product. Discussion of the causes of differences brought out that some mills had evolved new and better methods of operating. This knowledge, by becoming available to the upper management, then became available to all.

A farflung activity like a telephone system operates hundreds of telephone exchanges. "Measures" have been evolved for service, cost, and other performance factors. The resulting actual performances are published as "ratings," and the ratings for various exchanges are there side by side for comparison. The managers are obviously in competition with each other. The unique character of the telephone business means that the exchanges must compete with each other.

(All natural monopolies, as the telephone system was once in the United States, have this problem of lack of a market to serve as standard for comparison. Thereby, a major problem for all utilities is to find the equivalent of market competition. This must be done by *self-competition*.)

We see that the market standard concept serves to sensitize us to the existence of a *spectrum of performance*. All the potentialities of "the mighty spectrum" (page 139) become available to us. As we learn of our standing relative to others, we can better determine whether we are so far from the norm that we should inquire further. In turn, these inquiries permit us to discover causes of differences and to apply this knowledge to improving our own performance.

[8]For a full account, see Juran, J. M., "Quality Control Handbook," 2d ed., pp. 4-20 to 4-23, McGraw-Hill Book Company, Inc., New York, 1962.

Prefabricated Intercompany Comparisons

In some instances, compilations of intercompany data are worked up by the statistical departments of service institutions. National Safety Council works up data on accident rates. American Management Association works up data on executive compensation. Trade associations work up data on wage rates, hours, fringes, etc.

Information on company performance is available mainly at the top and at the bottom of the companies. At the top, there are available the financial ratios by industry, as worked up by trade associations and industry publications.

At the bottom of the company are the special productivity studies for various kinds of manufacture. For example, a study of shoe manufacture will publish the units per hour attained in various processes; material utilization; ratio of supervision to productive labor; rejections for quality. These productivity studies are invaluable for analyzing manufacturing costs.

In the middle of the company, studies are still mainly in the research stage. American Management Association's "Group 10 Project" years ago made much headway in defining categories of efforts (inputs) and results (outputs) of the "overhead departments." For example, inputs of the accounting department are staff-years. Outputs are such things as lines of billing and number of accounts receivable. The resulting ratios, such as staff-years per thousand accounts receivable, become the basis for intercompany comparison. As the research studies refine the categories and the data gathering, it may be feasible to create a new intercompany service.

The Giraffe's Heart

The "market" is a tricky standard. What someone else is doing is certainly informative, and it is usually pertinent. It may also be good for his or her situation, but not necessarily for our situation.

> During 40 historic days many kinds of animals were afloat on a certain ark. There wasn't enough to do, so someone organized study groups to make constructive use of the long hours. One of these groups got into a study of the hearts of the various animals. It turned out that there was immense variation. The big whales had huge pumps weighing over 400 pounds; mice had tiny hearts, three thousand to the pound. This was a variation of over a million to one.

Then a staff animal made a shrewd observation. "Naturally, big animals need bigger hearts. We should compare ratios—the ratio of heart weight to total body weight."

They tried it out, and it worked brilliantly. The per cent of heart weight to body weight ranged from 0.1 to 0.9, a range of only 9 to 1.

But the data threw consternation into the giraffe camp. Their 25-pound hearts were a thumping 0.9 per cent of their body weight. The giraffe Controller stated it eloquently: "Our ratio of heart weight to total body weight is twice as much as the market. We are carrying a lot of unnecessary overhead. If we could do with 15-pound hearts, we would be more in line with the market."

It didn't work. Nothing but a 25-pound heart was powerful enough to pump blood to the top of an 18-foot animal.

So the emphasis should be on "What is best for my health," not on ap-ing the other fellow.

Some years ago the life insurance companies established proof that overweight reduces the life span. In their campaigns to reduce mortality rates, the companies thereupon published tables of average weights of people. Through these tables, people had a target—get down to the average.

A few years later the companies published new weight tables. These new tables did not show the prevailing averages; instead, they showed desirable weights. The prevailing averages were too high and hence poor targets.

The Decreed Standard

The scene is the office of Big Sid, the plant manager. The door opens and there enters a well-padded suit of clothes containing the smiling body of Ray, the sales manager.

RAY: Relax, Sid. We got the Atkins job. Right on the dotted line.

SID: Good going. We needed that one to take up the slack.

RAY: It wasn't easy, and it still isn't.

SID: What do you mean?

RAY: We had to promise delivery in nine weeks. No fooling. Penalty clause.

SID: You're crazy. We can't deliver in nine weeks. I went through all that with you.

> RAY: It's this business that's crazy. Without the nine weeks promise, we would be out, and you would still have all that wonderful slack.
>
> SID: Even with overtime, we wouldn't have the boring-mill capacity. The subcontracting and the overtime will cost us a fortune. Even then we may not make it.
>
> RAY: If it were easy, we wouldn't need *you* on this job. A cluck could do it.

The decreed standard is imposed on us in various ways: by the customer, who for reasons of his own must have a particular date, quality, package; by the boss, who for reasons known best to him wants this report in the mail Thursday; by the general manager, who wants a new design ready in time for the semiannual trade show.

The decree at times has little evident relation to historical, engineered, or market values. The most obvious feature of the decree is its irritating arbitrariness. History, engineering, and the market, with all their deficiencies, do have a logic behind them. They also have an impersonal character. But the decree is a *personal* thing—it is traceable to some person who refuses to accept logic and who imposes his or her power on well-meaning, logical people. The decree is a government of people, not laws, and is resented aplenty.

> The Whidden Company's general manager performed high-level selling. He also made delivery commitments which could not be met. His subordinates dutifully went through the exercise of making up schedules which showed that the customer would get his delivery as promised by the boss. But only the customer was fooled. Everyone else knew the schedules were a fake and a joke. The managers took a lot of abuse because they seldom met the promises. They also derived some consolation from the hilarity of it all.

In the Whidden Company, and in similar situations, a sort of Gresham's law takes over. The bad standards drive out the good. A price war can drive out sound prices. A plant slowdown can drive out engineered labor standards. Dishonest appliance-repair shops can drive out the honest.

The Plan as a Standard

Many standards—budgets, schedules, quotas—are the result of a mixture of considerations. The budget is a good example.

A well-ordered budgeting procedure starts with defining the objectives for the year ahead—objectives in *deeds,* not money. These objectives may be things like: bring products A, B, and C to market; drop products Y and Z from the line; hold present share of market on the original equipment business; increase share of market in the replacement business from 10 to 11 per cent; consolidate the two Eastern plants; open up new sales branches on the Gulf and West coasts.

To do these deeds requires facilities, personnel, time, money. These needs are worked out by a study which combines use of history, engineered standards, market data, and that mysterious ingredient, business judgment.

Now the deeds are "dollarized"—they are priced out to see whether they make sense financially. Inevitably, it is found that we can't do all these things next year. Some are not economic; some do not give enough return; some must be deferred because we don't have the capital this year. Finally, the deeds and their financial implications make sense, and we have a budget.

The annual calendar of seasonal operations is another example of using a plan as a standard. The cardinal dates (the Christmas rush, harvest time, the trade show) are the D days around which events must be planned. Some of these calendars become elaborate, showing in great detail who is to do what and when. The Program Evaluation Review Technique (PERT) is an example of a highly formalized plan of this character.

Companies which are faced with repetitive introduction of new products or model changes evolve a plan for giving easy birth to the new family members. Timetables and roles are laid out for sales forecasting, product development, market testing, approval of samples, tooling, material ordering, fabrication, build up of inventories, sales promotion, packaging, selling.

The Plan also operates in microcosm. Many employees do their work without the benefit of a supervisor on the scene—the salesperson, the installer on the customer's premises, the plant maintenance person, the trucker. These individuals must be supervised by plan rather than by personal supervision.

These plans take familiar forms—the itinerary for the trucker, the call list for the salesperson, the daily schedule for the maintenance person. Where the plan is not worked out in advance, provision is made for call-in so that job-by-job supervision can be given (the two-way radio system used by the taxicab fleet, for example).

The control by plan extends to the methods used. "Standard practice" is the key phrase. As improved practice is evolved, whether by the engineers, the supervisors, or the employees, the improvement is woven into standard practice, the manuals, the procedures. So the better way becomes the regular way.

Subjective Standards

In a sense, these are simply the lack of objective standards. The boss says "Your costs are too high," which comes as a surprise to the underling. He thought his costs were pretty good (and he still thinks so).

Experience has shown that these subjective evaluations are mainly a curse. Human beings yield to pressures of the moment, so that what was good (subjectively) in lush times becomes no good in hard times. Our concepts of prices, quality, and service change remarkably depending on whether goods are scarce or plentiful.

Nowhere is the problem of subjective standards more a curse than in evaluation of human performance. Much of the impetus for seniority, work rules, etc., stems from the opportunity for arbitrariness which the subjective standard gave the supervisor. To this day the personnel people and the behavioral scientists are hard at work refining the performance-rating systems to make them more and more objective.

Standards for a Function[9]

With all the talk of the importance of standards, we are at our worst (in precision) when setting standards for executive performance—the very place where we need standards the most.[10] At the bottom of the company, the organization of work has generally been such that objective

---

[9]These standards are not to be confused with some related tools of the personnel trade. The contrasting definitions are about as follows:

Job description tells *what* is to be done, and spells out the authority and responsibility associated with doing it. The finished job description is built around various action words—inspect, pack, assemble, interview, contact, etc. Those writing a job description are trying to complete sentences of the form "The duty of this job holder is to...."

Job (or personnel) specification defines the background and characteristics of the person needed to fill a job: age, education, experience, skills. The effort is to complete the sentence—"The individual doing this job should have...."

Performance standard (our present subject) defines what are the essential results to be achieved, and the means for determining that these results have in fact been achieved. The effort is to complete the sentence—"A good job has been done when...."

Performance appraisal is the process of determining whether the results attained are up to standard.

For a comprehensive discussion of all aspects of this subject, see the 120-page research study: Enell, John W., and George H. Haas, "Setting Standards for Executive Performance," American Management Association Research Study 42, New York, 1960.

[10]For years it had been assumed that executive performance was *not* measurable. Such "systems" as were in use were methods of "rating" the individuals mainly for personal qualities (loyalty, leadership, integrity, etc.) with "quantity of work" and "quality of work" thrown in. During the 1950s there emerged a wide shift of emphasis from individual rating to performance rating.

standards can be set with confidence. As we get away from the countable, measurable activities and move more and more into variety, creativity, judgment, and leadership, our ability to measure seems to fade out. How then do we go about setting standards when we cannot measure the results? We go at it in several ways:

1. We set *quantitative* standards anyhow. An example[11] is that of a divisional area supervisor managing a pipeline for the Standard Oil Company of Ohio (now Exxon). Quantitative standards have been set for no less than 37 control subjects. Some of these are familiar enough:

3 safety standards, based on accident rates

2 personnel administration standards, based on idle time and overtime

14 maintenance standards based on labor cost, waste, total cost, etc.

10 operating standards based on costs, errors, waste, etc.

But some of the standards are less familiar:

4 "communications" standards based on numbers of training sessions, meetings, and visits

4 public relations standards based on numbers of visits to municipal officials, schools, other companies, and on number of newspaper stories

(Incidentally, the published standard includes a promissory note to develop similar quantitative measures for the activities of General Administration.)

2. We set *qualitative* standards. An excellent example[12] is that for a division manager in Inter City Paper, Ltd., of Canada. Some 34 control subjects have been identified, and for each there has been completed the sentence—"Performance is satisfactory when...." For example, with respect to work delegation, performance is satisfactory when:

(*a*) There is evidence of planning for the appropriate delegation of responsibility.

(b) Subordinates are informed of and understand their responsibilities and authority.

and so through *c, d, e,* and *f.*

3. We set *verifiable* standards. A good example[13] is seen in the standard for a Regional Manager of Smith, Kline and French Laboratories.

[11]Enell and Haas, *op. cit.* pp. 20–21.

[12]Enell and Haas, *op. cit.*

[13]Enell and Hass, *op,.cit.*

In this standard, 20 control subjects have been identified; for each there has been completed the sentence—"Performance is up to standard when...." Now, *in addition*, there is added the "method of determination" (the format of the published standard is specially designed to show this). For example:

The performance of a regional manager with relation to Supervision is up to standard when:	Method of determination
4. Representative's standards of performance are reviewed at least once a year	Standard-of-performance review report in representative's confidential file
	Check sheet in regional manager's confidential file
6. No major problems causing poor morale exist	District manager's report on regional manager's conferences, regional meetings, and field contacts in regional manager's confidential file

Generally, performance standards will consist of a combination of all these forms—quantitative, qualitative, and verifiable.

The unique nature of standards for executive performance has required that the approach be special. However, since formal standards for this purpose are still relatively new, the process for creating them has not yet been fully agreed on.

The one thing on which all authorities are unanimous is that development of these standards requires full participation of the people affected. Ideally, such standards should be developed by exhaustive discussions between (*a*) a number of people all holding like posts and (*b*) the boss or bosses of such posts. Staff people can be useful as catalysts and as professionals for consultation, but the main burden falls on the line managers. Moreover, since the standards are unique to specific job classes, the amount of time consumed is considerable.[14]

---

[14]Those who look on these activities as shocking expenditures of time might ponder on another emerging concept. These standards, along with job descriptions, union contracts, piece rates, etc., are all in the nature of establishing agreements between the company and the employees. These agreements concern "rights in the job," the industrial equivalent of rights in land. When we consider the effort which human beings have (during the agricultural centuries) put into setting boundaries, defining rights in land, formalizing transfers, etc., we can well conclude that during the industrial centuries we will see more, not less, of definition of rights in the job.

Beyond this unanimity, there is general agreement on some other elements of the approach:

the job descriptions should first be brought up to date.

there should be identified those elements of job performance over which the job holder is to have a substantial degree of influence.

for each of these elements of job performance a standard should be set, either in terms of the results expected or, alternately, in the indirect terms of what one should do to accomplish the expected results.[15]

the results expected should be defined either quantitatively or in terms of how they are to be verified.

the standard should be attainable by at least one member of the group who participated in developing it.[16]

the standard should be issued in a formalized manner, with an official approval.

there should be a provision for keeping the standard up to date.

Multiple Use of Standards

A widely prevalent fallacy is that standards are used only as a basis for comparison with actual performance. Standards are indeed used for this purpose. But standards have a much wider range of use, and this range should be understood.

For example, labor standards are used to judge the performance of operators and clerks. But these same standards become the basis for costing, for budgeting, for pricing, for judging potential cost reductions, for estimating labor requirements, for estimating machine capacity, for planning of inventories, purchases, money needs, and many others.

Standards for executive performance likewise serve a variety of purposes:

the very act of preparing the standard clears up many vague notions about the job.

---

[15]Indirect terms are an open-end approach. In lieu of results, we may dwell on the facilities, i.e., adequacy of labor, of physical facilities, of technology. Alternately, we may dwell on the process or method of approach, how he goes at the job, i.e., the clarity of his planning, the adequacy of his communication, the logic of his organized approach. We may dwell on the effort he has put in—the time spent, the money spent.

[16]Note again how most people are convinced of the value of something not by its logic but by the fact that others have done it.

the publication of the standard is an act of communication to many people on an important subject.

the published standard becomes a guide for selection of individuals for the post and for their subsequent training and development.

the standard becomes the reference for the boss in supervision of the job, in appraising performance, in merit reviews, and in salary administration.

The advocates of setting standards for executive performance feel that the exhaustive discussions which must precede the setting of such standards result in a new depth of understanding of the job, the responsibilities, the relationships, etc. This deeper understanding is so rewarding that a considerable body of opinion regards it as the main value of setting these standards.[17]

The multiple use of standards is also decisive in choice of dialect and terminology. For example, if standards were to be used only as a basis for control, the local terminology of vats, bays, stacks could become the units of measure, since the natives would understand the dialect. However, with broader usage, the units of measure must be in widely understood language—gallons, square feet, reams.

Before there is a big undertaking to set standards, there should be a look around to see just how widespread will be the use of standards. This spread will then decide how broad should be the participation and how broad (or provincial) should be the resulting concepts, language, and applications.

Tools for Standards Setters

Setting of standards can be a most elaborate activity. The annual budgeting preempts the time of many employees in the company, for many hours. Scheduling of a large construction project is a considerable feat. So is the scheduling of a mass-production and mass-marketing activity. A standard cost system requires a prodigious amount of detail work. So does a system of piece rates, of job evaluation.

Those who draft proposals for standards have by now acquired a proved kit of tools to aid in setting standards. For example:

---

[17]"Setting Standards for Executive Performance," American Management Association Research Study 42, pp. 103–114.

Tool	Used for
Engineering synthesis	Setting standards for material usage, chemical reactions, electric-power usage.
Time study	Setting standards for labor hours, machine capacity, machine time.
Statistical analysis	Clarifying history, discovering seasonal trends, variations by product type, etc. Analyzing engineering data to "purify" standards and make them applicable to various situations. Discovering what is the market.
Engineering or business judgment	Filling in the gaps not supplied by other, more objective means.

The emergence of modern high-speed computers has made possible the standardization work which heretofore has been too forbidding in time and effort. A familiar example is the scheduling of customer orders. Here, a computer carrying the parts lists in its memory "explodes" the orders into parts. These orders for parts are then analyzed in relation to the parts-inventory record, which the computer also maintains. Next, the production schedule is prepared from load vs. capacity analysis. Finally, the computer prints out the standard, i.e., the delivery schedules.

Additional tools for standards relate to the form of the standard itself. The variable budget is an example. It separates the constant from the variable expenses, and the job of standardization is greatly facilitated.

As in all other cases of uses of tools, no practitioner needs to do much inventing if he will but look around. An immense amount of effort has gone into invention of tools, and the results are available for the use of anyone who will trouble to inform himself or herself.

Statistical Aids in Setting Standards

When historical data are to be used as a basis for setting standards, some useful aids to judgment can be got by analysis of the data.

Historical data are usually derived from an assortment of experiences—data from many machines, many branch offices, many weeks of operation, many customers. There is "variability" in these data, and one of the needs is to discover what is "normal."

The statistician is able to analyze the data in a way which sheds light on the variability. He also has some clever tools[18] for distinguishing "abnormal" from "normal." Through this analysis, the makeup of past performance is better understood, and the determination of what is "normal" can be better defended.

So far, the procedure has dealt with doing a better job of understanding history. Now comes an act of judgment.[19] It is decreed that the standard for the future is to be either:

(a) The "normal" of the past

(b) The upper quartile of the past, i.e., the performance attained by the best 25 per cent of the weeks, offices, machines, or whatever

(c) Some other improvement over normal past performance

There is much to commend such an approach to setting standards. If the proposed standard has been met 25 per cent of the time, it can hardly be attacked as unattainable.[20] But let no one be deceived into thinking that use of a mathematical formula confers science or precision. The basic act of judgment in choosing the upper quartile is arbitrary. The soundness of the judgment is demonstrated by the subsequent results, not by the prior logic.

The Standard as an Anesthetic

One of the main purposes of the standard is to sensitize us to feel pain when the standard is violated. The reverse is also true. The standard has the effect of making us shockproof as to matters which are *not* a violation of the standard.

The factory process which had for years yielded about 90 per cent good product (p. 27) is a case in point. No one had been able to take the process to higher yield levels. In consequence, the 90 per cent came to be regarded as normal. A whole series of applications of anesthesia followed.

The standards for costs, machine capacity, and material usage were all set on the premise that 90 per cent was normal. The effect of the standards was to desensitize all organs. Only when the yields fell below the threshold value of 90 per cent were any alarms tripped.

---

[18]See, for example, the case of matching pennies, p. 331.

[19]This is similar to the act of engineering judgment discussed in The Engineered Standard, above.

[20]Many engineers of the Taylor school would contend that the result will be a loose set of standards. They would have ample experience to back up such a contention.

Participation in Setting Standards

There are strong arguments for giving, to the individual who is to meet standards, a voice in setting them:

1. The standards become more realistic (really attainable) if they have first been tested against the arguments of those who face the practical problems of meeting them. "Applicability" is a most sensitive area. The conditions under which the standard is to apply vary considerably. Total activity varies; there are variations in product type, process conditions, packaging. Unless the standard provides the necessary allowances or flexibility to handle these variable conditions, the resulting performance will, in part, measure these variations rather than the performance of individuals.

2. The psychology of participation makes for a genuine acceptance of the standard, and hence a genuine effort to meet it.

Despite these compelling reasons, there is much setting of standards without participation. Some of this is for reasons of principle. "The crew can't run the ship." Some is for reasons of classified information—a plan for abolishing or changing the jobs of the very people who would participate. Their first reaction could well be that they are being invited to dig their own graves. Some lack of participation is for pretty weak reasons—the boss is insecure, or closed-minded. Some is due to a confusion of "participation" with "consent." But some is done on the sound ground of experience. Many an executive can point to cases where his or her subordinates succeeded in meeting the very objectives they had once regarded as unattainable. These same executives point out that they retain the means for easing the objectives if the unfolding events show them to be really unattainable.

Even when participation is present, the biases show. Managers try to arrive at a budget which is attainable; so do salespeople respecting their quotas; so do factory hands respecting their piece rates. But in the absence of participation, mutual suspicion runs high. The lack of confidence then results in arbitrary setting of objectives, e.g., arbitrary cuts in budgets. In turn, those faced with the threat of arbitrariness set up defenses in the form of restricted production, padded budgets, etc. Some of the cases of fantastic military requisitioning during World War II were the result of each level adding a generous safety factor to the requisition submitted by the levels below.

In contrast, when participation takes place in an atmosphere of confidence, it is common for line supervisors to propose goals which seem surprisingly severe to the bystanders. When the supervisors are questioned about it, the response is in the form "We are the ones who really know what can be done." And often they are.

Participation is not merely a relationship between boss and subordinate; in many companies, the real problem is between the line supervisors and the staff specialists. Uninitiated staff people—industrial engineers, accountants, controllers, procedures analysts, etc.—can be so impressed by their own logic that they consider the standards they work up should be adopted forthwith. Upper managers seldom raise a hand in initiating these staff people, leaving the staff and line relationships to be "worked out." They do get worked out, but the process is long, and the casualties many.

The Budget as an Example of Participation

Some companies have traveled the long, flinty road of training their employees to understand the financial implications of their departmental activities. In such companies, the budgetary process becomes a form of major participation in setting standards of performance. To an important degree, each supervisor sets his or her own budget.

There is coordination and supervision, to be sure. The charts of accounts, the forms, the timetable have all been coordinated by the Budget Director (or similar title). But each supervisor drafts his own budget, using these tools to facilitate his own planning. He goes over this draft with his own department head, who supplies the first layer of broad coordination.

The coordination process broadens as the various rivulets of budgeting join to become broader streams. But each of them provided a high degree of participation by those who will, in due course, be held responsible for meeting it.

Consent in Setting Standards

The concept of consent involves a head-on contradiction of two great principles:

1. The needs for decisiveness and clear responsibility. To date, no way has been found to meet these needs adequately without use of a chain of command, and thereby, the opportunity for decision in the absence of consent.

2. The need for consent of the governed.[21] Inherent in the human sense of justice is the idea that laws are to be based on the consent of those who are to be governed. The human being who joins an industrial company brings this idea into the gate with him or her.

These two principles are so important that neither can be ignored. A manager may dismiss "consent" with truism that "the crew can't run the ship." But no one can brush off a basic human drive without paying the price. In the managerial levels, the spirited individuals may leave, lowering the average of managerial competence and morale in the process. In the ranks, the employees do not quit—they organize into unions, after which the boss jolly well discovers the meaning of consent.

An important factor in the need for consent is whether we are dealing with proved or unproved standards. By the very nature of things, we have already met most of the historical standards, many of the market standards, and some of the engineered standards. In contrast, we have not already met the plans for Breakthrough, or the decreed standards. These latter, untested standards require (and generally receive) more participation and consent than do standards proved by prior usage.

A further factor is the rigidity of the subsequent accountability for results. When review of results is done with fairness, the need for prior consent shrinks markedly. Undue rigidity at the top breeds blind obedience at the bottom, but only after the people of spirit get out. The habit of blind obedience has value only when the top person is all-knowing.

The dilemma of decisiveness vs. consent is probably best resolved by the concept of revision of standards.[22] When the results are up for review, one of the alternatives is revision of the objective. If the boss is flexible on this score, the need for prior consent again shrinks markedly.

Maintenance of Standards

Standards start to deteriorate from the day they are established. This deterioration continues as conditions keep changing. In time the standards can get badly out of date, unless provision is made for review and maintenance.

---

[21] "To secure these [inalienable] rights, governments are instituted among men, deriving their just powers from the consent of the governed." (The Declaration of Independence.)

[22] See Tight Rein and Loose Rein, in Chap. 20.

Some of this provision is made at the time of major changes. Part of the job of introducing a major change is to review the standards which might be affected, and to change them as well.

But there is also need for periodic review to deal with creeping and with undisclosed changes. Such reviews are known as audits, and are properly conducted on a scheduled basis—quarterly, annually, every 5 years, or whatever is deemed to be appropriate.

Maintenance of standards is greatly aided by adopting a formal approach toward standardization.

> Our basic problem was this:
> Manual-type information was being sent to supervisors from a number of different sources. Each source had its own numbering system, its own format and editorial practice, its own indexing system, and its own distribution system.
> Because of this circumstance, the position of the supervisor was needlessly difficult. It was difficult from the standpoint of keeping the material he received up to date. It was difficult from the standpoint of locating a particular piece of information when he needed it. It was also difficult because the information, when he did find it, was often not as simple to understand as it might have been.
> Having decided what the problem was, we made a rather simple decision. We decided to standardize on standards. All of this procedure and policy information was to be written up as standards. It was to mean that each of our supervisors would have his own standards book, to be used as his primary on-the-job reference. Just one book to look in; just one book to keep up to date; just one numbering system to become familiar with; just one index to refer to. That was the idea behind our original conception of administrative standards.[23]

And Now, How Are We Doing?

The standard becomes our decision of what we *should* be doing. Now we need to know what we *are* doing. Finding out what we are doing requires, in every instance, a device which scans or senses the deeds we are performing and converts this sensing into communicable language. We will call this device the "sensor," and it becomes, logically, the subject of our next chapter.

---

[23]Dalcher, L. M., "The Role of Administrative Standards in Business and Industry," American Standards Association, New York, 1951.

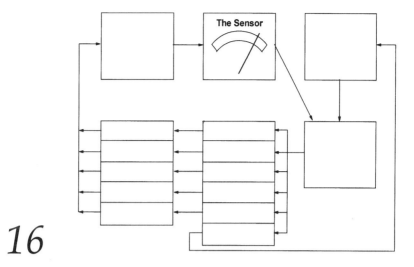

16

THE SENSOR

Behind the Instrument Panel

The simple automobile instrument panel, the very complex aircraft instrument panel, the manager's monthly reports, and the charts in the Board of Directors room are all the culmination of much detail. Every instrument, report, or chart is the end result of a *system of reporting* which has the same basic elements of:

A *sensor*. This device (also called receptor, informer, tale bearer, tattletale), senses what is taking place and registers it in a form ("information") suitable for transmission to the proper destinations.

A *transmission line*. This conveys information from the sensor to its destination, often through a series of relay stations.

A *receiver*. This converts the transmitted information into forms usable by the people (or mechanisms) at the destination end.

In this chapter we are concerned with the sensor. The transmission lines are discussed in Chap. 17, the receiving stations in Chap. 18.

What Is a Sensor?

It is a detecting device, highly specialized to recognize certain stimuli, and to convert the sensed knowledge (of the presence and intensity of the stimulus) into "information."

In the biological organism, some of the more well-known sensors are the myriads of tiny sense organs which transform heat, light, mechanical energy (pressure, touch), and chemical energy (smell, taste) into nerve impulses. In the company, the more familiar sensors are the clock cards, materials requisitions, inspectors' gages, sales call records.

The sensor may consist of mechanical means for sensing stimuli which cannot be detected by the unaided human being (magnetism, radiation). It may be a means for amplifying the human sense organs (thermometer, barometer). In any case, the detected stimuli must be converted into "on or off" signals, scale measurements, beeps, or other things the human senses can detect.

The sensor may also consist of a human being who is "plugged in" to do what, as yet, no mechanical instrument is able to do. The patrol inspector, the security guard on the beat, and the field auditor are all examples of human beings used as sensory devices.

> To study the effectiveness of conference leadership a trained observer sits in some of the conferences. He records the happenings. He then judges these against criteria for leadership, participation, and content.[1]

The industrial sensor is not necessarily located within the company. The sensors which detect changes in prices of materials, in business activity, or in cost of living may be maintained by a trade association, a government bureau, a business magazine. Through publication, the resulting stimuli energize various readers into action.

The sensor may be on a heroic scale. A wind tunnel creates an artificial environment. A "test town" is used to discover the probable effect of marketing a new product. A national test panel, of thousands of consumers or television viewers, is used to the same effect. The "polls" serve a related test purpose.

The Time Factor in Sensing

We have an option of sensing events before, during, or after they happen. The general relation of these options is shown in Table 16-1.

It is seen that *all* forms of sensing serve a useful purpose, but that each fits different circumstances.

---

[1]Harrison, Richard S., "Conference Timed-Analysis," *Personnel*, November, 1952, pp. 241–252.

Table 16-1. Time of Sensing Relative to Occurrence of Activities Being Sensed

	Before	During	After
Type of situation most appropriate	Prior to embarking on major programs; to defend against major disasters	For regulation of the "useful many"	For review of effectiveness of long-range programs
Type of sensor	Special, expensive, early warning, or predictive sensors	Simple. Often done directly from deeds without creating any data	Information systems based on data which are mainly a by-product of operations
Who collects the sensed information	Specialized personnel or departments	Mainly the regular operating forces	Regular statistical departments
Who acts on the summarized information	The upper and middle managers	Middle managers and people on the firing line	The upper and middle managers

Sensing before the Fact

This may be done for defensive (Control) reasons, i.e., predicting disasters before they happen. The symbol of early warning is the watch tower. The lookout is the human instrument used to detect those happenings which precede disaster. An unfamiliar ship on the horizon, or a wisp of telltale smoke, are signals of danger. The lookout sounds the alarm, and all hands race to man the defenses against the pirates, the conflagration, or whatever.

Sensing before the fact may also be done for offensive (Breakthrough) reasons, i.e., predicting the likely result of a new undertaking. The key word here is "forecasting."

In days of yore, the same sensors were used for both defensive and offensive prediction. The Pharaohs, Khans, Moguls, Emperors, and such all kept a stable full of astrologers, clairvoyants, augurers, diviners, oracles, seers, soothsayers, and entrail readers. These worthies were responsible for interpreting omens, dreams, or other potential early warnings of disaster, as well as for certifying the most auspicious occasions for breaking a mutual friendship treaty with a neighboring nation.

The modern manager likewise has need for prediction, both defensive and offensive. He also has, at his service, descendants of the foregoing worthies, as well as some new species. (Distinguishing the useful fore-casters and lookouts from the students and quacks is no simple task.) Collectively, the manager and his specialists have made some good strides in sensing before the fact.

On the Control side, extensive use has been made of the early-warning principle. Buildings are guarded against fire, using sensors which respond to temperatures below the ignition point. The health of people is guarded by the annual physical examination. The batch is processed only after a sample is checked for adequacy. The product is shipped to the customer only after an inspector has tested it.

Perhaps the most extensive use of the early-warning principle is in the very setting of a target, i.e., "management by objective." A stated objective carries within itself a stimulus to action. "Let's ship the machine by June 30" sets up a race against time. The grownup in industry can relive his youthful romping days by racing this one for keeps.

Such emphasis on a future target forces some useful habits to evolve. Each day of March or April contains as many hours as the dramatic day of June 30. So the early-warning principle puts the emphasis on the starting time, the milestones along the road, the rates of production, the expediting, the clearing of obstacles, all before D day. If these things are done, June 30 will be just another day on the calendar, and the machine will ship as just another event in a long series of events. The final birth of the baby is dramatic to the parents, not to the child.

Prediction for the purpose of taking the offensive has likewise made great strides. In extensive use are such technical sensors as:

Sensor	Used to predict
Cost estimate	Actual cost
Measure of machine capacity	Rate of production through a bottleneck
Measure of process capability	Ability of a process to meet tolerances for quality

In the broader area of business prediction, there is use of other sensors:

"Leading" economic indicators*	Extent of economic activity, i.e., contracts booked and unfilled orders "lead" the volume of construction and production

Study of market potential	Whether a proposed product line will do the company enough good to embark on development

---

*Our best industrial fog lights are those dealing with population trends. Once the babies are born, we can predict with accuracy how many will live to what stages. In broad terms we can predict the resulting extent of family formation, school attendance, etc.

But most of business "forecasting" rests on the judgment of what the future will bring. The record on this score is bleak. For general business conditions, the recently developed economic indicators have a probability of being right which likely goes beyond all earlier forms. In particular, it has been found that some series of statistics, the "leading indicators," are usually predictors of business conditions—they "lead" business.

The bigger the company, the more does it require that its executive instrument panel include an instrument which reads "Business Forecast."

See, for a good discussion, Platt, Henry M., "Economic Indicators," *The Management Review*, April, 1959, pp. 9–13, 67–80.

The early warnings do not come cheap. They are not a by-product of regular operation and hence require special effort to create and maintain. As a result, managers put forth this effort only if they have been bitten by failure to do so, if the stakes are uncommonly high, or if the manager is really a virtuoso in such matters.

Sensing during the Fact

Most managerial sensing of trouble is done during actual operation, and is a by-product of operation, or rather, of trouble encountered during operation.

> A customer phones that the shipment hasn't arrived yet, and that he or she is losing *his* or *her* customers.
> A shop steward advises that the pressroom employees will walk off the job if young Bill is laid off for alleged insubordination.
> The assembly line comes to a halt because the impeller shafts and holes do not mate properly.

In situations such as these, the respective managers have little need for sophisticated sensors. Things were going on in the ordinary way and suddenly there was a piercing scream.

Much sardonic humor has emerged from those living in the crisis-by-crisis world; e.g., "Why is there never time to do it right and always time to do it over?"

But this is an oversimplification. Obviously, in any *one case* of failure, prevention would have been cheaper than cure. But in the *entire class* of cases, the reverse might be true, since the prevention effort would have been spent also on many cases where it was not needed. It is rather like the cost of drilling for oil. The gushers must pay not only the cost of drilling for gushers, but the cost of drilling the dry holes as well.

In this way, the question of sensing before the fact vs. during the fact is really a question of:

(*a*) Applying the sensing before the fact to the entire class of cases, or

(*b*) Making a separation of the cases so that sensing before the fact is applied only to the "vital few" where it is economically justified.

Blind application of the idea of the early-warning principle to all members of a class gives rise to insufferable red tape, delays, and choking of channels and roads. Study of production capacity or process capability for every machine is largely a waste of time. Only a few per cent of the machines are that critical. So it is with market surveys, credit investigations, economic lot formulas, etc.

Sensing during the fact is commonly coupled with "direct control," i.e., control by deeds rather than by data. For example:

cardinal dates or events are identified. As these are reached, the supervision takes a look before authorizing additional work.

material is supplied only as needed to do the job with normal wastage. If there is an overrun, the fact comes to attention then and there.

machine time is allocated by specific jobs. At the end of the time, if the job is not finished, it comes to attention.

The minimum inventory is "sealed" so that it cannot be used without the dramatic breaking of the seal and associated reordering.

Direct controls such as these are as good as they always were. The entry of more sophisticated data processing does not reduce their value. Too many managers have missed this point.

Sensing after the Fact

A good deal of sensing takes place "after the fact." Many executive reports emerge monthly, meaning several days or weeks after the close of the month in which the deeds were done. Other reports are quarterly. Some are annual.

Such sluggish sensing is frequently under fire. "How can we control costs (or sales, profits, inventories, etc.) when the information we get is ancient history?" The answer is obvious. No day-by-day or week-by-week control can be exercised by such reports. These slow-paced reports are suited only for longer-range decisions on objectives, planning, etc.

Some confusion arises from failure to distinguish between sensors of deeds and sensors of finance. *The real things that happen are physical deeds.* The summarized reports convert these physical happenings into the common language of money so that the executives can make decisions optimizing the company's performance.

But sensors of deeds need not be tied to the accounting machinery. Costs show up in staff-hours spent, and in materials used, long before they show up in cost reports. Inventories show up in piles of stuff, long before they show up in the accountants' books.

> The superintendent of the rolling mill (p. 165) watched his inventory of copper rod by seeing the height of the physical pile. He even had upper and lower tolerances painted on the warehouse wall. He could and did see the pile daily, and he paid no attention to the accountant's report on inventory.

The disadvantage in sensing after the fact is not only in the slowness of detecting; the resulting self-excitation, or "hunting," can be worse. See, in this connection, Chap. 20, under Hunting, p. 370.

Which Form of Sensing?

Seldom does an agenda present topics such as:

Shall we, for this set of needs, do our sensing before, during, or after the fact?

Shall we, for this situation, sense from deeds or from data?

In many situations, practical people are guided by their instincts to practical answers, without framing such questions. But we are probably entering an era in which more precise answers are needed.

It will not be easy. Data processors, not responsible for the results of operations, tends to emphasize their language—dollars, accounts, accruals, variances. They also tend to urge control by data, not by deeds, even when it would be nonsense to do so. (Their logic is that a rejection of control through data is a kind of criticism of the data system, and hence of them.)

But the problem of the operating managers is to perform deeds and get results. Sales managers have a world of their own, in which quotas, volume, and commissions dominate. Plant managers live in a world bristling with tons, labor hours, quality, safety. They and their assistants want emphasis on these realities.

If there is to be a sensible scheme of sensing, reporting, and control, it must come from the joint determination of the data processors with the operating managers. The old approach of "You do your job and I'll do mine" has become obsolete—now the job is joint. Increasingly, the questions of design of information systems need to be set out in an agenda so that specific questions are put and positive choices are made.

Designing the Sensor

To do its job the sensor must be accurate,[2] precise,[3] reliable, economic, and still other things. To build all this into a sensor requires attention to much detail, so much that the manager may be unwilling to devote the time to it.

> We have seen (p. 232) that designing the sensor calls for precise definition of the control subject. "Number of employees" seems clear enough. But when you go to count, it gets complicated. If you make a "head count," how about the people on vacation, on jury duty, on sick leave, or at the ball game? If you give up on "head count" and count the employee files, again, what do you count? There are people on military leave, on pension, on strike, on disability leave.

The point here is that there is no escape from decisions on what to count, what to omit. The specialists who design the sensor know that these problems are there, and usually the specialists bring them up the line for decision. *If the managers do not decide these things, then, by default, the people down the line must.*

> The author has seen mature, competent managers in heated debates over how many employees are there, how many units did we make, etc. No one was dishonest, ignorant, or unable to count. They did have different concepts of what the sensor should measure or where the sensor should be plugged in. But they had not brought these different concepts out into the open so that the sensor measured in accordance with agreed concepts.

When the specification is clear, the specialists can take it from there. They design a black box which can do the sensing. The results can then be piped to various destinations in the system.

---

[2]"Accuracy" is the degree to which the sensor tells the truth. Accuracy is measured by the "error," which is the difference between the real conditions and what the sensor says they are. The sensor may be regarded as adequate for accuracy if the error is less than the "tolerance."

[3]"Precision" refers to the ability of the sensor to reproduce its own results.

The black box is sometimes intriguing. At a General Electric refrigerator factory, the author once saw, on the factory floor, a black
box into which an inspector fed information on the quality of refrigerators under test. The black box computed cumulative per cent
defective. This information was then displayed not only on the face
of the instrument; the instrument was duplicated in the manager's
office, hundreds of yards away. In other words, a distant manager
could look up at an instrument on his wall and read the current
quality on the factory floor.

Keeping the sensor accurate and precise requires an active program
of check and maintenance. The specialists sometimes guard against
sudden error through duplication; i.e., the sensor repeats its message,
inspects the product twice, adds the column twice, etc. Alternately, use
is made of redundancy, i.e., duplicate sensors. As in the case of multiple
eyes or ears, this redundancy not only is a form of duplication; with
skillful design, it adds a dimension similar to that of stereoscopic vision
or stereophonic sound.[4]

The designers of sensors have done their best work at the very bottom
of the company (with respect to materials, hours, processes, etc.) and at
the very top of the company (with respect to financial performance). In
between, there is a great need for sensors as well, to measure departmental performance, progress on projects, functional effectiveness.

An example on a grand scale is seen in the AMF stage system for
controlling progress of experimental engineering projects (p. 228).
The stage system can be regarded as a design of sensor for measuring this progress.

In experimental engineering projects, or other large, complex undertakings, the number of happenings is so immense that it is out of the
question to set up an information system to sense them all. Instead (as
is done in the AMF stage system) we identify the "vital few" check
points. Then we design sensors which can inform us as to progress relative to the vital few. The performance against schedule is measured by
what happens to a few critical operations. The performance as to cost is
measured by the success or failure of engineering decisions on a few
new, untried features. The quality performance is measured from a few
key qualities. By identifying these vital few features we do the sensing
without creating a huge activity which must collapse of its own weight
(as it has in some of the military programs).

---

[4]In Joseph Conrad's "Victory," there is persuasive debate that a ship may have one or
three but not two chronometers. If there are two, no one knows which is in error.

Sometimes the sensing must be done by indirect means.

A training program is conducted. How can we judge the effect of the program? One way is to compare the subsequent performance of the trained people with that of a "control group" of untrained people.

A related problem arises in appraisal of managerial performance. It is feasible to list the responsibilities of the manager, in action words of various sorts—communicate, plan, organize, etc. Appraising the subsequent performance is a widespread, recurrent problem, and several approaches have been developed as an approximation to measurement. One of these is the concept of "evidences of results."

One of the divisions of General Electric Company tabulates 11 principal responsibilities of a manager. Alongside of each of these are tabulated the "evidences of results" for carrying out that responsibility.[5] For example:

Responsibility	Evidence of results
9. Develop, promote, and negotiate improvements in union relationships toward the end of eliminating practices that will be restrictive to the successful operation of the business.	*a.* Skill in identifying and evaluating problems and successful implementation of programs. *b.* Judgment in determining and timing corrective action. *c.* Acceptance of recommended programs.

Perhaps the most elusive problem in sensing is the case where the act of sensing may change the thing being sensed. Common examples are the interview, or the attitude survey. The risks of getting distorted answers are so great that the amateurs should stay out of such situations. It is not only that current answers are distorted; an attitude survey may sensitize the people under study to a new level of expectancy. The professionals are unanimous in asserting "Do not conduct an attitude survey unless and until you are prepared to act on the findings."

The inventors have done a good job of simplifying some sensors for ready use. The ingenious tables, charts, and forms for working to a budget are an example. So is the Gantt chart (Fig. 48), an admirable way of depicting schedules as well as a simple way of recording progress. So is

[5]See, for a detailed discussion, Habbe, Stephen, "Rating Managers in Terms of Job Duties," *The Management Record*, October, 1961, pp. 23–29.

the Shewhart chart, a sensor used to detect "significant" change (see Fig. 42). The extent of these inventions and simplifications is so great that it becomes sheer waste for a company to do its own designing of sensors, from scratch. The literature, the seminars, and the information services are some of the ways of being briefed as to the state of the art.

The Tricky Ratio

A sensor in ratio form is actually measuring two separate things and then dividing one by the other. Usually the "things" being measured are streams of events. In such cases, the timetables for the two streams should coincide to avoid distortion.

> In some companies, the monthly profit varies sharply as between 4-week months and 5-week months. This is due to charging many fixed expenses (rent, monthly salaries) on a basis of a constant sum each month, whereas sales, income, and variable costs are allocated according to the actual dates of occurrence.

In like manner, absenteeism can drop because the data for the numerator of the fraction have not yet been fully processed. The inventory report shows there is 3 weeks' supply on hand but the bins are empty—the withdrawal requisitions have not been posted.[6]

The Human Being as a Sensor

The human being still plays a major role as a sensing "device" and will continue to do so for the foreseeable future. There are many forms of this, but for our purpose we will classify them as between:

(*a*) Cases in which the basic job of the individual is to be a sensor (accountant, inspector, investigator, auditor).

(*b*) Cases in which the basic job of the individual is something else, with his or her sensing duties being incidental. These cases abound.

In complex, unique situations (appraisals, investigations) we use the full-time human sensor for the simple reason that he or she can outperform any instrument devised to date. In repetitive situations (account-

---

[6]During World War II, the author, then a government administrator, faced the fact that, for some categories of products, the goods exported exceeded the goods manufactured. The explanation was simple enough: the paperwork for reporting exports moved more rapidly than the paperwork for reporting manufacture.

ing, inspection, internal auditing), the full-time human sensor can be given aid in the form of procedures, routines, patrol beats. His standards go by different names—the town ordinances, the process specifications, the standard operating procedures. He compares the actual happenings against standard, and records the differences. His record is again a variety of devices—the inspector's report, the security guard's log, the auditor's report.

In the extreme cases of importance and complexity, the human sensor may be an interdepartmental *team*. In the AMF plan for control of experimental engineering projects (p. 228), the team is plugged into the project at stated intervals to read either "go" or "stop."

In most situations of human sensing, the "real" job is something else; the sensing is only incidental. Clock cards, time sheets, and daily call reports are the most familiar examples. But there are many others—the ship's log, the police blotter, records of materials used, travel expenses, telephone calls, etc. There is widespread reluctance to do this "incidental" sensing. The "doers" tend to feel that record keeping is a nuisance, keeps them from their "regular" jobs, and is kind of low-grade stuff anyhow.

The generals and admirals have been among the most colorful rebels. Here is a letter[7] written (about 1810) by the Duke of Wellington to the British Secretary of War, Lord Bradford:

My Lord:

If I attempted to answer the mass of futile correspondence that surrounds me, I should be debarred from all serious business of campaigning.

I must remind your lordship—for the last time—that so long as I retain an independent position, I shall see that no officer under my command is debarred by attending to the futile drivelling of mere quill driving in your Lordship's Office—from attending to his first duty—which is, and always has been, so to train the private men under his command that they may, without question, beat any force opposed to them in the field.

I am,
My Lord,
Your obedient servant
/s/ Wellington

Salespeople have exhibited monumental resistance to becoming the field intelligence force of the company. They do not regard it as part of

---

[7]Quoted by Major General O. L. Nelson in "National Security and the General Staff," *Infantry Journal Press*, 1946, p. 465.

the job, meaning not only "it hasn't been part of our job" but also "we don't want to do it." Even more resistance is encountered when inspection or audit jobs (which have a connotation of spying on fellow employees) are first created in some organization. Securing acceptance of such responsibilities is not just a matter of convincing the sensor. It is no less a job of convincing those who are to be the subject of check that a constructive purpose is being served.

The twentieth century scientists look at record keeping with skepticism or even fine disdain. Here is an extract from a study of how scientific personnel were recording their time:

> All personnel are provided with a form on which to list the time devoted to:
>
> (a) Development projects
> (b) Service to Production
> (c) Customer service
>
> The actual practice is that a person devoting most of his time to one category charges all of his time to that category, regardless of the actual time distribution. Time distribution is supposed to be estimated to the nearest hour. Instead, time sheets are not filled out until the end of the week. In some cases, they are filled out completely at the beginning of the week.

Experience with getting "incidental" recording done has evolved some useful guides:

1. Explain the why of the records. Show the trail followed, who needs them, what he or she does with them.

2. Do a real job of minimizing the amount of recording needed. Avoid lengthy forms which deal more with the useful many rather than the vital few. Handle the former by sampling or the like. Provide for recording by checks or tallies rather than words or numbers.

3. Go as far toward push-button recording as is economic.

> In a plant making rubber products, there was a problem of recording the weights of sulfur, carbon black, crude rubber, etc., entering various batches. The weight records were used in several ways—for costing, for production control, for quality control. Getting the operators to record the weights was a problem, not only in getting it done at all, but in getting accurate readings, legible figures, clean records, etc.
>
> A solution was worked out by designing an attachment to the scales so that they would print the weight on push-button command. Now all was simplified. The operator first put the batch card

into a slot. Then he loaded the sulfur and pressed a button. The scale punched the weight of sulfur onto the card. Next the carbon black, and again a push-button recording. Then the crude rubber.

In like manner, some plants have solved the problem of controlling idle time of machines. So long as the machine keeps running, a recording instrument mounted on the machine causes a continuous line to be traced on a central registering chart. When the machine stops, the line on the chart is interrupted by an amount which can be read on the calibrated chart. Up to this point all has been recorded without the machine operator. He or she does play a role in recording the reason for the stoppage. This he or she does by dialing a code number on a telephone-type dial.[8]

4. Check periodically to see whether the data are actually used. If they are not, scrape them off like the barnacles they have become.

5. In dealing with variances or exceptions, assign the sensing to full-time sensors.

> The Nichols Company was facing a problem of disappearance of castings. The castings going into the machine shop were counted. So were the machined castings going to customers. So were the defective castings scrapped on scrap tickets. But what happened to the rest? Suspicion centered on the possibility that some scrapped parts were not coming through—they were being hidden, buried in metal turnings, dumped in the river. "When the snow melts in the spring, you'll see them in the yard."
>
> The routines provided that the shop operators make out scrap tickets daily, and bring the scrap plus the tickets to collecting stations. It turned out that this routine was unenforceable as applied to hundreds of operators. When the job of writing scrap tickets was turned over to the few inspectors, there was a considerable improvement in accountability.

Errors by Human Sensors

There are several varieties of these, ranging from felonies through misdemeanors down to dubious short cuts. They include:

willful errors of a criminal nature, i.e., fraud, collusion
willful errors for personal convenience

[8]Engblom, Alex N., "Mechanical Time Studies," *Mechanical Engineering*, July, 1951, pp. 549–553.

bias, coloration, and "noise"

blunder, fatigue, and other errors due to human fallibility

Aside from the spicy reading they provide, the errors of human sensors are important enough to merit careful consideration in design of control systems.

Fraud and Collusion

Our immense system of commerce is organized to act on paper symbols of the real thing. A credit card symbolizes the solvency of the bearer. A passport identifies him. A laboratory test certificate symbolizes the properties of materials. An auditor's certificate symbolizes the validity of the company's books.

The seamy side of our society has taken notice of this widespread reliance on paper symbols. If people pay so handsomely for symbols, why not forge the symbols? It is ever so much more economical than creating the solid stuff behind the symbols. Having reached such logical, reprehensible conclusions, our light-fingered brothers and sisters act on them with an energy and ingenuity which we must admire even as we put the authors away for the prescribed periods of years.

The more obvious cases are the faking of test reports, printing of currency, cashing of rubber checks. It is not too difficult to carry out a one-shot or several-shot form of deceit. The systems of alarms, checks, and balances of the victims are not nimble enough to respond to short-cycle fraud.

Fraud over a longer period of time requires precise knowledge of the alarm systems so that they can be desensitized at the critical spots. For example:

The procedure for paying invoices for purchased materials normally involves several participating departments, each creating an essential document or performing an essential service. They usually include:

Department	Provides or performs
Purchasing	Purchase order
Receiving	Report of receipt of goods from vendor
Inspection	Report of acceptability of vendor's quality
Voucher	Checking of vendor's invoice against purchase order, receiving report, and inspection report
Treasurer	Writing check to pay vendor
Accounting	Charging proper accounts with all transactions

If a conspirator set out to defraud the company by the device of having it pay for goods never purchased, he would have to understand precisely the sensory structure of each department. Obviously, a conspiracy of six individuals, each in the key job of each department, would permit creating all necessary documents and hiding the trail for some time. To the extent that the key people could not be enlisted, to that extent forgeries would be necessary, with added risks of detection.

Some of the really spectacular swindles of history have been achieved because the swindler understood just how the sensory device worked, and manipulated it to his purposes.

> Billie Sol Estes, a Texas industrialist, sold mortgages on some 30,000 ammonia tanks despite the fact that only about 1,800 tanks were in existence. The finance companies generally took the precaution of sending auditors to verify the physical existence of the property under mortgage. These auditors would ask to see tanks of various serial numbers. The Estes men became experts at changing serial numbers, painting them, and even making them look weatherbeaten, all in a space of several hours. During this time the auditors were subjected to plausible delays. The end result was that the finance companies' instruments (the auditors) were plugged into staged "facts."

Other forms of swindle have used different details of the same principle—plug the victim's instrument into biased data. The Musica brothers (who embezzled funds of the McKesson-Robbins Company) also faked the existence of an inventory (of crude drugs). In this case, the swindlers operated two fictitious companies in Canada. Actually, each of these companies had only one employee, whose duties were to send the unopened mail to one of the swindlers. He then sent back sealed replies to be mailed with Canadian postage. These one-woman offices served their purpose of throwing people off the trail.

Ivar Kreuger's now famous approach was to publish glowing statements which had little relation to reality, and to deny access to the basis for these statements. His labyrinth of companies shifted real and phantom assets from one set of books to another, and only Kreuger knew the score. His reputation, acquired on a sound basis at the outset, fended off inquiries by sheer bluff. It did not occur to his victims to question his financial statements.

Fraud and collusion can be minimized by:

> filling sensitive jobs only with persons of proved and sustained integrity

conducting unannounced checks to ensure that the established procedures are being followed

conducting periodic reexamination of the procedures themselves to judge them for "security exposure"

developing independent information sources which look for subsurface irregularities

In addition, some authorities urge that deliberate errors be introduced periodically to judge the competence of the regular system to deal with them.

Bias, Coloration, and Noise

To the engineer, "information" is what the sensor transmits to the destination. But information is made up of:

(*a*) "The message," i.e., what is really happening. The manager calls this "the facts."

(*b*) Noise,[9] i.e., unwanted signals.

The following actually took place in a division of a large company:

> The Vice-President at Headquarters phoned the Works Manager in the hinterlands. "How many ranges are you shipping today?" The Works Manager asked the Production Manager, who asked the Assembly Superintendent, who ask the Shipping Room Foreman, who asked Pete. Pete, being low man on the totem pole, had no one to ask. So he went out to the shipping platform and counted the ranges—in the freight cars, in the trucks, and on the platforms. There were 400 in all.
>
> Pete was no fool. He remembered that yesterday they had shipped 440 ranges. He also knew someone would ask "Why is today below yesterday?"
>
> He found the answer. There were 40 more ranges in a hold area. They had been assembled today, but they couldn't be shipped, because they lacked electric clocks. "We're just out of electric clocks. A truckload is on the road now, and is due here at 11 A.M. tomor-

---

[9]The early radio engineers encountered all sorts of hisses, crackles, and sputters in their earphones. These unwanted signals were called "noise," which they were. Later generations of engineers have used the term "noise" to represent any unwanted signals, i.e., "snow" on the TV screen. To the manager, "noise" becomes rumors, false alarms, and other signals not actually reflecting the conditions on the job.

row." In Pete's mind everything dropped into place. Those 40
ranges in the hold area were as good as shipped.

So he reported—440 ranges. And this information sped up the
line. 90 per cent message and 10 per cent noise.

There is a sharp distinction to be made between explanation and coloration. When Pete reported "440 ranges being shipped today" he used
coloration to the tune of 40 ranges. Had he reported "400 ranges being
shipped today, 40 more held up for clocks; will ship tomorrow," it
would have been explanation.

There should be an iron discipline restricting coloration, and there
should be no restriction on explanation. The purpose of asking "how
many ranges are being shipped" is ordinarily multiple, and looking for
Pete's scalp may have been in no one's mind. When Pete adopted his defensive posture, he may have fouled up someone else without knowing it.

But the defensive posture is not so easy to banish. Industrial human
beings are schooled and motivated to try to look good before their
bosses. Pete is not an unusual case—he is symbolic of Industrial Man.

The real remedy for coloration lies elsewhere. For really important information, connect directly to the source of the facts. The skipper on the
bridge does not call the engine room to ask for the propeller rpm. That
vital instrument is duplicated on the bridge.

The principle of direct connection is widely used. Numerous streams
of paper flow through the company—time tickets, requisitions, orders,
invoices, etc. The accountants, inspectors, human resources personnel,
etc., connect their sensors to these streams of data, and the resulting information is piped to all layers of bosses.

The future of direct connection is even more interesting. Today, a
black box enables the distant manager to read, from an instrument on
the wall, what is the quality of the refrigerators currently going through
the test line. Tomorrow other black boxes will enable the manager to
read what are the current costs, the current sales, the current profits!

An incidental value of direct connection is that of avoiding the psychological tension of "spying." The foreman respects the superintendent's unlimited right to be informed, including through direct observation, i.e., visiting his or her (the foreman's) department. But shop
protocol requires that the foreman accompany the superintendent during the visit. For the superintendent to come through alone and (worse
yet) without prior notice is spying.[10]

---

[10]This is not limited to industry. The General has the unquestioned right to visit the
camp. But protocol requires that he let the commanding Colonel know about it beforehand, and that the Colonel accompany the General on the trip.

But while a spying trip by the superintendent is resented,[11] *there is no resentment when the spying is done impersonally.* The reports on production, scrap, absenteeism may reach the superintendent at the same time they reach the foreman. But there is no resentment about the inanimate instrument being plugged in!

Those who deplore any interference from higher levels are simply not aware of what can happen. A vivid example[12] was related by a Polish engineer during the 1930s.

> He told about the pumps.
>
> In one of the mills, the *Amerikanskie* chart showed up at once the place where something was interfering with the free flow of work. This was where the wood was put into huge digesters. The way of doing this was for men to shovel in chips, then go in and tramp on them. This held up the work in the rest of the plant.
>
> The obvious way to solve that "bottleneck" was to install a hopper and a spreader which would feed in the chips automatically, without interruption.
>
> The plant manager, called to Warsaw and told to install such a hopper, replied flatly:
>
> "*Niewozliwy!*" (Impossible!) Such a hopper, he said, could not be run by their single pump.
>
> "Then install another pump."
>
> "*Niewozliwy!*" That would overload the electric generators.
>
> "Buy another generator," the Board of Directors was advised. "To get a free flow of work, we must consider nothing as static and nothing as impossible."
>
> When they went to plan for a new generator, they found there were *two* pumps, one being held for repairs, and both pumps were *driven by steam, not by electricity.*
>
> This was no reflection on the manager, the speaker explained. It was a reflection on blind acceptance of an old way of doing things. "In America," he said, "a manager has often worked his way `from the bottom up,' so that it is more usual for him to know what the facts are. Over here we are more apt to bring in someone who is highly qualified by education but who gets his information from someone beneath him and so down the line.
>
> "In that way a director in Warsaw may be told by a plant manager in the provinces who has been told by a superintendent who has been told by a foreman who has been told by a skilled worker who has been told by an unskilled worker that something is `impossible', until this becomes accepted and believed and defended by men of in-

---

[11]Or worse yet, a spying trip by an underling.

[12]Clark, Pearl Franklin, "The Challenge of the American Know-how," pp. 47–48, Harper & Row, Publishers, Incorporated, New York, 1948.

telligence. If they knew the facts, they would end the impossibility at once. But such type of organization does not permit those at the top to know what are the facts.

"Obviously, executives must get their facts from others. But there must be methods to make sure that the information on which they take action, is correct."

Blunder and Fatigue

There have been some measurements of the fallibility of the human being in his or her role as sensor.

The human inspector looking over many units of product finds about four of every five defects. He or she misses the fifth one. (Means have been devised for measuring inspector accuracy.) Similar errors are encountered in other forms of check, i.e., patrol beats, preparing reports, and especially, routine continuous vigilance.

Industrial psychologists have come up with a variety of ways for reducing such human errors:

1. Test the aptitude of people before assigning them to such tasks.
2. Provide means for reducing fatigue and monotony, through rotation of tasks and through rest periods.
3. Provide a check of work done to measure accuracy, and use these data to improve accuracy.

Now to the Use of the Sensor

With the availability of the sensor, we are equipped to create the system of measurement. In turn, this system will provide us with knowledge of what is our actual performance, and thereby, of our departure from standard.

Because the comparison of actual performance with standard becomes the basis for decision making, the next chapter deals with the manager's mobilization for decision making.

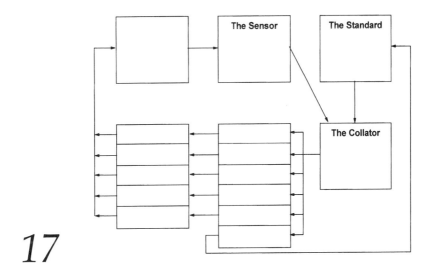

The Sensor

The Standard

The Collator

17

MOBILIZING FOR DECISION MAKING

All Roads Lead to Decision Making

The Control steps discussed thus far all have one common goal in mind—to bring, to a decision maker, the knowledge of what is happening compared to the standard of what should happen. With the availability of units of measure, standards, and sensors, it becomes possible to create the systematic approach by which the decision maker does receive this essential knowledge. What we will call "mobilizing for decision making" starts with this availability and ends when decision makers fully armed with the ingredients needed for self-control.

The broad features of this mobilization for decision making consist of:

1. Creation of the various measuring stations which collect the bits of knowledge
2. Creation of the analysis stations which receive these bits of knowledge and convert them into a form which facilitates interpretations (Chap. 18), decision making (Chap. 19), and action (Chap. 20).
3. Creation of the network of transmission lines to pipe all forms of information from the measuring and analysis stations to the usage stations at all levels of the control pyramid (Fig. 21).

Collectively these stations and their interconnection represent an extensive, complex piece of machinery. This must be designed, set up, staffed, maintained, and overhauled. The manager's role is to see that these things get done.

The sole purpose of setting up this elaborate machinery is to aid decision making. Since decision making is done at all levels in the pyramid, the information system must feed all these levels. In turn, each level must speak up so that the system design and operation meet all needs. In this connection, a special burden is placed on the upper managers.

Upper managers' most obvious responsibility is to see to it that they themselves are provided with the essential information needed for decision making. A shortage of this information becomes evident to the managers themselves. They feel pain, and they do something about it.

But managers also have the responsibility for seeing to it that subordinates are provided with the means for self-control. Here, any shortcomings in information are not directly evident to the managers—someone else feels the pain.

The Measuring Stations

We have seen (Chap. 16) that sensors are numerous and varied. Yet every single one of them, from the mechanical instrument all the way to the full-time human sensor, is involved in certain essential steps.

1. Each sensor must be plugged into the source of information.

The very act of plugging in raises the final questions of detail about where to plug in and just how to make the connections.

We decide to create a report on the number of appliances produced. Where do we plug in? Some of the options are shown in Table 17-1.

2. The connection must be secured. Not only must the sensor be plugged in at the right spot; it must be done in a way which secures an unbiased measurement.

Even a mechanical measurement can have trouble on this score. You have a thimble full of liquid and wish to measure the temperature. So you put the end of a mercury thermometer into the liquid. Now read the height of the mercury column. What do you get? You get a very dubious result—a composite of two temperatures (a) that of the liquid before the thermometer was plunged in and (b) that of the thermometer before it was plunged into the liquid.

Table 17-1. Where to Plug In?

Detailed definition	Where to plug in	Form of sensor
Number of chassis entering the assembly line	At the beginning of the assembly line	Count of the serial number plates used
Number of appliances assembled	At the point of transfer from assembly to test	Count of the assembly piece-rate coupons detached from the traveler tag
Number of appliances O.K. on test	Right after test	Count of the test coupons detached from the traveler tag
Number of appliances packed for shipment	Shipping station	Count of copies of packing slips

As we have seen, when human beings are used as sensors, the effect of bias is far greater. Such was the case of Pete and the appliances (p. 297); also the problems of the attitude survey (p. 290). The human sensor gives different information depending on who does the asking, e.g., the "low down," the "party line," the "brush-off," a "snow job," or still other varieties. The human sensor tends to give "information" as a form of propaganda for influencing action.

The existence of such problems makes it clear that the planners of the control system must be on the scene at the time of first plugging in. Only in this way are they assured that they understand the problem of sensing as it will be faced by the troops. Failing this, the troops are, by default, forced to make decisions on design of the information system.

3. The sensor must provide detail.

When measurement is done solely for automatic or operator control, many problems of analysis, transmission, etc., disappear. But when measurement is also to be the basis of informational control, a whole host of added needs are superimposed on the measuring stations.

The information system of the company rests on a foundation of "basic records." These are the records created by the fundamental activities or deeds carried out. These fundamental deeds are such things as spending time, making a sale, requisitioning material, buying services, shipping finished goods, repairing a machine.

We set things up so that whoever carries out one of these deeds leaves a paper trail of what he did. This trail consists of time sheets, customers' orders, material requisitions, invoices, shipping tickets, work orders, etc. The detail on these paper trails is decisive as to the content of the resulting reports. The reports can never bring out more information or detail than went in.[1]

Consider the problem of control of selling expenses.

Selling expenses are incurred for a variety of reasons. A typical "chart of accounts" will show categories such as salaries, commissions, travel, entertainment, samples, telephone, postage, rent, depreciation, advertising, sales promotion, insurance, social security, pensions.

These selling expenses are incurred by Jenkins, O'Toole, Lafferty, McNeeley, and other salespeople working out of the Boston branch; they are also incurred by salespeople working out of the other branches of the New England district—Providence, New Haven, Springfield, and Portland. There are additional branches in the other districts of the Eastern region—New York, Mid-Atlantic, and Southeast. Then there are the branches and districts of the other regions—Great Lakes, Central, Gulf, Southwest, and Pacific.

Nor is this all. Selling expenses are incurred for a variety of purpose classifications—by customer, by product line, by type of market. Our subsequent analysis of profitability may require such detail to discover whether we are making or losing money on the small customers, on the jobbing product line, on the discount-house business.

Nor is this all. Selling expenses are incurred virtually every minute of the working day. But supervisory review cannot be conducted every minute, at every layer of supervision. If not every minute, how often? Daily, weekly, monthly, quarterly, annually? These questions need answers.

4. Each sensor must be connected to the transmission network.
The sensor has the dual role of:

(a) telling the individual on the scene what are the facts so that he may control his job. This transmission commonly requires no record.
(b) providing the facts on which information control is to be based. This transmission does require a record.

In its most rudimentary form, the system of records consists of:

the basic record forms and instructions, which, if followed, will provide useful grist for the data-processing mill

---

[1] As one wag put it, we operate on a GIGO system of information—Garbage In: Garbage Out.

the intermediate summary forms which provide an early feedback for supervisory control as well as the input for the intermediate levels of control

the ultimate summary forms which provide the feedback for control at the highest levels

In addition, the measuring stations have, collectively, a very real problem of keeping their instruments in calibration. In the case of mechanical gages or electrical meters, the system for such maintenance is well developed, and consists of the following steps:

number each instrument.

establish a card record for each instrument.

establish a checking schedule.

provide for adherence to the checking schedule (this makes or breaks the system).

keep a record of the findings.

analyze the records to improve the system and to improve the design of the instruments.

This general approach applies, in theory, to the sensors used for managerial control as well. However, while mechanical instruments have no objection to being numbered, catalogued, and checked, human sensors do object. So we tread lightly.

The Analysis Stations

These serve the purpose of clearing away the underbrush which would otherwise entangle the decision maker.

In automatic systems the sensor makes its own decision. In operator control systems, the operator makes the decision direct from the data, without the need for separate analysis. But in informational control, the analysis problem becomes so complex that the decision maker cannot very well work direct from the basic data.[2] Instead, an analysis station is created to sort, summarize, calculate, correlate, present, chart, and otherwise simplify the assimilation of the original mass of data.

These analysis stations are staffed by human beings who exhibit all the traits of the species. Of this, more in Chap. 18.

---

[2]Of course he "can" if he has the time and skills. But many decision makers commonly need to work from the same basic data. It would be a chaotic waste for all these people to become duplicate data processors.

The Usage Stations

The end purpose of the effort of setting standards and measuring performance is decision making at some usage station. (How this decision making is done will be discussed in Chaps. 18 and 19.) Because the usage stations all have different decisions to make, the systems planners have a problem of piping the appropriate information on standards and performance to the respective usage stations.

In the short feedback loops (automatic control, operator control) the usage stations are coextensive with the measurement stations. As informational control takes over, the usage stations multiply and diversify. It becomes most desirable to "package" the information into modules or standard units. Through such modules, the job of assembling the various combinations required by the various usage stations is greatly simplified.

The usage station rests on a collection of control subjects. List the control subjects which are local to a usage station, and there will emerge a clear image of the pattern of information needed. From this list it is feasible to design the report forms and other tools actually used by the person in charge.

Unless the operating managers have a decisive voice as to what enters the usage station, the data system can run berserk and spew out a torrent of useless information.

> The Horn Man-Made Fibre Company established a Statistical Department to bring order out of the great volume of information which was then wandering aimlessly around the company. The Head Statistician set up procedures for flowing all data into his office, and for charting these data in time series, Shewhart control charts, and other statistical devices. When the author visited the company, there were 600 such series being maintained. A few of them were vital to the company's operations. Most of them were of local interest only—the need was solely for a short feedback right to the firing line.
>
> The statistician, with his staff of a dozen people, were busy as beavers maintaining their numerous series. They lived in a world apart, their walls covered with their 600 charts. Outside, the world of action paid no attention to all this. This situation of two separate worlds living apart could not go on. But it could have been avoided in the first place had the operating managers had an adequate voice in design of the usage stations.

The personal preferences of the managers who staff the usage stations should receive considerable weight, since these people carry the responsibility for results. If these preferences become burdensome to the company, it can be demonstrated to these same people that it is they who are carrying this burden in overhead charges.

The Transmission Lines

The utilities which provide telephone, electric power, gas, or water services have a whopping problem of "transmission." To deal with this problem they have created a new world of philosophic concepts, language, apparatus, literature, and detail. In these companies, transmission is the job of major departments, staffed by specialists who have devoted a lifetime to the subject.

The related problem of transmitting "information" has rapidly been following the same trail. In industrial companies, transmission of information has likewise become a whopping problem requiring the effort of special departments and the skills of specialists. A glimpse at the special character of this transmission can be seen from some of the concepts worked out by telephone engineers and being applied to transmission of information generally.

The amplifier. It restores the intensity of a signal which has become weak after traveling a long distance. The amplification takes place at *a relay station.*

The filter. It is a selective transmission device, designed to admit a selected part of the spectrum, and to reject all else—like the meshes of a sieve, or the ticket taker at the ball park.

Redundancy. It provides multiple transmission channels to increase reliability.

Shielding. It keeps noise from invading the message; keeps adjacent channels from whispering to each other ("crosstalk"); keeps the message secure from unauthorized listeners.

Managers do make some use of these concepts. They use "shielding" by classifying information, or by coding data. Where it is important to discover coloration and noise, they use redundancy.

In the days of foot soldiers and cavalry, the mounted general made his plans, issued his orders, and observed the progress of battle personally. The "measurement" was by direct observation. In those days the battles were limited to a front of a few miles; so a short feedback was feasible.

As the human race made "progress" in the form of bigger and better battles, this direct observation was no longer possible. Instead, commanders received reports from subordinates who received reports from *their* subordinates, etc. The risks of coloration and "noise" became high.

When Winston Churchill visited the Headquarters of Field Marshal Montgomery, he observed a redundancy technique in use by the Marshal. Montgomery was directing four attacking divisions along a huge front. He posted his personal observers (officers of about the rank of major) along various parts of the front. As personal representatives of the Commander in Chief, they had the authority to go anywhere, see anything, ask questions of anyone at all. Churchill's account notes that these observers, reporting one after another, occupied about 2 hours one evening in presenting their reports to Montgomery. This information was used as a cross check against the reports of the commanders.[3]

However, in the aggregate, the manager has done only a spotty job of using the available know-how, and even less of adding to it. Very likely this mixed performance is the result of the undramatic way in which the transmission problem comes up.

In most situations, there is no facing of the transmission problem as such. The company has long been evolving its information system, bit by bit. The new problems are presented bit by bit, and solved that way. None of this is conducive to an imaginative, fresh approach. Only when a revolution (i.e., electronic data processing) comes along is there a ready-made occasion for making a really fundamental reexamination. It could well be argued that a main contribution of a newfangled approach is that it forces a reexamination of the entire creaking, jerry-built structure.

What is the manager to do? Certainly, he or she should *not* invade the system on the basis of his or her personal expertise. He or she probably is no expert; if he or she is and spends his or her time redesigning the data system, he or she has, for the time, vacated the job of manager. Rather he or she should:

realize that *any* important matter which has long undergone bit-by-bit development is out of date

create the expertise needed in the company by sending the right people to school, or by importing experts

require that modernization of the data system be undertaken as a major topic on the agenda, not just as a by-product of other topics

preside over the undertaking through the usual managerial approach to Breakthrough.

[3]Churchill, Winston, "The Second World War," "Crossing the Rhine," "The Iron Curtain."

Presentation[4]

The work of the data processor comes to fruition in the "feedback" to the usage stations. Applied to information control, this feedback consists of a factual report, tailored to the needs of the usage stations as to content, format, and timing.

Content. This follows directly the choice of control subjects (Chap. 13). With respect to each control subject, the report brings together the information on standards and on performance, using the agreed format.

Format. Choice of format is not just a matter of taste. Format greatly influences usefulness of reports.

The most primitive format is a tabulation (Fig. 29) of numbers showing:

Actual performance
Target performance
Variance

This simple tabulation contains the bare elements of the control cycle, and some managers prefer it that way. Others object to the tabulations on a variety of grounds:

the tabulations show neither the historical trends nor the future projections.

fluctuations and trends are not evident; they must be recalled, from fallible memory.

---

[4]For some examples by leading companies (Burroughs, Carrier, Koppers, Thompson Products, Ford), see *Reports to Top Management,* American Management Association, 1953.

	Cost and Expense Report Department 392			Nov. 1962
No.	Description	Budget	Actual	Variance
20	Direct Labor	4093	3991	102
30	Indirect Labor	6740	6915	(175)
40	Indirect Material	850	824	26
50	Waste	517	488	29
60	Services	603	611	(8)

Fig. 29. Primitive report format.

in the upper levels, busy executives are submerged by the sheer number of tabulations. Only a talented[5] few thrive in such a medium. The rest want visual or other aids.

The use of charts and exhibits in executive report packages has become an accepted mode of presentation today. Its roots go back nearly three decades, when I wrote the following in the original edition of this book. (Naturally, the advent of sophisticated data processing and graphic capabilities has played a key role here). The basic chart form is seen in Fig. 30. The chart shows three time zones: (a) history, (b) current operations, (c) target for the future. The vertical scale naturally varies with the subject matter, but there is a standardization of the methods of presentation.[6]

The world of charts has some fascination as well as utility. It also provides a wide scope for originality, imagination, and even faddism. Consequently, there is a wide array of physical approaches to charting, the most usual being built around:

(a) A set of paper masters maintained by the issuing office. These are reproduced monthly, so that the old issues are discarded.

(b) A chart room built around large-scale charts which are exhibited to the executives during the review meeting. The best known of these is the chart room at the headquarters of the Du Pont Company. These charts are so sizable that they are hung from a monorail for mobility. Figure 31 shows a sample chart.[7] An alternative approach, used by

[5]Those who lack the talent generally deny that it is a talent.

[6]For a comprehensive manual on charting see "Time Series Charts—A Manual of Design and Construction," American Standards Association, or American Society of Mechanical Engineers, New York.

[7]For a full discussion of the Du Pont approach, see "How the DuPont Organization Appraises Its Performance," American Management Association, Financial Series, No. 94, 1950.

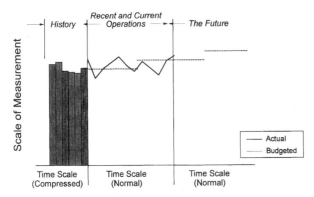

Fig. 30. Basic chart format for reports.

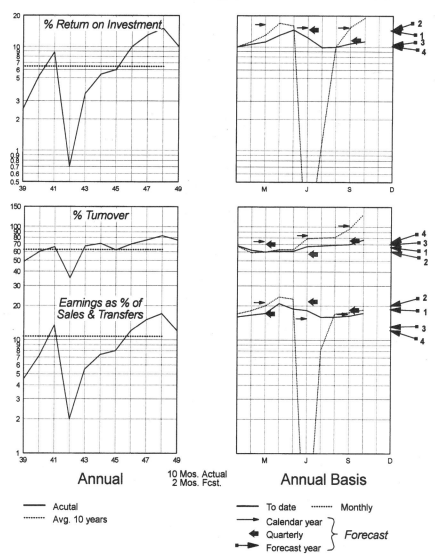

Fig. 31. A Du Pont chart format.

Thompson Products Company, is to put the charts on $8\,^1/_2$ by 11 transparencies and then to use an overhead-type projector for enlarging them to be viewed by the executive group. Figure 32 shows an example of the Thompson Products chart (an admirable format).[8] Still other forms are a set of flip charts or wall panels, brought up to date with colored tape.[9]

(c) Returnable books of charts which are brought up to date monthly.

The board of a company or the cabinet of the president, being mixtures of individuals from a variety of backgrounds, may want a variety of presentations—tables of figures, charts, associated narrative explanations. All have their place, and there are presentation forms which combine all of these. Figure 33 is an example from Koppers Company.[10]

Some presidents ride an instrument panel as quite a hobby. They have elaborate chart rooms, charts in bright colors, push-button display, and other evidences of preoccupation with the game aspects of the instrument panel. It doesn't matter; these elaborations seldom weaken the presidents' grasp of what the charts contain and often are part of a comprehensive enthusiasm for mastering the information.

The price of good format is surprisingly low.

> Pennsylvania Salt Manufacturing Company[11] used an executive instrument panel of 93 charts, in Kardex file size, showing monthly trends on:
>
> sales and profits by products (43 charts)
>
> expenses vs. budget (4 charts)
>
> production as a per cent of plant capacity (8 charts)
>
> hourly pay rates (8 charts)
>
> balance-sheet items (10 charts)
>
> common-stock items (4 charts)
>
> personnel statistics (4 charts)
>
> financial ratios (11 charts)
>
> Maintenance of the charts is estimated as 3 staff-days and $200 per month

[8] Brelsford, Ernest C., *Reports to Top Management,* American Management Association, 1953.

[9] For some details of construction, see Boylan, Howard D., "Financial Charting for the Board of Directors," *National Association of Cost Accountants Bulletin,* June, 1957, pp. 1304–1313.

[10] *Reports to Top Management, op. cit.*

[11] "Tools for Decision-makers," *Modern Industry,* Sept. 15, 1950, pp. 42–43.

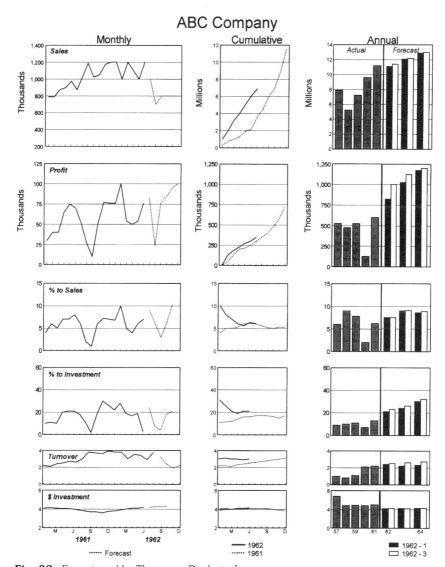

Fig. 32. Format used by Thompson Products, Inc.

Koppers Co., Inc. & Subs.

Earnings to Common Stock

Earnings per share of common stock exceeded the program by a wide margin in November. Although profit before taxes was substantially below program, profit after taxes was considerably above. This resulted from an excess profit credit of $_____ thousand additional, in November, to that programmed. In addition, tax adjustments applicable to Chilean income amounted to a reduction in taxable income of $_____ thousand. These factors tended to reduce the tax for the month; however, an additional amount $_____ thousand over program was provided in the reserve for tax contingencies, as was also done last month, and partly offsets these reductions. For the year to date, earnings to common are above those programmed by ___ per share outstanding.

Sales

Company sales dropped approximately ___ percent from the previous month but were, nevertheless, $_____ million in excess of the goal.

Table K1

Summary of Activities— November 1952			
		Actual	
Item	Program	Amount	Percent of Program
NET SALES	(In Thousands of Dollars)		
November	$	$	
January-November			
NET PROFIT*			
November			
January-November			
COMMON & SURPLUS INVENTORIES		(In Dollars)	
EARNED PER SHARE OF COMMON STOCK** (Bef. Spec. Items)			
November	$	$	
January-November			

* Before taxes and special items.
** Based on 1,867,125 shares.

Chart K1

Earnings per Share of Common Stock (Before Special Items)*

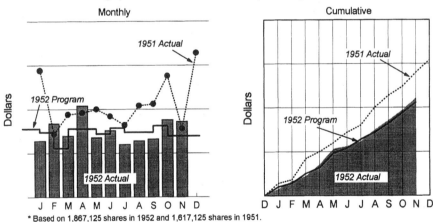

* Based on 1,867,125 shares in 1952 and 1,617,125 shares in 1951.

Fig. 33. Combination format used by Koppers Co.

315

One graduate student of the author's came up with an inventory of a company's reports to top management and the staff-hours for each. We will call it the Leaning Tower Instrument Company. It employs 900 employees and makes instruments for the military.

For this company, close to 4,000 staff-hours annually are used for executive feedback. See Table 17-2 for the details of this.

Copies to whom? There are advantages to wide distribution of reports—more people are better informed; there is more likelihood of agreement on common facts. There are also disadvantages—executives are swamped with mail they don't really need; there is greater risk that classified information will leak.

Solution to the problem of copies is twofold:

1. The reporting must be modular. The reports are prepared in logical sections, dealing with different subjects and at different levels of importance. Such a modular concept makes possible a selective distribution of those pieces needed by specific personnel. If the report is a single inseparable package, distribution must be on the basis of all or none.

2. A mailing list is worked up for each module. (This list must then be kept up to date.) In the Koppers example, about 160 copies of the "Progress Report" are issued. About 100 of these are complete; the rest are partial, being tailor-made to the needs of various recipients. Restricted reports are marked "Secret" or "Confidential," depending on the degree of security required.

Timing. The timetable for reporting affects all levels in the company. At the top, information must be timed to reach the directors and execu-

Table 17-2.

Nature of report	Annual staff-hours*
Economic climate: No report	None
Finance: Monthly balance sheet, profit statement, asset schedule, income schedule, cost schedule, source and application of funds	1,200
Contracts: Work load, backlog, under negotiation	144
Proposals: Schedule of those outstanding (weekly)	400
Labor: Wage rates and labor turnover vs. market	84
Production: Schedules, shipments, balances	1,324
Quality: Reject analysis	120
Engineering: Progress, by projects	600

*Annual staff-hours refers to the time required for preparation of the executive-type report from basic information. Time for preparation of the basic information is not included.

tives for their scheduled meetings. At the bottom, the work loads and due dates of the clerks, statisticians, accountants must be geared to meet the schedules at the top.

In some companies, a fully integrated timetable is in force. In the Koppers example, all dates work back from meetings of the Boards of Directors on the last Monday of the month. The Operating Committee of the company meets on the prior Tuesday. In preparation for these meetings, the "Progress Report" has been issued the Thursday prior to the Operating Committee meeting (see Fig. 34). In this way, the "Progress Report" issues 3 working days prior to the Operating Committee meeting and 7 working days prior to the Board meeting. The actual dates for issuing the Progress Report can be as early as the twelfth or as late as the twentieth of the month. Working back from these due dates, the schedules for feeder reports are worked out and routines are adopted so that the progressive scale of dates is met.

Generally the trend in reporting has been away from a scattering of reports throughout the month and in the direction of issuance of one comprehensive monthly report. The growing use of computers has been accelerating this trend. But the trend had been there before. Executives had found that the scattered reports gave only partial pictures and could not be related to each other. It was not fruitful to organize meetings for discussing a limited few reports, but it was decidedly fruitful to discuss the comprehensive package of reports.

A further aspect of timing is the difference in frequency at various levels. The shop operator, the salesperson, the laboratory technician—all are informed by the physical situation which confronts them, event by event: this machine is showing signs of need of first aid; this customer's shelf is almost bare; this shipment isn't going to raise the supplier's reputation.

At the next level people are informed partly by personal information, partly by hearsay, partly by written report. The foreman hears the chattering machine and gets after the maintenance department. The branch manager receives the salesperson's telephoned order and passes it on to

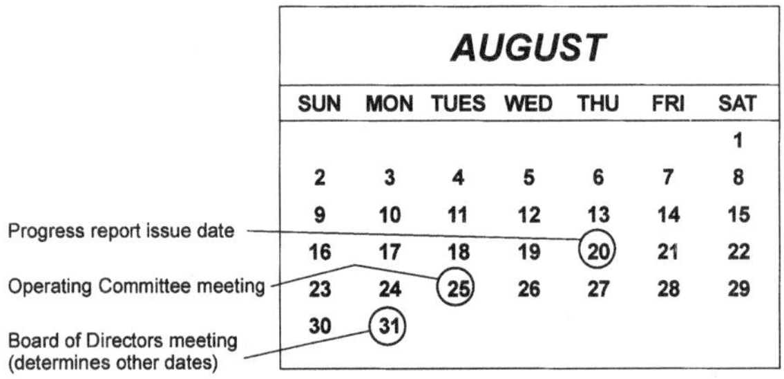

Fig. 34. Calendar of timing for reports.

be executed. The laboratory head reads the test report and makes a note to talk to the purchasing agent about this supplier.

Higher level personnel seldom get into event-by-event or even day-by-day matters. But they do get week-to-week information. The shop superintendent gets a weekly report on machine down time. The district sales manager gets a weekly report on the doings of all the salespeople. The Assistant Quality Manager gets a weekly report on all vendor rejections.

Instrumental Panel for Executives

At the highest executive level there is not only the need for selective, summarized, comparative information; there is even a real problem of how to "package" this information. The requirements of the "package" are fairly well agreed on:

> It should be limited to a comparatively few really important control subjects.[12]
> For each of these control subjects it should show:
>> Past performance
>> Current performance against goals
>> Future goals
> Each report should read at a glance.
> Collectively, the reports should have common format, common language, common timetable.

Ford Motor Company[13] has used a concept of financial reporting which dovetails both in time scale and in organizational level (Fig. 35).

At the base are the daily reports for the foreman—direct labor, indirect labor, indirect material, scrap, production count (Fig. 36).

The superintendent and department heads receive frequent reports also, but in condensed form (Fig. 37).

The plant manager receives monthly summaries of plant-wide performance, as well as analysis of results.

Divisional management, central staff offices, and top management receive reports and analyses which permit them to concentrate on broad review, planning, and action (Fig. 38).

---

[12]Those who cry for "just one sheet of paper" seldom mean it.

[13]*Reports to Top Management*, American Management Association, 1953.

Reports are Designed to Serve <u>All</u> Levels of Management

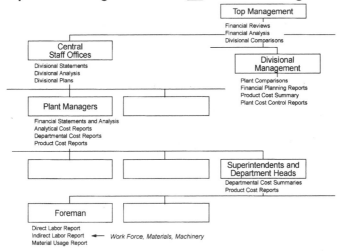

Fig. 35. Concept of reporting at various levels.

The Foreman Receives

Daily Production Count		

Scrap Report		

Indirect Material Usage Report		

Indirect Labor Report		

Foreman_____	Dept_____	Plant____
Direct Labor Report		

Classification	Authorization	Actual	Variance
Assemblers	17	16	1
Material Handlers	12	14	(2)
Sweepers	3	3	

Fig. 36. Schematic of daily reports for first-line supervisors.

The interrelation of these reports is shown in Fig. 39. Summaries for each level of reporting provide the grist for the next level.

A further contrast in control concept is seen in the extent of travel of a report to secure action. Reports should travel only a short distance (Fig. 40). Failing this, the scheme of control is cluttered up with innumerable copies of detailed reports going to levels far too busy to deal with them (Fig. 41).

The Superintendents and Department Heads Receive
More Condensed Reports

Departmental Cost Report			
Cost Trend Charts (by Foreman)			
Manufacturing Cost Performance Summary			
Dept._____ Plant_____		Date_____	
	Total Manufacturing Cost		
Foreman	Authorized	Actual	Variance
Jones	$32,014	33,419	$(1,455)
Smith	17,965	16,010	1,955
Brown	48,272	46,800	1,472

Fig. 37. Schematic of condensed reports for department heads.

Divisional Management Concentrate Principally on
Performance Reviews and on the Plans of the Various Plants

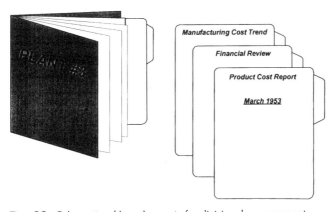

Fig. 38. Schematic of broad reports for divisional management.

The matter of detail reports cluttering the mails is surprisingly widespread. It often has its origin in some crisis, and then goes on and on after the crisis is past.

The Bridewell company endured a series of serious production stoppages because of inadequate plant maintenance procedures. The manufacturing vice-president got into the act and ordered that

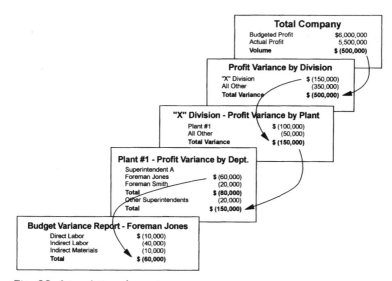

Fig. 39. Interrelation of reports.

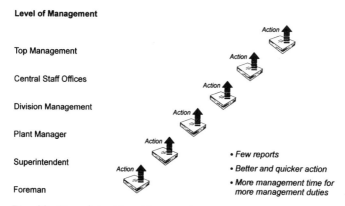

Fig. 40. Plan of short travel for reports.

a system of preventive maintenance be installed. The vice-president then required that copies of the *daily* reports of the various maintenance inspectors be sent to him. It was his way of being advised that the system of preventive maintenance was actually in use. Soon afterward he stopped reading the daily reports and just

Poor Financial Control

Level of Management							
				• *Too many reports go too far through the organization*			
Top Management	Action ↑	Action ↑				Action ↑	Action ↑
Central Staff Offices	Info ↑	Info ↑	Action ↑	Action ↑	Action ↑	Action ↑	Info ↑
Division Management	Info ↑	Info ↑	Info ↑	Info ↑	Info ↑	Info ↑	Info ↑
Plant Manager	Info ↑	Info ↑	Info ↑	Info ↑	Info ↑	Info ↑	◇
Superintendent	Info ↑	Info ↑	Info ↑	Info ↑	Info ↑	◇	
Foreman	◇	◇	◇	◇	◇		

Fig. 41. Effect of unrestricted issue of report copies.

piled them up. Then he asked his secretary to pile them up in her office. But he failed to shut off the valve.

Years later someone found that these daily reports by maintenance inspectors were still going to the vice-president, the works manager, and the plant engineer, none of whom had read any of them for years. Their secretaries just filed them.

Too many reports going to the manager is an old problem. Taylor observed it in the nineteenth century:[14]

> It is not an uncommon sight, though a sad one, to see the manager of a large business fairly swamped at his desk with an ocean of reports and letters, on each of which he thinks he should put his initials or stamp. He feels that by having this mass of detail pass over his desk he is keeping in close touch with the entire business. The exception principle is directly the reverse of this. It states that the manager should receive only condensed, summarized, and invariably comparative reports, covering, however, all of the elements entering into the management, and even these summaries should be carefully gone over by an assistant before they reach the manager, and have all of the exceptions to the past averages or to the standards pointed out, both the especially good and the especially bad exceptions, thus giving him in a few minutes a full view of progress which is being made, or the reverse, and leaving him free to consider the broader lines of policy and to study the character and fitness of the important individual under him.

[14]Taylor, Frederick W., "Shop Management," *Transactions of the American Society of Mechanical Engineers*, vol. 24, par. 288, "Exception" principle.

Who Does What?

It is now time to divide up the work of control.

This has been a bloody battlefield. The time-honored urge of human supervisors to command as much as they can has been in full play. But beyond this, there has been a really perplexing question of "Who *should* do what?"

It is no answer to say that "The line is responsible for running its job." "The Controller must control." "The inspector is responsible for quality." Such statements shed no light on what is meant by "the job," by "control," by "responsible." (Since the statements can be interpreted as self-serving, they are suspect anyhow.) There is no real understanding of "responsibility" *until we talk of decisions and actions.* To understand who should be responsible for control, we should talk of who is responsible for choosing control subjects, for creating units of measure, etc. So let's talk of these things.

Table 17-3 shows the general approach to organizing for control. The various steps in control have been broken down clear to the decision and action level.

The column "line" refers to the departments held responsible for meeting the goals established. The column "staff" refers to the service, planning, or auxiliary departments in their capacity of assisting the "line."

The most significant fact of the table is the universal provision for approval of all final actions by the line.

In a multilocation company, the problem is complicated by the question of local autonomy vs. central direction.

The Wheeler company runs several plants. Each requires the services of a clerical staff which keep various records and prepare various reports. The question is, should the clerks at each plant be supervised by:

(*a*) The local plant manager? He argues that only he can prescribe the priority of service needed; that all sorts of supervision as to hours of work, discipline, etc., must be done locally; plus a hundred other arguments.

(*b*) The chief accountant at company headquarters? He or she argues that the methods used must be uniform; that the plant manager should not be in the position of reporting on his own performance; that specialized supervision is needed; that clerks and accountants need their own promotion ladder; plus a hundred other reasons.

(A similar situation may prevail as to the Personnel department, the Purchasing department, the Industrial Engineers, etc.)

Our concern here is primarily with the reporting system. Should the plant manager be put into the situation of reporting on his or her own

Table 17-3. Who Does What?

	Staff	Line
Choosing the control subject:		
Nominating	X	XX
Reconciling	X	XX
Approval	X	XX
Creating unit of measure:		
Nominations	X	XX
Test of nominations	XX	X
Approval	X	XX
Choosing the standard:		
Study of history, market, work data	XX	
Proposals for standard	XX	X
Test of proposals	X	XX
Approval of standards	XX	XX
Creating the sensors:		
Proposals for sensors	XX	X
Tests of validity	XX	X
Approval	XX	XX
Measurement:		
Design of plan for measurement	XX	
Approval of plan	XX	XX
Carrying out the approved plan	Either	
Audit to see if the approved plan is being carried out	XX	
Data processing:		
Design of plan	XX	
Approval of plan	XX	XX
Execution of plan	Either	
Audit	XX	
Reporting:		
Reduction of data	XX	
Summary and analysis	XX	
Interpretation of results	XX	XX
Issuance of reports	XX	

XX=prime responsibility
X=supporting responsibility

performance? How about the coloration, biases, and other traps all will fall into?

Actually, it is possible here to have the best of both worlds—to provide for uniformity of system and unbiased reporting, while providing good service and local supervision. The solution requires that we separate "responsibility" into its elements as follows:

Responsibility for	Assigned to	
	Local manager	Central staff
Design of data-processing plan	X	X
Execution of plan	Either	
Audit of practice against plan		X

If the central staff has a full voice in the planning, plus responsibility for auditing, the actual processing of reports can be done either under the local manager or under the central staff, depending on the economics involved and on other considerations.

What Type of "Staff"?

The conclusion that some of these actions and decisions should be done by "staff" is not the end of the story. Clearly, "staff" means "not line." But there are various staff departments. They differ in their specialized orientation but not in their appetite for responsibility.

Look at some of the staff departments which have come to be "recognized" as proper for carrying out many of the responsibilities of measuring and reporting:

Department	Responsible for measuring and reporting
General Accounting	Company profit, assets, liabilities
Sales Analysis	Sales volume, expenses, etc., vs. budget
Cost Accounting	Cost of production vs. standards
Quality Control	Quality of product vs. specification
Production Control	Volume of production vs. schedule

This proliferation of staff departments is quite recent in industrial history. In the centuries dominated by the merchant, the vital control was the balance sheet and, to a lesser degree, the profit statement. To prepare these statements there evolved the specialist whose descendants are known today as General Accountants.

In consequence of this history, the most highly developed network of measurement and analysis is that relating to financial ratios. Generations of accountants, financiers, entrepreneurs have devoted themselves to perfecting the measures and analyses needed to work up these ratios. The schools of finance, accounting, business administration, industrial engineering, etc., have embodied all this lore into the curriculum. In consequence, many of the young people entering industry are already trained in how to collect and use this information. Through such means, use of financial ratios has been woven into the cultural patterns of many industrial managers, and they will pass it on to their apprentices.

As industry evolved further, the great trading companies were joined by great companies in manufacture, transport, communication, distribution, etc. The finance function, still vital, was joined by other vital functions—personnel, manufacture, research, etc.

These "nonfinancial" functions, having risen to prominence long after the trading and finance functions, have not yet perfected their methods of measurement, analysis, and control. These "nonfinancial" measures have, as yet, no clear-cut sponsorship from various professional groups. They have not yet become part of the curriculum which bright young people assimilate before they join companies. Yet these functions are of top-management importance, and it is essential that tools for their control be provided. How is this to be done? Unless top management is to get its financial measures from one source and nonfinancial measures from a variety of sources, there needs to be an answer to the question:

To whom should top management look for control information?

There have been several approaches.

1. Give the job to the Controller.[15] The results have been mixed. Most Controllers have pursued a career exclusively in accounting and finance. As with other lifelong specialists, they find it difficult to broaden their perspective to give balanced emphasis to matters not on the balance sheet or profit statement.

2. Set up a Statistical Department to deal with the nonfinancial information. Generally these departments have gravitated into specialized statistical studies (economic forecasting, market research, operations research). They have not generally been successful in providing management with control information.

3. Create a special department for control reporting. The classic example is Koppers Company's Control Section.[16]

When General B. B. Somervell became president of Koppers Company, he created a new "Control Section" as his reporting service.[17] This Control Section was made responsible for the staff ac-

---

[15]Generally his or her responsibilities include office management and data processing as well as General Accounting.

[16]Walker, George M., "The Control Section: A New Aid to Management," *Modern Management*, October, 1949.

Not many companies have followed the lead of Koppers. For another example, see "A Control Unit for Top Management," *Management Record*, October, 1961, pp. 10–13 (The Case of The County Trust Company, a bank operating in New York State).

tivity associated with preparing the monthly "Progress Report" for the Board of Directors and the company's Operating Committee.

Since the Control Section operated at the top of the company, it did no collecting or processing of basic records. Instead, it worked out with the company's operating divisions and staff departments the necessary arrangements for supplying the Control Section with the information needed.

4. Assign an "Assistant to the President" (or similar title) to do the job. There is sporadic use of a functionary for conserving the time of the executive by predigesting information for him or her. However, the one-person nature of the post has generally made it a temporary and unstable setup.

It must be concluded that industry generally has not settled the problem of "to whom should top management look for control information." It may take another decade or two before the experiments under way finally disclose the most useful setup. Meanwhile, in the absence of clearly designated prime responsibility, all involved are left to self-coordination.

Next Step, Interpretation

Whereas the sensor has provided us with communicable information, our mobilization for measurement has provided the transmission lines. Through our system of measurement, the myriads of drops of information collected by the sensors are pumped to the usage stations.

We had previously supplied, to these usage stations, the standard—the knowledge of what we *should* be doing. Now, the information on what we *are* doing flows in from the transmission line, and we have a comparison to make. The key word is now "interpretation," discovering what useful meaning we can derive from this comparison. So "interpretation" becomes our next chapter heading.

---

[17]It was also assigned some other duties which are not pertinent here.

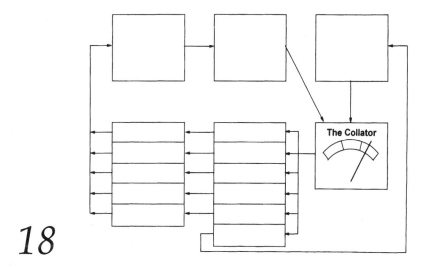

18

INTERPRETATION

The Purpose of Interpretation

Interpretation is an added, essential step on the road leading to decision making. It consists mainly of:

1. Verifying the validity of the alarm signal
2. Evaluating the economic and statistical significance of the alarm signal
3. Discovering the factual cause behind the alarm signal
4. Evaluating the alternative roads toward reestablishing the peace

In the absence of these interpretive steps, managers would stampede with every alarm signal, false alarms as well as others. They would make snap judgments, "correct" things which had no relation to the alarms, and mete out court-martial punishments for technical offenses.

The interpretive steps are not a procession of mechanical, impersonal actions following each other as in the automated assembly line. They are human actions, and they take place in an environment which may be favorable or hostile to objective interpretation. Before looking at the details, let us look at the environment.

Primitive Interpretation

When a primitive animal feels pain, it presumably does not engage in thoughtful reflection on the factual causes. It responds to its reflexes, and acts to shut off the symptoms.

In the company, which is staffed by more civilized animals, there is a residual disposition to do what the primitive animal does—stop the pain by shutting off the alarm signal. Argue with the scorekeeper. Cut the overhead by charging to some other account; forget to make out the scrap tickets.

Obviously, responses to the company's alarm signals should be directed at causes, not at symptoms. But the "obvious" will happen only if the company has established an environment of law and order. Under a system of law and order, the alarm bell signals a departure of performance from standard, i.e., a violation of an industrial law. In the outside community, the leading citizens determine, by their example, whether law and order are to prevail. In the company, the managers set the example. Lacking a system of law and order (or worse yet, having an unenforced system) the company becomes a jungle, with everyone for himself or herself. The veneer of civilization falls away, and *homo sapiens* reverts to the practices of his or her predecessor species. Reflexes, secrecy, and other personal defenses take over. When there is no law, people trust only themselves.

All along in this book, we have assumed that Control is to be taken seriously, that the standards are set with the intention that they be met. Now, as we come close to the action link of the feedback loop, we underscore this need for law and order. Without law and order, the system of controls is an organized approach to frustration.

Establishing Law and Order

The ingredients of an environment of law and order within the company are quite similar to those found outside the company. This is hardly surprising, since the same human beings inhabit both worlds. The ancestors of these people waded through bloody wars and revolutions to overthrow tyranny and to establish government by law. Their descendants would not, for long, check these hard-won gains at factory entrances.

Outside the company, the theoretical ingredients of law and order are obvious enough—the legislative, executive, and judicial functions of government. But the really decisive ingredients are the integrity of the leadership—the leading citizens, the public officials, the clergy, the intellectuals. Where these people do provide leadership and set the example, law and order are realities. Where the leadership fails, the entire system is corrupted.

Inside the company, it is no different. The legislative, executive, and judicial functions are all there, though organized along other lines. And the really decisive criteria of law and order are not the formal specifications, procedures, and other industrial laws; what is decisive is the spirit of compliance as exemplified by the actions of the leadership.

The managers decide, by their own respect for the industrial law, the level of compliance throughout. When the managers do nothing on evidence of budget overruns, late deliveries, or quality failures, the word goes down the line: The company doesn't regard these things as important. The deeds begin to follow these conclusions. If this goes on and on, the deeds form habits which take deep root. Thereafter, nothing short of "the earthquake treatment" can bring about an early return to law and order.

Participation

The environment of law and order is greatly influenced by the extent of interdependence of the managers. Where interdependence is great, a manager's performance depends, in large part, on what other managers do. The alarm bell rings in one department, but the trail leads to another. The alternatives for action become more numerous and complex. Arriving at a solution which is optimal for the company becomes a collective undertaking. The team, not the individual, gets the results. The key word becomes "participation."

In such a collective society, the timeless drives of human beings reassert themselves. "No taxation without representation" becomes "membership on the committee." Freedom from unwarranted "search and seizure" becomes the right to control what goes on in "his" or "her" department. The "Statute of Frauds" (a contract for sale of real estate must be sealed) becomes "requires the approval of...." These historical drives make it clear that it is against the grain for individuals to act on someone else's interpretation of what rang the alarm bell.

Some managers have missed the point because of a misunderstanding of the role of the scorekeeper. Clearly, he or she plays a vital role. He or she provides the numbers, guards their integrity, and interprets their meaning. This essential role of the scorekeeper has trapped some executives into concluding that the scorekeeper must be given a monopoly on interpretation. Such a conclusion is dangerous nonsense. It mistakes the evidence of deeds for the deeds, and it misses the important difference in outlook between the operating manager and the scorekeeper.

The operating manager looks to the reports for aids in making decisions, performing deeds, making corrections, explaining things away, keeping the peace. His or her interpretations are in the context of the operating situation and of the human beings faced with the realities of operations.

The scorekeeper emphasizes the numbers, the rules of the game, the procedural law and order. His or her interpretations are statistically oriented. The extremists make it seem that the purpose of the operations is to make the numbers come out even.

> An example (not restricted to extremists) is that of the two burden centers.
>
> Profit analysis in the Neader Company has shown that product A is not competitive. The main reason is process X. It is performed in department 12 where the burden rate is $16 per hour.
>
> The operating managers have for years protested this burden rate. They point out that process X uses none of the costly machinery which is the cause of the high burden rate. But the Controller has been adamant—so long as process X is performed in department 12, it must use that department's burden rate.
>
> But the Controller has a suggestion. Why not move process X out of department 12 and across the aisle to department 11, where the burden rate is only $5 per hour? The operating managers are flabbergasted. How can the same process, operated by the same people, cost less by moving across a factory aisle?
>
> Each says to the other: "You don't understand." And they don't, since they start with widely different premises.

Conceivably, the operating manager can, through personal contact, understand his or her operations without seeing the scoreboard. But no one else can. The scorekeeper may be content with knowledge of the meaning of the numbers. But no one else is. So we need the views of both. These needs are great enough to make us willing to put up with a few extremists rather than to miss the value of the interpretations of the many moderates.

Agreeing on the principle of participation is not enough; the means for participation must be worked out. Committees, task forces, and teams are the meetinghouse variety of participation, and they have their place in the company. Use of the staff specialist or the "assistant to" is also feasible provided that this individual serially touches base with all concerned.

Those of us who have seen many companies in action have been struck by the contrasts in team effort, or lack of it. The individuals in all companies have intelligence, energy, and drive. Where a team spirit has been established, the individuals fight the enemy—the competitors, the natural forces, the blunders. Where the team spirit is absent, the individuals fight with each other.

Verifying the Alarm Signal

> "I don't care what the report says. The bins are empty and that's all there is to it."

The design and installation of a reporting system has much in common with marketing a service (or a product). The service must be debugged to a point that the customers accept it as reliable. Thereafter, there is need for continued vigilance. Complaints about the service must be taken seriously. Chronic complaints must be rectified by fundamental changes in design or production. To anyone except a stubborn scorekeeper, the real signal given by a false alarm is that the reporting system is no good. The boy who cried "wolf" has many industrial descendants.

The scorekeepers in the company often fail to grasp the realities of this situation. They become deluded by their current monopoly, or by the current support they have from the big boss. These artificial immunities do not endure. If the scoreboard is allowed to deteriorate, the scorekeeper will in due course follow it into oblivion.

It behooves the scorekeeper to be the first to verify the alarm signal. If the false alarm is first detected by the operating manager, it is like the defect in the product being first discovered by the customer. It not only inconveniences the customer—it makes the entire system suspect.

Evaluating Significance; Tolerances and Shewhart Control Charts

Even before we get to the question of *cause* of a variance from standard, we look at the *size* of the variance. In two respects, the size alone may cause us to forget it:

1. The variance is economically insignificant. "It isn't worth looking into." "We have more important things to do."

Certainly, there is a sound principle behind these views. Increasingly, this principle is being put to regular use by the idea of a "tolerance." The engineers have long used the tolerance to designate acceptable variances in manufactured product. Company regulations often allow a fixed per cent of overrun on capital projects before there must be a resubmission for high approval.

Managers who are troubled by overattention to small variances might well consider use of the tolerance concept as a formal device for interpretation. It is already there informally.

2. The variance is statistically not significant. The word "significant" is here used in a special sense.

It is well known that nothing repeats itself precisely, whether monthly sales, hourly production on the assembly line, or dimensions of pieces turned out by a lathe. This "natural" fluctuation is the result of the interplay of numerous small variables and is called random or chance fluctuation, i.e., not traceable to any specific cause.

One result of the random fluctuations is that it does not pay to investigate any small fluctuation; the cause is obscured by the random variables.

> You are matching pennies. Your opponent wins three times in a row. You should not (yet) conduct an investigation to see if there is skullduggery. Chance alone will produce such a result once in eight times. This is not so unusual as to be suspicious.

Obviously, a really big fluctuation will have a "findable" cause. But how big is big? For once, we have a clear answer. The fluctuation is big if the odds are heavily against its having been caused by chance alone.

> You continue matching pennies. Your opponent has just won for the eleventh time in a row. (This too can happen by chance, but only once in 2,048 times.) You are now justified in assuming that chance is being helped along, and that there exists some "findable" cause.

This illustrates the principle of the statistical "test of significance." Over the last few centuries, mathematicians have learned how to calculate probabilities associated with various sizes of fluctuations, and have refined the tests of significance. But the effort to calculate and recalculate the probabilities was forbidding except in isolated cases.

In 1924, Dr. W. A. Shewhart of the Bell Telephone Laboratories invented a "control chart" which could be used as a convenient, perpetual test of significance. The probabilities are calculated once, and a pair of horizontal boundary lines ("limit lines") are drawn to show the range of fluctuation which could be due to random causes alone (Fig. 42). Then the actual performance (lot by lot, hour by hour, machine by machine, or whatever) is plotted on the chart. Points outside the limit lines are almost certainly due to findable causes.

To date, the widest use of the Shewhart control chart has been in connection with control of quality. However, it is a universal test device, and has been used in many varieties of control.

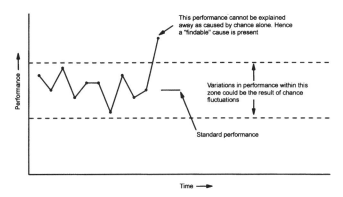

Fig. 42. The Shewhart control chart.

The tolerance is not merely a way to deal with deviations from standard; the very concept of tolerance is an expression of determination to remain the master of the system rather than to become its servant. It was aptly put by a company during a discussion of "red circle" rates (departures from the job evaluation system); "We run the system—it doesn't run us."

"Accuracy" in Interpretation

Some management decisions are based on small differences. One per cent or even less may be decisive in contract awards. Tiny differences in cash balances are tracked down ruthlessly.

This emphasis on small differences has its place. But it is out of place when there are large variables rampant. In such cases the experienced person turns his or her attention to the real variable rather than to an exercise in arithmetic.

> There are a dozen ways of calculating return on investment for capital projects. Scholars can and do get enmeshed in the differences. But the practical manager does not. He looks to see if return on investment is comfortably "in the ball park." If it is, he spends little time on arguing just where in the ball park it is. Instead he spends his time on the real variable—the "forecast" of usage of the proposed facility. This forecast can easily be so inaccurate as to lead to a wrong decision. In contrast, a failure to refine the calculations on return on investment will seldom lead to a wrong decision.

The drive for undue accuracy has another bad effect. It slows down the signals, and delays the interpretation. The main body of information comes out promptly; it is the refinements and discrepancies which take the time to track down. With or without the refinements, the managerial decision is usually the same. The intangibles which plague the manager are more important than the effect of ignoring the refinements.

"Preliminary" or "unaudited" figures are examples of the principle of gaining time by not waiting for the refinements. Use of the principle might well be extended.

Discovering Causes

At the outset, we recognize that there are various levels of investigation in finding the causes of departures from standard:

1. Finding the *presence* of the departure from standard. This can be done either by study of the reports of performance or by observation of actual events. The former, done in the office, is generally more sensitive than the latter, which is done on the scene of action (warehouse, district office, shop floor, etc.).
2. Finding the *concentration* of the departure, i.e., which account, product, department, etc. This likewise can be done either from the reports or from direct observation. Again, the reports are the more sensitive.
3. Finding the *causes* of the departure from standard. For the most part, this must be done from direct observation of events, and hence by the people directly on the firing line. The operator, not the scorekeeper, is in the best position to identify the deeds which might have damaged the score.

> In "The Bridge over the Drina," by the Nobel prize winner Ivo Andric, the brutish operating manager supplied his own interpretation as to the cause of the continuing sabotage of a bridge construction job. The theory of the villagers was that supernatural forces had decided there should be no bridge. But the cunning manager noted, after guards had been placed on night patrol, that the sabotage took place only on moonless nights. This convinced him the sabotage was of human origin.

By special effort, it is feasible to conduct the analysis of causes during regular operations rather than after the fact. In such cases, the analyses can be piped to the scorekeeper and summarized by him.

> The Aleph Machine Tool Company requires its salespeople to report on the reasons for losing sales: poor service; customer design

preference for competing machine; better delivery date by competitor, etc. (It took some doing to get the salespeople in the habit of reporting these things.) The resulting summarized and analyzed report is regarded by the executives as "about the best thing that ever came down the pike."

These several levels of analysis of deviations (finding the presence, the concentration, and the cause) are so interrelated that means must be found for pooling the knowledge and ideas from all sources. This pooling is done by a combination of two basic devices—the leg man (as I referred to it in the previous edition of this book) and the conference.

Interestingly enough, these two devices are repeatedly used in the stereotype of the mystery crime novel. The starting point of the mystery story is a departure from standard—corpses appear, or jewels disappear. Headquarters receives reports of this performance, and now the causes must be discovered.

A detective goes to the scene of action and thence to wherever the trail leads. Courteously and patiently, but firmly, he collects the facts, ma'am. (Would that all our industrial staff people exhibited such sterling qualities.) His painstaking work gradually enriches our knowledge and keeps narrowing the list of suspects. (The list also keeps narrowing of its own accord as the mysterious killer strikes again and again.)

Finally it is time for the Great Conference. The survivors are herded together into an appropriate setting and all exits are barred. Our hero now demonstrates what we had suspected all along—he is no slouch at rhetoric, suspense, and psychological trickery either. (These traits the industrial staff people can do without.) The grand climax bursts forth from behind the clouds. Performance returns to standard and peace once again descends on a grateful community.

Industry makes wide use of the scheduled performance review meeting:

the membership consists of a presiding manager plus his or her line and staff subordinates.

the agenda for the meeting consists, in part, of the performance report package which was distributed in advance.

each member is expected to contribute what added information he or she has, to aid in interpretation, and to propose alternatives for action.

These meetings take place at all levels, from the monthly meetings of the Board of Directors clear down to the factory floor.

In the late 1940s the author saw an unique review meeting. The time was Tuesday morning. The scene was a factory floor in the shops of Husqvarna Vapenfabrik A. B., in Sweden. Various supervisors and specialists surrounded a floor area in which all of last week's scrap had been collected. The staff people had determined which department was responsible and how much money had been lost. The supervisors responsible reported, one by one, what they were doing to prevent a recurrence. The whole atmosphere was one of earnestness and reality.[1]

The leg-man device is a supplement to the meeting device. The specialist makes the rounds, picking up facts, interpretations, and proposals. He weaves these into a report or newsletter which is supplementary to the package of facts, and which is made available to the interested parties. Since the device is built around one individual, his personal competence greatly influences the value of the results.

The leg-man device is at its best when dealing with interdepartmental problems—the alarm bell rings in one department, but the trouble lies somewhere else. In such cases the line supervisors are fatally handicapped. Only people who can bridge across departments can complete the study.

Untested Standards

It will be recalled that control means "holding on course" whether our course is to hold the status quo or to create change. In discussing interpretation of departures from standard, let us now look for a bit at departures from a planned or decreed course for Breakthrough.

We are now dealing with *untested standards*. (When we are trying to hold the status quo, we are generally dealing with proved standards.) The practical effect is that we are less insistent about meeting the standards. The failure to meet them may only prove they were no good in the first place.

A case in point is control over capital expenditures. Admittedly, it is inherently difficult to set standards for these projects—they are in the Breakthrough category. But there is much evidence that the available know-how is not being employed very extensively either.[2]

---

[1] There was also a complete absence of chairs, which likely contributed to the brevity of the conference.

[2] "See Improving Control over Capital Expenditures," *Business Record*, October, 1961, pp. 22–33. See also, in greater detail, "Managing Capital Expenditures," National Industrial Conference Board Studies in Business Policy, No. 107, 1963.

Managers are warranted in allowing more tolerance on performance against untested standards. But they should guard against an attitude which assumes that the only alternatives are to enforce or to change the standard. In a Breakthrough situation, nothing is really settled, and the opportunity for imaginative proposals is at its greatest.

Proposing Alternatives for Action

We have already seen several alternatives:

1. Forget it. The variance is not significant, economically or statistically.
2. Fix it. Train the new employee so he or she doesn't do it again. Resharpen the tool.
3. Challenge the standard. "Sure, it's off three months in a row. It just goes to prove the budget was cut too far."

This does not exhaust the list. Human ingenuity being limitless, the responses at review meetings are varied indeed. For example:

4. Following the leader. "The boss has told us to clean up the backlog. So we'll be over on costs for awhile."
5. Hoisting the all-clear signal. "I know all about it. Somebody misread the specification. It's all straightened out. Next month's report will prove it."
6. And so on and on.[3]

> The newspaper carries an account of how two youths, with mechanical skills bordering on the genius, and with the energy of beavers, worked out an amazingly effective gadget for thievery. It took them months to perfect their invention. Then they were caught because of some amateurish blunder in tactics. The reaction of many a law-abiding citizen is "If they had put half that much effort into an honest business venture, they would really have gotten somewhere."

---

[3]The industrial people are not the inventors of such responses. Common-law pleading includes such terms as:

demurrer, e.g., "even assuming I did call you a washed-up political demagogue, that doesn't give you any legal case against me."

confession and avoidance, e.g., "Yes, there was such a contract, but it was you who breached it first."

The manager finds himself or herself raising the same question with respect to ingenious alibis, theories, and other escape devices. If only all that energy and inventiveness could be turned to constructive purposes. "They spend more time hunting up a good reason for failure than hunting up a good road for success."

The Payson Company case (p. 182) is a good example of an imaginative solution. On the face of it, it is absurd for a company to compete with itself in the open market. Yet the analysis made this an alternative, and the employees were bold enough to try it.

Managers who brood over the lack of dash and ideas in their company would do well to question whether there is an environment of creativity.

> It probably dates from the time that Perry became the Vice-President. He was really a very capable guy, but his way of dealing with new ideas was murder. He challenged 'em all, with lots of seasoning and sarcasm. The few fellows who knew him well felt it was his peculiar way of bringing out all the pros and cons. But most men just wouldn't run that gauntlet more than once or twice. Instead, they just quit bringing up ideas. The Vice-President's meetings were about as lively as a wake. Finally Perry just cut them out and handled things direct with each individual.
>
> Now we have a new Vice-President and his approach seems to be different. But it will take him years to get the fellows out of that long hibernation.

So a worthy industrial citizen once told the author. The author had known Perry quite well. He was indeed capable—keen, dynamic, anxious to do a good job. And he was totally unaware that he was doing a lot of damage.

There are cases in which the top executives have become convinced that certain roads are closed to them, and have given up. This word goes down the line, and in due course, everyone else gives up. The barricade becomes permanent.

> An engineer for the Aqua Water Company made the following observations in a thesis he prepared as a graduate student of the author's:
>
> During early 195x, revenues were increasing, partly due to normal growth and partly due to an increase in rates which had gone into effect on Jan. 1, 195x. In spite of the increases, the Controller's report showed that costs were going up even faster. It became evident during the latter part of the year that the increased costs would jeopardize the company's ability to earn a fair return. Application was made to the State Public Service Commission for permission to increase rates again. This permission was granted effective the first of

the year, subject to investigation by the Commission to determine the justification of such new rates.

In most industries, it might be expected that the control system would give recommendations for improvement....In Aqua, the principal expense items are the payroll and the electric power required for pumping. With unionized employees and with pumping charges coming from another company, there is, in the opinion of the executives of the company, little chance for a rearrangement of personnel or the altering of pumping procedures....In fact, an interview with the Chief Engineer and the Controller indicated that neither could recall an instance wherein a truly positive cost reduction had been or for that matter could be effected.

In Aqua, they use a sort of "backward cost reduction" (i.e., getting rate increases).

The principal purpose of the cost data is to act as the watchdog over the expenses so that this negative type of savings might be effected when necessary.

Who Does What?

Our discussion of Interpretation has come up with a plan of responsibility somewhat as shown in Table 18-1. (Such a summary table still omits a good deal about responsibility, since it does not distinguish between levels of operating management nor between the different kinds of staff.)

The main arguments center around the role of staff. The staff is accused in both directions: they don't do enough; they do too much.

The "don't do enough" criticism is directed at the contention of some staff that their role is pure scorekeeping. "We are like an instrument

Table 18-1. Who Does What?

	Upper management	Operating management	Staff
Establish law and order	XX	X	X
Verify the alarm signal		X	XX
Evaluate statistical significance		X	XX
Evaluate economic significance		X	XX
Discover causes of variance, proved standards		XX	X
Discover causes of variance, untested standards		X	XX
Propose alternatives for action		XX	X

XX=prime responsibility
X=collateral responsibility

plugged in to read the score. We shouldn't set the standard. Neither should we get involved in what to do when the score is high or low."

If the premise of a role of pure scorekeeping is sound, then the logic is sound. What about the premise?

In the author's judgment, the premise is unsound as applied to all but small companies. In the small companies, the President can personally coordinate matters for the entire company. As the company outgrows this size, this coordination must be taken over by others.

In the small company, the accountant can be limited to a scorekeeping role because the President does the budgeting, financial planning, and such in his head. Beyond this size, if there is to be financial coordination, the accountant must expand his or her role to take a hand in planning the system of financial standards, designing a common language, establishing procedures, evaluating the operation of the system, and reporting on the validity of all this to top management. It is such an added list of duties which converts the Chief Accountant into the Controller. The same concept converts the Chief Inspector into the Quality Manager, etc. See, for a more extensive treatment, Chap. 21 under "Concept of a Control Function."

These disagreements over whether the scorekeeper role is too narrow are seldom acrimonious. An individual's motives are not suspect when he feels he would be invading someone else's responsibility. It is when he reaches out that the sparks begin to fly. Where the staff is accused of doing too much, emotions can run so high that they hide the merits of the case.

The focal point of excessive staff activity is in the "interpretation, decision, and action" part of the control cycle. Responsibilities for this activity are seldom well defined; so there is ample opportunity for a strong staff personality to move into a power vacuum. The resulting spectacle is infuriating to the line managers. To them, the controller (or some other staff villain) is in the position of authority without responsibility. He or she criticizes departures from standard without having had to face the realities. He or she proposes courses of actions, or vetoes others, again in an irresponsible manner. They know that much of it is a mistake, but they are unable to prove it.

A journalist, watching a review meeting attended by line and staff people, might well, report somewhat as follows:

> There were two kinds of people in the room, gladiators and scribes. The gladiators had just come from the arena, still covered with blood and sweat, still breathing heavily. But the scribes were cool, alert, and energetic.
>
> Now there were shown on the screen the pictures of what had gone on in the arena. Oddly, the discussion was limited to pictures

of faulty fighting. They had a name for this selection—it was called "the exception principle."

As these pictures were shown, the scribes would comment sagely. "That thrust was rather weak." "There you could have advanced." "That cut was not up to standard." The gladiators listened and grunted. Now and then they would try to explain that in the arena there is not time to think of all these things, that blood is slippery, that lions have their own ideas. But it was of no avail.

The gladiators were doomed to defeat. They were now fighting in an arena they did not understand. The weapons now were not the familiar swords and spears; the weapons were numbers, words, rhetoric. As to these weapons, the gladiators were no match for the scribes.

The meeting broke up and each group went back to its stations. The scribes retired to the safety of the stadium seats where they made themselves comfortable and ready to resume counting. The gladiators returned to the hot, hostile floor of the arena. They knew they had suffered defeat at the hands of the glib, clever scribes. But in their hearts they remained convinced that no one but a gladiator understands the problems of fighting in the arena.

Fantasies aside, the jurisdictional needs are clear. When there are doubts as to who should play the leading role in interpretation and decision, the doubts should be resolved in favor of the operating manager. There are persuasive reasons for this:

> the operating manager, not the scorekeeper, faces the pressure of conflicting standards. Frequently he is forced to violate one standard to meet another.

> the operating manager, not the scorekeeper, will take the final corrective actions. This is more likely to happen when he or she has participated in the interpretation and is thereby convinced of its merits.

In some of these jurisdictional feuds, the real culprit is upper management. The top manager, seeing a gap in the pattern of responsibility, should not just sit by and let the scorekeeper move in. The top manager should arrange to clarify the responsibilities. In particular, any responsibility of the staff person to move in to investigate in depth should be clearly defined.

Without being aware of it, the line manager also benefits from the fact that his or her boss has access to a staff department for analysis of performance. Look at the alternatives available to the boss when a manager's performance is poor:

1. Move in personally and try to find out why the performance is poor. Generally the boss has no time or disposition to do this.

2. Fire the manager. This requires the time of breaking in a new manager, yet with all the risks that he or she will be no better.
3. Endure the situation and hope it will work itself out. On the record, this doesn't look too promising.

Collectively, this is still a poor set of alternatives. Now, with a staff available, the boss has a fourth alternative.

4. Send the staff person in to obtain a new, different viewpoint. (It will often be unbiased as well.)

Many a situation has been saved because this alternative was used. Many a line manager has smarted under the humility of submitting to such a staff study, not being fully aware that it was the boss's only real alternative to taking him or her off the job.

Tools for Interpretation

Myriads of staff-hours have been devoted to interpreting data. A by-product of this huge effort has been the evolution of aids or tools for interpretation. By now these tools constitute a respectable kit. Some of these aids have attained the status of general-use tools. Others are still special enough to require extensive legwork on the part of the specialists.

The manager is well advised to have a speaking acquaintance with the general-use tools, and an awareness of the possibilities inherent in the specials. Through these tools he or she is provided with welcome alternatives to the extremes of (a) staring at a mass of meaningless numbers, or (b) reinventing tools which have long been in active use.

About a dozen common-use tools are discussed under that heading below. Following these, there are separate discussions of several special-use tools.

Common-Use Tools

These are numerous. The list below is confined to some of the more widely used.

1. Show the *trends*. The arguments for showing trends can best be seen by comparing Fig. 43 with Fig. 44. Figure 43 is the conventional comparison of this month's performance against standard. Figure 44

likewise shows this month's performance against standard. In addition, Fig. 44 shows:

whether the long-range trend is up, down, or sideways

whether the trend is steady or unpredictable

whether this month's departure from standard looks any different from those of months gone by

There can be no question that the presence of the trends in Fig. 44 greatly improves the ease and quality of interpretation.

2. Make the report *comparative*. The act of comparison is an act of interpretation.

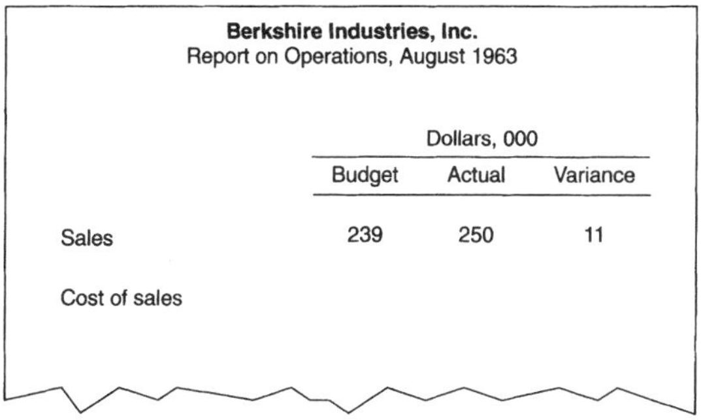

Berkshire Industries, Inc.
Report on Operations, August 1963

	Dollars, 000		
	Budget	Actual	Variance
Sales	239	250	11
Cost of sales			

Fig. 43. Simple report emphasizing current performance.

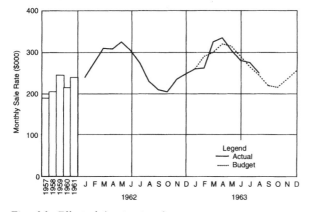

Fig. 44. Effect of showing trends.

A study[4] of controllers' reports showed that out of 428 devices used for interpretation, 153, or 36 per cent, took the form of comparisons (with last period, with the same period a year ago, with the budget, with some standard). Comparisons were the most popular single interpretative device. Others were cumulative figures, ratios, per unit reductions, charts, etc.

Edmunds[5] relates an example in which days of supply of new-car stocks is used as the sensory device for triggering action with respect to automobile production and sales. Evidently a "normal" or standard supply is 30 to 40 days' sales. Figure 45 shows how the rising trend during November of each year, to May of the next year sounded the alarm. Through various actions (production cutbacks, redistribution of inventories, and sales promotion), the balance was restored in a few months.

3. Make use of *summaries*. These take various forms: a straight total of many pieces of information; year to date figures; abstracts. The common purpose is to present a single important total rather than many subtotals; a single paragraph rather than a 6-page report. Through this summary, the reader is able to understand enough to judge whether to go into detail (which is often appended) or to skip on to the next summary.

To prepare summaries puts an added burden on the reporter. (Newspapers and magazines employ specialists to write headlines.) But the summary is a great time saver for the operating manager.

[4]Smith, C. Aubrey, and Jim G. Ashburne, "Internal Blueprint: The Controller Reports to Top Management," *The Controller,* December, 1951, pp. 558–562.

[5]Edmunds, Stahrl, "The Reach of an Executive," *Harvard Business Review,* January–February, 1959, pp. 87–96.

Days' Supply of New-Car Stocks in Dealers' Hands
At the End of the Month

Sales district	November	December	January	February	March	April	May
Boston	36	42	61	62	52	40	31
Buffalo	36	35	67	86	57	39	39
Cleveland	33	38	68	64	46	45	43
Twin Cities	33	24	40	45	53	41	43
Dallas	27	28	41	65	93	92	74
Los Angeles	38	34	52	73	76	58	44

Fig. 45. Alternative method of showing trends.

4. *Underscore the vital few.* "All districts were on target except Northeast, which was off 7 per cent." The detail shows too much, and the summary may obscure something important. Emphasizing the few really important matters is a sensible middle ground.

The underscoring may take the form of a separate report: the list of delinquent accounts; the back-order list; the FBI's ten most wanted criminals. It may take the form of "headlining."

> Glass bottles are subject to over one hundred "diseases" or defects during fabrication. In one factory, the inspectors at the cold end of the annealing conveyor send hourly reports back to the employees at the hot end. These reports state, for example: "During the last hour, 8 per cent of the ware was scrapped. The three principal defects, accounting for 5.7 per cent of the 8 per cent were...."

5. Report only on *"exceptions."* An alternative to underlining is to omit reporting on matters which are proceeding according to plan. Only the delinquents and laggards are reported. By implication, anything not on the report is doing fine. Adoption of this principle has resulted in some phenomenal reductions in cost of reporting, as well as aiding interpretation by concentrating attention on the topics needing it the most.

6. Make the reports *timely.* The search for causes involves a recall of past events to explain a current report. The shorter the elapsed time, the fresher the memory and the easier the recall.

7. Standardize the *calendar* so that the month begins and ends uniformly for all reports. Failing this, the relation of cause (the actual happenings) to effect (the score on the report) is influenced by the fact that events tend to congest at the end of the reporting period.

8. Adopt a standard *format.* Use the same size of sheets or charts. As far as possible, use the same scales and headings. Such standard format makes it easy to tune in and out quickly and reduces the chance of mistakes in interpretation.[6]

9. Record the major *explanations.* Reports going to upper management should include explanations of trends and fluctuations where there is a consensus. (Where the explanation is not yet available, that fact should also be recorded.)

10. Provide *prognosis.* When a reviewing executive sees a sporadic drop in performance, his or her main question is—have steps been taken to get back on target? Because correction is the cardinal purpose of the

---

[6]In this connection, standards for charting are available. See "Time Series Charts: A Manual for Construction," American Society of Mechanical Engineers or American Standards Association.

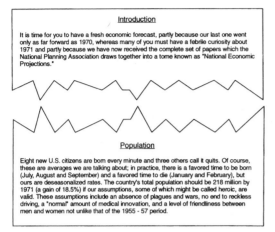

Introduction

It is time for you to have a fresh economic forecast, partly because our last one went only as far forward as 1970, whereas many of you must have a febrile curiosity about 1971 and partly because we have now received the complete set of papers which the National Planning Association draws together into a tome known as "National Economic Projections."

Population

Eight new U.S. citizens are born every minute and three others call it quits. Of course, these are averages we are talking about; in practice, there is a favored time to be born (July, August and September) and a favored time to die (January and February), but ours are deseasonalized rates. The country's total population should be 218 million by 1971 (a gain of 18.5%) if our assumptions, some of which might be called heroic, are valid. These assumptions include an absence of plagues and wars, no end to reckless driving, a "normal" amount of medical innovation, and a level of friendliness between men and women not unlike that of the 1955 - 57 period.

Fig. 46. Use of the light touch in a market-research study by Herbert L. Campbell, William A. Clark, Marlene S. Mills, and Henry J. Siegle, for Monsanto Chemical Company, St. Louis, Mo.

feedback loop, the report increases in value if it makes clear whether corrective action has been taken.

11. Serve with a dash of *humor*. Business is serious, even grim, but the human relations need not be (Fig. 46).

Artificial Units of Measure

The parent reviewing the child's report card is presented with a common language of reporting for a variety of subjects. Junior studies a wide assortment of subjects: geography, algebra, English, biology. But the grading language for all subjects is identical, A through F.

Some managers have also preferred to have a common reporting language for a wide assortment of subjects. To achieve this, their staff people have been obliged (1) to invent a common language or artificial unit of measure to fit all subjects, and (2) to do the detail work of converting the measure of performance of each subject into the common language. All this parallels precisely the approach used by the schoolteachers.

The literature reveals a variety of approaches used by companies to fashion a common reporting language. The most prevalent is the accountants' "per cent variance," i.e., the ratio of variance to standard.

Related to per cent variance are the systems which equate all standards to 100. It doesn't matter whether the control subject is the accident rate, the level of customer complaints, the cost of giving service. It doesn't matter whether the standard is historical, engineered, or based on the market. Whatever the type or source of standard, it is equated to 100. Performance at standard becomes 100. Performance 15 per cent better than standard becomes 115, etc.

An example is seen in Koppers Company's plan.[7] Here the universal character was achieved by converting everything into "per cent of program." All goals, whether for profit or sales, were expressed as "programs." Attainment of the goal became meeting 100 per cent of program.

Weighting

Summaries of unlike things soon run into the argument that you are adding horses and oranges. So there is need to find some index that gives horses, oranges, and anything else an appropriate weighting in the summaries.

Sometimes this can be done by natural weightings—the dollar value of each, the pounds of air frame, the feet of welding seam, the number of electrical connections, etc. In the absence of natural weights, artificial weights are created.

The Quality Control people have gone a long way down this road. Reports on per cent defective have traditionally been suspect because defects are unlike in importance. The quality control fraternity has attacked the problem by going over to demerit systems based on the seriousness of the defects. The common language becomes demerits per unit of product.

In personnel work it is common practice to secure answers to surveys on a scale of preference, for example: like strongly, like, indifferent, dislike, dislike strongly. To summarize these, resort may be had to an arbitrary weighting of numbers, i.e., 5, 4, 3, 2, and 1.

These point systems simplify matters for the reviewing executive, at a price. The original price is the staff work required for designing the system. There is also an upkeep price because of the inevitable built-in arbitrariness in assigning the points and the weights. In the traffic-violation penalty systems, how many parking violations are equal to one speeding violation? For the salesperson, how many new accounts are

[7]*Reports to Top Management,* American Management Association, 1953.

equal to meeting the quota for volume? The debate on these matters continues long after the original agreements have been reached.

When the Standard Is a Curve

A special problem in interpretation arises when the standard is a curve.

> A trainee is brought into the department. Past records show that there is a 16-week learning period in getting up to standard efficiency (Fig. 47). Progress of a trainee can be judged only by comparison with this learning curve. The trainee may improve week by week and still fail to make the grade because his or her performance curve is too far below the normal pattern.

The training or learning curve has many counterparts—debugging a new product, or a new process; developing an executive, or a team.

There are other forms of variable standards:

Seasonal fluctuations. The term "corrected for seasonal fluctuations" is in common use. Lacking such correction, the interpretation of statistics on sales, unemployment, etc., can be maddening.

Progress of a "drive." An essential element in a "drive" is a scoreboard. Sustained interest requires progress against a target—reduction of overtime, accidents, etc. But no one expects this reduction in the first week or month. The real goal is an *improvement curve.* Once again, the interpretation must be related to the curved standard.

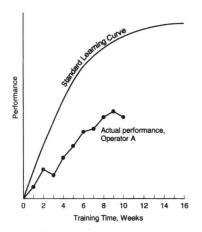

Fig. 47. The standard as a curve.

The Gantt Chart[8]

This ingenious device combines the activities of measurement, analysis, and usage in one "reads at a glance" chart. It was invented by Henry L. Gantt during World War I to aid in controlling the timetable of the American shipbuilding program. It can be used in all kinds of production control.

The chart (Fig. 48) consists essentially of equally spaced vertical lines. The equal spaces represent:

(a) A calendar of equal units of time (hours, weeks, etc.), *and*

(b) Equal quantities of *scheduled* production (pieces, tons, gallons, etc.), *and*

(c) Equal quantities of *actual* production.

A schedule is marked on the chart by "reserving" time (a horizontal distance) for the activity in question. Actual performance is then shown as a horizontal line, the length of the line being proportional to the amount of performance. Per cent of completion is then seen as the ratio of actual (the horizontal line) to schedule (the reserved horizontal distance). Extent behind or ahead of schedule is seen from the relationship of the righthand point of the performance line to "today" on the calendar.

The chart is designed so that it can be maintained with just a pencil and a ruler. A number of mechanical "boards" have been developed to avoid drawing lines at all.

[8]Clark, Wallace, "The Gantt Chart," The Ronald Press Company, New York, 1922.

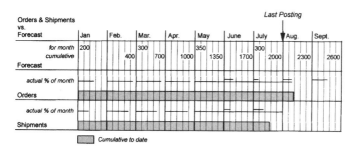

Status as of August 1st:

<u>Orders</u> - For year-to-date, one week ahead of forecast. Future orders light. Orders by month were less than forecast every month from Jan. through Apr. May order equalled forecast. June and July exceeded forecast.
<u>Shipments</u> - Total orders are behind forecast. Monthly shipments lagged - now exceed orders. Three weeks' orders to ship.

Fig. 48. The Gantt chart.

And More Tools

Since there is no known limit to human ingenuity, we may be sure that the parade of new tools for interpretation will continue. The staff people, especially, are in a position to come up with Breakthroughs here, and their record to date is quite creditable.

There is a further job to be done. As tools are proved to be useful on a broad scale, they should move out of the laboratory and into the main room. To do this requires that:

the tools be redesigned to make them simple, reliable, and foolproof

the people in the main room be trained in use of the tools

Staff people have no lack of zeal for wide dissemination of such tools. But too often the approach is to ask the line people to take courses in mathematics, or otherwise to try to complicate the users rather than to simplify the tools. This runs contrary to a rule of the anthropologist— "Strip off all cultural baggage not needed for introducing the change."

Managers should make no compromise with these tendencies. The salesperson must learn the language of the customer, not the other way about.

Next, Decision Making

Up to now all roads have converged. We have brought to each usage station the necessary battery of standards plus the associated array of performance measures. We have been put to a good deal of effort to achieve this convergence. However, we are repaid because we have brought, to the presiding agencies, the ingredients needed for interpretation.

The converged roads now travel together to the decision maker. He or she will choose a course of action. At that point the roads diverge again, since action takes many forms, and various actors are assigned the tasks of converting the decisions into deeds.

Logically then, our next consideration is decision making on the difference between the standard and the actual performance.

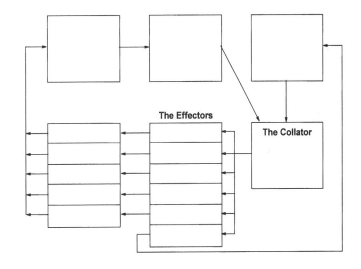

The Effectors

The Collator

19

DECISIONS ON THE DIFFERENCE

A Mysterious Process

We confess at the outset that we don't really know how decision making actually takes place. This is a pity, because decision making is a truly indispensable process. But pity or not, our ignorance is a fact. We do, of course, know a good deal about the steps which managers have found to be helpful as prerequisites for making decisions. So we will, in this chapter, confine ourselves to examining these prerequisites.[1]

The Need for Alternatives

Thomas Hobson was a sixteenth-century stable owner. He was also a firm believer in the first-in first-out principle. He rented his horses out to the U-drive men of that era on a strict basis—you take

---

[1]Many investigators, including this author, have hurled themselves at the question "What goes on within the decision-making process?" But not much has come of it. We can prepare a list "The nine elements of decision making are:..." We can talk a good game about this list. We can teach it to students so they can pass an examination in it (despite never having made a business decision in their lives). But until the behavioral scientists have told us a good deal more about how the human mind-brain complex performs its functions, we will make very little headway.

the horse that has rested the longest, or none at all. Hobson's customers might inspect all the horses, but they would "decide" to take Hobson's choice.

This spectacle goes on apace in modern industry. A key job suddenly opens up, and there is no one ready to fill it. No one. No one, that is, except maybe Stanley.

Stanley has been the corporal in this department for years. No one has ever thought of him as a candidate for the top job. No imagination, colorless, a plugger, a steady-Eddie.

But suddenly we are faced with a crisis. We must fill this job promptly because so many things are popping. We must decide right now. So we take a second look at all our candidates, namely, Stanley.

Stanley has played ball with the company. His attendance record is unique. He has never refused to pitch in in an emergency. He hasn't uttered a peep at being passed over for promotions. Shouldn't seniority count for anything around here? And how about that vanishing commodity, old-fashioned loyalty?

We labor to make it sound plausible. And we give the job to Stanley. Thereafter, for years, he does the job. No imagination, colorless, a plugger, a steady-Eddie. Exactly according to forecast.

We didn't "decide" to give Stanley the job. We had maneuvered ourselves into a situation where we had Hobson's choice.

The need is for alternatives. If we are going to fill a key job, we should have several competing candidates. If we are going to buy a house, elect a public official, award a construction contract, revise a process, we should have several competing candidates. Otherwise, we have Hobson's choice. Any pretense of "deciding" is just a pathetic ritual.

One of our alternatives is making better use of what we have. Remember the case of the phony figures (p. 136)? There we made an unfair comparison. We compared the proposed method operating at optimum efficiency with our present method operating at mediocre efficiency. Hence, an added alternative was to make no change in process, but to beef up the present process.

But what if there are no alternatives? Then, say many authorities, delay your final decision.[2] "We should make plans so that we may have plans to discard." Use the delay to create alternatives. Search for competing candidates. Assign people to work out competing proposals.

---

[2]"Delay your decision" isn't as bad as it sounds. See "How Much to Decide," below.

The alternatives may be there but we haven't smoked them out. One of our nine sales representatives is outdoing the rest, by a good margin. He did it by setting up a repair service which, though it is marginal for profit, has attracted a good deal of new business. But no one understands this. The "reps" know that there is a star in their midst, but they don't know just what makes him a star. (Neither does the star know—his books aren't that precise.) And we don't know, but we should. We have the most at stake, and we are in the best position to look into why these performances are different.

Conference leaders have long made use of the principle of competing alternatives. They stimulate people to talk, to come up with ideas, even if you are just thinking out loud. A good conference leader puts these ideas on the blackboard immediately, *without challenge*. Once these competing ideas are on display, they will be challenged, to the hilt. But they will also elicit support. The resulting contest will, of course, discard many ideas. But the surviving ideas will be the better for it, and there will be greater confidence that there has indeed been a survival of the fittest.

The ultimate in grasp of the principle of alternatives is reached when a manager's internal alarm system stops him or her in his or her tracks. "I'm in a fix where I have Hobson's choice. So I'll decide as little as I must. And I'll set the wheels in motion to develop alternatives as to the undecided residue."

The Right to Decide

The line manager, not the scorekeeper, is responsible for making the decision on what to do when performance departs from standard. There is fairly complete agreement on this principle. Otherwise we would be taking away with the left hand the responsibility we gave with the right hand.[3] The jurisdictional problem on decision making is rather among the various line managers. Some of this problem arises because the work of several line managers must be coordinated. But some exists as between the line manager and his or her boss.

The pyramid of control (Fig. 21) made clear that most control action takes place at the bottom of the company. It is inevitable that most decision making likewise must take place at the bottom of the company. This, if course, requires delegation of the *right* to make decisions. And it requires that those at the bottom be stimulated to be decisive.

---

[3]It doesn't follow that the scorekeeper has no responsibility for decision making. He does, but on matters other than what to do when operating performance departs from standard.

At one of the plants of International Harvester Company, labor grievances were being written at the rate of 300 per month. These written grievances satisfied no one. They were many months getting settled. Delays in settling one grievance would breed other grievances.

Company and union officials looked into ways to avoid this unwanted flood and pile-up of grievances. They came up with a proposal to speed up the decision-making process through "talk-outs" Under the proposal:

> verbal complaints are "talked out" at the foreman-steward level. If they do not agree, they do *not* write up a grievance to go to upper levels. Instead, upper levels are brought in for the "talk-out."
>
> written grievances are used only after the talk-out fails
>
> settlements are retroactive to the date of the talk-out, not to the date of the written grievance

They tried the proposal at one plant with stunning results. The number of written grievances dropped to 5 per cent of its former level, almost immediately. In consequence, they extended the idea to all plants.[4]

The fact of delegation is what counts; the form is optional. Delegation may be a matter of unwritten precedent; there may be a list of don'ts, with the implication that all else is delegated; or the delegation may be spelled out, with the implication that anything not on the list is reserved to the boss. Now and then there is an attempt to define everything (p. 144).

The Duty to Decide

We can pass quickly over the conventional establishment of the duty to decide. The job descriptions contain the proper clauses, and the usual motivations of reward and punishment are in the background. We might best devote our attention to the overshadowing force—the environment of law and order.

> A child is told by his mother "Don't bang on the piano. You'll be punished." He bangs on the piano but he is not punished. So he bangs on it day after day.

---

[4] "Talk-outs"—One Way to Settle Grievances Fast, *Business Management*, January, 1962.

The same child is told by his mother "Don't touch the hot stove. You'll be burned." He touches the stove and is burned. So he never touches it again.

The biggest factor in enforcement is the practice followed by the boss. In several ways he or she sets the pattern of responses which come from below:

he or she keeps out of situations which are running well, except to commend those involved.

he or she demonstrates his or her awareness of, and interest in, departures from standard by asking for explanations. The subordinates cannot provide the explanations without digging into it.

he or she demonstrates his or her determination to do something about departures which are not set back on the track. Either he or she gets into such cases personally, or he or she sends in a staff investigator. The subordinates do not care for either.

he or she follows the foregoing pattern so consistently that subordinates cannot misunderstand. "The way to keep the boss out of your hair is to keep things on target."

To some it may seem reprehensible for a manager to secure compliance by threat of invasion. But it is only an expression of a universal reality. (Nonunion shops may follow enlightened practices because of the threat of unionism.) The subordinate who is motivated to keep things under control has acquired skills and habits which will be increasingly valuable to the company and himself or herself.

How Much to Decide

A profound question in decision making is just how much to decide. The manager's range is wide. He can decide not to decide. Or he can commit the company to a considerable risk. The process by which he chooses a sector of this spectrum is still a mystery to us. But we might dwell on an important related matter:

future events have a way of sneaking in, as uninvited guests, behind today's decisions

Keeping these uninvited guests out is important enough, in enough cases, to warrant a question on the manager's agenda: "How much should we decide?"

The uninvited guests are of two main classes:

1. In deciding this case, we are committing ourselves to a "whole course of action."
2. In deciding this case, we are setting a precedent for a whole host of cases.

The usual approach to the "whole course of action" problem is to split the program up into logical steps. As each step is taken, we can review the situation and make a new decision on whether to proceed further or to call a halt. The AMF state system (p. 228) is an excellent example.

In effect, we distinguish between a plan of approach and a definite decision. This distinction, though widely practiced, is not well understood.

An example is the capital appropriations budget. This is prepared annually, based on anticipation of projects to be initiated or continued in the year ahead. The total is estimated, reviewed, and finally approved, *as a plan* or budget. This approval is *not* an authority to spend the money. The spending authority comes later, project by project.

There are managers and engineers who deplore this state of affairs. Why go through the ritual of approving something as a plan but withholding approval to spend the money? The reason is that new developments may require that we change our position. Between December (when the plan is approved) and a year from now, a product becomes obsolete, a key employee dies, a customer abandons us, a new machine comes on the market, a recession looms up. We must retain flexibility.

In the same way, some companies prepare sales forecasts for 5 years ahead. But the firm authority to produce per schedule may be limited to only the next quarter, or even to the next month. We know, from bitter experience, that we must retain flexibility.

Despite the absence of firm decisions, the planned approach has great value. It "combs out our thinking." We cannot prepare the plan without going through some wholesome disciplines of fact collecting, study, etc. Moreover, the plan is not an academic exercise. We intend to carry it out. If the conditions we had forecast actually come to pass, we do carry the plan out. Otherwise, we change the plan.

The other problem of uninvited guests is that of precedent. "If we do this in situation A, we will have to do it in all similar situations."

If the manager is afraid of precedents, let him talk to the lawyers. They have faced this problem for centuries. Under the Anglo-Saxon system of law, a decision becomes a precedent to be followed in the future in like cases. Otherwise the law will be applied unfairly and unpredictably.

The lawyer's solution is to get pretty precise. "If we do this in situation A, we do *not* have to do it in all similar situations; only in identical situations. We can seize on the differences to arrive at different answers."

A precedent applied to the vital few does not have to be applied to the useful many; the economic balance is different. What we do in the Eastern Zone does *not* have to result in the same action in the Western Zone, in spite of what some of the staff say. "The same action" might be the right thing to do. But not because it has rights as an uninvited guest. When we made our earlier decision, it was restricted to the case at hand.

The Time Factor

The effectiveness of a decision depends greatly on the timing. The proverbial "stitch in time" and "nip in the bud" have their counterparts in modern industry. A failure to lubricate ruins a good machine; slow settlement of a grievance loses a good employee; hesitancy in bringing out a product loses a market. The relative costs of badly timed to well-timed decisions can be enormous.

> In the late 1940s, the native population of Algeria made various demands on the ruling European minority. Rejection of these demands built up pressures which resulted in demands for full independence. Several bloody years later, the original demands looked astonishingly modest.

In other cases, time acts not as a magnifier, but as an evaporator. Many problems "solve themselves," meaning there are forces at work which don't need our help.

Discovering what kind of case we are dealing with requires that we know the time perspective, the trends. When we limit ourselves solely to control during the fact, we may look ridiculous several years hence. (Again, polishing brass while the ship is sinking.)

Training in Decision Making

We can divide the topic of training several ways:

> the mental decision-making process. We don't know enough about it, so we can't teach it.

> the preparatory steps to be taken prior to making a decision. We do know a good deal about these steps. (Some are discussed in this chapter.) Moreover, the steps are evident and lend themselves easily to a training program.

the willingness to decide. This is the elusive one, and warrants some elaboration.

On the face of it, there should be no problem of willingness to decide. Doesn't the human being get into the habit of decision making from childhood on? So he or she does, but there are differences. Consider some of the ways in which the pattern of decision making of the non-manager differs from that of the manager:

For the nonmanager, most decisions involve:	For the manager, most decisions involve:
A direct feedback from one's personal observation	Feedback through the intermediary of information
Control during the fact	Control before and after the fact
Accepting responsibility for one's own actions	Accepting responsibility for the actions of others

Collectively, these and other changes add up to a big change—far greater than is commonly realized.

The list also suggests that some main training needs are to be aimed at:

understanding the concept of control through information rather than solely through direct observation

participating in the setting of standards and goals

understanding the reporting system so that the significance of the numbers is understood and accepted

accepting personal responsibility for results

The acceptance of personal responsibility provides the push which sets all else in motion. Without this, the other things are of no avail.[5]

When managers are for a long time *prevented* from making decisions, they may become unable to make decisions. (Think of the ancient Far Eastern practice of binding little girls' feet to stop their development.)

McCormick & Company had for years been dominated by the founder, who ran it as a one-person show. On the death of the founder, he was succeeded by his nephew, C. P. McCormick. The new president had no inclination to run a one-person show. But he also concluded that the members of the Board of Directors "had

---

[5]The concept of personal responsibility can also be overdone, to the damage of the company. See "Optimizing Company Performance," below.

grown into the habit of confirming my uncle's judgments." To enlarge the source of ideas, he invented "Multiple Management," i.e., bringing lower levels of managers into decision making. This was done through an organized approach, the so-called "junior board of directors."[6]

Optimizing Company Performance

During the last two decades, managers have devoted an immense amount of attention to establishing and achieving standards of managerial performance. One by-product of this intense effort has been to obscure the original purpose of Control. Our real purpose is to optimize *company* performance, but we act as though our purpose were to meet *departmental* standards. They are by no means the same thing.

> The scene is the district sales office. The new recruit is making his first report to the district manager. The rookie is mighty proud. He has been on a selling spree. He has easily beaten his quota for volume of sales. He did it by: selling to known deadbeats; selling on absurd payment terms; cutting prices; offering all sorts of technical services. The rookie finishes his success story and waits eagerly for the boss's comment. The boss says: "You're fired."

It's a grotesque case, of course. But it emphasizes that meeting standards is child's play if we don't know what the effect is on company performance.

We can also meet standards easily if we put personal or departmental goals ahead of the common good.

> In the early days of fire fighting, the volunteer fire companies performed yeoman service for the communities. Their contests and rivalries resulted in improved equipment and technique. But in the cities, the rivalries intensified to a point of destruction. Rival companies rushing to a fire were deliberately directed to the wrong part of town; their equipment was sabotaged; their hose lines were cut. In other ways the rivalries became an end in themselves, with great damage to the community. The cities were forced to abolish the volunteer fire companies in favor of a single, tax-supported Fire Department.

[6]McCormick, C. P., "Multiple Management," Harper & Row, Publishers, Incorporated, New York, 1938.

The volunteer fire departments which attained a state of fanaticism[7] have their counterparts in modern industry[8]: the product development department which blocked a stunning project (p. 34); the controller's department whose adherence to the book flies in the face of common sense (p. 329). Those in such departments regard themselves as working for the common good. Often enough their departments are well disciplined, with a good deal of departmental pride, competitive spirit, and high morale. They would be astounded to be accused of acting contrary to the company's interests.

So we have a basic contradiction. Our real purpose is to optimize company performance. But the goals we ask workers to meet are individual or departmental standards. And when workers turn their energies to meeting these narrow standards, all too often the original purpose sinks to a secondary importance. Is there a way out of the contradiction?

Let us first review the train of reasoning which seems to have got us into this contradiction.

1. We know of no way to carry out the company's mission without organizing work into jobs, and jobs into departments.
2. Our experience has been that individuals (and departments) working under a control cycle for setting and attaining standards have outperformed individuals who do not.
3. Our experience also tells us that individuals and departments with proud traditions, competitive spirit, and high morale will generally outperform those who lack these things.

It seems clear that energy and zeal are increased by the use of narrow standards. The job is to direct this energy toward the common good rather than into destructive frictions. There are two main approaches:

1. Set up checks and balances in the form of multiple, interlocking standards.
2. Set up an environment of continuing awareness of the effect of individual actions on the common good.

These two approaches can be seen more clearly by looking sideways at a related problem.

---

[7]Recalling again the definition of fanaticism: redoubling your efforts after the original objective is forgotten.

[8]And out of industry. Witness the competition of the various services of the Defense Department and the resulting duplication and waste.

A government has the job of collecting taxes from individuals and organized groups. It can approach this job from two directions:

1. The hard approach: plug the loopholes by still more legislation; minimize freedom of action, i.e., collect at the source; apply rigorous enforcement and stiff penalties for evasion.

2. The soft approach: conduct educational programs to show how the common good is served; hold public hearings on tax measures; obtain appeals, by leading citizens, to the public conscience.

The industrial equivalent of plugging the loopholes is to establish interlocking standards.

The manufacturing job is mainly to meet standards of cost, quality, and delivery. Any fool or knave can meet any two of these standards *provided* he is allowed to ignore the third. By setting and enforcing standards for all three, we help to ensure a balanced performance.

In like manner, if the salesperson (rookie or otherwise) overemphasizes volume, we put in more standards. We give points for a balanced product mix, for opening new accounts, for holding down expenses, etc.

Optimizing company performance through interlocking individual standards is a limited solution at best. In the first place, we don't really know how to define the company's goals solely in terms of individual or departmental standards.[9] We can only approximate, and some of these approximations are wide of the mark.

Secondly, we are defeated by the ingenuity of man. He finds ways to squirm out of the interlock and so to continue his pursuit of provincialism.

Finally, some top managers contribute to the confusion by a wooden insistence on intense incentives for meeting individual and departmental standards. Such incentives tend to enforce the erroneous view that the purpose of these standards is to provide targets for provincial employees, rather than to help provincial employees contribute to the common good.

The "soft approach" is also widely used in industry. It includes such activities as:

preparing programs of education and enlightenment to help workers to understand and work for the common good

providing wide participation in the original setting of objectives and in the planning to meet those objectives, as a means of understanding the relation of departmental goals to company goals

[9]There are some managers, perhaps many, who would contest this assertion.

community review of results as a means of understanding the effect of departmental performance on the common good

The soft approach has its own array of deficiencies. Participation turns out to be like democracy—the concept soars through clean clouds while the practice slogs over dusty roads. The community pace can be exasperatingly slow, and the community members maddening in their bickering.

For the foreseeable future, we must use both roads. We must retain the individual and departmental standards. We should keep improving and refining them so that collectively, if met, the results do approximate the common good. But we cannot rely solely on these standards. We must, in addition, set up the environment which urges employees to channel their individual and departmental zeal (for meeting standards) into directions which optimize company performance.

Such an environment is not the result of slogans, exhortations, or other tools of propaganda. These tools are an aid for the real thing, which is the *role*.

Each individual is present in the company in two basic capacities:

(*a*) As a person with personal aspirations—a role brought in with him or her on the day he or she was hired. No action by the company is needed to give his or her awareness of this role.

(*b*) As a member of the company community, with a stake in the common good. The reality of this role depends on whether the employee is allowed to play it. Unless he or she is given the role in fact, it is nonsense to exhort him or her to subordinate his personal aspirations to the common good.

We will return to this dual role in Chap. 21, under the heading of "Control and Freedom." Few topics in this book are so farflung in their implications.

Action in Theory and Practice

With the decision and choice of action, the road diverges again. The designated effectors are energized and, in theory, we are on the way to restoring normality. Working this theory out in practice is, as always, a subject in itself. It is this subject, "Taking Action," which closes the feedback loop as well as our treatment of the Control process.

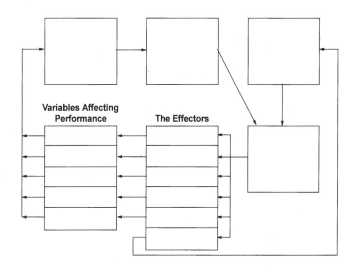

20

TAKING ACTION

The Last Lap

The final step in a series of events is deceptively dramatic. The birth date of a human being is celebrated year after year. But 9 months of awe-inspiring embryonic development had preceded the dramatic climax.

Our final step in Control is "action." Action, too, can be deceptively dramatic. It is the preceding steps, during months of painstaking effort, which have made possible the dramatic end result. If these prior steps have been executed with precision, the final result emerges triumphantly. The astronaut goes into orbit, cool and courageous. He makes it look easy. He returns, and we go wild. We break out the champagne. He proves his caliber by toasting the thousands who backed him up.

So our action chapter will be short. If we have done a good job in the preceding chapters, there shouldn't be much left to do here.

Action is the final lap of the feedback loop. The decision to act is transmitted to the person who can and should act. He becomes the industrial equivalent of the effector[1] muscle of the biological organism. Unless the muscles do their job, all prior activity is washed out.

---

[1]Synonyms for effector include actuator, corrector.

Most control action takes place in the lower levels of the control pyramid. There the loop is closed by a servomechanism[2] or a nonsupervisor. Added control is provided by the first-line supervisor through the loop of personal supervision.

Responsibility is now clear. (In the lower levels of the control pyramid it is seldom unclear.) The decision-making process has not only clarified what is to be done; it has necessarily clarified who is to do it.

It remains to see that the decision is carried out. This requires follow-through in any case, and coordination in those cases involving multiple muscles.

Follow-through

The vast majority of follow-through is done by waiting to see whether performance comes back to standard. If it does, it is taken for granted that the decision to act was carried out. Some sophisticated managers go further. Once an operation is "red-tagged" as "out of control," it must show a 3-month record of being in control before the red tag is removed.

Where multiple muscles are involved, the coordination may require that we keep book on the actions agreed on, and monitor these against the timetable. The monitoring will be resented by some. One of the justifications for monitoring such cases is that a failure to act affects the performance of more people than just the actor.

Universally, a failure to take agreed corrective action is a more serious crime than the failure which lost control in the first place. The latter is commonly assumed to be involuntary; the line of reasoning runs: there are many things which can go wrong; inevitably some of them do go wrong; it is not predictable just which will go wrong; hence there is nothing willful about it.

In contrast, a failure to take agreed action carries a connotation of willfulness about it. The matter had been up for specific discussion, alternatives had been considered, and a decision had been reached. While we can't expect some one to be everywhere at once, we can expect him to be in the very places we agreed should be acted on.

The extent of necessary follow-through depends largely on whether the actions taken are reversible or not. If the action is to throw away the old tool and use the new, there is no going back, and no need for follow-through to see if there was backsliding. But if the action is a change in human practice, backsliding is easy. Here the follow-through would in-

---

[2]The prefix "servo" is derived from the Latin *servus* meaning servant. The servomechanism is an automatic control device.

clude a periodic audit to check against backsliding until it was clear that the new practice has become rooted.

Motivation for Action

The motorist on the highway is commonly in a state of full responsibility, according to our formula (p. 147).

He or she has knowledge of what he is supposed to do, in the form of posted speed limits and such.
He or she has knowledge of what he is doing, through speedometers and personal observation.
He or she has the means needed for regulating the vehicle.

Whether he or she uses these means now depends on his state of mind—is he or she law-abiding, safety-minded, sober, courteous, considerate?

By a wide margin, the limiting factor for safety on the highways is the personal attitude of the motorist. Generally, the laws and the hardware are adequate.

In the company, there is also a big problem of attitude which we will now discuss. As we do so, let us notice that too often, managers will seize on employee and supervisory attitude as *the* problem and overlook the presence of a lot of unfinished business in standards, measurement, and means for regulation.

The Hades Machine and Foundry Company was losing a good deal of money because of quality rejects. Scrap was extensive, as was the amount of reworking of salvageable product.

The general manager had an idea. Why not dramatize these losses so that people would be shocked and do something about it?

With the aid of the Personnel Department and the Advertising Department, Hades ran quite a campaign. Scrap heaps were set up in the yard, with huge placards showing how much money was in the pile. In the various departments, similar heaps were piled up. The factory walls were papered with posters. "Quality depends on you"—"Let's cut down on the *waste*."

But nothing came of it. The scrap and rework remained right where they were, and it still required an army of inspectors to pick over the product to keep the defects from getting out to the customer.

Later, a study was conducted to find out how much of the money being lost was due to reasons under management control and how much due to the fact that the operators were not law-abiding. It was very revealing to see that of the total losses:

20 per cent were operator-controllable

70 per cent were management-controllable

10 per cent were undetermined

One of the biggest needs in supplying motivation is to set up the prerequisites without which motivation is academic. It is not necessary that this be done 100 per cent. Once we have separated the controllable from the noncontrollable to a point that the latter is a clear minority, a working agreement is in sight.

The very act of separating the controllable from the noncontrollable is an invaluable source of training and motivation. Discussion of what the foreman (for example) can control or not is itself of value in convincing him that he can, or convincing his bosses that he cannot. The scorekeeper should be a party to such training sessions. It helps him or her both in setting up the scorekeeping system and in interpreting the score. In turn, the line manager better understands the nature of the score and has more confidence in the scorekeeper's interpretation.

Competition among line managers can supply a great deal of added motivation if it is kept on a basis of good-natured rivalry. Competitive scores, published along the lines of sports events, are particularly effective.

The tactics of giving orders are an added influence in motivation for action. Much has happened to reaffirm Miss Follett's dictum[3] "One *person* should not give orders to another *person*, but both should take their orders from the situation." We saw an example of this in the spindle case (p. 177). It is a profound idea.

Finally, there are opportunities for motivation through increasing the opportunity for initiative. Time and again, practicing managers have come up with proposals such as:

never ask someone to do something without explaining why you want it done.

never tell someone how he or she should do something without first asking him or her how he or she thinks it should be done.

either tell someone what result you want and leave the method to him, or tell him what you want him to do and take the responsibility for the result yourself.

---

[3]Follett, Mary Parker, in Metcalf, Henry C., and L. Urwich (editors), "Dynamic Administration," p. 58, Harper & Row, Publishers, Incorporated, New York, 1940.

Confidence in the Standards

Knowledge of the standard itself is essential. Without it, people honestly doesn't know what he or she is trying to accomplish. But this knowledge may not be enough to supply motivation. The past record may be one of no confidence in the standard. "We worked like hell to meet the schedule but now the stuff just sits in the warehouse."

A campaign to raise "mindedness" should include an educational program to explain the control cycle. If the standards have had a checkered career, the problems faced in setting them should be made clear.

> The annual budget meeting was never complete without a review of the precision of prior sales forecasts. The self-appointed historian was Felix, the plant manager, whose comments were as well-spiced as they were lucid.
>
> This year it was different. The vice-president was waiting for him. "Felix—all of us want more reliable forecasts. Except for John (the market researcher) you have dug into this more than any of us. Now I'm assigning you the job of checking John's forecast. He'll make available to you everything he has, and get you anything else you need. Then we'll have two forecasts which we can check against each other.
>
> In subsequent years, Felix continued his interest in the forecast. He continued to challenge the figures. But now people had to choose their words more carefully. If anyone began to talk in terms of tea leaves or crystal balls, it was Felix who rose to John's defense—"You just don't realize what John is up against."

Industry teems with situations in which the standards are clear but there is no confidence in the approach to setting them: Budget cuts, sales commissions, tolerances in specifications, piece rates. Managers who have such situations in their own company have a constant uphill march because of this lack of confidence. They would be well advised to put on the agenda the problem of confidence in the standards.

A selective use of standards is usually based on a selective confidence on their validity.

> The Fly Hy Company is a well-known distiller. It maintains an extensive battery of engineered standards for shop labor and material usage. Departmental performance is compared with these engineered standards, and there is a high degree of conformance.
>
> For its broader controls, Fly Hy has an opportunity to make use of market standards based on performance of other companies. In this industry the government collects and publishes statistics on

process yields, etc., for various companies (who are not named, however). But Fly Hy is not inclined to use these figures because of differences, in method of operation, between companies. Instead, it uses its own history as a basis for comparison.

Tight Rein and Loose Rein

In Breakthrough projects, the standard is commonly "unproved." By its very nature, the unproved standard cannot command the same confidence as the tried and proved.

> At the outset of World War I, the German invaders at first made swift progress through the Low Countries. It was all according to plan, literally. Then, when the real obstacles arose, came the cardinal question—adherence to plan, or departure? Insistence on inflexible adherence to plan blunted the drive and contributed to the resulting stalemate.

The company is faced with meeting standards for both Breakthrough and Control. The latter should be administered with considerable firmness—the tolerances are small in relation to the quantities being controlled. In contrast, standards for Breakthrough require a more flexible administration. When we walk into a fog we cannot be sure what will loom up ahead.

But the same manager is called on to administer both kinds of standards. He must shift from tight rein to loose, and back again, as he moves from Control to Breakthrough and back again. It is easy to get mixed up, or even to drift into one common practice for these diverse situations.

One of the prime reasons for pushing the control mechanisms to the base of the control pyramid is to free the supervisors and managers so they can devote more time and energy to pursuit of Breakthrough. But we do not know how to liberate the manager completely from Control. So we must clarify for him the great differences between the two cycles of Breakthrough and Control, and how these differences demand differences in administration.

Pseudo Action

We don't know how to cure the common cold. But we are able to do something about the discomfort of its symptoms. So we take medicine to get rid of the symptoms. The cold runs its course in a week, after which we no longer need a medicine for the symptoms.

When we have a mysterious industrial disease, we also resort to fighting the symptoms. This takes place at all levels. The salesperson or piece-rate operator juggles his or her performance to avoid peaks and valleys. The department head authorizes overtime at the end of the month to beef up the month's performance. The president does the same in the annual report to stockholders, through judicious juggling of write-offs, and through other hat tricks. In some companies these practices go on year after year.

Obviously, all these people know that lighting a match under the thermometer changes only the evidence, not the results. What goes on then? Are we dealing with a deceitful breed?

The behavioral scientist tells us that such deceit is the result of insecurity. The culprit believes that the unvarnished facts, though not intrinsically bad, would just look bad. He knows from experience that things which look bad tend to attract attention out of which can grow investigation and criticism. If this train of events grows out of things *looking* bad, why not disguise them so they look normal?

If managers as a species had an invariable habit of studying the facts judiciously, and of dealing out even-handed justice, these insecurities would undoubtedly shrink drastically. But being human, managers have no such built-in stabilizers. Instead, they are subject to impulsive action.

The scene is the office of Wilmer, the president of Spurious Manufacturing Company. Wilmer is staring at a paper clutched in his trembling hand. It is a letter from a customer. It starts:

"Dear Wilmer:

I have been doing business with you for the last 27 years and your quality has been above reproach. But last week...."

With a heroic effort Wilmer pulls himself out of his chair, and careens down the hall into the office of Mac, his Manufacturing Vice-President. "Mac, look at what you've done to me...."

A relay race is now in full gait. The baton, in the form of a crumpled complaint letter, gains momentum as it passes to the Quality Manager, the Chief Inspector, the Assembly Inspection Foreman, and finally Eddie, the hapless inspector of 1A Gadgets.

Until it hits Eddie, the train of events is like a blow striking a row of billiard balls—each passes the shock on to its neighbor. But Eddie is at the end of the row, and the full impact of the shock sends him spinning. He "tightens down" on the things he customarily looks for. Production costs go up because of the higher reject rate.

Weeks later, when the fury dies down, the real cause of the complaint emerges. It had been a packaging blunder. Someone had crated up the day's rejects and shipped them to the cherished customer.

Wilmer's "stirring up the animals" is mighty annoying to those on the receiving end. They will have no compunctions about deceiving him. If Wilmer doesn't know how to react to bits of bad news, let's edit the news before it gets to him.

Employees know that the best way to keep out of trouble is to avoid these strange things coming to the boss at all. The "right" way is, of course, to fix them at the bottom so that there is no bad news to go to the top. But if those at the top exhibit impulsiveness and arbitrariness, the emphasis will shift to manipulating the news rather than the deeds.

Hunting

Hunting is an occupational disease of all control systems. Let's take an example:

> If the motorist's reflexes are sluggish, he or she will be slow to sense that the car is drifting off the road. When he does sense it, the drift is so great that he or she swings the steering wheel wildly. Now an over correction takes place, and the car begins to drift into the opposite lane. Again there is danger, and again overcorrection. This goes on and on if the motorist's responses remain sluggish.

Corresponding industrial examples of self-excitation are well known. Budgets are relaxed, followed by a drive on expenses. A drive to improve customer service is followed by a drive on overtime costs.

A maddening example is the spectacle of working overtime to build up inventories which then stand on the shelf while employees are working only 3 or 4 days a week.[4]

> We are giving poor deliveries to our customers, and the peak season is yet to come. So the orders go down—"build inventories." The production line goes into overtime and multiple shifts, and the stuff gushes out. But now the buying season is over, and the product

---

[4]Far more serious are the cases in which movements of goods within the channels of distribution, rather than usage by the customer, are regarded as a prime basis for action. The J. I. Case Company near disaster shows how serious this can be. The company "sold" heavily to its distributors, and outwardly increased its share of market. This went on at a pace much greater than the purchase of these goods, by the ultimate customer, at the other end of the pipeline. The consequences were nearly mortal.

turned out at such high cost begins to pile up in the warehouse. Now the order comes down frantically—"cut inventories." The production line goes into single shift, with short hours and layoffs. The inventories dwindle until we are ready to go into the same, idiotic cycle again.[5]

The engineer calls this "hunting," i.e., oscillating about the desired value. An overswing is sometimes called an "overcorrection."

The engineers' remedies for hunting are various: reduce the response time; provide damping, i.e., decelerate the corrective action as the standard is approached; etc.

The manager is well advised to look sideways at the engineers' solutions to the hunting problem. A long response interval is at the root of the trouble. Informational control may be unsuitable for nimble responses. Instead, the need may be for going to control direct from the deeds.

Training for Action

The pace of change which affects so much of the company's operations affects the ability to provide corrective action as well.

On the factory floor this change is obvious. Maintenance staff who once could fix any machine in the place stand in awe of some of the new machines.

Elsewhere the change may be less obvious, but it is there all the same. The supervisor now needs training in leadership as well as in the technical job skills. The key people need to understand much about the system of which they are a part, in addition to the details of their specific job.

These changes creep up on us week by week, a little bit at a time. Over a year or two, there are 50 or 100 of these bits, which amounts to quite a bit. The skills of workers have not necessarily kept pace, and we wake up to the existence of a wide gap.

The Technical Processes

Throughout this book we have said little about the *technical* processes which we must regulate if managerial control is to be translated into physical control. It is timely now to look at the relationship of the technical processes to the managerial Control procedure.

---

[5]One investigator has traced an amplification of "hunting" to the interaction of seasonal customer usage with sluggish responses at the levels of retailer, distributor, and factory. See Forrester, Jay W., "Industrial Dynamics," *Harvard Business Review,* July–August, 1958, pp. 37–65.

What distinguishes managing from all other activities is the fact that the manager gets things done by getting other people to do them. If these other people are also managers, they get still other people to take the action. But soon the nonsupervisory stage is reached where the human being takes direct action[6]—calls on the customer, throws the switch, adds up the column of figures.

The amount of direct action is today so immense that we have created machines and processes to do most of it for us. These processes are subject to ailments of all sorts. They get indigestion because we feed them tainted materials; they develop creaky joints and require lubrication; they wear here and there, requiring the equivalent of dentures and braces; they go berserk now and then, flying apart, writing checks for $999,999,999.99, and the like.

In this book, we are concerned with managerial control, not technical control. Hence we do not deal with the techniques of salesmanship, metallurgy, machine design, or tax litigation. Our concern is with the manager's role. He does have a role with respect to the technical processes, but the role is one of seeing to it that nonmanagers are around who can deal with these technical problems. More specifically, the manager sees to it that:

the duties needed to keep a mastery of technical matters are identified.

these duties become a part of specific job responsibilities.

individuals are selected and trained to carry out these responsibilities.

standards are set, performance is measured, etc.; i.e., the Control procedures are provided to enable these people to know what are their goals, are they meeting them, etc.

A Final, Panoramic View

Our study of the Control process started with a panoramic, bird's-eye view. From this, we returned to earth, and set out on foot to study the Control process, step by step. Now that our pedestrian study is concluded, let us take to the air again. In the next chapter, we will look at the great forces of Breakthrough and Control, and consider the extent to which managers can keep these forces in leash.

---

[6]The manager also spends part of his time taking direct action. He switches on his office lamp, calls on an important customer, or (in one riotous case) spends hours driving the new fork-lift trucks around the warehouse. During such activities he is not managing.

21

MANAGERS, BREAKTHROUGH AND CONTROL

Great Issues

We have come to the end. We have traced, in detail, the means by which the manager breaks out of a plateau to a new level of performance. We have also traced how he or she stabilizes at the new level by use of the tools of Control. We are aware that this stability may be short-lived. In centuries past there were long, static dynasties of Control punctuated by violent revolutions or invasions of Breakthrough. With quickening technology, Breakthrough is ever more frequent, and life on one level ever shorter. The pace of change is quickening, and there is properly much uneasiness about man's ability to keep up with the pace.

In this chapter we will examine the Great Issues posed by the endless stair steps of Breakthrough and Control. Where do they lead? What is the effect on the people involved? What are the deeper meanings for the manager? Some of these Great Issues will bear an obvious, direct relation to this month's bread and butter. Others will seem remote and philosophical.

We are fully justified in talking of Great Issues. The stakes wagered on ability to Breakthrough are unprecedented. National security, domination of the earth, even human survival are among the stakes.

Nor are the big stakes limited to Breakthrough. We might well conclude that humanity is just in the beginning stages of Control as a massive human effort. The human race has increasingly put itself at the mercy of the good behavior of products, processes, structures, political organizations, all designed, built, and maintained under human direction. Increasingly, we live behind an extensive system of protective dikes in the form of Controls on these man-made devices. Now and then we rediscover the importance of control of these dikes:

> A greedy financier outwits various auditors and makes off with huge sums of other people's money.
> A battery of tests fails to detect a monstrous defect in a drug. Thousands of infants are doomed to lead handicapped lives.
> A mad political organization gains command of an industrialized nation. Centuries of civilization collapse before the barbarian, and millions of lives are lost.

These gigantic shapes moving around in the background may not attract the attention of a manager wrestling with this year's problem. But the same yeast which is making these shapes move has brought about the manager's problem. And the implications for the manager are the same as for humanity:

> the pace of change is quickening.
> the penalties for failure are rising, as to both failure to Breakthrough and failure to Control.

In consequence:

> the energy which is devoted to Breakthrough and Control must rise in greater proportion than the energy required for operation.
> to direct this energy requires greater sophistication in the use of Breakthrough and Control.

We see numerous evidences of the growth of these consequences. Expenditures for research and development are at record proportions of the budget. Machinery, in both the office and the factory, is changing remarkably—for some, their brains are costing more than their bodies. The organization charts exhibit new department names which include the words "research," "planning," "control."

The issues are indeed great.

Control and Freedom

No seminar on Control is complete until someone has raised the question: Aren't controls an infringement on the freedom of the individual?

Control, staying on course, certainly requires that we restrain and govern individuals. So control does limit freedom *unless* the individual has consented to it, freely. This exercise of free consent, being itself an act of freedom, converts the restraint into a self-imposed restraint. So we must look at "consent."

The revolutionists of Western society established the principle that government must be by the consent of the governed.[1] This principle is no longer limited to political control; it has been extended to industrial control as well. Where, then, do we find in industry a basis for consent of the governed?

First, let us reject the notion that individuals do not want to be governed. Freedom is not simply opposed to tyranny; freedom is in the middle of a spectrum, with tyranny at one end and anarchy at the other. The following was the image of the Norris Company as seen by a graduate student of the author.

> Until recently there were no records. Raw facts were gathered on the spot as requested. Under time pressure, wild guesses were prevalent.
>
> The recent records have made raw facts more available and reliable. But there is no common language. "Work completed" means different things to different executives because there is no agreement on where completion takes place.
>
> There is no report system for summarizing records into executive reports. Instead, reports are prepared upon request. Mostly, facts pass orally from person to person, with glaring distortions during the transmission.
>
> Some men have set up informal sources of information and reporting in self-defense. Because of lack of definitions, standards, etc., the results do not dovetail with other men's sources. Debates on "what are the facts" are frequent and bitter.
>
> Lack of standards is the most serious indictment of the Norris company's "system" of control. Facts are so many numbers, without reference to what the numbers should be based on—last month, last year, some engineered standard or what some successful competitor is doing.
>
> Top management has no control over the company. For example, indirect costs are neither reported or controlled. The company is controlled by guess work.

(Soon thereafter, the author met the president of the Norris company. He was a dynamic, intense individual, but with an obsession on matters of management control. He had plenty on his mind. If he could only

---

[1]"...governments are instituted among men, deriving their just powers from the consent of the governed." The Declaration of Independence, July 4, 1776.

find good men who could take responsibility, employees who could stay on top of their jobs, and protect him from unpleasant surprises, he would be able to reduce his pace, maybe even take a vacation.)

In broad terms, we know very well the bases on which individuals consent to be governed. The consent has been based on a reward, or a cause, or a leader. People have died in battle, for example, as mercenaries, as patriots, or as hero worshippers.

In industrial history the consent was at the outset based on a money reward. The employment bargain was struck, and the employee consented to obey the orders of the owner (or his appointed overseer) in return for money.

In those days the power system was strongly allied against the industrial employee. The government, which was *not* based on the consent of the governed, was in league with the owners. Quite aside from this, the economic power of the owner was simply immense. In those days, the incomes of many people were below subsistence level. Holding this very job was often literally a matter of life and death.

So the owner was able to secure compliance without getting much involved in discussions about freedom and dignity of the individual. The available evidence suggests that the owners did not concern themselves too much with developing other bases for industrial government—loyalty to a cause and devotion to a leader. Presumably there was no need for it.

Meanwhile, history has marched on, and some big changes have taken place:

the political revolutions made governments more responsive to the views of the citizenry and thereby, of employees.

the neglected opportunities for securing consent of the governed (via a cause or a leader) were seized on by others—the intellectual, the union organizer, the politician.

the balance of power, previously tilted toward the employer, was turned through the force of collective agreements. These agreements were backed up by the force of governments now alien, if not hostile, to the employer.

the standard of living rose to a degree such that most employees were well above the subsistence level. For these employees, holding this very job was no longer a matter of life or death.

this same rise in the standard of living solved the problem of stark survival, and removed it from the agenda. In consequence, the unsolved problems all moved up a notch.[2] These unsolved problems in-

---

[2]This theme is brilliantly analyzed by Prof. Douglas McGregor in "The Human Side of Enterprise," *The Management Review*, November, 1957.

clude the need for belonging, for status, for "self-fulfillment." (These problems are not solved merely by money; they require that the employee become a team member, have a team cause to support, have the opportunity to respond to leadership.)

finally, the growth of industry, in size and complexity, has increased the requirement for team action. Increasingly, we must rediscover what is the effect on the common good before we decide what individuals should be doing.

(This may seem to be a long sojourn into history. However, much has happened, and these happenings have greatly influenced the freedom and consent problem. The answers to our question: "Aren't controls an infringement on the freedom of the individual?" have varied with the decade in which people live. The answers for the 1990s must be based on contemporary conditions, not on ancient conditions, or on wishful conditions.)

Evidently, we must separate "freedom" into some components.

The biggest single limitation on industrial freedom is the act of becoming employed. The consent for this is still based on contract.

Once employment is under way, the timeless needs of human beings work their way to the surface, look for leadership, and begin to press. The manager cannot ignore these needs—they just press on until he or she is forced to confront them.

Theory X and theory Y. An important fork in the road is the manager's premise on human motivation. He or she may subscribe to either of two theories[3] to explain the outward evidences of employees' indifference to work:

(X) Human beings are inherently lazy, so the manager's job is to fight this deplorable human nature through skillful use of the carrot and the stick.

(Y) Human beings are inherently willing to work, but industry gives them unchallenging, meaningless tasks. So the manager's job is to redesign work in a way which harnesses these unused capacities of people.

Under both theories, the manager sets up standards and measures of performance. Under theory X, review of results emphasizes informational control systems; formal reports; extensive use of staff personnel; rigid reward and penalty schemes. Under theory Y, review of results emphasizes self-control; personal supervision; informal reports, informality generally.

---

[3]These are paraphrases of theories X and Y as stated by McGregor, *op. cit.*

Companies live and presumably flourish under each of these theories. No one can say which is "better" without becoming enmeshed in endless argument. But in terms of "freedom," the contrasts are clear. Companies operating under theory X are definitely autocratic in nature. Goals, plans, controls are imposed from the top. The extent of restraints produces a reaction not only from the rank and file; the reaction comes from middle management as well. The reasoning which causes top management to adopt theory X causes restraints to be applied throughout.

An example of the case for theory Y is seen in "bottom-up" management as described by the American Brake Shoe Company.[4] The concept is stated by some of the key phrases: teaching rather than telling; freedom to fail; decentralized initiative.

It is easy to become emotional when human freedom seems to be the issue. Some of the advocates of industrial democracy have indeed become emotional about it. It is also easy to lose sight of the objective during the argument. The objective is to carry out the mission of the enterprise—to provide goods and services at costs and prices which will yield enough surplus to take care of all claimants. The choice of theory X or Y should be on the grounds of which will help us best carry out the mission of the enterprise.

Let us now return to the "cause" and the "leader" as bases for consent to restraints. These bases are interrelated; the company's operations are a team effort, and a team requires both a cause and a leader.

The teamwork argument is so compelling that one wonders why we have not made better use of it. The team member[5] is there in a dual role:

his or her role as an individual. Here he or she has duties and rights arising from (*a*) the employment contract, (*b*) his or her membership in the human race, (*c*) his or her status as a citizen.

his or her role as team member of the car pool, the Union, the lathe shop, the softball team, the executive dining table. Here he or she has duties and rights arising from having accepted membership on the team.

The dual role is the crux of it. It is in his role as an individual that he or she has the protection of the "consent of the governed." When he or she assumes a teammate role he or she consents to restraints on his or her role as an individual to avoid damaging the team, on which he or she also plays a role. The restraint is part of the price of admission to the team.

---

[4]Given, William B., "Freedom within Management," *Harvard Business Review*, summer, 1946, pp. 427–437.

[5]Some researches suggest that, at the nonsupervisory levels, employees may team up into "frozen" groups. Membership in such employee groups becomes a stronger motivator than anything management has to offer, excepting only employment itself. For an illuminating discussion, see Gellerman, Saul, "Motivation and Productivity," Chap. 4, American Management Association, 1963.

Such is the way it should work out, and sometimes it does. Where it isn't working out, we should look for one of several usual villains:

(*a*) The individualist who cries "freedom" but doesn't want to give up his team role. He wants to belong, but is too individualistic to pay the price. In athletics, he should be playing games which are one on one contests. In industry he should be on jobs of low restraint content (researcher, professional specialist). If he is an extreme individualist, he is out of place in a company. He should be a proprietor, author, professional individual, cab driver, professor, etc.

(*b*) The special pleader who agrees that controls are fine for the assembly line, the clerical force, the warehouse, i.e., the other person. But managing, selling, research, i.e., his or her job, is different. Take the researcher's line of argument—"how can you control creativity?" He or she is right in asking, but the question is not really in point. Research can fail because it is channeled into directions that lead to no market; because it duplicates what other people are doing; because there is no provision for taking projects from research to production; because it is costing more than it will yield even if successful; because the creative activity is not backed up adequately by the noncreative services of the laboratory; because morale among the researchers is so low that strife and frustration are draining off the creative energies. The real purpose of the controls should be the liberation of the creative energies, and the channeling of these energies into fruitful pursuits.

(*c*) The manager who points to accomplishments of individuals as evidence of the futility of team operation. "It looks like it's been designed by a committee." His conclusions may be in line with his experience. In his company, the climate for team activity may still be so adverse that team roles are so much added baggage. He is correct as to his company, but he is mistaken when he generalizes his experience to cover industry as a whole.

(*d*) The manager who cries "loyalty" and "good of the company," but who, because of autocratic beliefs, denies to individuals any role as a team member. This manager becomes terribly frustrated, as do the people around him or her. He or she is in a deep self-contradiction. He or she doesn't have a team; he has only a collection of individuals. They feel they have only one role—that of individuals. They do not respond to the "common good" because they have not been made to feel a part of it. Their advice is not sought. Their ideas are not considered. In numerous other ways, they are individuals carrying out orders; they have no other role.

Finally, we return to the question asked in all those seminars: "Aren't controls an infringement on the freedom of the individual?"

Indeed they are.

The individual starts it by bartering quite a chunk of his or her freedom for a job. He or she barters another chunk to belong to a team.

If the manager responds by living up to his or her end of the bargain, there are no hard feelings—everyone has gained. If the manager fails, the loss of freedom becomes conspicuous, and the trouble begins.

Controls from Outside the Company

Human needs are extensive, perhaps limitless. As the animal needs for survival are met, other needs are free to assert themselves—the need for security, for status, for belonging, for self-expression, etc. These needs are so strong that humans are willing to trade part of their freedom to meet them (just as they traded part of their freedom for the wages or salary required to satisfy their physiological needs).

> It is by no means clear that these higher needs can be met only by giving up more freedom. In "An Experiment in Management— Putting Theory Y to the Test" (*Personnel*, November–December 1963), Arthur H. Kuriloff indicates that the reverse may be true. The company (Non-Linear Systems, Inc.) jettisoned time clocks but retained a low absentee rate. They discarded their assembly lines and formal planning, replacing them with small assembly teams, and productivity went to record highs. They reduced the emphasis on formal written memoranda, and thereby opened up the channels of communication and understanding.

Whether the company can (or will) provide security, status, etc., is a separate question. If the company can meet these needs, individuals are willing to accept added controls. If the company cannot, the matter doesn't end there. Instead, individuals turn to other directions to get these needs met—the family, the PTA, the bowling league, the union, the American Society of Mechanical Engineers, the American Legion, the Young Presidents' Association, the basement hobby room.

Some of these other directions give the company little concern—they may infringe a bit on company time, bring in some unwanted mail or phone calls. But some directions give the company a lot of concern, because a competitive leadership arises. An outside institution makes itself felt; requests and demands are made on the company. In the resulting debate, the employee follows the leadership of the outside institution, and not that of the manager.

For managers it is a disheartening sight. Employees have surrendered part of their freedom, not to the company, but to the union, the professional society, the government. Employees have submitted themselves to control, not of the manager, but of the union steward, the code, the politician. It is easy for managers to become emotional over this disloyalty, this treachery. It is easy to cry "outside agitators" or worse. Then, when much of this outside leadership turns on the employees, tyrannizes them, plunders their pension funds, and betrays them for bribes, the managers' views appear to have been proved by the march of events.

In the judgment of the author, these dismal things are revolting. Certainly, the thieves should be dealt with. But we must also look back to the fundamentals—how did the manager ever get into such a mess? In retrospect, it all seems very obvious:

industrial employees harbor within them all the timeless needs of human beings. Preeminent on this list of needs is stark survival.

the company was willing to provide money, the means for survival, in return for control over much of the employee's time. He or she submitted to this control.

the company was unable or unwilling to provide the means for meeting the remaining needs of employees (these means could, in part, be met by money, but mostly by things other than money).

the unsatisfied needs became notorious, and new, outside leadership arose, promising to meet these needs.

employees responded to this outside leadership and accepted controls as a price for meeting the unsatisfied needs.

the outside leadership, backed by employees, successfully challenged the leadership of the managers.

If we retain a society which is responsive to the will of the majority, it is difficult (in the author's view) for any other power pattern to prevail.

But the manager broods heavily. He or she feels, with much justification, that:

the free industrial society has created the very affluence which permits individuals the luxury of pursuing needs beyond those of stark survival.

the key role in conduct of the industrial society is played by the manager; no one else understands so well how industry runs.

hence the leadership of the industrial society should be left to the manager, not to the politicians, the intellectuals, the union bosses, the hangers-on.

It is really a very logical position. But it ignores the fact that there are important needs of another cultural pattern, which needs industrial companies have not met and still are not meeting. It also ignores the fact that an earlier generation of managers stand blamed (rightly or wrongly) for having botched the job, so that the country endured a traumatic depression.

Can the managers regain the controls which others have chipped away? In the opinion of the author:

they can, by looking to the spectrum of human needs and meeting them on the job.

they won't, because the generation of managers now in power does not feel that it is the companies' responsibility to meet these human needs.

The foregoing discussion of "Controls from outside the Company" has emphasized controls arising from the manager's role as a governor of people. However, the manager is also faced with other outside controls. These arise from the manager's other roles, e.g., policymaker for the economic system, referee for division of the fruits of industry, leader in setting the pattern of ethical conduct. Outside controls have been imposed on every single one of these roles. Managers are alert to detect the excesses in these controls, the senseless extremes, the stupidities of bureaucratic administration, the perpetuation after the need is over. But managers have generally failed to avert these controls at the outset. In the judgment of the author, the failure is again the result of the managers' belief that it is not the companies' responsibility to provide leadership in these broad public matters.

Organizing

Here and there in this book we have considered various aspects of organizing for Breakthrough and Control. Now we might look at the organizing problem in perspective.

The Great Issues in organizing include the following:

control over widely divergent activities
sole responsibility for both Breakthrough and Control
control in small company vs. large
span of control

Widely divergent activities. Putting Tiffany and Woolworth under one roof would be asking for trouble. Here we have a drastic difference in merchandise, sources of supply, quality standards, packaging, pricing, complaint policy, credit policy. We also have a drastic difference in clientele, as to income class, buying habits, demands for service. Trying to meet these diversities with one store location, one decor, one sales force, one public image, etc., would be nonsense, which would be obvious to all.

Yet we have many such situations going on in industry, now. They are nonsense, but they continue on and on because the nonsense has not been dramatized and made obvious to people who can do something about it.

When we discussed "the mighty spectrum" (p. 137) we saw some examples of such nonsense. Using one pricing formula to *mis*fit a wide variety of services can often be remedied by more precise cost accounting. But we may need to go beyond this.

> A company making ball bearings for precise instruments loses its shirt on an order for ball bearings for roller skates. Reason: the inspector applied the quality standards used for precise instrument bearings to the roller-skate bearings.
>
> A company mass-producing standard motors loses its shirt on small orders for special motors. Reason: the same elaborate plans and procedures which are justified for mass production are being applied to the small specialty orders.

In such cases (which are legion) the heart of the problem is that we are asking the same person to think Tiffany in the morning and Woolworth in the afternoon; to think Quick Service Lunch today, and Leisure Continental Repast tomorrow; to think interchangeable mass production now, and handcrafted masterpieces next week.

We cannot, through cost accounting alone, solve the problem of split personalities. We may need to go deeper, and split the operations, or the business itself. Tiffany and Woolworth must be housed separately, in different locations, with different decor, employing different sales forces, exuding different public images. As yet we cannot give a formula for how far to go when we have only different quality standards, or service standards, or design standards. But there are numerous situations in which we should go beyond just cost accounting.

Here, to solve the problems of Control, we must reorganize the business!

Sole responsibility for both Breakthrough and Control. Is it a basic contradiction to make the same individual responsible both for preventing change and for creating change? If it is wrong to put Tiffany and Woolworth under one person, isn't it just as wrong to put Breakthrough and Control under one person?

The contradiction is not really as basic as it sounds. There is actually a common purpose—the health of the company. Control is necessary for the short-range health; Breakthrough for the long range. But the processes for achieving Breakthrough and Control are certainly widely different, as we have seen.

Our present concept of responsibility makes one chief executive responsible for the health of the company, whether short-range or long-range. So long as we retain this concept, there is no escape, at the top of the company, from sole responsibility for both Breakthrough and Control. Below the top, we have flexibility in dividing up the responsibilities. We have seen, throughout this book, examples of this division.

Our Great Issue here is whether we should move in the direction of:

(*a*) Perfecting our means for organizing work so we do not put the same person in the position of dual responsibility for such diverse processes as Breakthrough and Control, or

(*b*) Conducting our supervisory and executive development in ways which enable us to widen the assignment of such dual responsibility.

The division-of-work argument is based on the reality that many who now have the dual responsibilities do not in fact carry them out. They do what is urgent, or what they like best, etc. "Hence" the solution is to "organize around" these people, i.e., organize in a way which neutralizes their weaknesses.

The develop-the-individual argument is that the tempo of change is upon us, and will not leave us. Hence our managers must learn to make use of change as well as to defend against it.

It is informative here to look back at an earlier problem in massive change.

In the 1930s the great wave of collective bargaining broke across the industrial landscape. The arbitrariness which had been the basis of so many decisions in industrial relations was exposed to full view, and it could not survive in the glare. Something else had to take its place. Often that something else was provided by personnel specialists or by consultants, since the line supervisors' experience was from an out-of-date era.

In a short time, line managers found themselves in an impossible position. Those with no responsibility for operations were making the collective-bargaining agreements, settling grievances, and otherwise invading what had been a basic line responsibility.

The question came to a head: "Are personnel relations to be a line or a staff responsibility?" The decision adopted was "It's a line responsibility." But to make the decision effective required an immense amount of supervisory training.

In the judgment of the author, we should open up our supervisory and executive development programs to admit added training for dealing with both Breakthrough and Control. Whether such training would "take" broadly is not fully clear. But there are precedents which suggest that it is feasible, i.e., the Work Simplification training programs.

Such an approach through executive development would not preclude refining the organizational approaches. Experience shows that, as people are given responsibility, they look for ways of improving the organization form to carry out that responsibility.

Small company vs. large. Growth in size always brings complexity in kind. To build one automobile a month in the neighborhood garage requires a few good all-around mechanics. To build a thousand automobiles a month requires a bigger plant and more people, but that is only the beginning. Efficient operation requires specialization in functions, skills, machines, and tools. So complexity sets in. Unifying these diverse efforts requires plans and controls. So coordination sets in. Complexity follows size around, whether in an automobile factory, a department store, a university, a government, an organism.

Greater size *cum* complexity makes the company more vulnerable to failure. There is more to go wrong and there is more at stake. So we do something about it. We may cut the company up into autonomous units so that failure of one will not kill the rest. In a way, we take an elephant and reorganize him into a herd of gazelles. Then death of one gazelle does not kill the herd. We may also leave the elephant in one piece, but rebuild and rewire him so he is more responsive to danger.

Damage can be done either way. The president who built the big company from a little garage continues to run it as a one-man show (which a garage is). He or she may have the personal capacity to keep it up for quite awhile. The price is a good deal of personal wear and tear on all concerned, including himself or herself. And after him or her, the deluge.

No less damage is done by the small company manager who tries to adopt the airs of a giant. He sets up the eleven personnel forms needed by a giant when two are enough for a pygmy. He sets up informational reports on matters that should be handled by direct observation. He slows down the works by elaborate procedures. All this robs him of the inherent benefits of being small—the mobility, decisiveness, ease of adaptation, nimbleness in response to customers, to change.

Span of control. How many subordinates can a boss supervise effectively? This intensely practical question has long puzzled managers and has intrigued scholars.

Graicunas,[6] a French management consultant, turned a new, fascinating light on this topic. Instead of just counting the number of subordinates supervised by a boss, Graicunas counted the *number of relationships*.

For example, the boss has one subordinate. This gives the boss one direct relationship to supervise.

When there are two subordinates, the number of relationships does not merely double. The boss not only supervises A and B separately. Sometimes he or she supervises AB together. So there are three direct relationships, the boss to A, to B, and to AB.

For three subordinates, the direct relationships rise to seven; i.e., A, B, C, AB, BC, AC, ABC.

As the number of subordinates rises (by simple arithmetic) the number of relationships climbs geometrically, as in Table 21-1.

(This leaves out of account even greater numbers of cross relationships, but we have enough to work on.)

Graicunas, the author of this ingenious approach, made no extravagant claims for its usefulness. But (as sometimes happens) some of his followers have exhibited undue enthusiasm. This overenthusiasm has, in turn, brought equally vigorous reactions to the effect that the problem of number of subordinates is one for solution through experience and judgment, and that it is ivory-tower theory to believe that mathematics can have any role in the solution.

---

[6]Graicunas, V. A., Relationship in Organization, Chap. X of Gulick, Luther, and L. Urwick (editors), "Papers on the Science of Administration," Institute of Public Administration, Columbia University, 1937.

Table 21-1. Span of Control

Number of subordinates	Number of direct relationships
1	1
2	3
3	7
4	15
5	31
6	63
7	127
8	255
9	511
10	1,023
11	2,047
12	4,095

This tempest in a teapot has brewed up periodically, the participants seemingly oblivious to the fact that people are supervised not merely through personal supervision; *people are supervised mainly through impersonal supervision*. Most of the 8-hour day of an employee of industry is directed by the informal rules of past practice and precedent, and by the more formal rules of written routine, method, specification, manual, code, etc. Personal supervision is in the minority, and is used mainly in "new, different, exceptional" situations. This fact has defeated those who would convert Graicunas's brilliant contribution into a mathematical device for blindly solving organizational problems. Too little is known as yet about the quantitative ratio of personal vs. impersonal supervision.

Concept of a Control Function

We have seen that Control takes place at all levels of the Control pyramid. Most of it is at the scene of action, involves no separate information loop, and hence does not become enmeshed in the farflung information network. However, what is left, which is still a lot of activity, does resemble an interwoven network. The character, size, and importance of this network have given rise to suggestions that Control is a "function" like Personnel, Research, or other major staff activity. You can guess the rest. The advocates advance logical reasons for "tying this function together"; for giving one department the responsibility over the information network;[7] for giving the function an appropriate place in the sun. The opponents advance logical reasons for not doing all this and accuse the advocates of empire building.

The sensible middle ground, as always, is found by dividing the subject into pieces and deciding piece by piece. There *is* a need for coordination of the information system. But there are a dozen ways of meeting this need without giving one department command over all information activities. Such noncommand coordination permits the best of both worlds—the function is recognized and coordinated, while operations remain decentralized and responsive to local needs.

A remaining unification problem comes up in top executive reporting. If we are to have a single report package (or a chart room) who will preside over the package?

---

[7]There are companies who have actually made decisions that "all figures are to come from just one place."

To date, this is still a contest in the ring. The Accountant once had a monopoly on the package, since its contents were purely financial. But the contents have grown to a point that the nonfinancial tail is wagging the financial dog. Some Controllers have risen to the occasion and have equipped themselves to handle the entire package. And there are still other attempts at solution (p. 325).

The executive report package, while requiring an individual in charge, is still no basis for overextending the concept of a Control function. A few companies have, on the grounds of a need for a single package, given the reins of the entire information system to one person. It has usually been disastrous.

For the foreseeable future, coordination, not command, is the way of dealing with the Control function.

The Role of Top Management

The chief executive certainly needs a clear awareness of the mortal nature of products, processes, and procedures, as well as some concept of their time and life cycle. He probably needs some clarification of thinking about "improvement" so that Breakthrough improvement is clearly distinguished from operational improvement.

As we have seen, "improvement" comes from a number of sources:

1. Eliminating causes of variance from standard. This causes performance to rise from substandard to standard. This activity is handled mainly by unaided operating management.
2. Increase in effectiveness through greater diligence, making better use of existing facilities, know-how, etc. For example: selective increase of prices; change of vendor for better price; landing a few new accounts. These activities likewise are handled by the unaided operating management.
3. Establishment of a higher lever of effectiveness by Breakthrough of existing levels. Here operating management normally requires staff assistance.

The patterns of activities behind these results differ in important respects. These differences are so great that it is confusing to apply the single generic word "improvement" to describe them all. In fact, some of the existent terminology makes the distinctions as between 2 and 3. The former is commonly designated as an operating efficiency improvement. The latter, less commonly, is designated a method improvement.

These distinctions are not just of academic interest to the linguist; they decide whether managers understand each other on some matters of importance.

> In the Yates Company's budgeting procedure, a firm budget is prepared for next year, and a long-range plan for 5 years ahead. The budget as presented includes a paragraph dealing with "profit improvement," which is projected at 5 or 10 per cent better than last year.
>
> However, a look at the details behind these summaries discloses that the improvements are all in the nature of operating improvements in the absence of Breakthrough. Nothing new is taking place. *The company is standing still,* despite what the figures say.

It is essential for companies to grasp these distinctions, and to coin the necessary words or phrases to enable the managers to communicate effectively. Here are some nominations:

Form of improvement	Proposed terminology
Elimination of causes of adverse variance from standard	Ironing out variances
Greater effectiveness in the absence of Breakthrough	Operating improvement
Greater effectiveness as a result of Breakthrough	Breakthrough improvement

Next as to active participation. The chief executive does need to become personally involved in urging major births—new markets, products, acquisitions. He or she should also become personally involved in seeing to it that what is doomed does not linger on. (Few managers will put part of their job to death. In really big cases, the president himself or herself may shield a dying operation, so that Board intervention is necessary.)

There are individuals who, having gained the presidency, continue to devote themselves to their former tasks and interests.

> Bill Merton came up through manufacture. He had spent a lifetime cutting costs and raising productivity. When he became president, he continued to cut costs and raise productivity, and was unable to devote himself to other forms of improving the company's effectiveness.[8]

[8]Some industrialists who became government officials concerned themselves mainly with cost reduction despite the fact that the mission of their department was not being carried out.

Marcel Beauchamp, a lawyer-financier, came to the presidency of a good-sized company by pyramiding a series of mergers. He continues to spend his time in financial wheeling and dealing, while the company deteriorates for lack of sound management.

The chief executive should be familiar with, and acquire skill in, use of the levers of his office—setting the important goals, organizing to meet them, seeing that they are met.

We pass by a few matters which need attention but depend largely on the specific situation—centralization or decentralization; direct or informational control; much or little staff. Whether the chief executive personally gets much involved in these things also "depends."

But now we come to a fundamental, subsurface question which lurks behind quite a few exposed questions:

Shall we manage the business on the basis of theory X or theory Y?

In the author's judgment, the chief executive should personally get involved in this question. Whether we operate on theory X or theory Y affects:

whether we must use imposed plans and standards, or whether we can use a participative approach

whether individuals feel they have only a personal role to play, or both a personal role and a team role

whether loyalties are mainly to local groups or mainly to company performance

whether controls must be highly formalized, or can be highly informal

Anything which affects such a formidable array of topics is itself a formidable topic. Moreover, the decision of whether to go down the road of theory X or theory Y is necessarily a high-level decision. A middle manager who decided to take the other road would become too conspicuous to be tolerated.

The author happens to believe that theory X is unsound. So do some other practitioners. But there are many practitioners, very likely the majority, who follow theory X. So the author does not press the point. What he does advocate is that:

the question of theory X vs. theory Y is vital.

so vital a question requires the direct participation of the chief executive.

the question should be faced as a major topic on the agenda, not just as incidental to some current question.

Finally, the chief executive should see that there is a periodic check on the control machinery itself. The financial audit is the old, obvious example of this. But with controls having spread over a wide variety of functions, the concept of audit must be expanded correspondingly.

Cross Fertilization

During diagnosis for Breakthrough the managers learn much about the operation which they never knew before. This new knowledge is then used, not only to aid in Breakthrough; the knowledge is later put to use in various steps of the Control cycle.

The converse is also true. Investigation of causes of substandard performance can turn up information which becomes the basis for Breakthrough.

> Frederick W. Taylor conducted many studies to standardize metal-cutting tools and processes. The heat-treating of tool steel was one aspect of this. As was widespread practice in those days, such a detail was left to the smiths to handle, based on their experience.
>
> Taylor's studies showed that there was great variation in the cutting capability of tool steel, even as to tools made from the same bar of steel. In collecting information to establish standards for heat-treating temperature, he tried a temperature the smiths had previously avoided. Result—a doubling of the efficiency of the tool steel, and a patent for the Taylor-White process of treating tool steel.

Taylor's accidental discovery came while he was doing some studying on purpose. The frequency of similar accidents by other investigators is so high that the word "accident" begins to lose its meaning. The author (who is no slouch in such matters) has personally been involved in studies of variations which have led to basic improvements in processes for polishing optical lenses; for carding woolen yarns; for centrifugal casting of steel; for calendaring of various materials. When one has gone through a series of such discoveries he or she is no longer surprised at the fact of discovery even though he or she could not, at the outset, predict just what form the discovery would take.

The End Points for Breakthrough and Control

Do Breakthrough and Control ever end?

There is no limit to Breakthrough unless there is a limit to human ingenuity.

In any one case, Breakthrough may not be worth it; it will not pay for itself. The return on investment is too low. Such economic decisions sometimes evoke the comment "We've gone about as far as we can go." Actually, we might well brace ourselves for a flank attack from an unexpected quarter.

> The aircraft piston engine started as a cumbersome thing. A critical ratio, the horsepower generated per pound of weight, was in the range of 0.20.
>
> Then came technological breakthroughs, and the horsepower per pound of weight was increased again and again. At first the increases were large—from 0.20 to 0.35 in one jump. Then the increases were more modest—from 0.71 to 0.76. Finally, the increases were small (and hard to come by)—from 0.97 to 0.99. It was time to say "We've gone about as far as we can go." The curve had flattened out (Fig. 49).
>
> Then came the flank attack. Out of nowhere came the jet engine, which in one swoop raised the horsepower per pound from 1.0 to 2.7.

Is there an end to Control? In several respects, yes. We can end informational control by moving something down in the pyramid to personal control. We can end human control by automating the thing. We can end staff control by simplifying the control system and turning it over to the local operators. We can minimize the need for control at all by designing more stability and reliability into our organizations, systems, and structures.

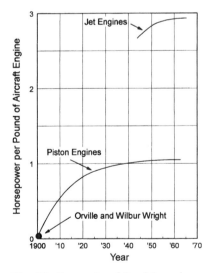

Fig. 49. Economics of Breakthrough.

There is also the economic limit—when does Control pay for itself, and when do we run into perfectionism?

Control does pay for itself within most of the range of operations. Within this range the added controls cost money but are more than paid for by reducing our losses (in bad debts, waste, poor deliveries, or whatever). Beyond this range, the added controls are not paid for, and we start to lose. These losses become greater and greater as we approach perfection.

Figure 50 shows graphically the interrelation between cost of control, and loss due to failure of conformance to standard, over the entire range of operations.

As we move to the right from no conformance, the cost of control increases modestly, with great reductions in the losses due to failure of conformance. This continues, but at a reduced rate until we reach the optimum. This optimum goes by various names ("point of diminishing returns") which all mean the same thing—it doesn't pay to go further. If we do go further, not only are our added costs not recovered; the added costs can be astronomical. Perfection, in the theoretical sense, costs an infinite sum. The cure is worse than the disease.

There is nothing theoretical about the losses due to perfectionism. Numerous paper programs which "fall of their own weight" have been swept out of industry. (Some are not yet swept out.) The cardinal figures to look at are:

the amounts still being lost because of failure of conformance;

the amounts being spent to keep the conformance at its present level.

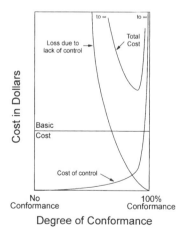

Fig. 50. Economics of control of conformance.

The Underdeveloped Areas

Our discussions of Breakthrough and Control have been on a universal plane. It doesn't matter what is the industry, product, process, function. The principles are universal.

> The author has conducted literally dozens of seminars, involving hundreds of managers, on the subject of Control and Breakthrough. These seminars commonly included people from various industries, companies, functions, and levels of authority. Yet there was no real problem of communication. They all faced similar problems, opportunities, and limitations.

It is a fact, however, that the *degree* of application varies widely. Some entire industries retain (with pride) a high degree of rugged individualism. Accountants look back on a long history of use of informational controls. Factory managers similarly have long been in the business of ingenious Breakthrough. As in all other human endeavor, there is the vanguard, and there are the underdeveloped areas.

It is a fascinating spectacle to see a technology lifted bodily from an industrialized country and applied to some country which is not using the technology. Supermarkets, vending machines, installment buying— it doesn't matter. The technology is already a proved success elsewhere. The job is one of selling, of adapting, of overcoming cultural resistance.

The manager who is looking for worlds to conquer might well look for the underdeveloped areas. There is much romantic precedent. The nineteenth century Englishman could go to India as a young man, and return several decades later, old, wealthy, and autocratic.

Today there are entire industries which are "backward" in the sense of Breakthrough or Control or both: hospitals, government at all levels; transport; building construction. Within any of these there are already islands of effectiveness; so that the job is one of use of available know-how.

What is true of industries is also true of functions. Some aspects of manufacture, notably direct labor, resemble a well-picked bone. But the services (maintenance, materials handling, data processing) contain plenty to chew on. Functions such as marketing or office management are well into the kind of revolution that overtook manufacture. Functions such as research and development, advertising or purchasing are as yet mainly inventing the concepts and tools needed.

The manager who has done well at Breakthrough and Control, and who is looking for new worlds to conquer might well look for the underdeveloped area. Like the Connecticut Yankee in King Arthur's Court, he will be able to outperform the local wizards, quite easily. But that is the end of the easy road. He will find the environment strange and the natives suspicious if not downright warlike. It is hardly a place for the person who likes predictable comforts, but it is certainly a place for the person looking for a challenge.

Research in Breakthrough and Control

We have learned to follow an accepted route in building a science. If we are to have a science, say of zoology, we:

1. Observe many animals in detail.
2. Classify our observations in various plausible ways.
3. Analyze these classifications to discover possible order or relationships.
4. Formulate theories to explain the relationships.
5. Test the theories by further observation and experiment, which starts the cycle all over again.

By analogy, if we are to have a science of management, we should:

1. Observe many management activities in detail.
2. Classify these observations in various logical ways.
3. Analyze these classifications to discover possible order.
4. Formulate theories to explain the relationships.
5. Test the theories by further observation and experiment.

This was, in fact, the procedure followed in evolving this book. In observing many examples of Breakthrough, the author discovered (or rediscovered) that they followed a common sequence of events. Hence he has stated this sequence as a theory. He also found that a different common sequence underlies all Control; so he stated that sequence as a theory.

As with all theories, these can be tested and confirmed, modified or rejected, based on subsequent observations. It is the hope of the author that many managers will undertake such a critique of these theories.

As it happens, we have in this case some potential help from other disciplines. Breakthrough and Control are found not only in management; they are found in engineering; in the behavioral sciences; and they are found, in great profusion, in biology. The presence of Breakthrough and Control in so many disciplines opens the way for broad interdisciplinary study. Some of this has already taken place, as witness the adoption of the word "cybernetics" as an interdisciplinary term in the field of Control.

Very likely we can learn the most from biology, as we discover where to look. Biology has its own dialect. It has its Breakthroughs, which are called mutations—"a sudden, well marked, transmissible variation in an organism, as distinguished from the gradual cumulative change over a long period." Biology has its controls, as, for instance, homeostasis— "the tendency of an organism to maintain a uniform and beneficial physiological stability within and between its parts; organic equilibrium."[9]

We might here briefly contrast the mechanisms of biological control with those of managerial control. It becomes immediately evident that they differ remarkably.

Biological control	Managerial control
Any sensor is single-purpose	Sensors are commonly multipurpose
Sensors never act; they only send impulses to one of several message centers	Sensors may either act or just transmit
Transmission lines are used exclusively either for sensory messages or for commands to effectors, never for both	Transmission lines often used to transmit either (a) sensory messages or (b) commands to effectors
Effectors are single-purpose	Effectors are multipurpose

In making this comparison we might well be mindful that managerial control is by human design, whereas biological control is based on the Grand Design. Look at a single, greatly simplified example of the results of the Grand Design:

> A human heart, beating at the rate of 60 to the minute, must, without failure, beat over *two billion* times if there is to be a life span of 70 years. This gives us a mere glimpse of the degree of reliability which is built into the biological control mechanisms.

As a project for research in management, study of the control mechanisms in biology would appear to be rewarding in the extreme.

A further interdisciplinary research is feasible in the area of human motivation. Breakthrough and Control are found in Political Science, in Cultural Anthropology, or in Clinical Psychiatry, to name a few. Introduction

---

[9]These definitions are from the Britannica Edition of Funk & Wagnalls Dictionary.

of technical change into a going culture is faced by agricultural scientists, by politicians, by the medical professions, by the ministry. A study across all these disciplines would be bound to clarify for the industrial manager the problems of introducing technical change.[10]

There is something else to be gained from the behavioral sciences—a scientific basis for participation, communication, incentives, and many other ingredients of human motivation. We can see this more clearly by contrasting the scientific bases for engineering and management, respectively.

Engineering is (essentially) the use of the forces of *nature* for the benefit of man.

Management is (essentially) the use of the forces of *people* for the benefit of man.

The forces of *nature* are discovered by the natural scientist—the mathematician, physicist, astronomer.

The forces of *people* are discovered by the behavioral scientist—the psychologist, sociologist, anthropologist.

The engineer, using knowledge discovered by the natural scientist, fashions the various tools of engineering—thermodynamics, machine design.

The manager, using knowledge discovered by the behavioral scientist, fashions the various tools of management—organization, motivation.

Both the engineer and the manager were in business before the scientist. As a result, much engineering and managing is done on practical, not scientific grounds. But it has been our experience that, when the scientists get around to do their discovering, some remarkable revisions in practice are in order.

It is in point here to return to the useful classification of management approaches or "schools" as made by Prof. Koontz:[11]

management process

empirical

human behavior

social system

decision theory

mathematical

[10]The author's paper, "Improving the Relationship between Staff and Line," *Personnel*, May, 1956, derived from a book *Cultural Patterns and Technical Change* by Margaret Mead, a cultural anthropologist, aroused wide interest among managers.

[11]Koontz, Harold, "Making Sense of Management Theory," *Harvard Business Review*, July–August, 1962, pp. 22–46.

It is significant that many, many individuals are now actively engaged in research in these and perhaps other directions. New tools and techniques are tumbling in profusion out of their research laboratories. A burgeoning literature has become so massive that managers are driven to the digests to keep up with it.

This movement toward research in management has some parallels to the growth of research in the physical and biological sciences. It was the Renaissance, probably the greatest Breakthrough in human history, which broke the bonds that for centuries had enslaved people's minds. Suddenly the way was open for scientific inquiry, on an unprecedented scale. In ever-increasing numbers, swarms of investigators have deployed along the widening frontiers of science. The fruits of these researches are now so extensive that we accept as commonplace the continuing flood of discoveries. Yet each of these discoveries would have merited the term "miracle" a few centuries ago.

There is much evidence that empirical approaches to management were used in all ancient societies. However, the early record of research in management is sparse. A known early, serious work is Niccolo Machiavelli's "The Prince" (again a product of the Renaissance). In "The Prince," Machiavelli snapped some long-standing, rigid thought processes. The prior beliefs had been those of "ascribing all things to natural causes or to fortune." Circumstances, not individuals, had been the masters. Machiavelli's contribution was to set out principles and methodology under which individuals could become the masters. The fact that his principles do not fit the twentieth century is beside the point. So is the fact that his applications were for political rather than industrial management. Machiavelli looked at management in the abstract, rather than as applied to his century or to his Florence. Like our early human in the cave, p. 13, Machiavelli was trying to find the law of 2 plus 3 equals 5, whether we are talking of rabbits, fish, children, or anything else.

For every Galileo we number today a thousand researchers in the physical sciences. For every Machiavelli we number today a thousand investigators in the field of management. To be sure, the physical scientists have handsomely outstripped the management scientists. But there are reasons for this, including the "procession of the sciences."

The sciences do not advance on a broad front; they move more nearly in single file. Some sciences must permanently await prior discovery being made in others. Progress in physics must always lag behind mathematics, which provides the analytical tools vital to theoretical physics. In turn, chemistry lags behind physics; physiology behind chemistry; and the behavioral sciences behind physiology. Management, which must derive its scientific base from the behavioral sciences, virtually brings up the rear of this long procession.

Whether at the rear or otherwise, management is in lockstep in this parade. Thereby management is inexorably being drawn into the same vortex of revolution which has already engulfed the vanguard of the awesome procession—astronomy, chemistry, and so on.

The furies of technological change wrought havoc among the empirical practitioners of these vanguard disciplines—astrologers, alchemists, and so on. Presumably, a like fate awaits the empirical managers, in their turn. Yet, if science can accomplish for management what it has done in other disciplines, we might welcome the result despite the havoc. Human beings' mastery in the vanguard sciences has increased enormously as the result of the revolutions. We could do with a good deal more mastery of the managerial process than we now possess.

As managers, we should like to be able to do with confidence many things we now do with apprehension. We would like to be able to:

launch our Breakthroughs with confidence that the great majority will reach the goals we set.

establish our Controls with confidence that they will take off our backs the great bulk of our burden of fire fighting.

design our organization of work so that the great majority of people will find, on the job itself, the challenges and satisfactions required by the human race.

Undoubtedly, our empirical ways have been moving us toward such goals, but no one is happy with the pace. Nor is the answer simply more laboratories and more investigators. The fact is that much of what the laboratories have already put out has not yet been assimilated and tried out by practicing managers. Between the two worlds of the researchers and the practicing managers there flows only a trickle of ideas and feedback. We need quite a few 6-inch pipe connections.

The pattern of effort toward research in management has been changing rapidly. The pioneering work in "Scientific Management" has been followed variously, first by practicing managers and later by the universities. Previously, much of the manpower, and perhaps most of the publications, came from the universities. Here and there, industrial companies have gone at research in management, in an organized way, but the resulting pools of findings have not been piped to managers generally. Institutions such as American Management Association and National Industrial Conference Board have increasingly been compiling and publishing summaries of current industrial practice. These summaries are invaluable both to the practicing manager and to the researcher. New forms such as the American Foundation for Management Research, Inc. (founded by American Management Association), are emerging and may become a force in establishing adequate connections between the world of research and the world of the practicing manager.

The author urges practicing managers to become well acquainted with what is going on in the world of research in management. This counsel, even if accepted, is not easy to follow. The things that are labeled "research" occupy the entire spectrum, from the scholarly works of an Elton Mayo all the way to the sheer drivel put out by eager-beaver consultants. But with practice, the manager increases his or her ability to discriminate. He or she will find a good deal of precious stuff amid the dross.

22

COMPLETING THE TRILOGY: QUALITY PLANNING

The final chapter of the original edition of *Managerial Breakthrough* began with the statement that "We have come to the end," having provided a comprehensive guide to Quality Improvement—"the means by which the manager breaks out of a plateau to a new level of performance"—and Quality Control—"how [the manager] stabilizes at the new level by use of the tools of Control." However, true to the cyclical nature of my thinking, reaching the end inevitably sends us back to the beginning. For what is missing from the original edition of *Managerial Breakthrough* is a discussion of the all-important discipline of Quality Planning—the third element of what has come to be called the "Juran Trilogy®," and in a very real sense, where Quality Management all begins.

Quality Control, as we have seen, involves developing and maintaining operational methods for assuring that processes work as they are designed to work and that target levels of performance are being achieved. Quality Control does not concern itself with improving a process, but rather with the execution of plans. Quality Control requires a carefully defined series of steps:

1. clear definition of quality
2. knowledge of expected performance or targets
3. measurements of actual performance

4. a way to compare expected to actual performance, and

5. a way to take action when measured results are not equal to expected results, or when processes appear to be drifting from their expected performance levels.

Quality Improvement is the discipline that concerns itself with *improving* the level of performance of a process.

The Quality Improvement process introduced in this book 30 years ago has been instrumental in helping numerous organizations achieve true breakthroughs in performance.

What is Quality Planning, and where does it fit in? *Quality Planning* is the activity of establishing quality goals and developing the products and processes required to meet those goals. These goals may apply to the features required to meet customer needs or they may apply to making these products and processes free from all deficiencies. Quality Planning precedes Quality Control and Quality Improvement, conceptually if not always in actual practice. Used at the very inception, Quality Planning is a precisely articulated guide to the development of whatever products—goods or services—are to be produced. Quality Planning can also apply to the development or the redevelopment of any process. Before there is a process that needs to be monitored (Quality Control) or improved (Quality Improvement), Quality Planning is the discipline that is used to decide what is going to be made in the first place.

How is Quality Planning different from traditional planning? Often, traditional planning is characterized by a process akin to "throwing it over the wall": someone begins planning the product in a vacuum, then tosses it to someone in the next department, who tosses it on to the next department, and so on. This is sometimes characterized by the process shown in Figure 51. Modern Quality Planning, in contrast, is a process of concurrent engineering, involving all of the people (or at least representatives of those people) who will ultimately be affected by the product, so that they can provide input and early warning during the planning process. This newer view is shown in Figure 52. Moreover, traditionally planning has been done by "designers"—experts in their particular function, but lacking the methodology, skills, and tools required to plan for *quality*. Many companies have tried to address this problem by making quality specialists available to the planners as consultants. This has met with limited success. What has proved far more successful has been to train the planners themselves in the use of quality disciplines—to equip them with the methods and tools needed to become professionals at Quality Planning. Quality Planning is not an esoteric discipline accessible only to quality specialists; it is a series of six logical steps, and a handful of basic tools, that can empower individuals throughout the various levels of the company hierarchy to plan for quality.

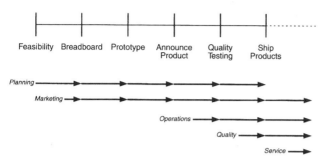

Fig. 51. Old development process.

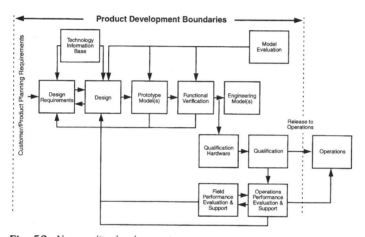

Fig. 52. New quality development process.

The six steps of the Quality Planning process are as follows:

1. Define the project.
2. Identify the customers—those who will be impacted by the actions we take to complete the project.
3. Discover customer needs.
4. Develop the product—features that respond to customer needs.
5. Develop processes that are able to produce those product features.
6. Develop controls/transfer to operations.

Figure 53 shows "The Quality Planning Roadmap," a graphic representation of this sequence of steps, and the way in which the output of each step serves as the input for the next step.

The Quality Planning process should be used for the development of both goods and services. In developing a new car, it is important to identify the customers, plan the features, design the production processes

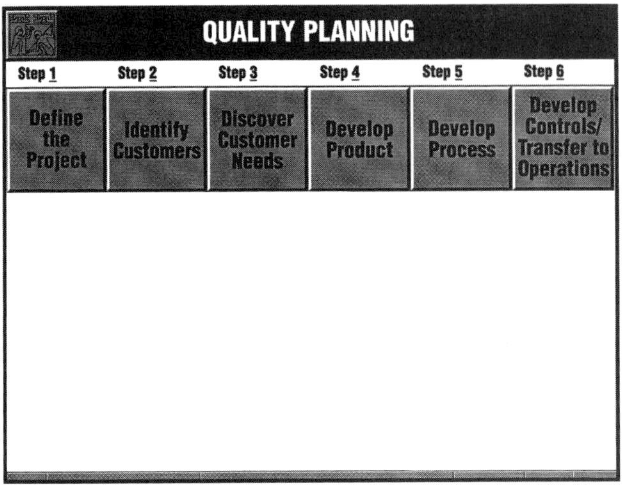

Fig. 53. The Quality Planning roadmap.

and process controls. The exact same steps are required for developing new services—whether that service takes the form of a credit card that earns frequent flyer miles, a pay-per-view cable TV service, or a call-answering capability offered by the telephone company. The focus of Quality Planning should not solely be on products sold to external customers but should also take into account the needs of internal customers, such as those who create the goods or deliver the service. They also have needs like those who purchase or use the product.

The Quality Planning process includes the design of invoices, reports, purchase orders. It also includes processes for recruitment of new employees, preparation of sales forecasts, production of invoices, and many other processes used by internal customers as well.

Why is Quality Planning so important? The marketplace—not to mention the public imagination—is littered with reasons, reminders of what can go wrong when a product is conceived, designed, and brought to market without sufficient planning. Most are examples not of bad products, but of the wrong product for the wrong time—the Edsel, Polaroid's Polavision, New Coke—and the dangers of failing to listen carefully to the voice of the customer. Other notorious examples are failures in the design of product features or operating processes such as Thalidomide, the Exxon *Valdez*, the *Challenger*.

This chapter will proceed through the six steps of the Quality Planning process, explaining the objectives of each step, the way in which the objectives are met, and the particular tools that are useful in meeting each of those objectives.

Step 1: Define the Project

The inputs to the first step come in part from outside the company: emergence of new technology; new government mandates; trends in the marketplace. Other inputs come from inside the company: the company's vision statement and policies; the company's strategic goals. Collectively these inputs demand action in the form of new projects to be undertaken.

Planning starts by defining the project—the end result or goal to be reached. The project may consist of a credit card system, a color TV set, a business process, an airfield. Definition of the project includes quantified goals for technological performance, cost, schedule, etc., and of course, quality. The presence of quality goals is what gives rise to the need for Quality Planning.

The question addressed in the first step of the Quality Planning process is, "What do we want (or need) to build? It is important to begin with this question because it is impossible to plan in the abstract; one can begin to plan only after a project or mission-specific goal has been established—taking the form of a specific, quantitative quality target, to be met within a specific time span. There are multiple sources of quality goals. They may derive from the strategic quality goals of the organization. Establishing such strategic quality goals helps translate an often vague vision—"to be the low cost producer," "to be the market leader"—into a specific plan of action. Some actual examples of strategic quality goals established as part of companies' business plans include Ford Motor Company's "Make the Taurus/Sable models at a level of quality that is best in class," Motorola's 1987 goal of "[Improving]

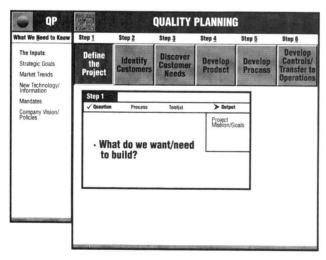

Fig. 54. Define the project.

product and services quality ten times by 1989," and 3M Corporation's "Reduce the cost of poor quality by 50 per cent in five years."

Most commonly, quality goals originate from customer needs—for example, a more easily programmable VCR, a luxury car at a price within reach, a cereal low in fat and high in fiber. However, sometimes quality goals derive purely from new technology or new information. Sony's original Walkman audio cassette player, for example, had nothing to do with "the voice of the customer;" indeed, the customer had no idea such a product was possible. When the Walkman technology was developed, Sony gambled that the product would create its own market—a gamble, as we now know, that turned out to be hugely successful. Yet another source of quality goals is mandates imposed by social forces: new laws and regulations (new emission standards for cars and gas mileage requirements; new services required by disabilities acts). New quality goals also result from the introduction of new technologies such as cellular phones, faxes, voice mail, and new electronic communications capabilities.

At each step of the Quality Planning process, certain tools are particularly useful—some of them are basic tools of quality management which have been introduced earlier in the volume; others are tools specifically tailored to the Quality Planning process. In the first step of the Quality Planning process, benchmarking and market research are extremely useful tools for gathering ideas about product goals.

Benchmarking is a label for the concept of setting goals based on what has already been achieved by others, rather than based on arbitrary decisions. A company benchmarks by going to other organizations and studying their products or processes that represent world-class standards. For example, when setting goals for the Lexus automobile, Toyota studied such companies as BMW, Mercedes, and Jaguar to see what features their automobiles offered, and to examine the level of quality of those features. At this stage of setting goals, benchmarking provides a point of reference, a standard against which to measure the new product. In addition to considering what has been achieved by external competitors, a company may benchmark against internal competitors as well: subsidiaries, other divisions, or other models. Benchmarking at this stage is especially important because it avoids the risk of using historical performance or arbitrariness as the sole basis for setting goals.

Market research is a way of listening to customers prior to creating the product, in order to determine whether there indeed exists a market for the product. (Note: In some cases—as we have seen, the Walkman is a classic example—the market for a product is a potential rather than actual one; the absence of a known market does not necessarily indicate that the product will fail.)

The next three tools are used for prioritizing product goals and keeping track of the process for establishing them.

All goals should be:

• Specific	*S*
• Measurable	*M*
• Agreed upon	*A*
• Realistic	*R*
• Time-phased	*T*

Fig. 55. Criteria for verifying goals.

The *SMART method* (Fig. 55) provides a clear set of criteria for setting goals that are specific, measurable, agreed upon, realistic, and time-phased.

The *tree diagram* (Fig. 56) is helpful in understanding the relationships among different quality goals; identifying and grouping the tasks involved in establishing goals, and establishing a time frame for the entire Quality Planning process.

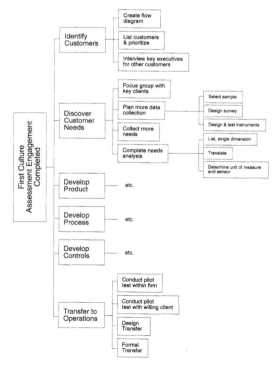

Fig. 56. Tree diagram for quality planning project.

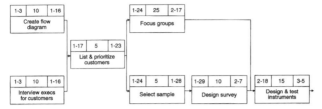

Fig. 57. Planning network.

A *planning network* is a project management tool for diagramming the entire process of Quality Planning (a partial planning network is shown in Fig. 57). It identifies all of the tasks that need to be performed, the sequence of those tasks, and the resources required to complete each task. The Planning Network keeps track of the increasingly complicated answer to the simple question, "What do we have to do and how long will it take?"

Step 2: Identify the Customers

Once the quality goal has been established ("What do we want/need to build?"), the next order of business is to identify the customers ("Who will we be building this for?). We are using the word "customers" in the sense of "those who may be impacted by our efforts to meet the quality goal." So "customers" may include external people, such as the merchant chain, suppliers, the public, the media, government regulators, etc. "Customers" also may include internal people such as subsequent processors, the workforce, the Union, etc.

Many managers simply assume that they already know who the customer for the product is, namely, the person who buys it. Although the buyer is certainly the most important single category of customer, in fact the buyer represents only a small percentage of the persons impacted or affected by the products and processes required to attain the quality goals. Simply putting the question on the agenda—"Who are the customers of this book, car, toy, dog food, heating oil, flight, courier service...?"—is a recognition that the buyer is but one of many customers, and a critical step in Quality Planning.

The proliferation of processes that are involved in creating a product creates a corresponding proliferation of customers. The most useful tool for discovering everyone who is affected by a product—in other words, for identifying its customers—is the *flow diagram*. Figure 59 illustrates many of the ways internal customers will be involved in developing a new product. In this case the new product is a workbook to be used in a class.

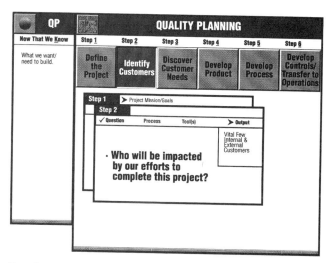

Fig. 58. Identify the customers.

Graphically representing the steps in a development cycle makes it easier to recognize all of the internal customers. A similar graphical display of all the customers of a product, including such "hidden customers" as the government, regulatory bodies, and the like would make it easier to identify these customers and their needs. Companies that make children's toys, for example, need to think not only of children (who, after all, are the ultimate customers or users of the product but seldom the purchasers of the product) and their parents, but of all the restrictions and requirements concerning toys. The product must be built for all of its customers.

A product has both internal and external customers. External customers include persons or organizations who are not part of the company building the product but who are impacted by the product; the most important external customer being, of course, the buyer. Internal customers include all of those people *within* the company building the product who are impacted by the product. "The customer" is typically a cast of characters; identifying that complete cast of characters not only improves decision making but reduces the risk of unpleasant surprises. One practical hospital administrator, for example, when faced with the need to build a new wing for the hospital, carefully planned a single room and collected inputs from a cast of characters that included the patients, family members who visited the patients, physicians, nurses, technicians who brought in and used test equipment, paraprofessionals, maintenance and cleaning personnel. Not until the administrator had accumulated feedback from the entire "cast" did he finalize plans for the new hospital wing.

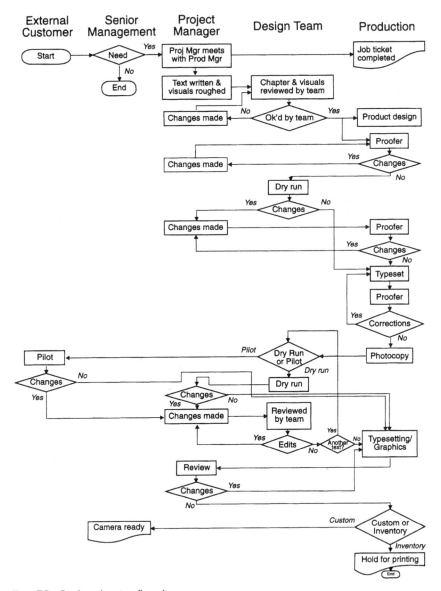

Fig. 59. Quality planning flow diagram.

After using these tools for the "divergent thinking" required to identify all of the potential customers of a product, it becomes necessary to move on to "convergent thinking," classifying the customers in a way that enables planners to allocate priorities and resources based on the relative importance of the customers and the impacts the product will have on each of them. *Pareto analysis* provides a useful way of classifying customers, separating the vital few from the useful many. For example, hotel rooms are typically booked by two types of clients—travelers who arrive one by one at random, and organizers of meetings and conventions who book blocks of rooms far in advance. The latter group constitutes the vital few customers; they receive special attention, while the former (the "useful many") receives standardized attention. Figure 60 shows the way in which Pareto analysis is used to classify all of the potential customers of a large hotel chain, and to identify the vital few customers whose needs should receive more attention and more weight in designing the specific features of the product.

Step 3: Discover Customer Needs

Once the customers for the product have been identified, the next step is determining customer needs ("What benefit do the customers want from it?"). In this way, the output of Step 2, a list of the vital few internal and external customers for the product, leads directly to Step 3, determining the customers' needs. We have seen that identifying the customer is a far more complicated task than it appears at first; similarly, determining customer needs is more complicated than simply asking. In order to simplify matters, it is useful to classify customer needs into five categories: stated needs, real needs, perceived needs, cultural needs, and needs traceable to unintended use.

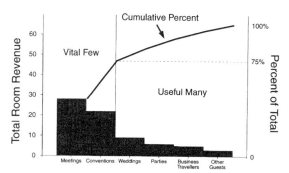

Fig. 60. Pareto analysis: hotel bookings.

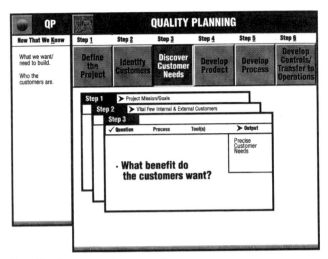

Fig. 61. Discover customer needs.

Stated vs. Real Needs. Customers typically state their needs in terms of the goods they wish to buy; however, their real needs are for the particular services those goods can provide. Failure to distinguish between the two can have serious consequences. In a classic example, two companies competed with each other in the 1940s for the market in women's hair-nets (yes, markets do come and go), focusing their efforts on such issues as fiber color, the process for making the nets, packaging, and sales channels. Both competitors became extinct, however, when a chemist invented a spray that could invisibly hold women's hair in place. Hair-nets were rather abruptly relegated to history; although the customer's *stated need* was for a hair-net, the *real need* was for an adequate means of holding their hair in place. In order to understand the real needs of customers—and to avoid the fate of the hair-net makers—one must ask not only "What product do you want to buy?" but also "Why are you buying this product?" and "What benefit do you want to gain from this product?" and "What service do you expect from it?"

Customers state their needs in their own language. Indeed, even within the same company, different people use their own local "dialect" to refer to the same thing in different ways. We need to capture needs in the "customer's voice" and then translate into our own organization's language. For example, the external customer's "I like this feature" may be the engineering department's "0.634." Especially at this step of discovering customer needs, it is of crucial importance that such differences not be "lost in translation." A *glossary*—a list of key terms and their various definitions—is a useful way of creating a common lan-

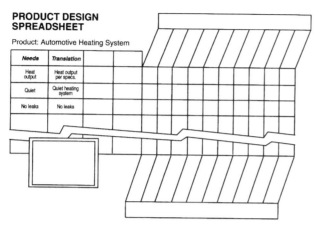

PRODUCT DESIGN SPREADSHEET

Product: Automotive Heating System

Needs	Translation		
Heat output	Heat output per specs.		
Quiet	Quiet heating system		
No leaks	No leaks		

Fig. 62. Excerpt from a glossary.

guage people can refer to, and of translating from one dialect to another. Figure 62 shows an excerpt from a glossary created in the development of an automobile heater.

Perceived Needs. Customers state their needs based on their own perceptions; some of them are product-related, while others seem to have little to do with the actual product. Consider, for example, two men in need of a haircut; one goes to a "barber shop," the other to a "salon." Although both receive professional haircuts, emerging with essentially the same outward appearance, there is a substantial difference both in the prices they have paid, and indeed in their perceptions of what "product" they have purchased. In another example, a candy factory produces chocolates which are then delivered to a conveyor belt, but at the end of the belt are two teams of packagers; one packs chocolates in simple boxes, the other, in satin-lined wooden boxes. Same chocolate? Yes. Same product? Not in the customer's perception, and (the customer hopes!) not in the perception of the ultimate recipient of the chocolates. Same price? Definitely not.

Cultural Needs. A great deal of failure to determine customer needs is traceable to failure to understand the nature and even the existence of cultural needs. For example, Bovine Growth Hormone (BGH), used to increase milk production in cows, may have been declared absolutely safe by the FDA; in the mind of some customer, however, it may still be unacceptable "Frankenfood." In another example, the Bank of Canada issued paper currency whose design mistakenly included a flag from the British colonial era; although the flag was visible only on close inspection, the French Canadians issued a sharp protest, and refused to use the currency.

Unintended Use. Finally, many quality failures arise because the customer uses the product in a manner different from that intended by the supplier. It is critical to take into consideration not just intended use, but actual use as well. Failures to do so provide useful examples of the importance of doing so: from the snowy northeast U.S., where automobile bodies rust because the designers are not aware that they will be exposed to use of salt on the roads; to the deserts of the Middle East, where luxury automobile engines and bodies fail because they were not designed to withstand the extremes of heat and blowing sand. During the Iranian hostage crisis, the rescue operations by the helicopters failed because the engines got clogged by sand.

Given the complexity of customer needs, what is the most effective way to discover those needs? A simplistic assumption is that customers are completely knowledgeable as to their needs, and that market research can be used to extract this information from them. On the contrary, the best way to discover customer needs is to be a customer. In any situation in which a worker performs a series of interrelated tasks—physicians, nurses, office workers—there is a daily opportunity to observe the effectiveness of the product, or lack thereof, and to modify the process used to create that product.

Another way to discover customer needs is to study customer behavior; it is a far better predictor of future customer actions than simply asking for customer opinions. A clear example of the value of studying customer behavior is the playrooms used by toy companies for testing new toys. Children are turned loose in a roomful of toys, while engineers with clipboards and stop-watches observe the play from behind one-way mirrors. Their observations answer a variety of questions relating to such issues as ease of use, risks of injury, lengths of attention span, and damage during use. Other methods of discovering customer needs include analyzing field intelligence, questionnaires, focus groups, and sampling.

Keeping track of customer needs in a format that enables them to be understood and analyzed can become a monumental task; the best tool for doing so is the *spreadsheet*. Figure 63 shows a spreadsheet used to keep track of customer needs in the planning of the automobile heater shown in the previous figure.

In the product design spreadsheet, the customers' needs are listed in the left-hand column; each horizontal row is devoted to a single need. The vertical columns of the spreadsheet are used to record the successive inputs from planning decisions. In this example the translation to

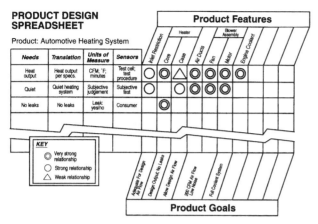

Fig. 63. Product design spreadsheet.

the organization's own language is shown along with the units of measure and the measurement device (sensor) to be used. The product features and their relationships to the product goals are also shown clearly.

The spreadsheet assembles a great deal of information into condensed, convenient form and is clearly an aid to a systematic approach. Through judicious use of symbols, a great deal of information can be compressed into a small space. However, it is also easy to be carried away by the elegance and convenience of the spreadsheet. The spreadsheet does not provide answers; it is simply a handy tool that allows you to record, maintain, and analyze information and data that you have collected. Often, people new to the Quality Planning process focus on the completion of the spreadsheet rather than on the creative process of planning. Although the spreadsheet is a useful matrix for determining which customers and which needs go together, the spreadsheet itself is no more than a convenient way of keeping track of data.

Step 4: Develop Product Features

Once the customer needs have been discovered—that is, a precise understanding has been gained of what benefit the customer wants from the product—the next step is to ask, "What will create that benefit?" The answer to that question will take the form of detailed product features and product feature goals. The ultimate goal for developing the product is to select the right features in response to customer needs. Then we must perform an additional step, what we call "optimizing"—that is, achieving a

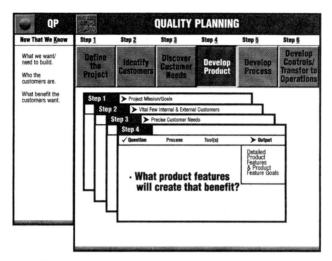

Fig. 64. Develop product features.

balance between customers' needs and suppliers' needs, and doing so at a minimum total cost.

The evolution of the videocassette recorder (VCR) is a useful example of a variety of ways to represent breakthrough thinking—constantly striving for better ways of meeting customer needs—all in response to the same basic need. One of the key customer needs for the VCR is "ease of programmability." In the first generation of VCRs, programming was done on the machine itself—not an optimal delivery system. The next generation had the capability for onscreen programming—a better solution, as it allowed the user to see time, channel, and so forth, and could guide the user through a series of onscreen prompts. The next step, VCR+, enabled the user to punch in a simple code of numbers, leaving the VCR to automatically program itself. The most recent delivery system is the voice-activated system, which requires no mechanical programming at all.

The numerous combinations of customers and needs necessitate a structured approach to product development. Earlier we saw that the spreadsheet was a useful way of keeping track of the numerous combinations of customers and customer needs. A second spreadsheet is equally useful for keeping track of the numerous combinations of customer needs and product features. This second spreadsheet is subject to the same caution as to the limits of its usefulness: it does not provide answers; it is just a useful way of keeping track of information.

The product features that result from product development are a mixture of (a) features carried over from prior products, (b) features carried

Methodology	Use When
Competitiveness Analysis	Comparing product features alongside those of your competitors
Salability Analysis	Evaluating which product features stimulate customers to be willing to buy the product
Value Analysis	Evaluating the interrelationships among: a) the functions performed by product features, and b) the associated costs
Criticality Analysis	Identifying "vital few" features that are vulnerable in the design so that they can receive priority for attention and assets
Failure Analysis	Identifying which product features/components might fail during service, how they might fail, and what should be done to prevent the failure

Fig. 65. Optimization tools.

over but modified to correct prior weaknesses or to adapt to new needs, and (c) features newly developed. Product development involves many different kinds of analysis; the following is a summary of the major kinds of analysis that should be conducted at this stage.[1]

Competitive analysis: evaluation of competitiveness of product features. This is done by tabulating product features alongside those of competitors, identifying such things as:

1. the presence or absence of specific features
2. the performance of specific features (e.g., comfort, fuel consumption, millions of instructions per second), and
3. customer perceptions of competitive quality

Competitive analysis can be used to evaluate not only product features, but features of the *process* used by competitors to produce their products.

Salability analysis: the extent to which the product features stimulate customers to be willing to buy the product. In the case of potential products based on new technology, the first and most basic question is, "If we had it, could we sell it?" In the case of a particular feature of a new product, the question becomes, "If we add this feature, will people pay for it?"

Value analysis: a process for evaluating the interrelationships among the functions performed by the product features and their associated costs. The aim of value analysis is to provide the customer with the essential

[1]For a more advanced, and a more complete, discussion of Step 4, see "Develop Product Features," *Juran on Quality by Design,* J. M. Juran (New York: The Free Press, 1992), pp. 159–217.

product features while optimizing the cost of providing those features, and to eliminate marginal product features. In terms of the VCR example, this would mean, "Building a VCR equipped with a voice-activated programming capability will cost an extra X dollars. If we add this feature, will the customer pay for it?"

Criticality analysis: to identify the "vital few" features that must receive priority of attention and assets. In criticality analysis, features are assessed with respect to the following criteria: essential to human safety, legislated mandates, essential to salability, demanding as to investment, demanding as to continuity, lead time, ethical sensitivity, and instability. Criticality analysis asks, "What are the potential failures, what are the implications of each of them, and what redundancy systems need to be built into the product?"

Failure analysis: looking at which product features or components might fail during service, how they might fail, and what should be done to prevent the failure. There are many different tools used in quality management for this step, such as FMEA (failure mode and effect analysis).

The above analyses provide comprehensive input for deciding on product features and product feature goals. The next step is, using this information, to "optimize the product design"—that is, to design a product that meets the needs of customer and supplier alike, and to do so while minimizing their combined costs. Doing so is a challenge; it requires overcoming the traditional urge of customers and suppliers alike to "suboptimize"—that is, to pursue local goals instead of the common goal. Finding the optimum involves balancing of needs, whether intercompany needs or intra-company needs. Ideally, the search for the optimum should be conducted by the joint participation and planning of all those who will be impacted by the design. The results of product development should be a written statement of goals for product features—the end product of Step 4 of the Quality Planning process. Writing out and publishing goals not only helps ensure that they are understandable, but also establishes their legitimacy.

At this stage many companies also develop models or prototypes to test and optimize product features. For example, in designing the new Boeing 777 airplane the designers tested whether the new door could be opened with one-quarter inch of ice covering the door.

Step 5: Develop Process Features

Once the product features have been identified, the next step is to develop the processes, both internal and external, that are able to produce the product features required to meet the customer needs. By the beginning of

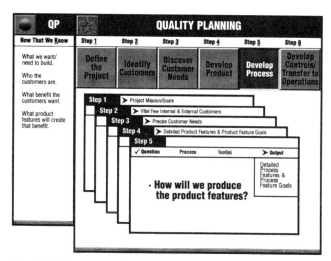

Fig. 66. Data process features.

Step 5, the product features and product feature goals have already been defined through study of who are the customers and what are their needs. The goals have been set out in such forms as product specifications, requirements, and objectives. The job of process development is to create the means for meeting those goals—to produce the product features.

A process is defined as "a systematic series of actions directed to the achievement of a goal"—in other words, all the things the customer *doesn't* see that go into creating the goods or delivering the service. In order to define the specific means to be used by the operating forces for meeting the product quality goals, we need to have knowledge of the product quality goals, the operating conditions, and whether the processes we plan are capable of performing as designed. Many of the kinds of analysis that were useful in determining product features (Step 4) are analogously useful in designing process features and process feature goals.[2] Examples of the kinds of analysis and the questions they seek to answer include:

Benchmarking: How does our process for producing the good or delivering the service compare with the processes of our competitors?

Carryover of process designs: Which of the existing designs (if any) should be carried over into the new process? If new designs are to be created, should they be of an evolutionary nature, or should they be

---

[2]For a more advanced, and more detailed, discussion of Step 5 of the Quality Planning process (especially on the topic of Process Capability), see "Develop Process Features," *Juran on Quality by Design*, J. M. Juran (New York: The Free Press, 1992), pp. 218–273.

radically new designs? Although the advantages of carryover are considerable—low cost of process design, predictable performance, operating forces already in place—the danger of carryover is that it may include chronic quality problems that have never been solved.

Critical factors: Which are the vital few critical processes which present serious dangers to human life, health, and the environment, or which risk the loss of a very large sum of money? Where might those processes fail, and what safeguards need to be built into the process?

Error proofing: Where in the process are the greatest opportunities for human error, and how can processes be designed to minimize error?

This step also offers the opportunity of using a third spreadsheet to keep track of the numerous combinations of product features and process features.

Step 6: Develop Controls and Transfer to Operations

The final step in the Quality Planning process addresses the basic question, "How do we make sure that the process works as it was designed?" Step 5 has two goals: to develop the process controls needed to keep the process in a stable state so that it continues to meet the product and process quality goals, and to transfer the planned process, along with its associated process control plan, to the operating personnel. "Process control" consists of three basic, interlocking steps:

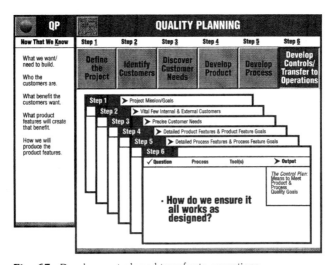

Fig. 67. Develop controls and transfer to operations.

1. evaluating the actual performance of the process
2. comparing the actual performance of the process with the process goals, and
3. taking action on the difference, to make sure that the actual performance of the process meets the goals that were set for it.

Process control takes place in a systematic sequence called a *feedback loop*. In its simplest form, the loop can be diagrammed as in Fig. 68. As the exhibit shows, we measure the actual performance of the process and compare to established control standards. If the process is within the established control zone, we leave it alone. If the process is not in control, we troubleshoot. This basic loop can take place at various stages in the process: at start-up (to make the "start" decision), periodically during the operation of the process (to make the "run or stop" decision), or after some amount of product has been produced.

The idea is to design processes for self-control and self-inspection, so that workers can easily determine their own performance (diagnosis), and make adjustments to the process (remedy) in order to bring it in line with goals. Self-control provides the shortest feedback loop, avoids use of a "policeman," and confers a sense of ownership of the process. To create self-control requires that we provide workers with means of knowing what is the target performance, means of knowing what is the actual performance, a known relationship between the process variables and the product results, and means for changing performance in the event that performance does not conform to goals.[3]

---

[3]For a more advanced, and more detailed, discussion of process controls, including Statistical Process Control as it applies to Step 6, see "Develop Process Controls: Transfer to Operations," *Juran on Quality by Design*, J. M. Juran (New York: The Free Press, 1992), pp. 274–298.

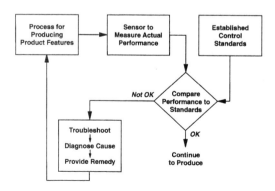

Fig. 68. Feedback loop.

Throughout all of the stages of process control, there is a need to gather and analyze the data required to evaluate both product and process performance. Responsibility for making the evaluations must be clearly assigned; sensors must be clearly defined, along with the means for maintaining their precision; and there must be a clear means of learning about the performance of the process from the data.

During this Step 6, there is again an opportunity to use a spreadsheet to keep track of the numerous combinations of process-features and process control features.

In addition to developing a clear and comprehensive system of process controls, it remains to take the final step of transferring the process design, along with the system of process controls, to the operating personnel. This is a transfer of responsibility from the planners to the operating managers. These managers understandably do not want to accept responsibility for results if the process cannot do its intended job—in our dialect, if the process lacks process capability or lacks controllability. So it is important that process capability be demonstrated to the operating managers.

Once the transfer has occurred, the operating personnel become responsible not only for producing the product but also for maintaining the process at its planned level of capability. It is important to design the control process in such a way that it provides the means for carrying out the activities within the feedback loop; these, too, must be carefully transferred.

During process design (Step 5), the planners acquire a great deal of know-how about the process. The operating forces could benefit from this know-how if it were transferred. There are various tools that help in making this transfer:

Process specifications set out the process goals to be met. This information is vital to the operating forces, but represents only the barest minimum of information they need.

Procedures, including instructions, cautions, and "the why as well as the how," are a welcome elaboration on the process specifications.

Briefings in which the planners meet face-to-face with the operating forces provide an opportunity for questions and discussion.

On-the-job training of operating supervisors by planners not only allows for complete and efficient transfer of know-how, but often provides valuable feedback to planners as well.

Auditing the transfer plan assures that the details of the plan are complete and have been carefully implemented throughout the organization.

Transfer to operations completes the Quality Planning process. Once again, "We have come to the end." Yet Quality Planning, like the overall discipline of Quality Management of which it is a part, is an interactive, very important process. Inevitably, along the Quality Planning journey, new things are learned—a new customer need is discovered, it is found that a carefully designed process cannot be controlled. That new customer need should not be ignored, even if it is discovered after Step 3; that uncontrollable process must be redesigned, even if its unruliness becomes clear only after several months of making the new product. Inevitably, as people start to see the end of the journey, they are anxious to arrive there quickly. It is all the more important, in the final stages of Quality Planning, to proceed carefully and take the time to test thoroughly. The "light at the end of the tunnel" just might be an oncoming freight train. All new information, about the product as well as the process for making it, is a valuable resource—to be fed into the process, rather than discarded or ignored as an inconvenience. After all, the end of the Quality Planning process is only the beginning of the continuous process of Quality Improvement.

Appendix A

TECHNICAL ADDENDUM TO CONTROL—
A PANORAMIC VIEW

Under this topic the author includes the briefest discussion on some of the technical aspects of the control cycle.

First, as to terminology.

Managers have to date held to a cavalier attitude on terminology for control, i.e., every person for himself or herself. This is wonderful for local freedom, but sets up a linguistic mine field in those conferences and seminars attended by managers from a variety of businesses.

The engineers have done better. In 1936, a formal committee[1] undertook to standardize terminology on automatic control. Table A-1 lists the engineers' terms relative to our eight elements of the control cycle.

(Lest anyone think the author has tried to make this sound complicated, may he note that the new standard on Terminology for Automatic Control defines no less than 275 terms. Sixteen of these are for varieties of "control system"!)

---

[1]This was the Terminology Committee of what has become the Instruments and Regulators Division of the American Society of Mechanical Engineers. The March, 1946, report, which contains the definitions listed here, has since been superseded (1963) by "Terminology for Automatic Control," American Standard ASA C 85.1-1963, available from the American Society of Mechanical Engineers, 345 E. 47th St., New York 10017-2392, New York.

Table A-1. Terminology for Control

Elements of the control cycle	Engineers' terms and definition
Control subject	Controlled variable. That quantity or condition which is measured and controlled.
Unit of measure	The engineers' list has no term for this. It seems to be taken for granted by engineers.
Standard	Desired value. That value of the controlled variable which it is desired to maintain.
Sensory device; sensor; receptor	Primary element. That portion of the measuring means which first either utilizes or transforms energy from the controlled medium to produce an effect in response to change in the value of the controlled variable.
Means for measurement	Measuring means. Those elements of an automatic controller* which are involved in ascertaining and communicating, to the controlling means, either the value of the controlled variable, the error,† or the deviation.†
Compare actual with standard	The engineers have no official terminology for this, but the engineers' servomechanism‡ always provides for it. At one time, the terms "memory unit" or "command station" were used to designate a unit which kept record of the standard, made the comparison, and decided on the action to be taken (see below).
Decide on action needed	Here again, there is no really equivalent terminology. The engineer may give the servomechanism a choice of what action to take, but the choice is not a matter of judgment—it is decided absolutely by the value of the controlled variable.
Take the action; effector	Final Control Element. That portion of the controlling means which directly changes the value of the manipulated variable.

*To the engineer, an "automatic controller" is a mechanism which:
 (a) Measures the value of a variable quantity or condition and
 (b) Operates to correct or limit the deviation of this measured value from a selected reference.
†"Error" and "deviation" correspond roughly to the accountants' "variance" of actual expense from budget.
‡Servomechanism—a mechanical device embodying the principles of feedback and power amplification, i.e., both brain and muscle.

The biologist also has a dialect. Of interest to us are:

sensor, which corresponds to the sensory device (or primary element of the engineer).
effector, which is the "take the action" part of the cycle—the final control element of the engineer.

Next, as to some distinctions between informational control and direct control by the sensor.

In the engineer's dialect, the flyball governor is an analogue-type computer. It converts one physical quantity (speed of rotation) into another (valve motion). It is simple but inflexible. The receptor, "translator," and effector are unique to this job. The analogue mechanism can do this job and no other.

The analogue device, through its great simplicity, is the most economic for many applications. It also works on "real" time—it relates to what is happening right now. But the analogue device also has some serious limitations. It is limited as to the size of the job it can do and as to the complexity it can deal with. It is also troubled with "noise" (false signals). When these limitations become important, resort must be had to separating the information system from the action system. The analogue controller is also a routine worker. It cannot deal with emergencies.

The digital computer is an example of use of a separate information system. The act of separation introduces much complication. Now we need logic units, storage units, and control units, in addition to the receptors and effectors we need in any case. However, the digital computer is not a one-job device. It can be programmed to deal with any problem, even with emergencies. It has no limit on size or complexity of task, and it is free from "noise." It is uneconomic for the simple jobs, which are best handled by analogue means. But the digital computer can "orchestrate the joint behavior of many analogue controllers."

Finally, a bit on control before, during, and after the fact.

The early-warning controls are those which introduce a *time lead* so that the alarm signal gets there well before the calamity.

A fire-alarm system is set up to be actuated by a rise in temperature to a value which is still well below the ignition point. The manager would say *this is acting on the trend,* and he would be right. Such a system would really set up a race between the rising temperature and the pace of the signal. The signal must win the race, and sound the alarm before things burst into flame—early enough so that action is taken to prevent the fire from happening at all.

The engineer's dialect for time lead is "phase advance." The engineer has ways of getting such time leads. He may use electrical capacitors; the current in such a capacitor leads the applied voltage. The engineer may use acceleration as the energizing phenomenon; acceleration leads velocity, hence to tie an alarm signal to rate of acceleration is to sound the alarm before the worst has happened.

The most elegant time lead is found in biology. When sensory organs of animals are stimulated, they respond by sending a series of pulses down the nerve fibers. These pulses are more frequent for a rising stimulus than for a falling stimulus (as the legendary idiot discovered when he stopped hitting himself with the hammer). The peak of the response occurs before the peak of the stimulus. Biologists call this anticipatory response. As yet they don't fully understand how the organism does this.

Appendix B

THE JURAN TRILOGY®

A company that wants to chart a new course in managing for quality obviously should create an all-pervasive unity so that everyone will know which is the new direction, and will be stimulated to go there. Creating such unity requires dealing with some powerful forces which resist a unified approach. These forces are, for the most part, due to certain non-uniformities inherent in any company. Such an obstacle can be overcome if we are able to find a universal thought process—a universal way of thinking about quality—which fits all functions, all levels, all product lines. This is the concept of the "Juran Trilogy" (Fig. 69). There

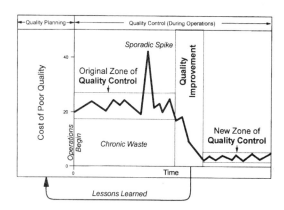

Fig. 69. The Juran Trilogy.

are three quality processes that make up this trilogy. *Quality Planning* identifies the quality features to be provided and plans for delivering them without deficiencies. *Quality Improvement* reduces or eliminates deficiencies in current goods, services, or processes. *Quality Control* maintains the results achieved through Quality Planning and Quality Improvement.

SUGGESTED READINGS

The field of quality has blossomed and much has happened in the last 30 years, including the establishment of the American Society for Quality Control with current membership that exceeds 120,000. Therefore, as an aid to the reader, a listing of useful references has been provided here. No attempt has been made to cross-reference these sources. They are presented simply as additional information in the burgeoning field of quality.

Albrecht, Karl, and Lawrence J. Bradford. *The Service Advantage.* Homewood, IL: Business One–Irwin, 1990.

Albrecht, Karl, and Ron Zemke. *Service America!* Homewood, IL: Dow Jones–Irwin, 1985.

Atchison, Thomas A. *Turning Health Care Leadership Around.* San Francisco: Jossey-Bass, 1990.

Aubrey, Charles A. *Quality Management in Financial Services.* Wheaton, IL: Hitchcock Publishing, 1985.

Aubrey, Charles A., and Patricia K. Felkins. *Teamwork.* White Plains, NY: ASQC Quality Resources, 1988.

Berry, Thomas H. *Managing the Total Quality Transformation.* New York: McGraw-Hill, 1991.

Berwick, Donald M., A. Blanton Godfrey, and Jane Roessner. *Curing Health Care.* San Francisco: Jossey-Bass, 1990.

Boyett, Joseph H., and Henry P. Conn. *Workplace 2000—The Revolution Reshaping American Business.* New York: Dutton, 1991.

Byrne, John. *The Whiz Kids: Ten Founding Fathers of American Business—And the Legacy They Left Us.* New York: Doubleday, 1993.

Camp, Robert C. *Benchmarking.* Milwaukee, WI: ASQC Quality Press, 1989.

Caroselli, Marlene. *Total Quality Transformations: Optimizing Missions, Methods, and Management.* Amherst, MA: Human Resource Development Press, 1991.

Covey, Stephen R. *Principle-Centered Leadership.* New York: Simon & Schuster, 1991.

Covey, Stephen R. *The Seven Habits of Highly Effective People.* New York: Simon & Schuster, 1989.

Couch, James B. *Health Care Quality Management for the 21st Century.* Tampa, FL: American College of Physician Executives, 1991.

Deming, W. Edwards. *Out of the Crisis.* Cambridge, MA: Massachusetts Institute of Technology, 1982.

DePree, Max. *Leadership Is an Art.* New York: Dell Publishing, 1989.

Dertouzos, Michael L., Richard K. Lester, and Robert M. Solow. *Made in America.* Cambridge, MA: Massachusetts Institute of Technology, 1989.

Drucker, Peter F. *Innovation and Entrepreneurship.* New York: Harper & Row, 1985.

Garfield, Charles. *Second to None.* Homewood, IL: Business One-Irwin, 1992.

Garvin, David A. *Managing Quality: The Strategic and Competitive Edge.* New York: The Free Press, 1988.

Hammer, Michael, and James Champy. *Reengineering the Corporation.* New York: HarperCollins, 1993.

Harmon, Roy L. *Reinventing the Factory II.* New York: The Free Press, 1992.

Hayes, Robert H., Steven C. Wheelwright, and Kim B. Clark. *Dynamic Manufacturing.* New York: The Free Press, 1990.

Heskett, James L., W. Earl Sasser, and Christopher W. L. Hart. *Service Breakthroughs.* New York: The Free Press, 1990.

Hutchins, David. *In Pursuit of Quality.* London: Pitman Publishing, 1990.

Ishikawa, Kaoru. *Introduction to Quality Control.* Tokyo: 3A Corporation, 1990.

Ishikawa, Kaoru. *What Is Total Quality Control? The Japanese Way.* Englewood Cliffs, NJ: Prentice Hall, 1985.

Kane, Victor E. *Defect Prevention: Use of Simple Statistical Tools.* New York: Marcel Dekker, 1989.

Kanter, Rosabeth Moss. *When Giants Learn to Dance.* New York: Simon & Schuster, 1989.

Kilmann, Ralph H., and Ines Kilmann & Associates. *Making Organizations Competitive.* San Francisco: Jossey-Bass, 1991.

Main, Jeremy. *Quality Wars.* New York: The Free Press, 1994.

Marszalek-Gaucher, Ellen, and Richard J. Coffey. *Transforming Healthcare Organizations.* New York: Jossey-Bass, 1990.

Mills, Charles A. *The Quality Audit.* New York: McGraw-Hill, 1989.

Morita, Akio, Edwin M. Reingold, and Mitsuko Shimomura. *Made in Japan.* New York: Dutton, 1986.

Onnias, Arturo. *Language of Total Quality.* Castellamone, Italy: TPOK Publications on Quality, 1992.

Peterson, Donald E., and John Hillkirk. *A Better Idea: Redefining the Way Americans Work.* Boston: Houghton, Mifflin, 1991.

Phadke, Madhav S. *Quality Engineering Using Robust Design.* Englewood Cliffs, NJ: Prentice Hall, 1989.

Phillips, Donald T. *Lincoln on Leadership: Executive Strategies for Tough Times.* New York: Warner Books, 1992.

Porter, Michael E. *Competitive Advantage of Nations.* New York: The Free Press, 1990.

Roberts, Harry V., and Bernard F. Sergesketter. *Quality Is Personal: A Foundation for Total Quality Management.* New York: The Free Press, 1993.

Scherkenback, William W. *The Deming Route to Quality and Productivity: Road Maps and Roadblocks.* Milwaukee, WI: ASQC Quality Press, 1986.

Schonberger, Richard J. *Building a Chain of Customers.* New York: The Free Press, 1990.

Schonberger, Richard J. *World Class Manufacturing.* New York: The Free Press, 1986.

Seghezzi, Hans Dieter, ed. *Top Management and Quality.* Munich: Hansers Publishers, 1992.

Senge, Peter M. *The Fifth Discipline.* New York: Doubleday, 1990.

Spechler, Jay W. *When America Does It Right.* Norcross, GA: Industrial Engineering and Management Press, 1991.

Stalk, George, Jr., and Thomas H. Hout. *Competing Against Time.* New York: The Free Press, 1990.

Starr, Martin K., ed. *Global Competitiveness—Getting the U.S. Back on Track.* New York: W. W. Norton, 1988.

Steeples, Marion Mills. *The Corporate Guide to the Malcolm Baldrige National Quality Award.* Homewood, IL: Business One—Irwin, 1992.

Stoner, James A. F., and Frank M. Werner. *Finance in the Quality Revolution: Adding Value by Integrating Financial and Total Quality Management.* Morristown, NJ: Financial Executives Research Foundation, 1993.

Stoner, James A. F., and Frank M. Werner. *Remaking Corporate Finance.* Edited by Fred D. Baldwin. New York: Fordham University Press, 1991.

Stratton, A. Donald. *A Quality Transformation: Success Story from StorageTek.* Milwaukee, WI: ASQC Quality Press, 1994.

Tjosvold, Dean W., and Mary M. Tjosvold. *Leading the Team Organization.* New York: Lexington Books/Macmillan, 1991.

Walton, Sam, and John Huey. *Sam Walton, Made in America, My Story.* New York: Doubleday, 1992.

Welch, Cas, and Pete Geissler. *Bringing Total Quality to Sales.* Milwaukee, WI: ASQC Quality Press, 1992.

Wheelwright, Steven C., and Kim B. Clark. *Revolutionizing Product Development: Quantum Leaps in Speed, Efficiency, and Quality.* New York: The Free Press, 1992.

Yasuda, Yuzo. *40 Years, 20 Million Ideas: The Toyota Suggestion System.* Translated by Fredrich Czupryna. Cambridge, MA: Productivity Press, 1991.

Index

About the Author

J. M. Juran, a world-renowned name in management studies for more than 50 years, has published the leading international reference literature and training media on quality and management. He is also the author of the best-selling *Juran's Quality Control Handbook*. His lecture schedule has taken him to companies and universities around the world.